RECORDS

OF THE

COURT OF ASSISTANTS

OF THE

COLONY

OF THE

MASSACHUSETTS BAY

1630—1692

VOLUME III

AMS PRESS
NEW YORK

RECORDS

OF THE

COURT OF ASSISTANTS

OF THE

COLONY

OF THE

MASSACHUSETTS BAY

1630-1692

VOL. III. PRINTED UNDER THE SUPERVISION OF

JOHN F. CRONIN

CLERK OF THE SUPREME JUDICIAL COURT

VOL. III.

BOSTON
PUBLISHED BY THE COUNTY OF SUFFOLK
1928

Library of Congress Cataloging in Publication Data

Massachusetts (Colony). Court of Assistants.
Records of the Court of Assistants of the colony of the Massachusetts Bay, 1630-1692.

1. Law reports, digests, etc.--Massachusetts.
2. Massachusetts--History--Colonial period--Sources.
I. Title.
KFM2445.A15 1630b 929'.3744 70-172853
ISBN 0-404-07350-6

Reprinted from the edition of 1928, Boston
First AMS edition published, 1973
Manufactured in the United States of America

Trim size of the original edition: 6 1/8" x 8 7/8"
Trim size of AMS edition: 5 1/2" x 8 1/2"

International Standard Book Number:
Complete Set: 0-404-07350-6
Volume III: 0-404-07353-0

AMS PRESS, INC.
New York, N. Y. 10003

PREFACE.

This volume is intended to complete the publication of the Records of the Courts held by the Governor and Assistants for the Colony of the Massachusetts Bay from 1630 to 1692. In the preface of Volume II. of these Records, known as the Records of the Court of Assistants, Mr. John Noble, Clerk of the Supreme Judicial Court, stated that, although he intended originally to include what is now published in this volume as Part Three of Volume II., he found that it contained such an amount of matter as to make a third volume necessary and it is accordingly now being issued as Volume III.

When Mr. Noble resigned from office on June 15, 1908, because of ill-health, most of the work of collecting and preparing the material for this volume had been done by him, with the assistance of Mr. William P. Upham, both now deceased. No funds, however, were available for completing and publishing it. Since then numerous requests were made for the necessary appropriation, but without success. Finally, in the year 1925, largely through the efforts of the late Ex-Mayor Nathan Matthews, who for a long time had manifested great interest in the project, the attention of Hon. James M. Curley, Mayor of the City of Boston, was obtained and, at last, after many years of delay, through his good offices, the City Council of the City of Boston, acting as County Commissioners for the County of Suffolk, appropriated the funds needed to meet the expenses of completing and publishing these records in book form.

I should not conclude without acknowledging with appreciation the able and devoted services of Miss Josie Murphy, a clerical assistant in this office, who assumed and carried on the compilation and correction of the material in this book, from Mr. Noble's resignation until her death in 1918; the services of Miss Madeleine Connors, who succeeded Miss Murphy and who has read the manuscript with its proof, and finally prepared it for the printer; and the constant and generous assistance, advice, and suggestions of Mr. Henry A. Macdonald, a member of the Bostonian Society.

JOHN F. CRONIN.

SUPREME JUDICIAL COURT,
OFFICE OF THE CLERK,
MARCH 7, 1928.

COURT OF ASSISTANTS.

RESTORED FRAGMENTS OF RECORDS FROM 1642 TO 1673.

EXPLANATION OF MARKS AND CHARACTERS.

MARKS.

A mark over a letter indicates an omission of one or more letters.

A caret ^ indicates one or more words omitted in the original.

Brackets [ ] indicate words or letters in the original which are illegible or doubtful or apparently erroneous.

Parallels || || enclose words interlined in the original.

CHARACTERS.

ff signifies ff or F.
n̄ " ner, nor, or no.
ꝑ " par or per.
ꝓ " por or pro.
Ꝑ " Per.
ū " ver.
&c " &c. (etc.)

COURT OF ASSISTANTS

RESTORED FRAGMENTS OF RECORDS

1642–1673.

[Taken from certified copies of judgments, verdicts, executions, etc., found among the Court Files in the offices of the several Counties, in the State Archives, among ancient manuscripts in the possession of the Massachusetts Historical Society, and in various other places, giving authoritative information as to the action of the Court of Assistants during that period. The place where each of these fragments of the record was found is indicated by a memorandum within brackets at the beginning. In some cases additional information obtained from contemporaneous sources is added in a note to explain or amplify the record.]

I.

[Essex County Court Files, Vol. VII., Fol. 127. Humphrey's Adm^rs^. & Maverick &c., June 1662.]

Att A Court held at Boston 6th. day of ye 7/mo. 1642.*

Mrs Lyddia Bancks ag^t^ m^r^ John Humphrey for plt. dam̄ 100^£^: costs 13^s^.

at ye Same Court

M^r^s. Bancks ag^t^ m^r^ Abra: Oatley : confessed a judgm^t^ of 20^£^ & such dam̄ as appears.//

These are true Copies taken out of the Courts booke of Records y^t^ m^r^ Nowell kept as Attests Edw. Rawson Recorder

NOTE.

It appears, from the fact that the above copies were used as evidence of title in the suit between Humphrey's adm^rs^. and Maverick &c., inhabitants of Marblehead, that, by virtue of these two judgments of the Court of Assistants, Mrs. Lydia Banks became possessed of the farm in Marblehead, known as the "Plains Farm," granted by the General Court to John Humphrey at the May session, 1635, with

---

* See Vol. II., page 125, for record of a Court of this date.

the proviso that "as the inhabitants of Marble Head shall stand in neede of it, the said John Humfry shall parte with it, the said inhabitants alloweing him equall recompence for his lab^r & cost bestowed thereupon." At the session in March 1637–8, a committee appointed for the purpose, in a report laying out the bounds of the grant, describe it as beginning "at the clifte, in the way to Marble Head, wch is the bound betwixt Salem & Linn, & so along the line between the said townes to the rocks, one mile by estimation, to a great red oake marked from wch the said marked tree, all under & over theise rocks vpon a straight line to the rum̄ing brooke by Thomas Smyths house, all the wch said ground wee alow him for his owne & so from Thomas Smyths to the sea, in case the ground appears to bee Mr Humfreys vpon wch Thomas Smyth & Willi: Wytters houses stands, wth the ground wch they have broken vp by their houses." (See Mass. Col. Records, Vol. I., pp. 147, 226.)

In accordance with the proviso in the grant to John Humphrey, William Hathorne as "one of the attorneys of Mrs. Lydia Bankes late of Salem," by deed dated 24 Sept. 1645 (see Court Files, Suffolk, No. 215) conveyed for £123 to Mr. Moses Maverick "and other the inhabitants of Marblehead all that farme called 'the plaines farme lying in Salem & adj^g. to m^r Peters farme being 400 acres more or less wth all ye houseing" &c. "excepting * 50 acres & two ponds formerly granted to m^r Downing."

At the Essex County Court at Ipswich in March 1662, by writ dated 19 March 1661–2 an action of trespass was brought by "Mr. Joseph Humphrey and Mr. Edmond Batter, administrators of the estate of John Humphrey Esq., deceased," against "Mr Moses Maverick, William Charles, John Peach and John Bartoll" "for possessing & feeding & otherwise occupying of a farm neer Marblehead containing seven or eight hundred acres more or less formerly in ye possession of ye above named John Humphrey Esqr. deceased."

By agreement the case was transferred to the Court to be held at Salem in June 1662. At that Court "ye attachment with what other evidence in ye case produced were read committed to ye Jury & are on file. ye Jury find for ye Defendant costs of court 26^s." It is among the papers on file in this case that our first Fragment of the Court of Assistants Record was found.

The following depositions were used at the trial. (See Essex County Court Files Vol. VII., Fol. 126, and Court Files, Suffolk, No. 448.)

"The deposition of daniell Salmon aged about ffiftye yeares testifieth and saith that that land in controversey between m^r. Humprey and m^r maverick and others that the said m^r Humpreys ffather did Inioy att his ffirst coming over peasabell with out aney molistation to my best knolidg severall yeares.

Sworne in Court at Salem 26: 4: 62
atestes Hilliard Veren Clericus"

---

* (See Suff. Reg^r. Deeds, I., p. 52.)

"The deposition of Nathaniell Pickman Agede 47 yers

This deponent sayth that a bout twenty thre years a goe that m^r John frende [builte?] a fram of a howes at the plaines for m^r John Humphrie esqur: & did other Work at his howes in Salem: & for this worke donn by the saide m^r frende: m^r Adam Oatly solde vnto m^r frende the Howes & grounde of m^r Humphries for payment: & the Remainder of w^t his work did not com vnto he was ordered by m^r Oatly to pay it vnto John Deacon of lin whether it was fife pounds or seven pounds I do not justly know & that the saide m^r Oatly did akt for m^r Humphrie when m^r Humphrie was in New England: about fineshing of the sayde Howes at the plaines: for I worked ther severall times & m^r Otly payd me som pay in part of w^t work I did at the Howes

Sworne in Court 25 : 4 : 62

Atestes Hillyard Veren Clericus."

"The Deposition of John Deacon aged 60 yeares sayth m^r Adam Oatly about 20 yeares agoe told this deponent that he had sold a peece of land & a house to one John ffreind, of Salem, for twelue pounds, & further saith, y^t m^r Humphrie when he went for England owed this deponent seauen pounds which m^r Oatly paid him, by the said John freind out of the said twelue pound, which debt of seauen pounds m^r Humphrie at his goeing awaye came to the house of this deponent & ordered him to receaue it of m^r Oatly: (which sd land is y^t land that is now in controversy & further sayth not.

Sworne in court 25 : 4 : 62

Atestes Hillyard veren clericus"

"The Deposition of Hugh Alley aged fifty three yeares or thereabouts Sworn saith y^t John Humfrey, Esqr., deceased, did posesse ye Plaines farme as we goe to Marblehead adjoyning to Mr Peters his farme & y^t the said Humfrey kept servants at his house one ye said Land and this deponent sayth alsoe y^t he earned seueral pounds for worke done there on ye Plaines farme which was paid him alsoe by the said Humfrey & when ye said Humfrey went for England [he] left his son in law Otley at ye house when he went for England

Sworn in court at Salem 26 : 4 : 62

atestes Hilliard Veren Cleric."

No. 5423, Court Files, Suffolk, is a deposition relating to the same land.

"John Putnum of Lawfull age Testifieth & saith y^t to his sartain knowledge about Sixty years scence Collo^ll John humphrys did liue one and Improve the plaine farme or farme commonly Knowen by the name of M^r humphreyes plaine or farme Lyeing neare unto marble head: & bordering on mr. petters farme & forrest River; I this deponent did work one sd farme for diverse years together: in carting Timber &c., and did frequent mr humphrys house one sd farme in the above sd time and farther I the Deponant doe Testifie y^t Coll^ll Humphreys did improve sd farme by building plowing and fenceing of sd: farme and was reputed his for Diuerse yearse; and never knew anything to the Contrary and farther adds that this farme was called plain farme near to a farme called Swampscutt where the Lady Moody lived and to the Eastward with ~~Divereuxes~~ Peters farme

Ipswich May 21. 1702 Sworne in [Court]
Attest Elisha Cooke Cl[er]"

In Thomas Lechford's Note Book, p. 249 of the printed copy, is a lease of the Plaines farm by John Humfrey to Zacheus Goold for 10 years from 29th Sept. 1640; and on page 355 is another lease of this farm and also of the Ponds farm, so called.

The following extract from Marblehead town records, of which No. 6592 of the Court Files, Suffolk, is a copy, gives the names of the purchasers from Hathorne.

"1646

The names of Those which did Purchase the ffarme of Capt. William Hathorne

Imp^{r} m^{r}.	William Waltown *	£10	0 0^{d}
	Moses Maverick	15	
	John Peach Senr.	5	
	David Corwithy	10	
	William Charles	5	
	Richard Norman Senr.	5	
	John Hartt	5	
	Aurther Sanden	6	
	Abraham Whitt:haire	3	
	Henry Stacey	2	
	Edmund Nicholson	4	
	Francis Symson	4	
	John Lyon	3	
	John Bartoll	3	
	Richd Cooke	5	
	Nicholas Merritt	5	
	Wasingham Chilson	4	
	John Peach jun^{r}.	5	
	Rich^{d}. Curtice	2	
	Thomas Hix	3	
	William Barber	2	
	Thomas Boweing	3	
	John Northy	5	
	James Smith & Richard Rowland	8	
	Joseph Doliber	4	
	John Legg	3	

* Walton.

Erasmuss James	1 10
William Chichester	5
John Stacey Senr.	1
	£136 10

A True Coppy of The persons names, and Respective Sum̃es Each man paid towards The Purchase of the plaine farme in Marblehead as it Standes Recorded in s^d. Townes book of Records for Landes dated Marblehead 8^ber. 12 1705

John Browne Town Cler. MHead."

II.

[Files of the Inferiour Court of Common Pleas 1699. Office of the Clerk of Courts, Salem — Case of Menzies vs. Pudney &c. — as to Humphrey Pond Farm.]

At a court at Boston the 6° of the (10) month 1642*

M^r. Robert Saltonstall ag^t. the estate of M^r. Humphrey in an action of debt to the vallue of two hundred & eighteen pounds m^r Otley alleadged thatt the goodes attached were nott m^r Humphryes butt farmer Dexters. Goodman N[a]sh testifies thatt m^r otley denyed thatt he had sold those Cattle to farmer Dexter butt sent them to farmer Dexter to prevent m^r Saltonstalls attachment. The Jury found for the plantiffe one hundred Twenty eight pounds Damages & ten shillings Costs. Moreover it is to be noted thatt of thatt 218^li there was 90^l. appeared to be discharged

The abovewritten is a true Coppy taken out of the Courts booke. being therewith Examined & Compared

Novemb^r pr° 1695 Attest Joseph Webb Clerk

Copia vera Exam^d ꝑ Steph Sewall Cler.

NOTE.

This suit by Menzies against Pudney &c. was brought "to recover possession of Margaret Willies moiety or half part of ye pond farme heretofore Mr. Humfreys farme." The whole farm contained about fifteen hundred acres, and included the great pond now known as Sun-

* See Vol. II., page 128, for record of a Court of this date. These two fragments, I. and II. contemporaneous with the record printed as Part II. of Vol. II., but not mentioned in that record, prove that there was, as stated in the Preface to Vol. I. (p. XII.), a separate record for civil suits at the Court of Assistants, which is now lost. There are other indications that such a separate record was kept. See, for instance, an account of the proceedings at the Court of Assistants, 3 Sept., 1640, in "an action brought by William Cole & Eliz: his wife against Francis Doughty," Mass. Col. Records, Vol. II., p. 205. The certification of the fragment II. shows that the lost record was in existence in 1695, and in the keeping of Joseph Webb, Clerk of the Suffolk County Court.

taug Lake, partly in Lynnfield and partly in Peabody. It was granted to John Humphrey by the General Court in May, 1635, and was laid out by a committee 12 March, 1637–8. (See Mass. Col. Records, Vol. I., pp. 147, 226.)

Among the other papers in this case is the fragment of record above given and also, on the same paper, the following copy of a deed by Robert Saltonstall.

"7 (4) 1645 —

Mr. Robert Saltonstall of Boston granted unto Mr. Stephen Winthrop of Boston a certain farme called Ponds farme together with the buildings thereon & all meadowes & other appurtenances thereto belonging according to the limits sett by the Court in th[eir] grant to Mr. Humphrey att a generall Court held at Boston 12 (1) 1637. Which lands were delivered to Mr. Saltonstall by execution according to a Judgment of Court 6° (10) 1642. As also the great Pond itself, And this was by an absolute deed of sale dated the 7° (4) 1645.

A hand & seale

Acknowledged & sealed
before Mr. Winthrop Dep^t. Govr.

The above written is a trew copy taken out of the Book of Records for deeds lib. pr°. p. 60.*

Nov. pr° 1695 Attest Joseph Webb, Cler.
Copia Vera Exam^d ꝑ Stephen Sewall Cler."

It appears by the following papers in the case that the only heirs of Stephen Winthrop were his daughters Margaret and Judith, between whom the farm was divided in 1690, Margaret's portion being the Northeasterly half and Judith's the Southwesterly half. Margaret married Henry Ward and afterwards Capt. Edmund Willie. Judith married Richard Hancock.

Deposition at Guildhall, London, Feb. 23^d, 1683, by "William Rainsborrough of London, gentleman, aged 38 yeares or thereabouts, John Leech Cittizen & frameworknitter of London aged thirty seaven yeares or thereabouts & Hannah Green wife of John Green of London gentleman aged thirty yeares or thereabouts" — Rainsborrough and Leech say "that Margarett Ward the wife of Henry Ward of London, framework knitter, and Judith Hancock wife of Richard Hancock cittizen & clothworker of London (which said Margaret Ward & Judith Hancock are now both liveing) are the reputed lawful natural & only daughters & children of Stephen Winthrope late of the Parish of St. Margaretts Westminster in the City of Westminster, Esqr deceased;" and Leech and Hannah Green say that on or about Jan. 29, 1676, "these deponents were present in the parish Church of Allhallowes in the wall, London, when the above named Henry Ward and Margarett were there lawfully according to the practice of the Church of England Entermarried. And this deponent Hannah Green for her

* See Suffolk Regr. Deeds, Vol. I., p. 60.

self further saith that about the month of July in the year of our Lord one thousand six hundred seventy & seven she this deponent was present in the parish Church of Allhallowes in the wall aforesaid where the aforesaid Richard Hancock & Judith were likewise lawfully according to the practice of the Church of England intermarried."

Deposition before the Lord Mayor of London Feb. 29, 1691–2, by "Judith Hancock aged 33 years, or thereabouts wife of Richard Hancock of Spittlefeilds in the Parish of Stepney in the County of Midd^x^. Packer and John Percivall Parish clark of St Buttolphs without Algate London aged fifty yeares or thereabouts," that Margaret Ward, widow, daughter of Stephen Winthrope of Jamestreet, Westminster, Esq. deceased, married with Edmund Willie of London, marriner, July 16, 1685.

There is also on file in the case a power of attorney and a copy of a deed of Margaret's half of the farm. The power of attorney is from Margaret Willie to her husband Edmund Willie, dated Nov. 29, 1697, to sell and dispose of "that Messuage or Farmehouse with all and singular the Barns, Stables, Outhouses, Edifices, & Buildings" "with several pieces or parcels of land containing by estimation Fifteen hundred acres of land be the same more or less situate lying and being at or in a certain place commonly called or known by the name of Lynn or Salem."

The deed under the power of attorney is dated 23 Aug. 1698 and conveys, for 300^£^, to James Menzies of Boston, Gent., "the moiety or one half part of that farme commonly called and known by the name of the Pond farme or Humphreys farme situate lying and being partly in the township of Salem and partly in the township of Lynn, both in the County of Essex in New England, containing by estimation the quantity of six hundred acres, be the same more or less, howsoever limited and bounded as the same was ascertained according to the Division between Bartholomew Gedney and Richard Hancock in the year of our Lord one thousand six hundred and ninety" &c.

The deed of division referred to has not been found or any record of it, but it is mentioned in a deed dated 31 Oct. 1695 and recorded with Essex Deeds, Book 11 Fol. 264, by which Richard Hancock and Judith his wife convey, for 165^£^, to Bartholomew Gedney "a certaine tract & parcel of land upland & meadow containing by estimation four hundred & twenty acres be the same more or less being two third parts of one moiety or halfe part of Humphreys Farme, so called, scituate lying & being partly in ye Towneship of Lynn & partly in ye Towneship of Salem" &c. "bounded Northeasterly with ye land of Edmund Willey & Margarett his wife ye other daughter & coheir of ye said Stephen Winthrop dec^d^. being a streight line from a stump and heap of stones on the Southwesterly side of Hither Stones Meadow, so called, to a stake & heap of stones standing about forty rodds Northeasterly of ye house where Peter Twist now dwelleth wch is ye Divisionall line" &c. Reference is made "to ye Division & partition made thereof between him ye said Richard Hancock & Judith his said wife & m^r^ Thomas Cooper & m^r^ W^m^. Harris of Boston in New England, merchants as Attorneys vnto m^r^ Edmund Willey & Margaret his wife as by ye Map or platt thereof reference thereto being had more fully may appeare."

The division between Margaret and Judith is also referred to in the suit above mentioned where this judgment of the Court of Assistants, 6 Dec. 1642, is found. The suit was in 1699, at the December term of the Inferior Court of Common Pleas for the County of Essex, by James Menzies against John Pudney and Daniel Mackintire, to recover possession of Margaret Willies "moiety or half part of ye pond farme heretofore Mr. Humphreys farme" partition thereof being already made &c. being 700 acres mostly in Salem a small part in Linn, bounded as followeth, viz., "on the Southwesterly side with land of Richard Hancock and Judith his wife the other daughter and coheir of said Stephen Winthrop, deceased, the Division line extending from a stake and heap of stones Northeasterly about 40 rods from the house wherein Peter Twist now dwelleth streight unto a stump or heap of stones which is ye Northerly bound of said Hancocks part and from thence Northeasterly about 50 rods, thence bounded on the lands of Moses Ebornes turning Southeasterly about 100 rods to a great rock from thence Easterly about 90 rods to a black oak, running thence Southerly about 90 rods to another black oak, bounded on Common land & so running Southward from bound to bound, the Easterly side being bounded with Common land vntill it comes vnto a white oak which is the Southeasterly lower bounds & is alsoe a corner bounds of ye lands of Mr. Gedney, and bounded on ye South with ye land of said Gedney now in possession of said Peter Twist, according to ye survey plat & division lately made of s^d^ farme leaving ⅔ parts of a broad meadow being ye Southwesterly part thereof to be & belong to Mr. Hancocks part of the Southwesterly division."

There is on file in the same suit a lease for one year, dated 20 March 1687, by Edmond Willie and Margaret, wife, and Richard Hancock and Judith, wife, to John Pudney of the whole 1500 acre farm.

By deed dated 27 Oct. 1693, and recorded Book 10, Fol. 67, Richard Hancock and wife Judith convey to John Pudney Senr. of Salem "the one halfe part or Moyety of a certain farme or tract of land lying and being in ye County of Essex aforesaid called or knowne by ye name of pond farme alias Humphreys containing by estimation seven hundred and fifty more or less acres of land according to a grant of Court to m^r^ John Humphreys & recouered by law from ye said Humphreys by m^r^ Robt. Saltingstall and by him sold vnto Stephen Winthrop aforesaid Esq."

"Memorandum it is agreed by ye parties abovesd that ye aboue said Farme is to be on ye North side of ye pond which is in ye whole tract of land fifteen hundred acres by estimation."

By deed dated 24 Dec. 1694, recorded Book 11, Fol. 28, John Pudney Senr. re-conveyed the said half part to Richard Hancock.

III.

[Middlesex County Court Files. "John Glover vs. Henry Dunster. County Court, April 1, 1656, p. 77."]

At a Quarter Court at Boston the 4th. 4/mo. 1644. mr Henry Dunster, mr Wm Hibbines, Increase Nowell, & Captaine George Cooke, being comittees of the Court, Agst the estate of mr Joseph Davis: for the pl. 1018£. 10. 2d. & Judgement for what is in the Country for mr Dunster to be disposed as the Court shall direct.*

IV.

[Middlesex County Court Files. "Collins & al. Exors. of Henry Dunster vs. John Humphrey's admrs. Dec., 1662, p. 227."]

To ye much honored Magistrates at Boston.

The petition† of us whose names are underwritten, Sheweth,

That wheras John Humphry late of Liñ Esquire Borrowed of Christopher Chadleigh, servant to Mr Davis, ye Sum̃ of eighty pounds in cash, ffor the repaying whereof ye said Mr Humphry passed over for certaine yeares his wind-mill at Liñ, wth a ffarme there and some cattle thereon. The wch cattle were sold away by some of his Agents, and therby the sayd ffarme made useless. The Mill also by reason of another water-mill yt was sett up in the Towne, being of little use and no proffit in yt place, whereby ye aforesayd morgage is altogether insufficient to pay in ye use of the sayd Sum̃ much less the stock; Wherupon Mr Oatly frequently solicited us yt wee would giue way to ye Selling of ye windmill for ye discharge of ye foresayd Sum̃ as far as it would go & having found us a chapman yt was willing to giue ye full worth of ye same wee could do no less yn assent to his reasonable request but understanding yt unless yrselves do cōsent ye sale of ye sayd mill will be invallyd, Therefore albeit a contract wth Samuel Beñet of Lin be made for ye same mill, yet before wee do fully rattyfy

---

* This paper has no other writing on it except the two following endorsements "Judgmt. at Boston" and "Verdict." The suit, in 1656, was an action of the case for an account of estate in hands of Henry Dunster and refers to the will of "Joss Glover" and his wife, Elizabeth, &c. There are other papers on file in the case.

† See also Essex County Court Files, Vol. VIII., F. 77, for a copy of this petition.

& confirme it unto him we humbly desire your assent unto the sayd Sale.

Increase Nowel
Will. Hibbins
Henry Dunster

We do conceive y[t] it wil be to M[r] Humphryes advantage (& y[t] w[ch] we are perswaded he wil allow of) that y[e] mill should be presently sold to help redeeme y[e] land morgaged.

Tho: Dudley, Gov[r]
John Winthrop
John Endicott
Herbert Pelham
Rich Bellingham
Rich Saltonstall
Samuel Simonds

This is a true Coppye of y[e] Original on file as Attests Edward Rawson Secret[y].

NOTE.

There is no date to the above paper, but the answer to the petition being signed by Dudley as Governor and by Herbert Pelham (Assistant), the date must have been 1645 or 1646. There is in the same file a copy of a mortgage of his "farme, lands and milne" by John Humphrey to Increase Nowell, for the term of twenty-one years, to secure the payment of 80£ to "m[r] Joseph Davis," dated "25 8[ber] 1641." There is also a copy of a deed by Increase Nowell and Henry Dunster to Francis Ingalls, dated Oct. 25, 1647, also depositions showing that the farm was unimproved and that another mill (a water-mill) was made use of generally in the town of Lynn about 20 years before 1662.]

By the record of the County Court at Charlestown, Dec. 16, 1662, it appears that the executors of the will of Henry Dunster dec[d] brought an action against Joseph Humphrey adm[r]. to the estate of John Humphrey dec[d]. for detaining stock and cattle &c. The verdict was for the plaintiffs, damages £34, 4s and costs of Court.

There were also two other actions relating to Humphrey's windmill farm at Sagamore Hill in Lynn. The first was at the County Court at Ipswich 30 Sept. 1662, by the administrators of the estate of John Humphrey, plaintiffs, against the executors of the will of Henry Dunster, defendants, but this action was withdrawn. The second action was at the County Court at Salem 25 Nov. 1662 by Edmund Batter and Joseph Humphrey, adm[rs]. of the estate of John Humphrey Esq[r]., against Edward Collins and Joseph Hill, exec[rs]. of the will of Henry Dunster, being an "action of the case, for y[t] y[e] said Dunster sould awaye a windmill of ye said Humfreys, Esqr., & a farme of his ye said Humfreys in Lynn, with a barne not deliuered vp according to covenant." The record of judgment is as follows: — "ye atach^t^. with other evidence in ye case ꝓduced were read, comitted to ye Jury & are on file, ye Jury brought in theire verdict: viz: they find for ye plt. the farme to be delivered vp with ye app^r^tenances & to pay 40£ for want of ye barne & milne, & costs 4£ — 4^s^ — 8^d^." The defendants appealed to the Court of Assistants. There are a number of papers on file in this case (see Essex County Court Files, Vol. VIII., Fol. 75, &c.). The first is the writ which is followed by three accounts and a bill of costs. The sixth paper is a copy of the petition by Increase Nowell &c. given above, and the seventh and eighth are copies of the mortgage to Increase Nowell 25 Oct. 1641, and of the deed to Francis Ingalls 25 Oct. 1647, mentioned above. The ninth paper is an agreement by Samuel Benet, of Lynn, dated 13 Dec. 1644 as to paying for "ye windmill y^t^ standeth on Sagamore Hill in Lin." There are also eight depositions some sworn to at Ipswich Court Sept. 1662, and others at Salem Nov. 1662. One of these is as follows: —

"The deposition of Clement Coledome adged thirty seven yeares or thereabouts sworne sayth y^t^ ye windmill now in Controuersie y^t^ was m^r^ Humfrey his mill (to his owne knowledge) this deponent sayth y^t^ ye windmill was worth one hundred pounds sterlling when m^r^ Henry Dunster posest her & allsoe when he sould her: & was of much use in ye Towne of Lyn more then any other mill: ye water mill being frozen up in winter time: & in sumer time not water to driue the same: & when the windmill of m^r^ Humfrey was sold ye towne was put to such a streight as was forced to build another Tyde mill.

Sworne in Court held at Ipswich 30 Sept., 1662.

Robert Lord cleric."

V.

[Notarial Record of William Aspinwall. Boston Athenæum.]

[page 5. (1645)] 22 (8) Major Edward Gibones & Richard Russell haveing received power from the owners of the ship Gilbert * inhabiting at Dover to demand the said shipp, Seized at Boston (by the Court) as a malignant Shipp, wth proviso, that Shee should be restored if the owners within 13 months after did cleere it that shee did not belong to any ꝑsons or place at enmity against the K. & Parliament at the time of the seisure, wch they say they have duly ꝑformed vnder the hand & seale of the Major of Dover; & therefore the ship being denyed them,

* For orders of the General Court as to the ship "Gilbert" see Mass. Col. Records, Vol. I., pp. 113, 132, 218.

they Professe themselvs against the Court so farr as they conceiue the said Order is not fulfilled toward them : & the Cause being transmitted hence th[ey] professe theire dislike & Protest they shall waite for further remedy to recover of the Court the said Shipp wth all just damages that hath befallen them by theire denyall of the said Shipp. Whereto the Court gave this Answer (after I had wth theire leave reade the same) That the testimony given did not satisfy the Court & therefore they referred the Cause to the High Court of Admiralty in England.

[page 10.] 25 Dec. 1644 [1645 ?] A ꝑtest made by m[r] Tho: Clarke in behalfe of the owners of the ship Gilbert called the Exchange, against major Edward Gibones.

VI.

[page 10.] 1645. 25.(10) A Copie of an order of Court made betweene m[r] ‖Ed:‖ Parks & Capt Georg Cooke the 22 (10) 1645. by Joh. Winthrop D. Gover.* Herbert Pelham Richard Bellingham & Increase Nowell. That Capt Cooke shall make a sure Conveyance of the house & 32½ Acres of marsh meddow & 2 Acres vpland vnto m[r] Parks & pay him 7£. 16[s]. 1[d] w[ch] is remaineing due vppon Account. & m[r] Parks to giue Capt Cooke a discharge.

[Same page further down.] 25 (10) A Copie of the Order of Court betweene m[r] Edward Parks & Capt Cooke, wherein it is Ordered that Capt Cooke shall make him a firme Conveyance of the house & 32 Acres of land & 2 Acres of vpland, & m[r] Parks to giue him a discharge.

VII.

[page 13.] 9. (1) 1645. [1645–6] ‖For m[r] Yale.‖ A Copie of a Judgment of Court in a case betweene Joshua ffoote plaintiff & George ffoxcroft defendant both of London merchants. wherein the Jury found according to the forfeiture of 3 bills 14 C pounds damadges, but the Court moderating it in way of Chancery gaue Judgment only for 492[li]. 16[s]. 9[d] damadges & 20[s] costs. & ordered that m[r] Yale Agent to m[r] ffoxcroft should either satisfy the same w[th]in 6 dayes after demand or giue in vppon oath what estate he had of m[r] ffoxcrofts in his hand at the

* Deputy Governor.

serving of the Attachment vppon wch the Tryall was made; or if he refused oath then the execution to be laid vppon such estate as he possessed either in m^r ffoxcrofts right or his owne. And that m^r Hues Agent for m^r ffoote should give security for what he receiued to saue m^r ffoxcroft & his executors harmles.

9. (1) 1645. Two Copies of the same Judgment to m^r Hues for the use of m^r ffoote.

[Same page further down.] 10. (1) 1645 A Copie of a judgm^t of Court betweene m^r ffoote & m^r ffoxcrofte as aboue ffor m^r Yale.

[page 14.] 24. (2) 1646. A Copie of the Order of Court made in m^r ffoxcrofts case at the Court 3 (1) 1645 [1645–6]

VIII.

[Mass. Archives, Vol. 59, No. 25.]

To the honoured Governo^r Deput Governo^r & Assistants, the humble petition of William Toy

ffforasmuch as my calling & imployment is in Distilling of Strong Waters, & many neighbours & others haue occasion for theire necessity to send for a glasse more or lesse as theire necessity & ability doth require; my humble Requeste is that I may haue yor Worshipps approbation to sell it forth in such considerable proportions not keepeing any tippling or drinking thereof in my house.

granted 4th 1 m^o 1645/1646
Increase Nowell Sec

IX.

[Waste Book, County Court, Salem, 1638–1647–8. p. 194. Office of the Clerk of Courts, Salem.]

" ffrō p. 167.* wherin is a speciall verdict brought in ꝑ Jury in the Court held 31–10m^o – 44 betweene m^r Tayler & m^r King.

More att Boston 7. of 3 m^o. 1646.

That after m^r Kinges Bull had his horns cutt, my self being on horsback wth my wyfe behind mee, ye sd Bull stood in the high way as I was riding a Longe when I cam vp to the Bull not knowing whos

* Pages 165 to 170 are missing in the Waste Book.

beast it was neither thinking of any opposition, I struck at the bull wth my stick to put him out of the way. ymediatly y^{e} bull made att my Mare & placed his horns vpon her $should^{r}$, & had well nigh ou^{r} throwne both the mare & hir riders & although I endeuoured to shunne y^{e} bull yet he still $p^{r}st$ vpon mee, y^{t} I cannot but conceaue, had not the herdsman bin att hand to beat him offe y^{t} some hurt had been done either to $o^{r}selues$ or my mare or both but gods good hand $bette^{r}$ ꝑvided.

Robt: Bridges

This Case being propounded to y^{e} magistrats assembled at Boston 7. (3) 46: and being by them throwly debated, & all cercumstances considered, It was agreed that in the Judgment of Lawe it is to be concluded* that y^{e} bull did kill y^{e} mare, & y^{t} y^{e} owner of the Bull (vpon such notice as he had) ought to have taken order to $p^{r}uent$ any future mischiefe

Increase Nowell secret

The Magistrates assembled at Salem doe Judg y^{t} m^{r} King shall pay halfe the vallue of the mare vnto m^{r} Tayler, wch is Judged to bee $7^{£}$ that is according [to] the rate of $14^{£}$ for the mare shee being great wth foale wth a mare foale. & the Mare adjudged to be at Least worth that some by such as well knew her. And that hee shall pay m^{r} Tayler costs wch amounts to — $1^{£}$. 12^{s} — 0^{d}.

gr. exec. 18. 5 m^{o} 46 "

NOTE.

Record of the "Court held at Ipswich the 29th (7) 164[6]"

"1 Dan. King pl. agst George Taylour in [an] action about the death of a mare by a bull

Withdrawne cost alowed 14^{s} 6^{d}"

"At a Court held at Salem the 28th 10th mo: 1647"

"2 Danyell Kinge plaint Contra George Tailer deft. in an action of review on the Case: The Jury finde for the plaintife damage ~~9^{li} 11^{s} 9^{d} and costs Court.~~ 12^{li} 10^{s} 7^{d}

Provided that if after vppon $furth^{r}$ considerc̄on it be found equall for m^{r} Kinge to lose his chardge in the former action then m^{r} Kinge is bounde to repaye it"

Essex County Court Papers Vol. I., Fol. 29.

(Miscellaneous 1644.)

"That [w^{ch}] Anne Knight can testify in the cause betwixt m^{r} Taylor and [m^{r}] King about the killing of m^{r} Taylors mare by

---

* On the evidence of Anne Knight?

m^r Kings bull the wch she will giue in vpon oath wen shee is called to it is as followeth

Shee dwelling then wth m^r Taylor did see the mare aliue the euening beefore eating chaffe wheere they had bene winowing corne, and the next morning about breake of day shee saw the bull in the houell whee^re the mare vsed to ly, and the bull seeing her went away shee thinking nothing of any harme done by him, then going in the house wth a few stickes for the fire shee came p^rsently out againe and saw the mare lying in the houell [her filly ?] lying on one side wth her [gutts] out and there was no other cattell then in the yard but only the [rent ?] of that mare. Shee also testifieth that shee had helped to dresse the same mare of a former wound that was very deepe. Ane Knight.*

"I William Worcester doe testify that m^r Taylor came to my house this last 6th day purposely to fetch Ann Knight now dwelling wth me for to bee a witnes for him at this court: but my wife beeing very ill and myselfe beeing warned before to this Court for a witnes made him † willing to spare her going: [then was ?] hee minded to haue caried her to Ipswich to haue taken her oath of these things beefore the magistrates, but the weather ꝓued wett and stormy and likely to so continue: [ ] hee was content to leaue her at home and to haue her testimony vnder her hand wch was done in my p^rsence

William Worcester

Salisbury 6th of the 5 mo^th 1644"

[Endorsed] "Ann Knight testimony taken vpon oath 31th 10th m^o. 1644 in Court

Dan^ll [King]

de ye Mare & Bull"

X.

[Middlesex County Court Files. "County Court, 1653. Blanchard *v.* Barnes, p. 27."]

At a q^rt^r Cort the 7th of the first m^o. 1647 or 1648 John Grout being alowed guardion to Rich: Barnes recd in money thirty six pound, & five pound in goods, hee doth resigne up that charge of guardion, the said Barnes is not to be disposed of without the consent of Thomas Blanchard.

by me Increase Nowell.‡

---

* The margin has the following entry: "An Knight.
Deposed or sworne in Court the 31th of 10 m^o. 1644
Ra[lph] ffogg."

† Mr. Taylor?

‡ See below, Fragment XIII., as to agreement between John Grout, guardian, and John Bent, 7th of the 1st month, 1649.

XI.

[Mass. Archives, Vol. 38, B., No. 57.]

At a Co^r^te of Assistants the 5th of the 7th m^o^ 1648 Rob^r^t Knight comencing an action agst John Treworthy Nicholas Shoply, & Nicholas Treworthy the Jury found for the plaintiffe damages one hundred eighty three pound nineteene shillings, & two pence & costs twenty one shillings & three pence.

this is a true Coppy by me

Increase Nowell

NOTE.

At the session of the General Court in May 1653, the following order was passed: —

"In ans^r^. to the peticons of Mr Niccolas Shapleigh and Mr Robt Knight, the Court granted a hearing of the case betwixt them; and, on the hearing and examination of all the evidence produced in Court, the Court judgeth it meete to reuerse the judgment of the Court of Assistants, the 5th of the 7 m^o^, 48, so farr as it any way respects the sajd Mr Shapleigh." In the margin, "Mr Knights judgment agt. Mr Shapley reu^r^st." See Mass. Col. Records, Vol. IV., Part I., p. 138.

XII.

[Notarial Record of William Aspinwall, pp. 188–190.]

Massachusetts in New England in America.*

At a Court of Assistants holden at Boston the sixth day of the fourth month called June in the yeare of o^r^ Lord 1648 according to the Account of England.

The Companie of the seamen belonging to the Shipp Planter of London, being there in the harbour at Boston aforesaid, brought an action as well against Robert Risbie master of the sd ship, & Thomas Gainer merch^t^ of the same, as against the shipp it selfe, for wages due to them for theire service done in the sd shipp, for divers months then past: wch being matter of Account, the Court appointed Auditors, vizt, m^r^ Duncan Auditor Generall, m^r^ Allen & m^r^ Addington to examine the ships accounts &c, & to certifie the Court. The returne accordingly was made as followeth, vizt, that there was due to the sd master Robt Risbie one hundred & eight pounds; To m^r^ Robert ffen one of his

---

* In the margin.

mates ninety one pounds : To Joshua Maid another of his mates fourty two pounds eight shillings : To Richard Holt Boatswaine fourty six pounds eight shillings : To John Carman Gunner fifty two pounds seven shillings : To Leonard Sergeant Chirurgeon fifty four pounds & to the rest of the seamen according to theire severall ꝓportions, amounting in all to seven hundred & eight pounds seven shillings & a penny. Wch being given in evidence to the Jury, they found for the plantieffs theire severall & respectiue wages, & costs of Court, & judgment was entred accordingly, & execution granted against the said Risbie & Gainer & the said shipp Planter. But because the said Risbie & Gainer had no visible estate in this Jurisdiction wch might answer the Judgment, the execution was laid vppon the said Shipp, wch by apprizall of three able & indifferent men, chosen according to lawe, was valued at seven hundred & thirty six pounds fourteene shillings, & at that rate shee was publikly offred to sale by the space of fourteene dayes or thereabouts. But none appearing to buy her at that price, a motion was made by the sd Shipps Companie at the Court held at Boston the 27th of the fifth month called July 1648. that the said ship might be putt vppon a new apprizall or delivered to the sd plantiefs in Satisfaction of theire wages ; wch was ordered accordingly ; & being apprized by able & indifferent men the first of the sixth month called August 1648 at six hundred pounds, was sould by the vnder marshall to major Edward Gibons for fyve hundred & fifty pounds, because no man would give so much, supposeing her to be over valued. Where vppon by Authority of this Court the sd sale of the sd Ship Planter is allowed & ratifyed to be good & effectuall in Lawe, to the said major Gibons & his Assignes, & to his & theire ꝓper vse & behoofe, & the sd fyve hundred & fifty pounds the ꝓceed thereof, to be distributed to the * sd shipps companie, according to theire severall ꝓportions, every of them giueing a receipt & acquittance for the same according to Lawe. In testimonie of the truth whereof I John Winthrop Gov. of the Colonie aforesaid have herevnto sett my hand this 2 of the 11th month called January 1648. [1648–9]

John Winthrop Governor.

108 .0 .0 Robert Resby against Tho: Gainer is granted one hun-
91 .0 .0 dred & eight pounds. Robert ffen is granted ninety
42 .8 .0 one pounds. Joshua maide is granted fourty twoe
52 .7 .8 pounds eight shillings.

* Here in the margin is entered, "I attested a Copie hereof for mr Gainer 10 (3) 1649."

18.18 .0	Rich. Holt is granted fourty six pounds eight shillings.
31 .7.10	John Carman is granted fifty two pounds seven shillings
17 .2 .0	eight pence.
28.16 .0	John Barre is granted eighteene pounds eighteene shill-
27 .0 .0	ings.
19.16 .0	Wm Joyce is granted thirty one pound seven shillings
54 .0 .0	ten pence.
19.16 .0	Wm Croucher is granted seventeene pounds twoe shillings.
42 .5 .0	Thos: ffoster is granted twenty eight pounds sixteene
22.15 .0	shillings.
31 .3 .9	John Perry is granted twenty seven pounds.
00.10 .0	Wm King is granted nineteene pounds sixteene shillings
————	Leonard Sergeant is granted fifty foure pounds.
*653.13 .3	Abraham Knight is granted nienteene pounds sixteene shillings.
	John Sparke is granted fourty two pounds fyve shillings.
	Wm Berry is granted twenty two pound fifteene shillings.
	Richard Haselwood is granted thirty one pound three shillings nine pence & ten shillings to be added to the whole.

To the marshall or his deput.

By vertue hereof yow are required to levy of the goods & chattles of mr Robt Risby, mr Thomas Gainer,† & the shipp planter to the value of six hundred fifty three pound thirteene shillings & three pence wth 2s. for the execution to satisfy each ꝑticular as aboue for a verdict & Judgment granted at the quarter Court held at Boston the 6th present. hereof not to faile. Dated the 12th of the 4th month 1648

By the quartr Court Increase Nowell Secret.

Richard Burges granted twenty one pounds.
George Smith granted twenty one pounds twelve shillings.
Raph Cox granted twelve pounds twelve shillings.

By the Court Increase Nowell Secret.

---

* The Rich. Holt 46£. 8s was omitted in the list.

† or Ganier.

XIII.

[Middlesex County Court Files. "County Court, 1653, Blanchard v. Barnes."]

The agreement Between John Grout Guardion of Richard Barnes and John Bent of Sudbury the 7th of the first m°. an. 1649. I John Bent of Sudbury out of my respect to Richard Barnes and out of other considerations do freely promise and ingage my selfe to giue unto John Grout for Richard Barnes good security to pay unto Richard Barnes or his assignes the sume of Twenty pound sterling, in good marchantable cattle and corne at or uppon the time, or shortly after that the said Richard shalbe of age, or would be if he Lived, Also to deliur to John Grout for Richard his use the moyety of the goodes of agnes Bent deceased lying in my handes and also two Silver Spoones, two brasse kettles a holland pillow beere and a table cloath, prntly uppon the Honored Magestrates approbacon.

John Bent.

And this offer wee John Grout guardion of Richard Barnes with the full consent of the said Richard and John Rutter do promise, (upon the Courts approbation held at Boston) to giue unto the said John Bent a full discharge or acquittance for the Twenty pound, and these goodes due to the said Richard by debt, or legacy

John Grout
Richard Barnes
John Rutter

Acknowledged and alowed by the Magestrates in Court
This is a true coppie Increase Nowell Secretary.*

NOTE.

It seems that Thomas Blanchard desired to secure for his wife's son Richard Barnes twenty pounds in money and certain goods which had belonged to his wife. Accordingly it was delivered to "Mr Peter Noice" and by him to John Bent of Sudbury an uncle of said Richard.

Among the papers is the following: —

"A Note of the Particulars of the Covent wch was concluded vpon betweene Tho: Blancher of Brantrey & John Bent of Sudbury, Concerning Richard Barnes sonne in law to the sd Tho: Bl: & sisters Sonne of ye sd John Bent about ye 3 mo: A°: 1646.

* This paper is a copy made by Thomas Danforth, Recorder. See also above, Fragment X., record of 7 March, 1647-8.

"1. The sd John Bent doeth acknowledge himselfe indebted to the sd Richard Barnes ye sum̃e of twenty pounds wch his mother gave him before shee married to the sd Tho: Blancher and xvi£ was part of his Grandmothers estate due to the sd Richard Barnes as her executor and oth^r^ goods wch was his part of the divid^t^ made betweene him and the oth^r^ executor wch Mr Noice was to put into an Inventory.

"2. He bindes himself his executors & adm^rs^ to pay all this to the sd Rich: Barnes at the Age of xxi yeares.

"3. The sd Tho: Blancher was to haue ye sd Rich: Barnes to bring him vp to the Age of 21 yeares. And was therefore to pay in Ry iij£ to release him from his pnt.prentiship. and vij to the boy at the end of his terme of 21 yeares.

" Witnes Mr Durand Scr.
" Mr Noice
" Goodman Rutter

" It was read & is remembered by Mr Bellingham. Mr Aspinall was to record it, but did not, but remembers it. There was a Petition presented wi^th^ this Coven^t^ to the Court "

The following petition by Thomas Blancher (or Blanchard) is probably the one referred to (see Mass. Archives, Vol. 9, No. 4.) : —

To the Honored Governo^r^ with the Deputy Governo^r^ and Assistants at this Present Quarter Court
Assembled in Boston (2^d^ of y^e^ (4) 1646)

The humble peticõn of Thomas Blauncher
Presenteth ;

That whereas Anne Barnes of Way-hill in Hampshire in the Kingdome of England in consideration of her nā̄all [natural] affection to her sonne Richard Barnes did giue and graunt vnto the sayd Richard the full summe of 20^lb^ sterl., And likewise Anne Bent grandmother to the sayd Ri: Barnes did giue & graunt vnto him 16^lb^ sterl. and certaine other goods, To haue & to hold the sayd sum̃es of mony, and goods to him the sayd Richard Barnes his heyres & assignes for ever, wch mony and goods are paid in and Com̃itted to the trust of John Bent with whom also the sayd Richard Barnes hath bene mainteyned hitherto since his com̃ing into N. England wch is about 7 yeares.

Now may it please this Honoured Court, yor pet^r^ with the consent of the sayd John Bent and the rest of the frinds of the sayd Richard Barnes, hath receiued the sayd Richard as his Apprentice, withall vndertaking the Guardian-ship of the sayd Richard during his Nonage, with this agreem^t^. That the sayd John Bent shall giue security for the payment & deliuery of the sayd sums of mony & goods to the sayd Richard Barnes, at the time of his age, 21 yeares.

All wch yor. pet^r^ in ye name of the rest of his frinds humbly presenteth to this Honored Court to be Confirmed (if so it seeme to the

Court to be just & equall, if other wise, are ready to obey further order about y[e] p[r]mises./

And shall pray &c./ Signed

Tho [a mark] Blauncher
Peter Noyes John Bent

[Endorsed — Tho: Blancher Pet. 1646]

In the Middlesex County Court Record are the following entries, of which there is also a copy on file in the case : —

"At a County Court held at Cambridge the 6[th] of the 2[d] mo: 1652 :"

"Richard Barnes plive agst Tho: Blancherd Defft for withholding a debt of Twenty poundes given him by his mother whiles shee was a widow, The Jury found for the plive, damages twenty pounds and costs of Court Thirty Shillings :"

"Richard Barnes and the wife of John Rutter executours of the will of Agnis Bent, plives agst Thomas Blancherd for withhoulding a debt of six pound due to y[m] lent to him by the said Agnis Bent, The Jury found for the plives, Damages Six pound, & costs of Court eleven shillings :"

At the next Court, held at Cambridge 5th of the 8th month 1652, both the above cases were again heard in review. In the first case the former verdict was again found. In the second case the Court reversed the former judgment for six pounds & costs.

XIV.

[Mass. Archives, Vol. 38, B., Fol. 30[1].]

Whereas the Magistrates finde by experience that much inconvenience is apt to arise by giving counsell concerning cases propounded to them in matter of law, they being to be Judges oft tymes when accons or crimes (grounded vpon their answeres) are brought before them to be heard, & determined. It is agreed by comon consent amongst themselves, that henceforth they will not give any counsell to any pson, concerning any accon, or case, to be heard, & tried. Provided that this restraint shall not extend to any officer of any Court that shall desire any direccon concerning his place for his proceedings. And this the Magistrates the rather agree vpon because there are now divers worthy men in the Country able to give good advise in such respects.

NOTE.

The above paper which appears to be in the handwriting of Samuel Symonds has no date or certification. The agreement not to give counsel was perhaps made at the same time, May 1649, that the General Court passed the following order making it unlawful to ask counsel of the magistrates: — (Mass. Col. Records, Vol. II., p. 279.)

"Forasmuch as it is found inconvenient and very burthensome to the magistrates that many persons have recourse to them for advice & counsell in cases which are afterwards like to come to their cognizance in a legall way, —

It is therefore hereby ordered, that, after one months publication hereof, it shall not be lawfull for any person to aske counsell or advice of any magistrate, in any case wherein afterwards hee shall be a plaintiffe, under penalty of being disinabled to prosecute any such action (that he hath so propounded or taken advice in, as aforesaid) at the next Co^r^te where the case shall come to tryall, being pleaded by way of barr, either by the defendant or any on his behalfe, in which case the said plaintiffe shall pay full costs to the defendant; and if the defendant aske counsell or advice, as aforesaid, he shall forfeit ten shillings for every offence."

In the margin of the order is the entry "None to aske counsell of iudges."

This question whether the magistrates ought to give private advice was debated in 1641, but an order which was proposed to prevent the practice was opposed by the magistrates at that time for various reasons, chiefly on account of the want of "lawyers to direct men in their causes." (See Winthrop's Hist. of New England, Vol. II., p. 36.)

XV.

[Court Files, Suffolk, No. 103.]

The 7th of the 10th Mo^th^ 1647. At a Court of Assistants

John Hatley Comencing an action agā^st^ John Coggan the Jury [found] for the Plaintiffe dam̄ two hundred fifty three pounds fifteene shillings & two pence, & costs twenty one pounds four[teene] shillings & two pence.

The 29th of the 9th mo 1649.

John Coggan agā^st^ John Chidley atturny of John Hatley vpon [w^ch^ ?] the Jury found for the plaintiffe dam̄ sixe pounds fifteene shillings & ten pence, & costs foure pounds

By the Court Increase Nowell

This is a true Copie compared wth y^t^ wch was left in Court as Attests Edward Rawson Recorder:

M^{r}. Hatley being to giue security to procure a sufficient discharge vnder his fath^{rs} hand, & seale, or saue m^{r} Coggan harmeles, & procure bond to repay or cause to be repayd what John Coggan shall within two yeares, make proofe to haue beene payd to m^{r} Hatley or by his order & appointm^{t}, more then what appeared to the Court then to be voyde

By the Court Increase Nowell

This is a true Copie compared wth y^{t} wch was left in Court as Attests Edw Rawson Recorder

---

XVI.

[Mass. Archives. "Council Records 1650–1656," on the 9th leaf from the end of the Volume.]

24 : $\frac{3}{\text{mo.}}$ 1650 In the tjme of the Generall Courts Sitting A particular Case was determined by the magis^{ts}.

Present
The Gou^{r}n^{r}
Dep^{y} Gouno^{r}
m^{r} fflynt
m^{r} Symonds
m^{r} Hibbjns
Capt Bridges
Capt Wiggen

There being a case betweene w^{m} Osbourne Agent for the Iron Works for the tjme being and charles hooke by mutuall Consent referred to the magistrates to be determined vppon hearing thereof the magists. doe thus order it That the sajd charles shall serve till he hath acomplished the full terme of nyne yeeres according to the tennor of the Indenture yett so that as soone as the sajd charles shall bring to the magistrates the writing it selfe or other sufficjent evidence whereby it may Appeare to be for a lesse terme as the sajd charles pretendeth that the magistrats will dischardg him of any further service thereby and take order that he shall haue due Recompence for his service in the meanetjme beyond the terme Agreed vppon: And also in Case he the sajd charles hath neglected to serve he shall make vp the same at and after the end of his terme. / Subscribed

Tho. Dudley Gou^{r}n^{r}
Jo: Endecott Dep^{t} Gou^{r}n^{r}.*

---

* For the original of this order, in the handwriting of Endicott and signed by Dudley and Endicott, see Mass. Archives, Vol. 9, No. 15.

XVII.

[Mass. Archives. "Council Records 1650–1656," 9th leaf from the end of the Volume.]

The magis[ts]. in a Court of Asistants held at Boston: [ ] of September 1651: After supper in hearing of the difference betweene m[r] Coggan & his majde servant mary godfry for ye losse of 2 months & five dayes & his laying out for hir diett in prison twenty eight shillings & nine pence. they determined she should serve m[r] Coggan after the end of hir terme one whole yeare on the same termes as now she doth by virtue of hir Indenture.

XVIII.

[From the Chamberlain Collection, Boston Public Library.]

2 : 1 : 1652/53

We y[e] Grand Jury for y[e] Commonwealth of y[e] Massachusetts upon o[r] oathes doe present John Betts late of Camebridge, Husbandman, for not having y[e] feare of God before his Eyes but being led by y[e] Instigačon of y[e] Divil and y[e] wickednes of his owne Heart upon y[e] 16th day of y[e] second moneth last or thereabout, in y[e] feild of y[e] sayd Betts in Camebridge aforesayd, in and upon one Robert Knight his servant then and there in peace, out of his rash anger did make an Assault and stroacke him wth a greate plough staffe and allso gave him severall Blowes wth y[e] great end of a Goad upon y[e] Backe, both which we find to be unlawfull weapons to strike wth all: also he gave him two Blowes wth his fist felling him to y[e] Ground wth one of them, and that he did beat him wth anoth[r] sticke, and that he neglected him and cruelly used him in his sicknes, and also that y[e] sayd Knight on his Death Bed affirmed that his sicknes came by y[e] Blow his mast[r] gave him wth y[e] plough staffe and upon y[e] Twenty [eighth] day of y[e] eight moneth last died. Vpon which Testimoneys we present him for his horrible wicked Crueltys and leave him to further Triall

Edward Jackson in
the name of the rest

NOTE.

It appears from the following record of the General Court (Vol IV., Part I., p. 145) that at the trial of John Betts at the Court of Assistants upon the above presentment the jury brought in a verdict which was not received by the bench, and so the case was carried to the General Court.

"Jn° Betts, of Cambridge, being at a Court of Asistants, on his triall for his life, for the cruelty he exercised on Robt Knight, his servant, striking him with a plowstaffe, &c., who died shortly after it, the jury brought in theire verdict, which the Magis^ts not receiving, came, in course, to be trjed by the Generall Court. Jn° Betts, the prisoner, came accordingly to his triall, submitted himself for triall to God and the country, & pleaded not guilty to his indictment. The evidences against him being examined and heard, the Court proceeded to censure him."

The original draft of the sentence (Court Files, Suffolk, No. 168, 10th paper) is as follows: —

"28 May 1653

The Genall Courte ||doe|| not find ~~ing~~ John Betts, Legally guiltie of ye murderinge of his Late Ser^te. Robert Knight: But for asmuch as ye evidence brought in ag^t. him, houlds forth vnto this Courte, stronge p^rsumcons & greate pbabillities of his guilt of soe bloody a fact, & y^t hee hath exercised & multiplied Inhumane cruelties vppon ye said Knight, This Courte doth therefore thinke meete y^t ye said John Betts bee sentenced (vizt) —

1. That ye next Lecture day att Boston, (a convenient time beefore ye Lecture beegin) the said Betts haue a rope putt about his necke, by ye Executioner, [an]d soe from ye prison y^t hee bee carried to ye Gallows, there to stand vppon [the la]dder one hower by ye glasse, wth ye end of his rope throwne on the gallows :/

2^ly. That hee bee brought backe to prison, & ymediately after ye Lecture to bee sevly whiped

[one line cancelled and now illegible]

3^ly. That ye said Betts shall pay all ye witnesses brought in ag^t him 2^s p day for soe many dayes as they haue attended vppon ye Courte of Assistants, & ye Genall Courte, vppon his triall

4^ly. That he shall pay 15^lb into ye Country treasurie, for, & towards ye Charges ye Courts haue binn att, vppon his triall *

5^ly That ye said Betts bee bound to ye good beehauio^r for one whole yeare in ye some of 20^ll.

The magists have Agreed wth yeire bretheren the depu^ts only ~~Releast~~ Judge it meete to be entred in the Reccord in this forme if the depu^ts Consent heere to Edward Rawson secret^y

The deputyes consent hereto

William Torrey Cleric"

[Endorsed] "[Betts sentenced] p Curiam"

* At the same session of the General Court it was ordered that the fifteen pounds "due to the country from Jn° Betts' be pajd to the survejor generall, to purchase powder wth all."

The following depositions were used at the trial at the Court of Assistants in March 1652–3 and at the General Court May 25, 1653. (Court Files, Suffolk, No. 168, first nine papers) : —

the testimony of m^r Alcock chirur Haueing occasion to visit Goodwiffe Betts being sick after it had pleased ye lord to grant hir some measure of health shee desired me to see a sicke man of hirs I told hir (or to y^t purpose I would, we went or my selfe alone to see him I cannot say absolutly which) wn I came vnto him I asked him how he fared, where sicke or affected, he told me & Goodwiffe betts both his backe was broken I presently looked vpon it found an imperfect dislocation of ‖ one of ‖ ye vpper vertebre or Spondells of ye backe bone which I doe not remember but noe Tumor no discolouration nor soreness materiall. after I had thus Looked on ye man I asked him why he had noe Empł Confirmat: applyed to ye dislocatiō he told me Either he had one before & lost it or worne out or he annoynted it & an Empł his chirurgiō thought not materiall of noe Greate Benefit or vse: At this first vew of him I then thought wth Good attendance & meanes the man might haue liued some yeares allthough I looked on him as vtterly disinabled by it Either to doe himselfe or others any Good. I likewise advised him to beware of all violent excercise or motiō of his Body or strain[e]ing of it and soe parted with him at y^t time

Not long after I came to see ye said Goody betts againe And occassionally saw ye man, it seemed to me (vizt his back & ye dislocatiō) to be much worse then [y^y w^r] before: I told him I feared he had vse[d] some violent Excercise: he told me he had pitched pease into a carte How many I doe not remember whether he loaded the whole Load or noe.

Being at another time wth Goodwiffe Betts vpon ye occasion before mentioned, Capt. Googing Came together wth his wiffe, and after some discourse wth Goodwiffe betts Concerning hir health and with my selfe ‖ Concerning a ‖ a daughter of his (‖ w^ch ‖ I remember not well, he began to discourse Concerning ye Sicke mā in which discourse he told hir) whether he ‖ G Betts ‖ was theire then I doe not remember y^t it stood them in hand to be very Carefull and diligent in ye vse of all meanes y^t may tend to ye mans health vrgeing it once & againe Seriously wth this y^t in case ye man should dy & any negligence proued it would goe hard wth hir husband Not long after I came againe to visit Goodwiffe Betts whoe againe desired me to see hir man. I did soe. we found him in a little Roome without a fire, ‖ Layd ‖ vpon his Bed & not in bed to my best remembrance, he put out his foote & it quavered exceedingly, his body pale & wan, much maciated & decayed, strength [in]ye inferiour Limbs much decayed & somew^t paralitick

I saide little y^t I remember to ye man But told G. Betts theire was an apparent obstructiō of nutriment & Spirit to ye Lower parts ffrom ye Spinall Marrow, or impostumatiō or both ye first very apparent. told her I would doe soe much for hir & hir man as informe mt^r Clarke in wt Conditiō his patient was on ye morrow morning, haueing occasion then to meet & speake wth him, which I did; whoe told me he would see him ye next day.

after which time I see him noe more. taken upon oath the 2d of the first month $\frac{1652}{1653}$ in Corte

Increase Nowell

[Endorsed] mr Alcocks test

The deposition of Thomas Peirce aged about sixty years testifieth as followeth

That he saw John Betts strike his man once with his fist upon the middle of the back downe to the ground, & when arose, he strocke him again that he had much adoe to ~~rise~~ ‖ recover falling ‖ the second time, And further this deponent saith not

taken upon oath the first of the first mo 1652 or 1653 Increase Nowell

Affirmd on oath before ye ‖ genll ‖ Court 25 may 1653

Edw Rawson Secrety

[Endorsed] Tho Pearce test

the testimonie of William Manninge concerninge Robert Knight late seruant to John betts sayth that he knew the sayd Robert in the tyme of his health to speake often tymes very false & that a litle before he complained of his hurt he did with many biter & dreadfull wishes vpon him selfe deny the takinge a knife out of the house of the said William Manninge which seuerall in the house knew ‖ by consequense ‖ he had taken & which he did after ward confesse he had taken whenas the sayd William Manninge had threatned to call him to giue acount thereof before the magistrate

Sworn before ye Court 25 May 1653. Edward Rawson secrety

[Endorsed] Mannings testimo.

Gilbert Cracbone aged aboue 40 yeares testifieth in the case betwen John Betts, & Robt Knight as followeth Robert [Knight and my]self wth diūs others happening to [ ] wa[g]es, wee obserued yt the [ ] performe his Labor whereuppon [we asked h]im the reason thereof he answered bec̄: his mr had broaken his backe, ‖ wth a Plough staffe ‖ at wch wordes we desired to see it, and found a kibe or knub about the upper ꝑt of his backe, and wished him hearing his complaint to complaine to ye magestrates

1. (1) $\frac{53}{52}$ Gilbert Crackbone

taken upon oath in Corte dicto

ꝑ Increase Nowell

Farther he saith [ ] saw [ ] Kni[ght] was not able to: putt of the earth from y [ ]

The testimony of Goulding Moore aged aboue 40 yeares I Comeing in to Goodman Betts house, ~~and~~ ‖ I found‖ Robert Knight Lying on a bed in a pantre and I asked him how he did, and he answered me very nume in my nether parts, and I know not why onely since m^{r} Clearke ‖ gave me a plaster for my backe ‖ I am much worse, also he told me yt he had hurt himselfe by a fall of a lather that he had formerly had by wch he said he had harme & did not mention any blow given by his master.

1. (1) $\frac{52}{53}$

By me Goulding Moore

Sworne before the Court 25: May 1653

Edward Rawson secret^{y}

[Endorsed] Goulden Moores test

furth [ ] llbert Crackbone sayth that [ ] [t]inge in the highwayes the sayd John betts [did charge] mee with wickedness that by my counselinge him he refused to labor & was the worse in his worke that he the sayd John betts was the worse by forty pounds alsoe another tyme he caled mee in to the house & charged the sayd Knight with counterfeit which he dyd seuerall tymes al along his sickness but this [last tyme was a]bout three weekes before [ ] house & alsoe [ ] this deponent that Rob [ ] ladder 3 staues high or fo[f]urther this [dep]onent sayth not Gilbert Cracbone [again be]fore ye Gennerall Court 25th of may 1653 [affir]med ye whole evidence to be true

Edward Rawson secret^{y}

[Endorsed] Crackbo[ne's] test

m^{rs} Renew Andrewes ‖ aged nere 60 ‖ comeing before me Increase Nowell the 10th of the 10th m^{o} 1652 saith that she many times going unto the house of John Bets saw hee was a furious man, & would be charging his man Rob^{r}t Knight wth dissembling, & telling her his man Kni[ght] could stirr if hee would, & it was onely lasines, that hee would not stirr, so shee went to the fellow, & desired him privately to tell the truth wheth^{r} hee did dissemble, & tould him if hee did God would find him out, & plague, or punish him for his dissembling the said Rob^{r}t tould her he did not dissemble, but wished I would I were dead, she replied thou art not fit to dye he said no he was a poore miserable creature, & wept, she many times put it upon the said Robrt for dissembling but he still gave the same answer as before, she further tould him she thought his m^{r} would free him, or put him to his trade & Robrt replied hee could not by reason of his weaknes ‖ do anything at his trade ‖ she hath further seene him in the place wch his m^{r} made for him to stand in to cry out, & would be let downe, & his m^{r}, & dame tould her it was by m^{r} Clarks direction, that they put him there the said Robrt would tell, hee was in great misery in that place, & could not tell what to do, & she would say canst not ease thy selfe with [thy] armes hee replyed no she farther saw John Bets when he ~~called to~~ ‖ pulled ‖ the fellow to come out of the pantree where hee lay & said hee was resolved to have him out, the servant intreating to forbeare hee was so full of paine the m^{r} said it did him hurt to lye, and therefore he was resolved to have him out taken upon oath the day before mentioned before me Increase Nowell

Affirmd on oath to be true before ye Gennerall Court 25 may 1653
Edw Rawson Secret^{y}

Richard French aged 27 yeares, or there about saith that hee being at carting saw John Bets strike his servant Robrt Knight with a stick wch hee held in both his ‖ hands ‖ wth all his force as hard, as hee could, & the stick seemed to bee a ‖ good ‖ big one, this was the last spring, & hee gave him at least six blowes so that the said Robrt began to cry out, but he did not see the said Robrt give him any iust cause but was at worke, onely the said Bets thought he did not work hard enough, hee hath heard the said Bets charge the said Robrt with Dissembling calling him Dissembling rascall, & said hee would go, & get leave of the magistrates to whip him with a rod till hee made him run about the house this was about a fortnight, or three weekes at the most, before the said Robrt Dyed, the said Bets tould the said Richrd hee had devised a way to scare his man Robrt Knight, & make him to run by putting a light into a dogs head, & conveying it secretly into his sight to scare him, & so make him to run, & if hee got him up hee would keepe him up, hee would warrant taken upon oath the 8th of the 10th m^{o} 1652 before me Increase Nowell

Affirmed on oath to be true before ye Gennerall Court 25th may 1653 Edward Rawson secret^{y}.

Ann Williamson aged about 16 yeares comeing before me Incre[ase] Nowell the 10th of the 10th m^{o} 52 saith that her mrs Andrews willing her to help the wife of John Bets to wash ~~she~~ ‖ her mrs ‖ was not willing to let her wash Robert Knights cloaths they smelt so strong, so John Bets bad Thom: Abbot set the keeler to Robert Knight that hee might wash his owne cloaths, & John Bets said hee would make the said Robrt to wash them, but Thom: Abbot going out she the said Ann set the keeler to Robrt, & the wife of John Bets did looke up the cloaths of the said Robrt that hee might wash them the said Robrt cryed, & said it was not fit for her ‖the said Ann ‖ to do, ~~yet~~ ‖ & ‖ did what hee could, & this was about tenn dayes before the said Robrt dyed

taken upon oath the day before mentioned before mee
Increase Nowell

Affirmd on oath to be true before ye Gennerall Court 25 May 1653
Edward Rawson Secret^{y}

(Endorsed) Left french mrs Andrew^{s}. & Ann w^{m}son test.

The testimony of Thomas Abbot Servt to John Betts aged about twenty yeares.

This deponent testifyeth that the same day wch Robert Knight his ffellow Servt. complained that his master had broaken his backe by a blow wth the plow staffe, that He being at worke wth the said Knight and his mr; his mr John Betts put forth his hand to strike this * ‖ deponent ‖ where uppon he escaped out of his reach, and as his mr was houlding the plow and the sd Knight driueing, his mr, wth the plow staffe as it were with a swinging blow, (and not a full upright stroake) did strike the sd Knight vppon the hips or the lower part of his backe he knows not wch, but, that it was not by much so high as the place that Robert ‖ Knight ‖ complained to ‖ be ‖ broaken he saith he is sure and certeine, also he doth apprehend the blow was but slight, and not a full blow, and that the sd Robert Knight was almost out of his reach, also he testifieth that his mr laid downe the plow staffe, and tooke up the goad, which was a greene smal ‖ warnut tre ‖ goad and wth the smalest end did strike the said Knight 2 or 3 blowes, and the goad did claspe round about the body of the sd Knight and that it was the smalest end of the goad he saith he is sure & certeine ffurther he saith that after this he went Home for a shovell, and when he returned againe his mr being absent, the said Knight told him that as he was lifting at a stone his master strook him uppon the backe, wth the great end of the plow staffe, and that he thought his master had broaken his backe, and He himself obserued that when he stooped downe, he did rise with his handes on his knees and so rose by degrees for the space of a weeke, but afterwards ffor a good space he did not complaine of it, but caried 2 bushels of Corne to milne on a wheelebarrow, 3 mile [&c.] and did his labor as formerly wthout any complaint,

ffurther he testifieth that the said Knight w̄ he came Home to dinner the same day complained to his dame that his master had broaken his backe, and desired her to looke on it, who accordingly did, and this deponent being prsent as also mrs Sarah Simes they Saw uppon the upper part of his backe a smal kibe, but no blunes or rednes, or any thing that did betoken any stroke or bruse, but apprehended that the kibe or nub that was on his backe was no new thing.

ffurther this Deponent testifieth that the said Knight told him about the latter end off ffebruary or ye beginning of march before this wch was about 2 monthes, that he went up a ladder that stood uppon the barne floare, and when he was up nine or ten staves, the 10th staffe broake and ‖ he ‖ fell between the ladder sides and slipt downe till he rested uppon the midle of his body, and then fell backward that so his shoulders first pitched on the grownd or barne floor also the said knight added that he thought he had broaken ~~his~~ two of his ribs, and that he had hurt his shoulder

ffurther this deponent saith that after this he saw the said Knight w̄ he sat downe he would set stooping, and w̄ his dame spake to him

* Them changed to this.

he would then complaine of his side, and for 3 or foure dayes he kept his bed, and was not able to labor, not any at all of 3 or foure dayes, and not as formerly of a month

ffurther this Deponent testifieth that about 2 dayes before the said Knight complained y[t] his m[r] had broaken his backe this Deponent and the said Knight were Spreading of doung to gether, and this deponent obseruing that he did twice or thrice as much as the said Knight, he asked the said Knight how it was y[t] he could spread 2 or 3 hills of mucke to his one, and the said Knight answered, y[t] he had such a paine on his side y[t] he could not perform his labo[r].

also this deponent saith that this he obserued the whole time betwen the fall that the said Knight had of the ladder, and the day that he complained of his m[r] for breaking his backe, that the said Knight altho he was for y[e] latter ꝑt able to do such labo[r] as did not occassion him to bow his body yet w̄ he had occassion to do any labo[r] that did occassion him to bow his body he eu̅ more complained, of his side:

ffurther this deponent testifieth that the said Knight often times told him that he was resoloued y[t] he would neu̅ learne to do husbandry altho his m[r] would learne him, and he gaue this reason bec̄: he had such a mind to his trade v[zt] a weau̅ and that the said Knight was so deceitfull that his m[r] could not trust him so much as to give the cattle meate, and also that uppon a time the said Knight was sent by his m[r] to giue the cattle some meat, and he came In again and said he had done it, and yet afterward being examined confessed that he had lied, and that he had not giuen them any meat at all, and y[e] like he did often, so that by reason thereof his m[r] was much inraged agst him, and agst himselfe vz[t] this Deponent also, who must needs confesse that they were both deceitfull in their labor and did plot by all meanes they could to get away and be ffreed ffrom their master being much moued thereunto by reason of there masters passion w̄ he was moued by their deceitfullnes in y[r] labor

ffurther this Deponent testifieth that the said Knight was much giuen to stealing and lying and cursing himselfe.

as once he did steal a knife from a neighbor and denied it, and wished that if he had it, y[t] it were in his bellie and y[t] he might neu[r] speake word more, and y[e] like, and yet afterward confessed that he had it, and at another time he did steale a paire ^ gloues, ffrom one in y[e] meeting house ‖ on y[e] Sabbath day ‖ (as himselfe after confessed) and yet said that they were given to him.

ffurther this deponent saith y[t] this testimony aboue written is the truth of w[t] he knowes concerning Robert Knight and the blow y[t] his m[r] gaue him, and the cariadge of the buissines untill the time that the said Knight made his complaint to y[e] magistrates, and further he saith not.

ꝑ me Thomas Aboot:

10. 12. 1652

ffurther he saith concerning the said John Betts, and Robert Knight dureing the time that the ‖ said Knight ‖ continued after he came Home from ye Magestrates as followeth vzt That after the returne of Robert Knight, untill the time yt ye said Knight fell bedred, his mr caried it very well towards the sd Knight, but after yt his mr called ye said Knight dissembleng wretch, rascall, and bloud soucor, and yt he did wt he could to take away his life, with other words of ye like nature, which wordes, ye said Knight being troubled ‖at‖ tould his dame, and said yt he did freely forgiue his mr any wrong he had done him, and desired no revenge of him, also he testifieth yt the sd Betts when ye said Knight was lying on ye bed, tooke hould of ye sheet, and dragged him of ye bed by ye sheet: & for this reason bec̄: ye said Knight did not rise so soone as ye sd betts did desire, also ye said Betts made ye said Knight a place betwen 2. railes as high as his armes, wherin he did set him up some times in ye morning & let him so stand fast tied yt he could not set downe, untill noone and some times made him stand ye like time in ye after noone onely some times his dame & some times my selfe did let him downe, also ye said Betts did study by all meanes to affright him and make him stirre conceiueing ye said Knight did counterfeit, also ye said Betts threatned to whip ye said Knight if he would not stir, and Robert ‖Knight‖ sd if he did [it] he could not helpe it, also on a sabbath day morning, ye said Betts being ‖formerly‖ ꝑvoked with ye said Knight by fowling his bed, and ye house by his excrements and conceiuing him to Counterfeit, did take some of his excrements, and put the same into ye mouth of ye said Robert Knight, also sometimes ye said Betts would take ye said Knight by ye Chin and hould up his head, & sometimes giue him a box of ye eares and sometimes when he lay on ye ground he would giue him a kicke, with his foote, also at a time w̄ his dame had a washer of her fowle cloathes, ye said Betts said that the sd Knight should wash them himselfe, & Robert Knight answered ay let me do them for its fit for no body else to do them, but my dame said he should not, and yet ye said Knight sd, let me do them for they are not fit for any body else.

also yt on a Satturday at night about a fortnight before ye decease of ye said Knight this deponent saw yt ye secret members of ye said Knight were much mortified, the wch he imediately tould his ~~master~~ dame and from yt time untill the death of ye sd Knight ye said Betts did his uttermost endeaur to get up the Chirurgions, and yet neū the lesse ye said Betts would affirme yt ye sd Knight did dissemble euen unto his dying day, and further this deponant saith not

1st (1) mo $\frac{52}{53}$ By me Tho. Abbott:
Affirmed upon the oath formrly taken
the first of the first mo 1652 or 1653
Increase Nowell

Affirmed on ye former oath to be true before ye Gennll Courte 25 May 1653 Edw: Rawson secrety

[Endorsed] Tho Abbotts test

Agedd about (50 yeares

The Testimony of William French concerning John Betts & his servant Robert Knight deceased

Testifieth that John Betts often endeauored to ꝑswade me that his seruant Robert Knight did conterfitt & dissemble & that it was Lasynes & Idlenes yt caused him to lye abed & say he could not stirr his lower parts, but felt numnes & deadnes in them; vpon wch ocation among [ot]hers my selfe & capt Gookin went to the fellow to his maste[rs] house where hee lay in his bed complaineng of his paine & weaknes; my selfe & the captine solemnely chardged him with conterfeiting & disembling also inioyneing him carfuly & conscientiously to declare to vs whether his masters blows hurt his backe or that it came any other way; as his master aledged by a fall of ~~the~~ a ladder in the barne ye winter past, the said Knight answered yt what hee spake of his paine & [num]nes both in his backe & lower parts were true & reall: & yt hee had no hurt in his backe by his fall of the ladder wch was not aboū 3 or fower Rounds of the ladder from the ground & yt hee had no hurt in his backe therby but only a litle pane in his side ‖ & that ‖ hee after was recouered of it ‖ the man ‖ stedfasly auerring that it was his masters blow wth the plow staffe yt hurt his backe, wch was the ocation of his prsent weaknes, annother time ‖ about ‖ two dayes before his death captane Gookin Decon Bridge & my selfe was with the said Robert Knight where wee solemly requird him to deale truly wth vs; concerning what his master had said of him viz that he dissembled & conterfeited also wee Inioyned him As hee would no‖w‖ a‖n‖swer before the Lord whether the cause of his misery came from his masters blows or by any other cause, he confessed his euell in lying in pilfering in some acts of wilfulnes; all wch he bewaild especialy his hard hart yt he could not more bewail ym; but yett still said yt his complants & paines were true & reall & yt his masters blows were the first cause of the weakenes in his backe yett he sayd hee ffrely forgaue his master; moreoū on that day beeing alone wth the said Robert endeuoring to draw forth truth from him & that his soule might be healed, ~~the said yonge man told me~~ I questioning of him how twas with his poore body he Answerd twas bad enough; but I leaue all to God & freely forgiue all wheron I required him yt if their were any thing yt did greue him yt hee would declare it his answer was yt one Sabbath day morning about a fort[ni]ght before; his master came in & tooke hold of the sheet vnder him & draged him about [the] house, & their left him, and att ‖an‖other time hee beeing sett vp by his master in a place hee had made for him to stand in hee stood so long vntill he felt no flesh he had he was so benumed; and yt at some such times his ‖master‖ would [durst] him & spurne him; & also yt hee made ‖a‖ whipp wth one cord & threatened to whip him wth it & to make him stir & hee said yt he gaue him 2 blowes wth ye said whip

William ffrench

[In margin]

Taken vppon oath the 8th day of 9 month 1652
before mee

Daniel Gookin

25 may 1653 Affirmd on ye form^r^ oath before ye Genl Court
Edw. Rawson secret^y^
(Endorsed) William French his Testimony Concerning old Betts

XIX.

[Middlesex County Court Files. "Wm Johnson vs. Woburne, 1662, County Court April 1, p. 201."]

Att A Court of Asistants held at Boston the 6th of ye 7th mo: 1653

The Court Graunted Administration of the estate of m^r^ Nicholas [Trerice] deceased to m^rs^. Rebeckah Trerice his widdow to pay as farre as the [estate] will goe, the Inventory being thirty sixe pounds tenn shillings. This is a true Copie taken out of the Courts booke of records as Attests

Edward Rawson Recorder.

NOTE.

This case "Wm Johnson vs. Woburne" was an action brought at the Middlesex County Court, April 1662, by William Johnson against the Town of Woburn and related to the title to 45 acres of land in Woburn, described as follows in a copy of a deed on file in the case: — "abutting to ye lands of Prudence Wilkins and James Hubbard Nor West, and to the land of William ffrothingham North East, and to ye land of Thomas Lynde and Hutchinson South East, and to ye land of Robert Shorthose South West." The deed is by Rebeca Trerise widow of Nicholas Trerise, marriner, of Charlestowne Deceased, to William Johnson of Woburn and is dated "26th of ye first moneth 1662." The copy is attested by "Samuel Phipps Cler."

XX.

[Mass. Archives, Vol. 10, No. 304(4) and No. 308(3).]

[304 (4)] Vpon the presentment of Benjamin Sawser by ye grand Jury we the Jury of life and death finde not the bill of the grand Jury, but finde the sd Beniamin Sawser vpon euidence, being in drinke to haue spoken profainely & Ignorantly Blasfemus words In saying Jehoua is the Devel, & he knew noe god but his sworde and that should saue him.

7 — 7^m^ — 1654. Edward Hutchinson foreman
by Consent of ye Jury

[308 (3)] In Sawcers case

Whereas the grand Jury did leave out certayne words mentioned in the lawe against blasphemers yet did finde the prisoner guilty of speaking that which we apprehended amounteth in substance to what the lawe expresseth so farr as to make the offence capitall; And whereas this bill soe found was comitted to the Jury of life & death and they have acquitted the prisoner vpon poynt of ignorance & we finding testimony that he the prisoner did at or about the tyme of vttering the words speak rationally: vpon these grounds the magistrates doe dissent from the verdict of ye Jury.

consented by the Corte of Assistants
Increase Nowell

NOTE.

The following paper (Mass. Archives, Vol. 10, No. 303 (2).) was probably the draft of a bill, but not the one actually found by the Grand Jury, as appears by the papers given below and by the fact that it has no signature or certification: —

"Boston the 27th of the 4th mo. 1654

Wee the Grand Jury for the Comon Wealth do present Benjamin Sawser a souldier for not haveing the feare of God before his eyes that vpon the 14th of this present 4th month in Boston hee did wittingly and willingly blaspheme the sacred name of God in saying Jehova is the Devill, and hee knew no God, but his sword, and that should save him, contrary to the law of God, and laws of this Jurisdiction sufficiently published"

The following paper (Mass. Archives, Vol. 10, No. 305 (1).) relates no doubt to this case: —

"The grand Jury for the Commonwealth did present B [C] * according to lawe for blasphemy:

The bill of Indictment was drawne according to the word of the Capitall Law provided in that Case.

The grand Jury did not bring in theire verdict according to the termes of the sajd Lawe but altered the termes from (wittingly & willingly) to willingly & prophanely.

The magistrates put it to the trjall of the Jury of life & death:

The Jury of life and death brings in theire verdict not making the blasphemye Capitall: The Court receiveth not yr verdict

1 — The question is whither the gennerall Court will be pleased to heare ye whole Case.

2 — or whither the prisoner ought not further to be proceeded against by way of Jury for ye Capitallitje of ye Crjme

---

*B. S.?

3 — Thirdly if Acquitted from a Capitall Crjme whither such blasphemous expressions should not be punished otherwise & what his punishment shall be.

The magist^{ts}. desire theire bretheren the deput[ies] to Consider & Resolve these questions in ye 1st place.

Edward Rawson Secret^{y}

The Deputyes think meete to heare the whole Case if o^{r} hourd magis^{ts} Consent hereto

William Torrey Cleric.

21 (8) 1654

Consented to by ye magis^{ts}

Edw: Rawson Secret^{y}"

Accordingly the 25th of October 1654 was appointed for said hearing. There are several depositions sworn to on the 31st of Oct. and the 1st of Nov.

A petition by the prisoner to the General Court appears in Mass. Archives, Vol. 10, No. 306, as follows:—

"To the Honoured Generall Court in Boston

Bee pleased to suffer a poore prisoner that hath a long time layne in chaines, and fetters; in misery, and in a sad condition to spread his case before you: I hope it will not trouble or grieve you: I intend it not: but my misery and sad distresse I am in, in the condition I now stand in makes mee bould to present these few supplicant lines to you. It is well knowne that I am a true borne subiect of England: a subiect to his Highnesse Oliuer Lord Protector: of England: Scottland: and Ireland: and to the States of England: for whose sakes I haue not thought my life to deare, often to uenture it in their cause and quarrell, as tendinge and mindinge the good of the English nation in generall: in prosecution of my employments as a souldier: I was moued to take a uoyage to New England: to serue his Highnesse in some seruice that might tend to the good of this country: which seruice I cheerfully vndertooke: in the prosecution whereof I meet with many difficulties distresses, and perills, and dangers at Sea: but in God's time I arriued here joyfull that I was in a capacity to serue my nation in these remote Corners of the world. It soe fell out that being occasionally a shoare (hauinge beene before a longe time on Shipboard) and meetinge with divers of our fellow souldiers, wee were to free in our mirth and drinke, by reason whereof some takinge notice thereof as it seemeth, fell a discoursinge with mee, and as they say beinge hasty and proud, returned vnseemely, and vngodly, and as they say diuelish language. It is most certainly true I am shamefully ignorant of God, and you may wonder it should bee soe, but soe it is though I haue had some meanes of knowinge more than I doe, and I thanke God I now know more of God then I did when hether I first came, and I dare not speake or thinke euelly of the name of God soe farre as I know him. I am apt to thinke St. Paul knew more of God and Christ in his worst time then I did, yett you know what hee sayeth as in other places: Honoured S^rs. you cannot but know how long I haue beene a prisoner, in what Case and condition I haue layen in these many months. I haue runn the Risque of my life by submittinge to the Current of Justice as settled amongst your selues, and by that way I conceaue accordinge to Law ffreed, yett by some fewer parties dissentinge am still kept in misery in prison and what you intend with mee I know not. My Commanders that brought mee out desired to free mee accordinge to that Law appoynted for mee and my fellow souldiers in any transgression that should fall out: I would haue submitted to it but could not obtaine it, what will bee done with mee I know not. But thus I am a free borne subiect of England, and was sent out as a seruant employed in the service of his Hignesse, and the State of England: I am noe inhabitant of this place, therefore giue mee liberty without offence: in the presence of God and this assembly, to appeale vnto the State and Gouernment, to whom I doe belonge: and I doe hereby appeale to his Highnesse, and the State of England.

[306(2)] If I haue wronged any mans estate, or done iniustice to any, I am ready to answer it, to satisfaction. where I haue offended God I hope hee will abundantly pardon. Thus begginge the blessinge of God amongst you, in your proceedings: I rest

Your poore prisoner

Beniamin Sacer

Dat: Octob. ye 25th 1654."

The following is in Mass. Archives, Vol. 10, No. 308: —

"The Deputyes in the case of the blasphemer passinge a vote therevppon the howse was Equally devided, & doe desire it should now be determined by the whole Court together which we are ready to attend if o^r hono^rd magis^ts Consent hereto

William Torrey Cleric."

The case appears to have come to the General Court for determination Nov. 1, 1654, but before sentence the prisoner escaped whereupon the following orders were passed. (See Mass. Col. Records, Vol. IV., Part I., p. 213.)

"Benjamin Saucer, a souldjer, was indicted at the Court of Asistants in September last for vttering most ꝓphane and vnheard of blasphemy, saying y^t Jehovah was the divill, that he knew no God but his sword; the bench & jury differing in the verdict whither the crjme was capitall or not, ye case came to the Court in course to be determined; the sajd Saucer appeared before the Court, and pleaded not guilty; the evidences were heard against him; but before the Court came to a sentence, the said Saucer made an escape out of prison.

It is ordered that George Munnings, the keeper of the prison, shall be called to an account about the escape of the prisoner, Benjamin Saucer, and that he shall answer for the same at the next County Court at Boston, vnto whom power is hereby given to deale with him as they shall see the merrit of the cawse, either by fine, displacing of him, or otherwise, if he give not a sufficijent sattisfactory answer.

Itt was voted by the whole Court, that Major Robt Sedgwick should be sent vnto, and in the name of the Court desired to send vp Benjamin Saucer, the blasphemer, that he may be deliuered into prison and to the keeper, from whence [he] made escape. The Courts minde was sent to Major Sedgwicke accordingly."

In the Deputies record (Mass. Col. Records, Vol. III., p. 368) is the message sent to Major Sedgwick, in which he is described as "commander in chefe of this fleet."

XXI.

[Middlesex County Court Files, "Margerum v. Brown, County Court 1655."]

To the marshall or his Deputy

By vertue hereof you are required to levy of the goods, & chattels of mr William Browne to the value of eleven pounds foure shillings, & a penny wth 2s for the execution to sattisfy Richard Margerum for a verdit granted by the Corte of Assistants the 6th prsent hereof not to faile Dated the 16th of the first mo 1654 *

By the Corte Increase Nowell

If goods appeare not take
his person in execution
Idem In. Nowell

Will. Toye Jon Ridgway Jon: [H]aitfeild these three tooke oath the 14th ofthe 3d mo 1655

Before mee Increase Nowell

This execution was leuied vppon the estait of mr Will. Brown the value of eleuen pounds six shillings, & a penny; this 14: 3: 1655

Per me Ri. Wayte Marshall

NOTE.

Among the papers on the Middlesex Files in this case is the following execution and levy thereon: —

"To the marshall, or his deputy

By vertue hereof you are required to levy of the goods, & chattels of mr Willi[am] Browne to the value of one hundred fiftye eight pound eleven shillings, & seaven pence wth 2s for the execution to satisfy Richard Margerum for a verdit granted at a Corte held at Boston the 14th prsent hereof not to faile dated the 18th of the 9th mo 1654.

By the Corte Increase Nowell

If goods appeare not take
his person in execution
Increase Nowell"

---

* 1654-5.

[Endorsed] "Delivered to Ri: margerum a house & ground & all the apportenacis thervnto belonging of m^r will Broune of Salem which house is in Boston to the value of one hundred and twenty fiue pounds: this 8 : 10 : 54.

The remainder of this execution was leuied vppon the Estaite of m^r Will Brounes this 14 : 3 : 1655.

Per me Ri Wayte:

Isack Collins Henery Brigham & Thomas Joy were sworne as apprisers this 8th 10 m^o 1654 before mee Natha: Duncan Cōmissioner"

The following order of the General Court, in May 1655, probably relates to this case. (Mass. Col. Records, Vol. IV., Part I., p. 237.)

"In ans^r to the peticon of Richard Marjerum, the Court judgeth it meete to refer the peticoner for releife in his case to a Court of justice."

The same order is given more fully in the Deputies Records: — Mass. Col. Records, Vol. III., p. 388.

"Richard Margerum, p^rfering a pet. for releife, in respect of an estate, as he affirmes, vnjustly detayned from him by Mr Wm Browne, of Salem, is referd for recouery of the same to a course of law in a Court of justice."

In the record of the Middlesex County Court held "at Charlestowne 25th 10th month 1655" is the following: —

"Ri: Margerum plaintiffe agst m^r Wm Brown Deff^t, in an accon of the case vppon acc^t. The Jury findes a non liquett."

There is also on the Middlesex Files a copy of writ and attachment "Richard Margerum vs. m^r William Browne" of Salem, returnable at the "next County Court to be held at Boston on the 14 day of this 9th. month" and dated 4th. 9th. mo. 1654; also a copy of a similar writ dated "23 (11) 1654." Both copies are attested as follows: — "This is a true copie compared wth. the originall wch I had on the file kept by the late honnored m^r Nowell as attests Edw: Rawson Secret^y."

XXII.

[Court Files, Suffolk, No. 262, 10th paper. Estate of Gibbons, appellant, against Stoddard, &c., appellees.]

this : 3 : of y^e : 7 : mo^th we find a spe[c]iall virdict we finde a moregage made by : major Edward Gibons to the defendent * of one eight parte of the mills : and also the originall deede made by John millam to major Gibbons : in ye hands of ye defendent : we find ye morgage Recorded by ye publicke notary : but we finde not the morgage acknowledged before a magestrate : as for ye legallity of the Recordinge

---

*** Defendants on appeal.**

of it we leave it to the Judgment of the ~~corte~~ binch to determine.*
|| The bench finds for ye defendants † & confirmes the Judgment of the former County Court: y[t] Possession be Given the defendants of ye sd eight p[t] of ye mill mill howse dames &c. and Costs of both Courts.

4 Septemb[r] 1656 Edw Rawson Secret[y]."

[Endorsed] Speciall verdict in m[r] Stoddards case.

NOTE.

This judgment of the Court of Assistants was given on an appeal from a judgment of the County Court at Boston in April 1656. The first paper in the case (No. 262) is a copy of the writ wherein it appears that the suit at the County Court was by "Anthony Stoddard, Hezekiah Usher, and John Johnson and Thomas Bell, junior, attorneys for Thomas Bell, senior, in an action of the case for full possession" of one eighth part of the "water mill or mills scittuate and being in Boston, with the mill house or mill houses, dames, sluces, water cources and other appurt[ces] heretofore belonging to the late Major Edw[d] Gibbons and by him mortgaged & sold to m[r] Anthony Stoddard, m[r] Thomas Bell & m[r] Hezekiah Usher for certaine sums of money, as in that deede bearing date the 4th of November 1651 more amply appeareth" the same having been "forfeited four yeares since and vpwards, & so owned by the said Major Gibbons that gave vp his originall deede thereof vnto the said Anthony Stoddard, Hezekiah Usher and Thomas Bell which yet notwithstanding the Administrators of the said Major Gibbons Estate hath since his death wth held and denyed to giue full possession thereof"

The second paper is a copy of an order of the County Court at Boston, 28 December 1654, providing for equal distribution of the estate of the "late Major Generall Edward Gibbons" among his creditors, administration on the estate having been "lately granted to m[r] Thomas Lake, Ensigne Joshua Scottow and m[r]. John Richards"

The third paper is a copy of the record of the County Court in said case 29 April 1656. "The Jury found a speciall verdict viz. wee finde a mortgage made by majo[r] Edward Gibons to the Plaintiffs of one eight part of the mill & also the originall deede made p John Milam to majo[r] Gibons in the hands of ye Plaintiffs. Wee finde the mortgage recorded by the publicke Notary but wee finde not ye mortgage Acknowledged before a magistrate as for the legallity of the Recording of it wee leave it to the Judgment of the Court. This is a true Copie of ye Jury verdict as Attest Edw. Rawson Recorder.

At an Adjourment of ye County Court held at Boston 17 May 1656. Att w[ch] time the Court mett Againe & vejwing the speciall verdict in the case betweene Anthony Stoddard, Hezekiah Vsher Tho. Bell ag[t] the mill mill howse &c. of the late major Gibbons. The Court

* From here the handwriting is Rawson's.

† Stoddard, &c., defendants on appeal.

i.e. the bench of magistrates found for ye Plaintiffs. The defendants m^r Lake and Ensigne Scottow Appealed from the Judgment to ye next Court of Asistants & gaue Security Accordingly. This is a true Copie taken out of the Court booke of Records as Attests

Edw: Rawson Recorder"

The fourth and fifth papers contain the two answers to the reasons of appeal,* in which among other things it is claimed that the recording of the mortgage, though not acknowledged, rendered it good against the mortgagor and his heirs and also against his administrators, and that these administrators have no right to take or hold the mortgaged estate for the benefit of creditors; the mortgagor having retained possession only by favor, and having delivered the title deed to the mortgagees.

The argument used was that the deed and the mortgage mentioned in the judgment of the County Court "are and were both recorded, & that by the Recorder for the time beeing, & that in such a way as he did vsually Record which was without the acknowledgment before a magistrate, he not observing the punctillio of law, doth not so much invallidate the Grantor's Right &c as indanger himself by layeing himselfe open to the censure of the Court for the neglect of his duty. ffurther the Major hauing not only passed his right in the mills to us, but deliuered vs the originall deed, we see not but wee beeing secured from him and his heires are sufficiently secured from his administrators to whom the p^rmisses were neuer conveyed." It was stated that as a matter of accommodation the mortgagor was allowed to take the rents, but it was denied that "the p^rmisses conveyed away by the Maior in his life time & possession by the originall deed to vs by the Maior" would "after his death fall into any administrator's hands, nor doe wee beleiue any Court will assume to themselues such power as to deliver houses and lands so made away by a man in his life time into the hands of administrators."

The sixth paper in the case is a copy of a deed dated 12 Oct., 1649, from John Milam (or Millam) of Boston, cooper, to Major Edward Gibbons (or Gibons) of Boston, for 350^£, of "one quarter or fowerth part of the water mill or mills & of all the watercourses mill dams" &c. in Boston "and one quarter or fowerth part of all the lands howses" &c. appurtaining to the "said mill or mills and now in the tenure and occupation of the said John Milam and Thomas Clarke merchants or either of them" The witnesses were John Dand and James Mills, and there is a certificate of the recording by "William Aspinwall Recorder" 15 Oct. [1649], but the deed does not appear to have been acknowledged.

The seventh and eighth papers are depositions in the case and the ninth paper is a further order of the County Court at Boston 1 February 1654–5, as to the distribution of Major Gibbons' estate among the creditors.

By a deed dated Jan. 23, 1656–7, the defendants on the appeal in

* The "Reasons of Appeal" is not among the papers.

this case, Anthony Stoddard and others, convey the said eighth part of the mill &c. to Capt. Thomas Clarke, reference being made to the Judgment at the Court of Assistants, Sept., 1656, confirming the judgment of the County Court "that possession of the said eighth part should be given to the said Anthony Stoddard &c." (Suffolk Registry Deeds, Vol. II., p. 341.)

XXIII.

[Court Files, Suffolk, No. 259, 32d paper.]

In the action of apeale m^r^ Robert Patteshall plaintiue against John Gerardie wee find a Spetiall verdit: wee finde that at a Spetiall Courte held at boston the 18th of August 1656 that theare was a Judgment granted against m^r^ Robert Patteshall for one hundred and seauentene pounds aeight shillings and seauen penc half peney: with Cost of Courte three pounds fower shillings:

the legallatie of which wee doe not vnderstand: not finding any euidence to guide vs theare in and thearfore wee leaue it vnto the Bench to determine the Case

Richard Cooke in
the behalf of the rest

Note.

The above verdict is not dated but it was evidently rendered at the Court of Assistants in September 1656, as appears from a deed by Robert Pateshall to John Joyliffe, dated 29 Nov., 1656, and recorded in Suffolk Registry of Deeds B. III., p. 97. That deed recites that "Thomas Scott, atturney to John Gerardy," "at a speciall Court held at Boston, obtained a judgment against the said Robert Pateshall for detaining the goods of Roger Kilvert, which judgment was afterwards confirmed at a Court of Assistants in Boston, aforesaid, the fowerth day of September," 1656, "against the said Pateshall, and execution thereupon awarded."

It appears from the papers in the case, No. 259, where the above verdict is found, that there were two actions, one between Kilvert and Gerardy, tried at a Special Court in July 1656, and the other between Pateshall and Gerardy, tried at a Special Court in August, 1656.

Among the papers the "Reasons of Appeal" by Pateshall, being the first paper in No. 259 is as follows: —

"[ ] Reasons of Appeale by Robt [Pateshall in the] Accon of Jno. Gerardy pplt against [Robt] Pateshall Deft. in an Accon of the Case, for detain[ing] the Cargoe, or loading of the Galliott, the value of 120 li

ffirst when the Galliott came to Boston, shee was ffree from any engagemt. or cleyer from beinge under any Leagall power, for ought any man knew, whereuppon the said Robt Pateshall, did disburst, a Considerable, Estate, to sett her forth to Sea, lookinge uppon the vessell, & ꝑduce [as] sufficient securitie,

Secondly The said Robt: Pateshall uppon her Returne, did disburst, a Considerable sume of mony more, to pay Seamen's Wages, And provissions, & other disburstmts., without wch, the Cargoe could not, have bin recd,

Thirdly The said Robt: Pateshall, did Receave the said Cargoe accordinge to agreemt. out of the said vessell, And did dispose of it, to seu'all men, before any demand, or Attachmt. as goods Propperly belongeinge to him, for his disburstments — And owned and alowed of in Court, by Roger Kilvert, That it was for sattisfacon of the said Robt Pateshalls disburstmts.

ffowerly that the Jury did bringe in theyr virditt, and doe rate all the Coales sould at Three pounds the Chaldron, And it will appe, a good pt. of them were sould for ffiftie shillings ꝑ [Chaldron]

ffiftly I desire you to Consider there was no Estate, at all, but what I disburst, to fetch & hew the Coales out of the Beach, but what I disburst to obtaine them, by settinge forth the vessell, and hyeringe the Seamen to goe to fetch them

Therefore I hope neyther law, Equety, reason, or iustice, will take away the Cargoe, or my iust disburstmts, from mee, All wch I leave to yor grave & serious Considracons, restinge

Yors Robt. Pateshall"

The answer to the above "Reasons of Appeal" is No. 26717, Court Files, Suffolk, and is as follows:

"An answer to the Resons of mr patishalls appeall

First whear as mr patishall saith that the Reson that he laied out his estate vpon the Galiott was because: that it was not knowen to him that shee was vnder any legall power: (to wch I answer): that its sufitient for vs, that we haue allredy prooued that shee was vnder the pour of the law: at that time: and thearfore if mr patishall be disapaynted thearby: I shall willingly grant him leve for to imput it to his owne ignorance concerning the Condytion of the vesell: as indeed he doth:: but I Conceave this Reson to be of no valew: becaus mr patishall doth not appea[ll from] that virdictt which gaue vnto vs the Galiott and hur Cargoe, but from that Court or virditt: which only tooke the quantity of the Coall so far as was both prooued and acknowledged then in the Court: and allso sumed vp; what thay amounted vnto according to the pric thay ware sould at: as did then appear in Court

Secondly: whear as he doth aleadg that he did disburst a considerable sum of mony to pay seamen and provistion and other disburstments with out wch the Cargoe Could not haue bin receud I answer: that m^r Killuert is the more ingaged to m^r patishall: [yt] in that the Cargoe was thearby freed: and so Capable of answering m^r Killuerts honist and more antient dabts: furder it did neuer yet appear that eyther Galiott or Cargoe was ingaged for to answer any disburstm^t of m^r patishalls notwithstanding it haue bin twic in adgitation: in two Speciall Courts and thearfore as I conceue it was concleuded and determined: and that according to law and reson:, according to verditt we haueing first recouered this estate by a Course of law; this estat appeearing to be properly m^r Killuerts: and not any way ingaged to m^r patishall: the sd patishall haue yet the same liberty that we haue had: for to prosecut the law against m^r Killuert, wch yet he hath not don: for according as m^r patishall did Creditt m^r Killuert vpon his [leter or] note: whear in he doth not ingage his vessell: but him: self: and accordingly m^r patishall Chargeth the sd Killuert dabter at this time for theis disburstments: as doth appear in his accoumpts:: I do also Conceaue this reson to be of no vallue: because as I said before the appeall was not from that virdict that gaue us the vesell and Cargoe: but from that virdictt which did only sum up what: it amounted vnto:

Thirdly: whear as its aleadged that m^r patishall receaued the sd Cargoe according to agreement out of the sd vessell: and disposed of it to seuerall men before any demand or atachment as goods properly belonging to him for his disburstments; and owened and alowed of: in Court by Roger Killuert: and that in satisfaction of the sd patishall disburstments: I answer: that this reson as its beside the Case in [hand so it] agrees not [nyther] with truth nor honesty: for: neuer yet did any agreement appear [ ] the asignement: which was made to oulld m^r Killuert: if so: then it Coulld not be to [ ] as his oune property [and] in satisfaction for his disburstments: and whear as he saith that [ ] killuert owened it in Court: its not true for he owened [ ] into m^r patishals hand by that asignement: to his father: and to that: end: to preuent m^r Gereardy and also [ ] then did and now doth owen himself indabted to m^r. patishall: according to the sd patishalls account Charged vpon the sd killuert:: this reson of m^r patishall I doe allso conseue of no valew and that for the Considerations giuen before,: it not tending to the case

fourthly whear he aleadgeth that according to the virditt the Coalls ware rated at three pounds the Challdron: whearas sum of them as he saith ware soulld for fifti shillings the Challdron; I answer that it was both prooued and acknowledged: in the Court: both by m^r Killuert and m^r patishall that thear ware forty Challdron soulld for three pounds the Challdron which amounts to more then the verdit: and: in Case m^r patishall hath soulld any of them at an vnder: rate out of sum priuitt respects to himsellf: or to plesure his friends that Conserns not vs

fifttly whearas he doth aleag that thear was no estate at all: but only what he the sd patishall did disburst whear by this Cargoe was procuered I answer: it Concerns not vs: by whose means or by what hallps and forederanc m^r^ Killuert did obtaine and procure this Cargoe of Coale its sufitiant that we haue allredy prooued it to be m^r^ Killuerts oune proper estate and that it appeears not: that it was aniwais ingaged to anyman: nayther hath m^r^ patishall nor any other sewed or recouered any judgment against it according to law: nayther hath thear bin any Convayenc of it out of m^r^ Killuerts hand: but only by that fraudelent asignement whi[ch] was made voyd by the Speciall Court houllden about the 3^d^ or 4th of August last: from whenc m^r^ patishall doth not appeall: all wch I doe humblely p^r^sent to the Consideration of the honered Court:

yours to Com̃and
Tho Scott"

The 27th. paper in No. 259, which appears to be an account by Patteshall, is as follows:—

"An acco^t^. of the Issues of Coales d^d^. out of the Galliott in Boston 1656

d^d^. Jno. Baker 10 Chaldrons at 3^li^: 50s^s^ in mony and the rest in Provissions, the mony hee pd Roger Kilvert - - - - - - - - - - -	30:	00:	0
To Dan: Turyn 10 Chaldrons vppon the same Tearms the money pd to Roger Kilvert - - - - -	30:	00:	0
To Geo. Halsall 5 Chaldrons in like prize - - - -	15:	00:	0
To Tho Baker, & Hawkins 2 Chaldrons - - - -	05:	00:	0
To [Hen.] Kemble 6 Chaldrons - - - - - -	15:	00:	0
To Alex: Addams 2 Chaldrons for a bill hee Trimed the Vessell for before shee went for the Coales - -	05:	16:	9
To m^r^ Evan Thomas 4 Chaldron 5 bu. at - - - -	10:	10:	0
111^li^: 06^s^: 9^d^			
	111:	6:	9

Toto 39 Chaldrons 5 bushells in all Issued to my knowledge besides the six the seamen had

[On back of paper]

An Acco^t^. of Coales sould,

pd 5s^s^ to gett Geo: Halsalls Coales out & 6s^s^ for hands to gett Kembles Coales out & measured"

The following is the 33d. paper in the case.

"ite for Coming hether and waighting hear one month - . - - - - - -	[		]
ite for two atachments and seruing them - -	00	[	]
ite thre warrants for witnesis - - - - -	00	[	]
ite thre witnesis tending the Co[urt] - - -	000	0[	]
ite Entring two actions - - - - - -	000	05	0
and what the Court Charges will com to I know not [*wch is for ye Jury - -	002	08:	0 —
charges of ye howse - - - - - -	001.	04	:
Allowed E R R.]	9	08	0"

This paper is endorsed "Gerard ag^t^. Kilve[rt] Speciall Court July."

The following paper (Court Files, Suffolk, No. 26701), is the bill of charges by Thomas Scott, who was the attorney for John Gerardy, at the Court of Assistants. Its allowance indicates that the judgment was in favor of Gerardy.

	s.	d
"Tho Scott his bill of Charges tending the Court fiue dais - - - - - - - - -	7	6
	1	6:

Allowed E R S:

I haue also tended only vpon this acation euer sinc the last Speciall Court wch was one the 18th of Augst last which hath bin great Chargis and damagis which I doe humbly intreat your worships to Consider and alow me sum satisfaction if it may bee

yours to Cōmand Tho Scott:"

[Endorsed] "Scotts bill of Costs"

XXIV.

[Essex County Court Files, Vol. XXIX., Fol. 137. Thomas Dexter's admin^rs^. v. Selectmen of Lynn, Nov., 1678, 4th paper.]

Att A Court of Assistants held at Boston the 1st day of September 1657.

Thomas Dexter plaintiff against Thomas Layton George Keysar Robert Coates & Joseph Armitage deffendants in an Accōn of Appeale After the Court & Jury had heard all the euidences produced at the County Court at Salem the Court Appealed from read which are on

* This last part is in Edward Rawson's hand.

file the Jury found for the deffendants Costs of Court seventeen shillings & sixe pence.

That this is a true Copie taken out of the Courts Records Attests
Edwd Rawson Secret^y.

Note.

The following papers are copied from the original records and files relating to the different actions in the County Court and Court of Assistants as to the title to Nahant, which was the subject to which the above judgment of the Court of Assistants related.

Record of the County Court at Salem 26 : 9mo. 1678.

"10 — Capt: James Oliver & Thomas Dexter Junr: Administrators to the estate of Thomas Dexter Senr: deceased, plts: agst: the Township of Lin, or Capt: Richard Walker, Thomas Leighton, William Bassett, Andrew Mansfield, Nathaniel Kertland, John Burrell & Ralph King : Select men of the Towne of Linne defts : in an action of review of a judgment granted against ye sd. Tho: Dexter Senr. in his life time at a Court of assistants held at Boston : ye 1 : 7 mo 57 : &c: acco: to atach^t: dated 20 : 9 : 78 : The atach^t. &c: ^

The Jury brought in theire verdict : they find for the def^t: cost of court 4^£ : 11^s : 06^d

The plantiffe by their Aturney Leift: Richd Waye apeales from this verdict, to the next Court of Assistants and the said Leift: Richard Waye, m^r Jonathan Ting & Joseph Webb doe acknowledg themselues to stand bound in twenty pound bond Joyntly & Seuerally, to ye treasurer of this County : the Condition is that the plts shall prosecute theire appeale to effect."

Essex County Court Files, Vol. XXVI., Fol. 149.

"To the Marshall of the County of Suffolk or Constable of the town of Lyn —

You are hereby Required in his Maj^ties name to attach the Goods, Estate, or lands of the Township of Lyn & for want theirof the bodyes of the Select men of the said Towne namely Thomas Layton Capt Richard Walker Capt Thomas Marshall Ralph King Samuel Cobbat, William Bassat, John Lewis, in the name & behalf of the towne of Lyn and take bond of them or either of them to the vallue of ffive hundred pounds for their and either of their appearances at the next County Court to be holden at Ipswich the last tewsday of this Instant September, Then & there to answer the Complaint of Captain James Olliver & Thomas Dexter junio^r Administrato^rs to the Estate of Thomas Dexter Senio^r deceased In an action of Review of a Judgment Granted against the said Dexter Senio^r in his life time at a Court of Assistants in Boston the first of September in the yeare 1657 which action then tryed was an action of Apeale from the judgment of Salem Court held the 30th of the 4th mo: 1657 being greatly to the damadg of the persons concerned. And so make a true return hereof under your hand Dated the 20th. day of September 1677

By the Court William Chard"

[Endorsed] "September 20th. 1677

I have attached the Common land neer to the Meeting house belonging to the town of Lin which Lt Richard Way shewed mee to be the town com̄on, and likewise Robt Coats and mr Thomas Laiton owned to be the com̄on land of the town of Lin, and gave a sum̄ons unto mr Thomas Laiton, Capt. Thomas Marshall and William Basset the day and year above written : ꝑ me Joseph Webb Marshall"

Record of County Court at Ipswich Sept. 25, 1677.

"4. Capt. James Oliver and Thomas Dexter Junr. Administrators to Thomas Dexter Sen: deceased plt: agst the Towne of Lynn & Thomas Layton &c. [Selectmen] defdts. in an action of Review of a Judgmt granted agst Thomas Dexter Senior &c. acording to attachmt The action being called the plt. was nonsuted vpon account the attachmt was made by a clerke of the writts in another Towne and not in the Towne whereof of he is clerke of the writts

The plt appeales to the next Court of Assistants at Boston

Left Rich: Way Atturney to Capt: James Oliver and Thomas Dexter Junr administrators to Tho: Dexter Senr deceased and Thomas Moore acknowledged themselues to stand bound to the tresr of the County in 20£. The Condition is that the sd Capt. James Oliver & Tho: Dexter shall prosecut there appeale at the next Court of Assistants at Boston to efect acording to law & abyd the order of Court therin."

Essex County Court Record (Court at Salem)

"30 : 4om° 1657

7 Thomas Dexter plat: against Thomas Laiton, George Keaser, Robert Coates & Joseph Armytage in ye name [& behalf of the towne of] Lynn defnts in an accon of ye Case conserning ye title & Interest of the said Thomas Dexter unto a ꝑcell of grownd or land Com̄only called Nahant, & for trespass done thereon by keeping of Cattle & cutting of wood & giuing out Lotts for building of houses & planting thereon to ye Injury of the sd Tho: Dexter.

Jury ffinds for the defendts: 9li: 6s. 2d. Cost of Court The defendt appeales from this sentence unto the next Court of assistance held at boston & Thomas Dexter & Richard Woody his son in Law binds themselues in tenn pounds apeece to prosecute this appeal to effect"

There are four papers on file in this case in Essex County Court Papers, Vol. III., F. 118.

"The deposission of John Ramsdell aged fifty fiue years or there abouts sworne saith that about fiue and twenty years since this deponent being a seruant vnto Capt Torner that this deponents master and seuerall other inhabbittance of Lynn as now is: that being before it was a toune, did fence in Nahant together euery man (or the most) that weare housholders and soe all those put in cattell upon Nahant upon the interest of fencing and noe man did troble or molest any by any claime in spessiall to him selfe and soe it was continued from yeare to yeare for many years, and this being the truth to the best of my knowledg and further saith not

Taken upon oath before the Court the 30° 4 m° 1657

ꝑ Elias Stileman Cler."

"This I Christopher Linsie doe testifie that Thomas Dexter bought Nahant of Blacke Will or Duke William & Imployed me to fence ꝑte of itt when I liued wth Thomas Dexter.

This is A coppie of an oath taken before me ffra: Johnson Comissiono[r] 15th: 2[mo]: 1657. Memorand: Lindsy denyed in Court that he was euer present at any bargaine &c."

"The testimonie of William Winter Aged 73 years or theirabouts, Testifieth that Black Will or Duke William soe Called came to my house (w[ch] was two or three miles from Nahant) when Thomas Dexter had bought Nahant of him for a sutt of Cloths, the said Black Will Asked me what I would giue him for the land my house stood vppon, itt beinge his land, and his ffathers wigwame stoode their abouts, James Sogomore & John, & the Sogomore of Agawame & diuers more, And George Sogomer being a youth was p[r]sent all of them acknowlidginge Black Will to be the Right owner of the land my house stood one & Sogomore hill & Nahant was all his and further saith not

This is A Coppie of an oath taken before me ffra: Johnson

Comissiono[r] 18[th] 2[mo] 1657"

"John Ledg* aged forty [seuen] years or there about sworne saith that aboute twenty fiue years since my master as then was m[r] Vmphries with seuerall others of Lynn as now is did fence in nahant and upon the right of his fenceing did put in cattell upon nahant and further saith not:—

Taken vpon Oath the 27 of 2: mo. 1657

Before mee Thomas Marshall Com[r]

linn"

There are forty-three papers relating to this case on file in Essex County Court Papers, Vol. XXIX., Fol. 137, etc., as follows:—

First paper. Writ by the administrators of estate of Thomas Dexter Sen[r]., dec[d], against the Selectmen of Lynn, Nov. 1678. in an "action of review of a judgment granted against the said Dexter, Sen[r]., in his life time at a Court of Assistants held in Boston the first

* Legg? See another deposition given below.

of September 1657, which action then tried was an action of Appeale from the Judgment of Salem Court held the 30th. of ye 4th. month 1657, which concerned a parcell of land lying near the Town of Linn, namely, a Neck of land commonly called & known by the name of Nahaunt." The writ is dated Nov. 20, 1678.

Second paper: —

Writ against "Thomas Laughton George Keaser Robert Coates and Joseph Armitage, in the name and behalfe of the Towne of Lynn and for themselues in speciall" to answer to Thomas Dexter senio^r^ at the next Court at Salem "in an action of the case concerning the title and interest of the said Thomas Dexter vnto a ꝑcell of ground or Island com̄only called Nahaunt and for trespasse done thereon by keeping of Cattle and Cutting of wood, and giueing out Lotts for building of houses and planting thereon to the injury of the said Thomas Dexter." Writ dated "24: 4: 57"

Third paper: —

"The Reasons of ffarmer Dexters Appeale in case wherein he is Plaintiff, Against the Inhabitants of Lynne Concerning his Interest in Nahaunt

1 The p^l^. pleadeth his right therein and thereto by purchase of the Indians, aboue 26 yeares now past, who were then the lawful own^r^s thereof

As by the test. of { John Leg
William Witter
George Sagamore
Sagamore of Agawam }

2 The p^l^. pleadeth his possession thereof by fenceing and other improvem^t^, as by test of William Witter and John Leg Capt. Traske, and m^r^s Whiteing

3 The p^l^. humbly Com̄endeth to the Consideracõn of this honno^r^d Court

1. That this purchase was by no Lāw then ꝓhibitted and made voyd, but hath since by act of the genn^r^all Court Octo: 19: 52 written Lawes beene Confirmed, as being according to Gods word Gen. 1; 28: chap 9: 1: psal 115: 16: also divers examples that might be instanced of sundry ꝑsons that doe enjoye those lands wch in the infancy of these plantations, they came by theire possession in like manner

2. That as yet no act or instrum^t^ made or signed by the p^l^. hath appeared to manifest any allienation thereof to the deff^ts^.

3 That they are parties which testifie against the p^l^. and that for and in there owne behalfe, and many of them such as haue in a disorderly manner ingaged themselues in a speciall manner against the plaintiff and his right as may appeare by the Testimony of Richard Woody, theire Combination of assaulting his person &c.

4 That if there be no remedy but what they will sweare must passe as truth (although the plaintiff conceiueth it to be very false) yet neuerthelesse the plaintiffe conceiueth himselfe to be wronged, in that he had no part found for him, when as by theire owne Oath and Confession he was an Inhabitant of Lynne so he had a share with them, the which as yet they haue not sworne, as he conceiueth, that he either gaue it them or any other, and therefore seeing he sued but for his interest therein, whether more or lesse, he marvailled that such a verdict should be brought against him, and humbly intreateth releife therefrom by this Honno^red Court

24 : 6 : (57) Thomas Dexter

This paper was deliu^red to me by Thomas Dexter the 26th of August 1657

Daniel Denison

Copia vera Attest. ꝑ Edw: Rawson Secret^y."

The fourth paper is the copy of the judgment of the Court of Assistants 1 Sept., 1657, (Fragment XXIV). The fifth paper is a copy of the judgment of Salem Court 30th of the 4th. month, 1657, given above. Then follow other papers in the following order : —

Power of Attorney by James Oliver of Boston, merchant, admin^r. to the estate of Thomas Dexter late of Boston, dec^d., to Richard Way dated Sept. 1677 — Record of appointment of Capt. James Oliver, son in law, and Thomas Dexter, junior, grandson, as administrators of the estate of Thomas Dexter, Senior, late of Boston, dec^d., Feb. 19, 1676. Bill of Costs for the Town of Lynn — total amount 4^£ 11^s 6^d. Order of the General Court 2 Oct. 1678 as to the case between Capt. James Olliuer and the Towne of Lynn authorizing a withdrawal with " liberty to begin *de novo*." Orders of the General Court as to bounds of Lynn, 13, 12mo., 1638 — 14 June 1642 — 13, 1st. mo., [1638] — and as to bounds of Humphreys grant " in the way to Marblehead "

Thirteenth paper : —

" The Deposition of Nathaniell Bacor Aged sixty six years or thereabouts

testefieth & saith that In the yeare (1632) or In the yeare (1633) I this Deponent mett with An Indian Called by the name of Black will: who had on A stuff sute of Cloaths that were pinkt, I this deponent Asked him said Will where he had those Cloaths, he said he had them of ffarmer Thomas Dexter Senior who then liued Att Saugust which Is now Called Linn, I Asked him what he gaue him for them, he said he had sould him Nahaunt, Afterward I being att ffarmer Dexters, saw him pay to Sagamore George sum Corn In part of pay for Nahaunt, which sd. Sagamore George Acknowledged to Receaue as part of pay for said Nahaunt, And sum short time After said farmer Dexter ffenced in the said Land on Nahaunt, & It was then Allwais owned to be the Land of said ffarmer Dexters, And Salem men for About two or thre years hired pastoredge of said Dexter for horses & Cattle vpon the said Nahaunt

Taken vpon Oath Sep^{t} 21th 1677 before me

Edward Tyng Assis^{t}."

Fourteenth paper: —

"I George Keser Sener Aged About sixty fiue or sixty sixe yeares or thereabouts saieth that I being an Inhabitant in Line when m^{r} Humphery Dwelt there, I being Present at A Towne Meeting, Mr Humphery maied A Moshen to the Proprietores of Nahant, that If they woold yealld vp there Right in Nehant to the Towne of Line hee woold yealld vp all his Right to the Towne of Line. Mr Thomas Dexter Sener beeing Desiered by Mr Humphery and some otherės then at the Towne Meeting did yealld vp his Right and Intrest to the Towne of Line that hee had in Nehant, this was about fiue and therty yeares A goe to my best memory.

Sworne in Court at Salem 27 : 9 : 78

Atests Hilliard Veren Cler."

Fifteenth paper: —

"The testimony of Captaine Richard Walker, Aged sixty five or thereabouts, testifyeth (that being one of the first inhabitants of the towne of Linn alias Saugus) that upon our first setling there, wee covenanted agreed and bought of an Indian called Black William (whoe was owned by the Sachem and all ye Indians to be the proprietor and owner of that place called Nahant) which place wee purchased of him and have had the possesion and use of the same for many years afterwards as the towne did increase, wee y^{t} were the ould inhabitants and purchasers, did fully and freely surrender all our right and title unto the towne of linn to whom justly now it doth appertaine —

Taken vpon oath : 22 : 7 mo: 77 :

Wm Hathorne Assist."

Sixteenth paper: —

"Richard Church of Hingham aged fortye eaight years or therabout testifieth that I the sd Richard Church heard George the Indian say vnto ffarmer Dexter that the sd Dexter did buy the land Called Nauhaunt of his Cozzen and further he the sd George Said that all the pay for the said land was not paid vnto his said Cozzen but he the said George beinge the next heyer ffarmer Dexter paid the Remainder of the pay to him and the sd. George ffuther saith that when some ꝑsons in linn desired to buy the said land of him he told them he could not sell it for the said land was ffarmer Dexters and ffuther this deponent saith not. this was about a yeare and halfe [since*.] Dated the 27th day of Aperill 1657 — this was taken vpon oath the day aboue written before me Joshua Hubbard"

* Written over "agoe," cancelled.

[Indorsed] "A testimony consearning Nahant taken upon othe before Captin huberd"

Seventeenth paper: —

"The testimony of Edward Holyoke

27. 4 mo. 1657.

About the yeares 1642 or 1643 mr Humfrey & Mr Thomas Dexter the Elder did instigate me earnestly to joyne in sute wth them about Nahant, because mr Dexter sayd I had a proprietie in Nahant as well as them, my selfe purchasing what right Captaine Turner had in Sawgus alias Lyn: but I durst not embrace that ꝓject because divers of the Inhabitants gaue forth that Nahant belonged as common to the plantatiō of Lyn, & for that the contending for Nahant would haue beene as for Naboths vineyard.

Taken upon oath before me
June 27 1657 Daniel Denison."

Eighteenth paper: —

"Jonathan Negus aged about 56 yeares and John Williams aged about 22 yeares doe both joyntly testifie, that Thomas Dexter and Joseph Armitage meeting by a providence together at the said Jonathan Negus his house, and they falling into some discourse concerning the suite that the said mr Dexter did intend to prosecute against the Inhabitants of Lynn concerning Nahaunt, wee these deponents heard Joseph Armitage tell the said mr Dexter that which side soeuer he the said Armitage tooke he would cast the case, and this is the truth to our best remembrance

Sworne before me Richard Parker Comissr
the 12th of the 4th 1657
Copia vera Attest ꝑ Edward Rauson Secrety."

Nineteenth paper: —

"The Deposition of Clement Couldum Ageed about fiuty [fiue] years sayth

That about thirty four years since I this Deponant liued with ould Thomas Dexter and the sayd Thomas Dexter Comming from the town meeting tould mr Sharp of Sallem In my hearring that for the Encoragment of the Town of Line he the sayd Dexter had Giuen all his Right and title which he had in Nahant vnto the town of Lyn and for ther vse in Generall and that the Town had Giuen him a Considerable tract of land on the back syd of his ffarm in Lew of it wich would be better to him then Nahant and ffurther sayth not

Deposed in Court at Salem 27 : 9. 78
atestes Hilliard Veren Cler"

Twentieth paper: —

"The testimony of Henery Vaine of Boston aged 72 yeares or there abouts in the case depending betweene mr Thomas Dexter and the Towne of Lynn saith that I haue heard many men of the Towne of Lynn say that Nahaunt is the ffarmer Dexters, the men which told me so that Nahaunt was the said Dexters are mr Sadler mr Otley Goodman Armitage Michaell Lambert ffrancis Linsey Goodman Riches. In a discourse two yeares agoe or there about, when the said Riches was working about a great Elme, which he or some body else had feld, he then said to me that Nahaunt did belong to ffarmer Dexter, and that he the said Dexter had bought it of the Indians, and farther said that he for his part was willing that ffarmer Dexter should haue it, for he should haue as much profitt of Nahaunt, if Dexter had it as if Lynn had it ffarther I heard mr Keaser say that Nahaunt was ffarmer Dexters, in the house of Michaell Lambert and further saith not

Master Keaser said before Michaell Lambert and his wife and Christopher Linsey and me Henry Vaine in Michaell Lamberts house, that they were ffarmer Dexters tenants for Nahaunt was ffarmer Dexters

Henry Vaine tooke his Oath to the whole writing aboue & Michaell Lambert to that part of it which differs in the writing before the Court 30 : 4mo: 57

p Elias Stilman Clarke

Copia vera Attest

p Edwd Rawson Secrety"

Twenty first paper: —

"The deposition of Ensigne William Dixy aged 50 yeares or there about, sworne saith, that about twenty eight yeares agoe, mr Isaack Johnson being my master writt to the Honrd: Gouernr: as now is mr Endecott for a place to sitt downe in, vpon which mr Endecott gaue me & the rest leaue to goe where wee would, vpon which I went to Saugust, now Linne, & there wee mett with Sagamore James & som other Indians, whoe did giue me & the rest leaue to dwell there or there abouts where vpon I & the rest of my masters company did cutt grass for our cattell, & kept them vpon nahant for some space of time, for the Indian James Sagamore & the rest, did giue me & the rest in behalfe of my master Johnson wt: land wee would, where vpon wee sett down in Saugust, & had quiett possession of it, by the aboue said Indians, & kept our cattell in Nahant the sumer following: Depo: 1: 5mo: 57

p Elias Stileman Cler:

Vera Copia atest: Hilliard Veren Cler:"

Twenty second paper: —

"The testimony of George ffar aged 63 yeares or thereabouts testifyeth that Blacke Will, or Duke William so called was the true owner of Nahaunt (as far as euer I heard) and Thomas Dexter bought Nahaunt of him and by that purchase fenced it in, and had full possession of it, and I helped to fence it in.

15 : 2 : 1657 This is a Coppie of an Oath taken before me ffrancis Johnson Comissionr.

Acknowledge that he knows not that Thomas Dexter bought, and expressed it when he tooke his oath before m[r] Johnson=

Copia vera Attest. ꝑ Edw[d] Rawson Secret[y]"

Twenty third paper:—

"Wee George Sagomore and the Sagomore of Agawam doe testifye that Duke William so called did sell all Nahaunt vnto ffarmer Dexter for a suite of Cloathes which Cloa[thes] ffarmer Dexter had againe, and gaue vnto Duke William so called 2 or 3 Coates for it againe and this they say they will sweare to as wittnesse our hands this 30: 4[mo] 57

the marke of S Agawam Sagomore

the marke of /|\ George Sagomore

They say they heard Blacke William say he sold Nahaunt to ffarmer Dexter this is all they meane

Copia Vera Attest. ꝑ Edw[d] Rawson Secret[y]."

Twenty fourth paper is a copy of the Deposition by Wm. Winter before Francis Johnson 15: 2: 1657, given above.

This copy is attested by Edward Rawson, Secretary.

Twenty fifth paper:—

"The testimoney of John Witt aged 40 or thereabouts Saith that Christopher Linsey told him that he neuer knew that farmer Dexter bought Nahant, but as it was said: & further not: I Daniel Salmon doe testifie the same aboue there written.

Mark Graues 35 yeares old or thereabouts, saith that being at Boston with Michaell Lambert, the said Lambert Meeting with Thomas Dexter, Sen[r]., asked if he had noe ꝑt in Nahant, that he might help him now in trouble, the said Tho: Dexter Answered, I should haue some share there for said he I paid some corne for a share there, & said he thought the rest that had ꝑt with him paid nothing & further saith not. Depo: in Court: 1: 5[mo]: 57: ꝑ Elias Stileman Cler:

Vera Copia atest: Hilliard Veren Cler:"

Twenty sixth paper is a copy of the deposition of John Ramsdell before the Court at Salem 30th. 4th. mo., 1657, as attested by Elias Stileman, Clerk. (See above)

This copy is attested by Hilliard Veren, Clerk.

Twenty seventh paper:—

"I John Legg aged 47 yeares or thereabouts doe testify that when I was m[r] Humphrerys Servant there came vnto my masters house one Blacke Will as wee called him an Indian, with a Compleate suite on his backe I asked him where he had that suite, he said he had it of ffarmer Dexter, and he had sold him Nahaunt for it

This is a Coppie of an Oath taken before me

ffrancis Johnson Cōmission[r] 7 of Aprill 57

Copia Vera Attest. ꝑ Edw[d] Rawson Secret[y]."

Twenty eighth paper is a copy of the testimony (see above) of Christopher Linsey before Francis Johnson 15 : 2 : 1657, (with a memorandum)

This copy is attested by Edwd. Rawson Secretary.

Twenty ninth paper : —

" Edward Ireson aged 57 yeares or thereabouts, sworne saith that liueing with m^{r} Thomas Dexter, I carryed the fencing stuffe, which Master Dexter sett vp to fence in Nahant, his part with the rest of the Inhabitants, & being & liueing with m^{r} Dexter I neuer heard him say a word of his buying of Nahant, but only his interest in Nahant for his fencing as the rest of the inhabitants had, this was about 25 yeares since, & after this fence was sett vp at Nahant, all the new comers were to giue two shillings six pence a head or apeece vnto the setters vp of the fence or inhabitants, & some of Salem brought cattell alsoe to Nahant which were to giue soe, & further saith not : Lynn : 27 : 2mo: 1657 : taken vpon oath before me

Tho: Laughton Comission^{r}

Vera Copia atest : Hilliard Veren Cler."

Thirtieth paper : —

" This I Joseph Armitege aged 57 or thereabouts doe testifie, that about fifteene or sixteene yeares agoe : we had a generall towne meeting in Lin at that meeting there was much discource about Nahant, the men that did first fence at Nahant, and by an act of the Generall Court, did apprehend by fencing, that Nahant was theires, myselfe by purchas, haueing a ꝑt therein, after much agitation in the meeting & by ꝑswasion of m^{r} Cobbitt, they that then did plead a right by fencing, did yeild vp all theire right freely, to the inhabitants of the Towne, of which Thomas Dexter Senr was one, & further saith not

Depo: in Court : 30 : 4mo: 57 : ꝑ Elias Stileman Cler:

Vera Copia atest : Hilliard Veren Cler: "

Thirty first paper : —

" The deposition of Daniel Salmon aged about 45 yeares Saith, that he being master Humphryes seruant, & about 23 yeares agon, there being wolues in Nahant, Comanded that the whole traine b[o]nd, to goe driue them out, because it did belong to the whole towne, & farmer Dextors men being then at training went with the rest & further saith not : Depo: in Court : 1 : 5mo: 57 : ꝑ Elias Stileman Cler.

Vera Copia atest : Hilliard Veren Cler: "

Thirty second paper : —

" Joseph Redknap aged about sixty yeares, sworne saith that about two & twenty yeares since the inhabitants of Linn as then were did injoyne me to fence in my ꝑt of Nahant fence as I was a inhabitant, which fence I sett vp, & there I kept the Towne cattell, since it was a towne, & soe it has beene a place as the Towne cattell haue beene kept from time to time, this fencing which I sett vp, was in repairing of an old fence formerly sett vp there:

Lynn 27 : 2mo: 1657 Taken vpon oath before
me Tho: Laughton Comiss^{r}.
Vera Copia atest: Hilliard Veren Cler:"

Thirty third paper: —

"The Testimony of Samuell Whiting Senr: of ye Towne of Linne Saith that m^{r} Humphries, did desire that m^{r} Eaton and his Company might not only buy Nahant but the whole Towne of Linne: & that m^{r} Cobbet & he & others of the Towne went to m^{r} Eaton to offer both to him & to comit themselues to the prouidence of God, and at that time there was none that laid claime to, or pleaded any Interest in Nahant, save the towne, & at ^ time farmer Dexter liued in the Towne of Linne.

Samuel Whiting Sen:
Sworne in Court ye 1 July 1657:
ꝑ Elias Stileman Cler:
Vera copia atest: Hilliard Veren Cler:"

Thirty fourth paper is a copy, attested by Hilliard Veren, Clerk, of the deposition by John Ledg (Legg?) before Thomas Marshall, Comm^{r}., 27, 2d mo., 1657 (see above).

Thirty fifth paper. —

"William Harker sworne saith that vpon ocasion, the Honrd Gouernour as now is, was at Sawgust or Linn, where there was an action comenced against one Linsey for liueing at Nahant where vpon I said I thought, that Lynn had not to doe with Nahant, the said Gouern^{r} said for that matter, he knew the contrarye for said he I know that Nahant is the Towne of Linns, & further saith not:

Depo: in Court 1 : 5mo: 57 : ꝑ Elias Stileman Cler.
Vera Copia: atest: Hilliard Veren Cler:"

Thirty sixth paper: —

"The testimony of George ffarr, saith y^{t} all the Inhabitants of Sagust y^{t} fenced at Nahant had propriety in Nahant, & y^{t} he knoweth not that euer Thomas Dexter bought Nahant, but that with the rest of the inhabitants he had a share by vertue of fencing there, & that he kept Cattell there for those Inhabitants that then liued in Saugust & saith that when Capt: Turner with the rest [went] to see where to make the fence, Capt: Turner said lett vs mak[e] hast, least the co[u]ntry should take it from vs: This 27 : 2mo: 1657:

This taken vpon oath before
Tho: Laughton & James Axey Com[^{rs}.]
Vera Copia atestes Hilliard Veren Cler:"

Thirty seventh paper : —

"The deposition of William Traske aged about 69 years saith that Jn° Balch my selfe and many others of Salem had leaue of Thomas Dexter Senio[r] late of Lynn to putt o[r] young Cattle to feede in the sumer neere 25 yeares since into Nahaunt

Taken vpon Oath 22 : 2[mo]: 1657
before me Edmo[d]: Batter Comissio[r]
Copia vera Attest. p Edw[d] Rawson Secret[y]."

Thirty eighth paper : —

"William Edmonds aged 47 yeares or thereabout, sworne saith that about twenty & one yeares since I kept cattell in Nahant for the Towne of Linne one sumer, & those as owed the cattell paid me for my paines: Linne 27 : 2[mo]: 1657

Taken vpon oath before
me Tho: Laughton Comission[r]:
Vera copia atest: Hilliard Veren Cler:"

Thirty ninth paper : —

"m[r] Daniell King aged 55 or thereabouts, saith that Thomas Dexter Sen[r]: comeing vnto his house, & asked him if he would Joyne with him in comencing a sute with him against the Towne of Linn for Nahant, m King answered him noe he would not, & further saith nott.

Depo. in Court 1 : 5[mo]: 1657 p Elias Stileman Cler.
Vera Copia atest : Hilliard Veren Cler."

Fortieth paper : —

"Robert Driuer aged 65 yeares or thereabouts, sworne saith that about 25 yeares since, most of the Inhabitants of Lynn as then was did Joyne together & fenced in Nahant, & did put in cattell vpon it, & soe from time to time it has beene a place to keepe the Towne cattell. Lynn 27 : 2[mo]: 57 : taken vpon oath before me

Tho: Laughton Comission[r].
Vera copia atest: Hilliard Veren Cler:"

Forty first paper : —

"The testimony of John Sibley: saith that about 28 years agoe dwelling with S[r] Richd: Saltingston,* y[t] my masters cattell with m[r] Johnsons, was kept in Nahant without molestation by the Indians or any other, & further saith not:

Depo: in Court : 1 : 5 [mo]: 57 : p Elias Stileman Cler.
Vera Copia atest: Hilliard Veren Cler:"

Forty second paper : —

"Joseph Redknap & Edward Richards sworne saith, y[t] at a generall towne meeting in Linn, m[r] Leader desired to haue the wood of Nahant,

---

* Saltonstall.

vpon som consideration, wherevpon, farmer Dexter, or mr Thomas Dexter did request of the Towne, that they would be pleased to consider him & giue him the runnings out of the pine trees in Nahant, mr Richard Leader said, he did not care whoe had the runnings out, if he might haue the runnings in & the Towne would not grant mr Thomas Dexter his request: John Tarbox doe alsoe witnes vnto this aboue testimony. Lynn 27: 2 mo: 1657: Taken upon oath before me

Thomas Laughton Comissionr.

Vera Copia atestes Hilliard Veren Cler."

Forty third paper: —

"The testimony of William Witter: saith that all those Inhabitants that liued in Saugust, that fenced in Nahant, had a proprietie at Nahant, & that mr Humphryes by vertue of fencing had a propriety in Nahant, and this deponent saith he bought Nahant & Sagomer Hill & Swamscoat of Black William for two pestle stones: ye 27: 2 mo: 1657: Taken vpon oath before

Thomas Laughton & James Axey Comissionrs.

Vera Copia atest. Hilliard Veren Cler."

XXV.

[Court Files, Suffolk, No. 270, 1st paper.]

Wee the Grandjury of this [Commonwealth doe present] Gregory Cassell for not having [the feare of God before his] eyes and being seduced by ye instig[ation of the divill did in] or about the midle of October 1[654 by] wound the head of Mathew Cannidge & divers [times] beate ye said Cannidge so as that the sd Cannidge dyed [ ] wound as Appears by seuerall evidences. ^ verdict of a [jury] of Inquest given in 4th $\frac{10}{mo}$ 1654. Contrary to the law[es of God] and this Jurisdiccon:

September 1. 1657

Wee fynd this Bill according [to]
the Containts thereof
Edward Breck foreman
in the name of the rest

Note.

By this bill of indictment found by the Grand Jury it would seem that the case came for trial before the Court of Assistants in September 1657, but it was probably transferred to the General Court at its session in October 1657, as appears from the following record (see Mass. Col. Records, Vol. IV., Part I., page 318): —

"In the case of Gregory Cassell, the Court, vejwing and considering of the evidences on file against him, the cheife whereof being out of this jurisdiccon, & not to be had, the Court judged it meete to discharge him at present, he giving in his owne securitje to value of one hundred pounds, that, on notice from authoritje, he shall appeare to answer what shall be lajd against him in reference to the vntjmely death of Mathew Cannige."

The following return of the jury of inquest is the second paper in No. 270, Court Files, Suffolk: —

"4: 10 mo, 1654

We whose names ar vnder ritten; being Called to veue the Body of Mathew Kehnige and to make in Qiuery of the suddinnes of his Deth and the cause ther of

by serching of his body we finde on his heade on the left side, a wounde wich wounde we sawe oppenned and ther was corupt blude: and towe small holes out of wich Blude Eissued forth and by what we sawe and by the witneses Brought in on oth we finde that that wounde on his heade as neare as we can Judge was a cause of his Deth

James Euerill
Samuell Bidfilld
Nathaneel Wales
Barnabas ffawer
John Phillips
James Mattocke
hugh Drury

Peter Pl[ace]
his **P** marke

Danil turell

Sammuell **S** Sendall
his marke

Godfry *A* Armitage
his marke

Henry Blague."

The third and fourth papers in No. 270 are as follows: —

"Thomas Michell Aged 26 yeares or thare: a Boutes: Testifieth and saith. y[t]: I being at: munhiging and cuming Into the house of Mathew: Cunnig and I saw mathew Cunnig Bledeing and I asked the young man y[t] struck him whey he lifted vp his hand a gainst an old man and y[e] said grigrey Answered It was dun and It Could not: be vndun or to y[t] purpos. And further saith not: sworne In Court 28 July 1657:

Edw: Rawson Recorder."

"The depositions of Nathaniell Gallop & Samuel Gallop about 26 years do both iointly testify That theise deponents beeing at Monhiggin about the middle of October last past hearing the report that was vpon the Island that Mathew Cenidge had received a blow by Gregory Castle vpon the head by a hammer, Theise deponents say that they heard the said Mathew Cennidge say that he had bled about 2 quarts & the said Castle had vndone him & that he should neuer recover the blow, & when the said Cennidge came on board the Barque of theise deponents in the evening went into his Cabbin very sick his sences beeing gone from him about an houre ~~and so continued all the voyage vntill his death tho not so ill as when he first came on board the Barque~~ ‖ and Contenewed sicke till hee Came to boston and there Contenewed ell till his death ‖ and further theise deponents heard the said Cennidge say that if he had the said Castle in place where ther was any government ~~they~~ he would trouble him for it & further saith not.

7—10—54 Sworne before [me]
Ri: Bellingham Govr

It must be farer written over"

The following papers from the Chamberlain Collection at the Boston Public Library relate to this case: —

"John Barker aged 27 yea. or thereabouts saith that math. Keninge was master of the boate Gregory Cassell and John Short were the boates crewe, and this deponent was Headman to the boate, and they began a voyage about January last and continued till Nov. last in wch tyme math Keninge and Gregory Cassell had many fallings out the sd. Cassell beinge for the most part the occasion thereof: and beinge too strong for Keninge (being an old man) [ ] beate him with his fist, but nowe at last about the middle of october last the sd Cassell in his presence (John Short alsoe beinge present) did strick the sd Keninge wth the broad end of an Ham̄er a stronge blowe ye old man sd. what hast thou done to me and said to this deponent and to Short beare wittnes. y^{n} sd. Cassell what care I if I had killed him it is all one to me. y^{n} the old man bledd ‖about‖ tow quarts and they used means to stop it but could not in ~~an~~ ‖three ‖ howre[s] after the old man cold rest but litle that night about [s]om dayes after the old man helped w^{t} fish into the barke to come for the bay and that night he was neare death talked idly for space of an howre, lost his sences for the tyme after the old man was ill all the voyage and was scarce able to stand up after comeinge to boston about three weeks after he dyed but before often desired that Cassell might be here to haue the lawe against him [the depo]nent further saith that he hath often heard the old man complain of the stopinge at his stomake before the voyage and since

attested on oath this 6–10–5[4]
before me Ri. Bellingham
[Govr]"

"the deposition of mathew Coy being triming of mathew Canigey ‖Canninge‖ going to come his head desired mee to let it alone by reson of his head being broke and his hare being clotted with bloud I asked of him how hee goot the blow hee tould mee by an [an untowerd] fellow which I thought never no harme by I asked of him whether hee was in drink or no and hee replied hee was as well as I am at this present I [fee]ling vpon his sore it was light or pussy

Sworne before me 7–10–54
Ri. Bellingham Govr"

"4–10–1654

Whereas we whose names are heerevnder written were required to take a view of ye Body, & especially of ye head of Mathew Cannedge (sodainely) deceassed. This is to certefye in dilating the left side of ye head, much corrupt & contused bloud came forth. So the skul being made naked or bare there seemed to be a litle cracke by, or through wch cracke, out of it issued a litle thinne [bloud although]away frō ye skul yet notw^th standing it [kept]wheezing forth And wheras ye sd Mathew [ ]ednes, or blacknes in ye face, the said blacknes much diminished after ye corrupt bloud was come forth by reason of ye sd incission of ye head. So y^t we conclude it is possible that ye said Mathew his dayes might be shortned by reason of that stroke wch is reported was given him vppon ye head wth ye ham̄er.

Comfort Starr

I doe agree to what is aboue riten. and also furder doe think it not only possable but very likely to be the cause of his death

John Clark

m^r: Clark and m^r Starr both were sworne to the truth of ye premis[es] before me
7—10—1654 Ri. Bellingham Govr"

"Peter warren of ye Age of twenty sixe yeares saith that he Coming vpon occasion to the house of Mathew Cannege found Gregory Cassell John Short John Baster who was then the shoarman at that tjme the said Cassell was in drink and did quarrell [w^th] the sd Mathew Cannege and did strike him on ye nose and made him bleed: After this deponent went abroad to shoote and came in about an hower after and then found many people there and saw mathew Cannege all bloody about his necke and sawe his blood Issuing out still. and this deponent further saith that mathew Cannege told him that Cassell had strucke him on the head wth an hammer as he was about to mend his shooes so others in the house sajd Also: this deponent further saith that he being at dinner there the sajd mathew came and sate down wth them, and his blood dropped on the chest on which there meate was; and the house floor was bloody. further this deponent that night see him put of his shirt which was very bloody, and that night mathew Canneg Complayned of great payne in his head the next day Intending to Come to Boston. and Carriinge some fish on a barrow. he could not by reason of his faint[ing] ‖nes‖ doe it for this deponent helped him downe wth his fish to the barke

Jur: Coram me 25 $\frac{5}{mo}$ ~~1656~~ ‖1657‖
Ri: Bellingham Dep. Gov[r]."

The following is found in Vol. 3 of Suffolk Probate Records, Inventories 1653–1660, on the blank page preceding the first page of the index: —

"[ ]
Gregory Castwell being comitted by y[e] Gou[r] [ ] acknowledged he knew mathew Kennige f[ ] y[t] he fisht wth mathew Kennig one season from [the spring] to August: denjd y[t] euer Mathew Kennige & h[e] euer fell out [ ] y[t] they were loving friends = y[t] y[e] sd kennige was an old man"

XXVI.

[Court Files, Suffolk, No. 271, 1st paper.]

Wee the Grand Jury for this Commonwealth doe present Rob[ert]* Quimby for not having the feare of God before his eyes and being seduced by y[e] Instigation of the divill did in or about the 17th of Aprill last in Salisbury Riuer thrust Henry Horrell in to the Riuer or Sea: so as he was drowned & not heard of or taken vp till about a moneth after as Appeares by seuerall Eviden[ces contrary] to y[e] lawes of God & this Jurisdiccon in such Case p[rovided]
Boston 2[d] September 1657

On y[e] Examinations produced & [hearing] of the Evidences in y[e] Case of the sd Quimby wee cann[ot finde] the said Robert Quimby Guilty of ye death of henry Horr[ell] although wee finde some suspition thereof.

Edward Breck fforeman in ye
name of the rest

Note.

The second paper in No. 271 is as follows: —

"The 17th day of April 1657 I John Lewes was at Salsbury readie to come away but was stopt Two dayes by a contrary wind and in ye evening vpon Saterday night my man was with me & went abord my vessell well; vpon ye Lords day morning lookeing for my man to come to meeting m[r] Carre sent vnto me his son so when ye youth came he told me that his father had sent him to me to haue me come downe and looke after my man. so forthwith I went, & goeing to m[r]. Carrs his

---

* Robbin?

servant mett me before I gott to ye howse and told me that my man was drown[d] wherevpon I asked him where was Robbin & he said he was within so in I went, and when I came into ye howse m[rs]. Carre was cryeing and wringing her hands and m[r]. Carre very sollentary and Robbin setting in ye Chimney so I askt Robbin where was Henry; his answer was he could not tell; I said to him it was best for him to know where he was, & further I askd him what business he had abord that day being Lords day, so then m[r]. Carre & I went out of doores & he spoke to me to goe to ye Iland where they two had bin, where was a place wch had bin scrabbled with hands by ye waters side; so I told him I would goe, and m[r]. Carr askd me what I would doe with Robbin and I said I would doe well enough with him, for he should goe along with me; so I returnd into howse & spoke to Robbin to goe along with me, so away we went and Tooke another man of m[r]. Carr[s]. with us, & comeing to ye Iland I could not see the place wch m[r]. Carr Told me he see vpon ye sands scrabbled, in reguard ye Tide was then come vpp, but lookeing along ye water side I spide ye print of a mans foote in a banke, comeing downe forward into ye water; Then I charged Robbin that he had Thrust him downe in that place into ye water; and further I asked him how far he saw him swim̄ and Robbin said to me he swam̄ to ye wallo[r]. of six or seuen rodd; & I askd him how he did swim̄e, and he said he swom̄e on his side after such a manner as he neuer saw any one swim in his life, & I askt him where his hatt was and he said vpon his head & I said to him why did not you make vse of ye skiffe that was by you or call for some help to saue ye mans life, and I askd him whether he see him sinke or noe & he said noe; Then away went I downe ye riuer neere about a mile to see if I could see his hatt, or an oare, or himselfe, but could see none; onely ye other man that was with me found ye step of a mans foote, wch he showed me asking me what I Thought that was; so we looked if we might haue fovnd more, but could find none; Then I said to him we will returne and goe vp to ye Towne; and comeing to m[r]. Carr[s] Told him I could find nothing, but would now goe to ye Towne in ye mean Tyme gott James ffreeze wch was m[r]. Carr[s]. man; to step to ye meeting howse to see if my man were there, whiles Robbin and my self staid till his comeing backe so he told me he was not there, and I said vnto them we will goe to ye farme, wch was about a mile off to see if he were there; so we went but he had not bin there so backe we went and com̄itted Robbin into ye Cunstables hands but all this tyme he neuer told me that he knew of his death."

The following papers are in the Chamberlain Collection at the Boston Public Library: —

"The testimony of James ffreese aged about sixteen years who examined & sworne saith that he saw Robert Quenby vppon y[e] last Sabboath day morning betimes aboard of Jn[o] Lewis his boate wth y[e] sd Lewis his man Henry Horell: & saw them both goe out of y[e] boate into y[e] skiff, & they going of & Henry going to rowe, he fell backward

& yᵉ oare slip out of his hand into yᵉ River, then he saw Horrill scull the skiff a shoare, butt fell to leward, & saw them goe a shoare, & saw ȳ together vppon Ram Iland coming vp towards yᵉ end of yᵉ Iland. afterwards he heard one hollow 2 or 3 tymes, so hee went downe in a boate wᵗʰ his master to yᵉ Iland yᵉ Indian being also wᵗʰ ȳ in yᵉ boate, & when we came downe towards yᵉ Iland hee saw Robert Quenby Walking alone vppon Ram Iland shoare, & when they were almost a shoare his master ask[t] Robert wᵗ was become of Henry, or wher he was, yᵉ sd Quenby said he was gon into yᵉ River & said wᵗ shall wee doe for him, & his master answered, hee must looke to that for if hee were drowned, he (yᵉ sd Quenby) must bee hang'd for him; then his master bad him & yᵉ Indian looke for him wᶜʰ wee did & searcht yᵉ Rocks & yᵉ Iland butt could not finde him, then his master cald them againe, & bid vs looke, looke, vppon a place of yᵉ flatts hard by yᵉ channell, neare the banke where Quenby said yᵉ said Horrell fell [in] & hee sawe vppon the sd flatts the markes of one scraping or scrabling wᵗʰ [the] hands to gett to the shoare wards. yᵉ [markes went] so farr from yᵉ water that ꝑᵗ of his body might be vppon yᵉ flatts. after wards in yᵉ house the sd Quenby told my master yᵗ Horrell went downe vppon his hands & knees into yᵉ water, & yᵉ said Quenby said, prithie Harry come ashoare good Harry come a shoare, & said yᵉ sd Harry told him he would come a shoare again. also the deponent saith he saw Quenby pull off his gloues, when hee cam ashoare vppon his masters Iland & further saith nott

Jurat Corā me Tho: Bradbury
Comissionʳ of Salisbury
the 20ᵗʰ of Aprill 1657.

The examination of Rob̄ Quenby who saith that Henry Horrell servant to Jnᵒ Lewis desiered mee vppon Satterday att night last being yᵉ 16ᵗʰ day of this pʳsent Aprill, to goe aboard wᵗʰ him to drinke a cup of strong waters, but he refused to go yᵗ night wherᵥppon he desiered mee to come aboard on yᵉ Sabboath day morning to drinke a cupp & then they would goe to yᵉ meeting together, so both of vs going aboard the skiff from yᵉ boat one of yᵉ oares slipt out of Horrells hand whervppon wee were driuen to luard before wee could recover the shore. then they went a shoare together & after they went a shoare yᵉ said Robert made fast the skiff & hee going before mee I followed him by the water side, but before I could come vpp wᵗʰ yᵉ sd Horrell by aboue a rodd hee was slip downe a steep banke vppon his side & by that tyme yᵉ sd Robert was gott to yᵉ banke yᵉ said Horrell was about halfe a rodd in yᵉ water from yᵉ banke side & after ward saw him plunging vppon the water, while he came agᵗ yᵉ great Rock being about 10 rodd from the place wher hee fell in, after wᶜʰ tyme he never saw him more. the sd Quenby also saith that he conceiues they drunke about a pint of Strong Liqʳˢ. the sd Quenby denied that hee had any gloues.

Taken vppon examinacōn before mee
Tho: Bradbury Comissionʳ of Salisbury

Robt Quenby further examined, denyed that euer he sd Horril went downe on his hands & knees into the water as also that he euer spake to Horrill Good Harry come out of ye water and Horrils answer that he would come out againe, wch are both testifyed by James Freese and affirmed to be true by George Car,

before vs Samuel Symonds Daniel Denison

Robt Quenby bound himselfe in to this goverment
bound himselfe in 10^li that
Court of Asistants or sooner
as authority shall appoint to answer what shall be objected ag^t him concerning the death of Henry Horril
Dated April 21 1657

John Lewes bound himselfe in 5^li to this goverment to prosecute his complaint ag^t Robt Quenby at the next Court of Asistants or sooner being called by authority.
Dated April 21 1657

These acknowledged before vs
witnesses m^r Carr & his family Samuel Symonds
Daniel Denison"

XXVII.

[Essex County Court Files, Vol. III., Fol. 152. "Miscellaneous Papers 1657."]

Att the Court of Asistants held at Boston 2^d Sept 57.

The Case of Richard Pitfold accused by Ruben Guppy for Beastiallity &c was referred to Salem Court next to be examined & proceeded wth according to law. And Ruben Guppy is hereby enjoyned to prosecut at the sajd Court. This is a true Copy taken out of the Court Records as Attests Edward Rawson Secret^y.

a Cording to my order
I have worned thes too
Richard Pitfold
and Rubbun Guppi: to the Cort

NOTE.

The return of the summons, written under the above extract from the record of the Court of Assistants, is not signed. The following from the record of the "County Court, Salem, 1655–1666" shows the action by the Salem Court in the matter.

"At a Court held In Salem: 24: 9: m^o 1657"

"25. Richard Pitfold being referd by the geñ Court* unto this Court to be examined for beastiallitie & ꝓceeded with accordingly, this

* Error of the record for Court of Assistants.

Court accordingly hath examined the case, & finds not ye accusation true, doe therefore acquit the said Pitfold.

26. Ruben Cuppie accusing Richard Pitfold of beastiallite & not making the same to appeare, wch had it been true would have indangered the sd Pitfolds Life This Court doth sentence the said Cuppie to be whipt & to pay the charge of the Constable & y^{e} said Pitfold hath been at aboute this business, wch is 2$^{£}$: 19^{s}. 10^{d}. the execution of the sentence is referd to Major Hathorn to se it done next 4th day not exceeding 20 stripes."

XXVIII.

[Suffolk Registry of Deeds, Vol. IV., p. IX.]

To Edw Michelson marshall Gen^{ll} and his deputy. Yo^{w} are by virtue hereof Required to Levy on y^{e} Goods & Chattells of Samuel Archard of Salem to value of tenn pounds thirteene shillings & fower pence & deliuer the same to Edward Lane of Boston merchant wth two shillings for this execution & is in sattisfaction of a Judgment Graunted & Confirmed to him for so much by the Court of Assistants held at Boston [the 7th September 1658 Dated at Boston] * the 12th february. 1660. If yo^{w} finde not Goods yow are to seaze his person.

ꝑ Edw. Rawson Secrety

underwritt

This Execution is fully sattisfied this 10 Aprill 1661 : & deliuered to m^{r} Edward Lane ꝑ me Rich. Wayte marshalls deputje

Entered & Recorded : 21st. may 1661 when Returnd

ꝑ Edw Rawson Secrety

XXIX.

[Court Files, Suffolk No. 2233, 1st paper.]

At a Court of Assistants held at Boston the first of march : 1658.†

A Petition from m^{rs}. Anna Laine was presented to this Court which is on file wherein She desires the favour of this Court to free hir from hir pretended husband m^{r}. Edward Laine. After the Court had read the petition they sent for the said m^{r}. Lane who appearing the question was put to him whither that was true which is inserted in the petition : i : e : That from first to last since his marriage he hath bin deficient in performing the duty of a husband After a considerable

---

* See a second record of this execution on page XII. of Vol. IV. Suff. Deeds. †1658-9.

pause his answer was that he must speake the truth he could not say he had performed the office of a husband = The Court on due consideration of the petition of m^rs^. Anna Keayne lately married to m^r^ Edward Lane declares the marriage to be null and according to her petition declares hir free.

That this is a true Copy taken out of the Courts booke of Records being therewith compared. Attests. Edward Rawson Secret

Copia Vera attest^s^. Is^a^. Addington Cler
Copia Vera attest^r^. Edward Rawson Secret.
Vera Copia ꝑ Is^a^. Addington Cler.

Note.

The above judgment for divorce is cited in a petition by Edward Lane to the General Court in May 1659, as having been passed by the Court of Assistants "sitting at Boston the second of March last past." (See Court Files, Suffolk, No. 2233, 8th paper. See also Mass. Records, Vol. IV., pt. I., pp. 369, 391, 392, 395; also Mass. Archives, Vol. 9, No. 31 — Copy of contract of marriage; and Vol. 9, No. 32 — Petition for divorce by Anna Lane to the Court of Assistants.)

XXX.

[Court Files, Suffolk, No. 329, 2nd and 3d papers.]

[2nd paper] "To the Constable of Boston.

Y^w^ are by Virtue hereof Required forthwith in the absenc of the executione^r^ to procure a meete ꝑson to execute the Judgment of y^s^ Court ag^t^ w^m^ Robbinson seuerly to whip him wth twenty Stripes for his Rayling & Contemptous Carriage & speeches ag^t^ the whole Court & chardging the Gouerno^r^ in ye face of the Cour^t^ to be Guilty of blood & would no^t^ be silenced by the Court ‖ but Continued Interupting y^r^ hon^rs^ in giving sentance ‖ hereof yo^w^ are no^t^ to faile dated 8th september 1659: at Boston: By ye Cour^t^

E. R. S:"

[3d paper] "To the keepe^r^ of the p^r^ison.

Yo^w^ are by virtue hereof Required forthwith to dischardge the prison of w^m^ Robbinson marmaduke Stephenson mary Dyer & Nicholas Davis who were found by the Court & Jury, by theire owne Confessions words & Action, to be Quake^rs^ & had sentenc pronounc^t^ agt them to depart this Jurisdiccon on pajne of death & y^t^ if after the fowe^r^teenth of this Instant Septembe^r^ they or any of them be found wth in this

Jurisdiction or any ꝑte thereof they are to be Comitted to prison & suffe[r] death according to lawe: that they may depart accordingly at theire perrill dated at Boston the 12th of septembe[r] 1659.

ꝑ Edward Rawson Secre[ty]."

NOTE.

The first paper in this case (No. 329, Court Files, Suffolk) is, like the other two papers given above, in the handwriting of Edward Rawson, and is as follows :—

"Att A County Court held at Boston 16 June 1659:

Nicholas Davis an Inhabitant of Bastable being Comitted to Prison for a Quaker, And w[m] Robbinson & marmaduke Stephenson Quakers coming into the Congregation at Boston ^ 15th Instant June endeavoring to make disturbance before the Congregation was dismist was Comitted to prison = The Court sending for the sajd Nicholas Davis w[m] Robbinson ^ marmaduke Stephenson & patience Scott after theire owning themselves Quakers by theire words & behaviour & considering of theire bold & abusive carriages coming into this Jurisdiction pretending theire Imediate Call from God to beare testimony ag[t] our Lawe for persecuting the Saints &c. Ordered them to be comitted to close prison according to the lawe ag[t] Quakers made in october 1658 & y[t] warrant Issue out Accordingly: wch was donne:"

"Att A meeting of the magistrates 21th of July 1659

Mary Dyer the wife of w[m] Dyer of Road Island a Quaker being brought before the magis[ts]. openly Profest that hir coming into these partes was to visit the Prisoners the Quakers now in hold[[g]] & y[t] shee was of the same Religion y[t] Humphrey Norton was of wch she affirmed was the trueth & Refused to Giue a direct Ans[r] to what was proposed to hir or w[t] other occasions shee came hither for Affirming the light wth in hir is the Rule &c. the magis[ts] ordered hir Comittment to close prison according to Lawe till the next Court of Asistants: warrants Issued out accordingly"

No record has been found of the sentence of banishment referred to in the third paper in the case, which was pronounced, no doubt, by the Court of Assistants in September 1659. The General Court in October 1659, after a full hearing, passed sentence of death against these three Quakers, William Robbinson, Marmaduke Stephenson, and Mary Dyer, they having been "banished this jurisdiction by the last Court of Asistants on pajne of death," but being "now in prison for theire rebelljon, sedition, & presumptuous obtruding themselves vpon vs," notwithstanding the said sentence, and having "acknowledged themselves to be the persons banished." Mary Dyer accepted the proffer of "liberty to depart within two days," but the others were executed; and Mary Dyer upon afterwards returning again was also executed in accordance with this sentence of the General Court. (See

Mass. Col. Records, Vol. IV., Part I., pp. 383–390, 419.) (See also below. the case of William Leddra. Fragment XXXV.)

XXXI.

[Court Files, Suffolk, No. 349, 1st paper.]

Att a Court of Assistants held at Boston 6 of March 1659 *

Thomas Dyer plaintiffe against Sampson Sh[oare] defendant In an action of the Case wch was trjed at the County Court in Boston in Nouember last for wthholding & denying to giue possession of the dwelling house he now liues in & the appurtenances [and priviledges] thereunto belonging wch h[ouse] & appurtenances belong to him the sajd Diar as appear[eth] by deede of sale or mortgage as he is Assignee of the sajd Addams And for detajning two yeares rent & more for the sajd dwelling house &c according to ye Attachm^{t} dated 29 5 mo 1659. wch being read wth the evidences in the Case presented comitted to y^{e} Jury & are on file The Jury found for y^{e} Plaintiffe the mortgage Good in Lawe & that possession of the house & land be deliuered accordingly & Costs of Courts i. e. three pounds two shillings = Vera Copia.

NOTE.

The above copy of a judgment of the Court of Assistants is not signed, but is in the handwriting of the Secretary, Edward Rawson. There are eight other papers on file in this case, as follows: —

"To the marshall of the County of Suffolk or his Deputy.

Yo^{w} are by virtue hereof Required by way of execution to levy & enter into the dwelling house of Sampson Shoare y^{t} he now Inhabitts and dwells ^ wth the land thereto belonging nere Adjoyning to the Coue & neere the Conduit in Conduit street in Boston the said land being in breadth thirty foote from ye late major Edward [Gibbons] his warehouse bounded on ye west wth ye said warehouse ye said land wth the said house front next ye streete towards the north the Coue on ye south the land of John Low on ye west contejning thirty foote in breadth to the waterside together wth the liberty or priviledg of water at ye well & giue full and peaceable possession thereof to Thomas Dyar assignee to Samuell Addams according to a deede of sale or mortgage bearing date 14 July sixeteene hundred fifty & sixe wth. three pounds two shillings as Costs. Graunted to ye sayd Dyar by the Court of Asistants held at Boston the.[6th] of march 1659 & is in sattisfaction of ye deed or mortgage wth two shillings for this execution. h[ereof] yow are not to faile. Dated [at] Boston 15 [March 1659]

[Edward Rawson]"

---

* 1659-60.

"I haue Attached ye Goods debts or estate of Samson Shoure this 21 mo a parcell of land lying in Boston together wth his dwelling house & Ground in Boston to the Value of one hundred & fifty pounds also I haue Attached the body of Samson Shoare this 21 $\frac{5}{mo}$ & haue taken bond of him to the Value of one hundred pounds

p me Rich Wajte marshall

This is A true Copie of the Returne made by the marshall on ye bakside of left Cooks Attachment agt Samson Shoare bearing date 21 July 59 as Attests

Edw. Rawson Record^{r}"

"Att A County Court held at Boston in New England 22th of Nouember 1659 Tho: Dyre Assignee of Samuel Addams Plaintiffe agt Sampson Shoare defendant in an action of the Case for witholding & denying to give possession of the dwelling house he now liues in & the appurtenances and priviledges thereunto belonging wch house & appurtenances belong to him the sajd Dyre as appeurs by deed of sale or mortgage as he is Assignee of the said Addams And for detayning two years rent & more for the said dwelling house &c. according to Attachm^{ent} dat 24th $\frac{5}{mo}$ 1659 After the Attachment & other evidences in the Case produced were read Comitted to ye Jury & are on file The Jury brought in their verdict they found for the Plaintiffe the house land & Appurtenances mentioned in the mortgage & that possession be given ye said Dyre accordingly & Costs of Court The bench Refused the verdict & so it falls to ye next Court of Asistants This is a true Copie of the Courts Judgment taken out of the Courts booke of Records as Attests

Edward Rawson Recorde^{r}

"To ye marshall of the County of Suffolk or his deputy or Constable of Boston

you are required to Attach the goods, and for want thereof the body of Sampson Shoare and take bond of him to the value of two hundred pounds wth sufficient surety or suretjes for his personall appearance at the next County Court to be held at Boston to Ans^{r} the Complaint of Thomas Dier Assignee of Samuel Adams in an Action of the Case, for witholding and denying to give possession of the dwelling house he now lives in, and the appurtenances & priviledges therevnto belonging which house & appurtenances belonge to him the said Dier as appeares by deed of sale or mortgage as he is Assignee of the said Samuell Adams, and for detayning of two years rent and more for the said dwelling house and the said appurtenances & priviledges and for some injury donne to the premises & due damages, and so make a true returne there of under your hand dat 29 $\frac{5}{mo}$ 1659

By the Court Jonathan Negus

Endorsed I have Attached the body of Sampson shoare this 29th 5 mo and have taken bond of him to ye volue of two hundred pounds
p me Rich. Wayte marshall"

"Wee Sampson shoare & willjam Hudson & Richard Cooke doe bind ourselves heirs & executors unto Rich. Wajte marshall in the some of two hundred pounds upon condition the said Sampson shoare shall appeare at the next County Court to be held at Boston to Ansr the Complainte of Thomas Dyre according to the tennor of this Attachment & that he shall abide the order of the Court & not dept without license as wittness our hands 15 6 mo 1659

Samson Shoare
William Hudson

This is a True Copie Compared wth ye originall on file as Attests
Edward Rawson Recorder"

"Know all men by these presents that I Samuell Addams of Charlestowne merchant for & In Consideration of the some of one hundred pounds well & truly long since pajd by Thomas Dyre of Weimouth in New England aforesaid on the tenth of the eighth month 1657 did Give Grant Assigne Sell Enfeoffe Confirme & release & by these presents from the sajd tenth of octobe r 1657 doe Absolutely Giue Grant sell Aljene Assigne enfeoffe Confirme & release vnto Thomas Dyer above mentioned all that right title Interest Clayme & demand that I had haue might or ought to haue in the dwelling house of sampson shoare scittuate in the Conduite streete in Boston in New England aforesajd wth all the libertjes priviledges & Appurtenances to the said house & land belonging or in any wise appertayning by virtue of a deed of sale from the sajd Sampson shoare to me the said Samuell Addams my heires & Assignes bearing date the fowerteenth day of July sixteene hundred & fifty & sixe Refference being thereto had more amply appeareth To Have & to Hold the sajd dwelling house & land wth liberties & priviledges & appurtenances thereto belonging to him the said Thomas Dyer his heirs & Assignes forever according to the above mentioned deed in all respects and to all Intents & purposes whatsoever that I the said Samuell Addams by virtue of that deede haue had might or ought to haue to him the said Thomas Dyer his heires & Assignes forever free from all & all manner of Clajms title Intereste demands that the said Samuell Addams my heirs or Assignes or any Clajming In by from or under me or them thereto In Wittnes whereof I have Againe hereto sett my hand & seale this twenty eighth of July one thousand sixe hundred fifty nine

Signed Sealed and deliuered in
presence of vs ffrauncis Norton
ffaithfull Rause

Samuel Addams

this is A true Copie Compared wth the originall on file
as Attests Edward Rawson Recorder"

"Joshua Scottow Aged forty three yeures or thereabouts sworne saith That he this deponent was Called ouer to Sampson shoares house to wittnes a deed from himself to Sam. Addams of charlstowne, where perceiving that this deede or mortgage was to prevent the seisure of the said house unto one Aron Cooke of Conecticott and that the said Shoare was not Indebted unto the said Addams one halfe of the hundred pounds which by the sajd deed he acknowledged this deponent Advised that for the strengthening of the said deed that the said Adams would signe bills of paymente to as many of the said Shoares Creditors as would make up the hundred pound, which was Consented to by the said shoare & Adams, Provided that the said bills should not be binding unto the said Addams unlesse the said deede were acknowledged before a Magistrate & also that if the mortgage were deliuered up by the sajd Addams to the sajd shoare, then that these bills were to be deliuered & not to be of force against the sajd Addams, the sajd deed was acknowledged before the Honnored Gouerno^r^ the mortgage was not deliuered up: by the sajd Addams and so the bills Came in force against the sajd Addams, the payment of one of these bills wch was made to Assigne of this deponent was not made sundry mounthes if not best part of a yeare after they were signed & due and when pajd was discharged in Corne at sixe pence upon bush dearer than he tooke it of others And further saith that he drew up an agreement betweene Samuell Sendall & the sajd shoare for the price & payment for the sajd house which was to be two hundred & odd pounds what hindered the Compleating of the bargaine Knoweth not but haue heard It was from G: Djar And further saith that the sajd Samuell Adams did at the first signing of the sajd deed & [since] promise the sajd shoare that the sajd deed should be Cancelled upon the payment of the hundred pounds & Advantage not taken upon the forfeiture or words to that purpose
Sworne In Court 23^d^ 9th mo: 1659 ꝑ Edward Rawson Recorde^r^

That this is a true Copie Compared wth the originall on file

Attests Edw: Rawson Recorde^r^"

"July 26. 59

The testimony of Samuell Sendall Aged thirty & nine yeares or there abouts who testifieth and saith . . that about october or Nouember sixteen hundred fiffty seven I was in dealing wth Sampsen shoare about his house and wee came to an Agreement of price for the house and the priviledges there unto belonging and there was a writting drawn up Concerning the sajd bargaine by Ensigne Scottow and I was to give the sajd Sampsen two hundred twenty five pounds and In the sajd bargaine It was the principall Care of sampson shoare to pay a debt of a good some to Thomas Dyar of weimouth who happened to be in the house at a Certaine tjme in our treaty; and hearing our Conference about it and that wee were like to Come to Agreement he sajd to me Friend you were best to Consider what you doe for you Can have no good Assurance without me and that if Goodmon shoare should make me a deede It would be of no Value for the house was made ouer to him he told me and as I Understood by goodwife shoare he persuaded Goodwife shoare not to give any Consent to the sale of it so I told him that [l]ooke what was to be paid unto him I should engage to pay so much to him according to the Agreement between me & sampson shoare but he the sajd Thomas Dyar was not willing to it nor would not accept of it and so our bargaine was made nothing by means of him and he might haue buin pajd & further saith not

Sworne In Court 26th July 1659

This is a true Copie of the deposition of Samuell Sendall Compared wth the originall on file as Attests

Edw Rawson Recorder"

"the testimony of Isack wooddy Aged thirty yeares or thereaboute saith that I being present when Samsen shoare mortgaged his house to mr Samuell Addams of charlstoune I heard Samuell Addams say that if the sajd sampson shoare did gett cleare of Captaine Cooke & those writtings which the sajd Addams had made to pay some of his engagements that he the sajd Addams would deliver up the mortgage againe & further that the sajd Addams sajd that those writtings were to be left with the wife of Samson shoare to keepe & I heard mr Addams say yt he had no other Intention in the mortgage but to keepe the house cleere from Capt Cooke his Attaching of it & further that these writtings were made for this end that mr Adams might say that he had engaged for the whole mortgage & further saith not

Sworne In Court 23. 9 mo 59.

Edw. Rawson Recorder

This is A true Copie of the deposition of Isack wooddye being Compared wth the originall as Attests

Edward Rawson Recorder

See Mass. Records, Vol. IV., Part I., p. 436. Order of the General Court Oct. 16, 1660, on petition of Sampson Shoare, that said Shoare "doe forthwith giue possession of the house wth inmentioned vnto the wth in named Thomas Dyer, according to the Judgment of the Court of Assistants" &c.

XXXII.

[Court Files, Suffolk, No. 26414.]

Hen. Bennett being convicted of slandering & open traduceing ye Court of Ipswich, referring to a case depending ‖ between ‖ him & Wm fellowes. This Court do sentence him to make acknowledgmt of ‖ his ‖ offence yr in to ye sattisfaccon of this Court and also ‖ ye same acknowledgmt ‖ at ye next Court at Ipswich and also to pay a fine of

5^{li}. to ye vse of ye Country & In case he shall refuse to mak such acknowledgm^t he shall pay a fine of 20^{li}. E. R. S.*

[Endorsed, in handwriting of the Secretary, Edward Rawson,] Court Judgm^t ag^t. Bennet 20^{li}.

NOTE.

The above judgment of the Court of Assistants, which was passed probably at the March Term 1659–60, is written on a paper which though not signed appears to be a statement or plea by Henry Bennett in connection with an appeal in a suit between him and William Fellows (see Court Files, Suffolk, No. 351). The following is the statement by Bennett: —

"may it please the Court and Jury I haue giuen in divers grounds of my apeale and what is in them it is in your selus to Judge

But that which I thinke is the Cable to the vessell that will hold against all that hath bin sayd, I desire may not be least atended and that is the first ground which holds Closse to the action for which I am sued and put to this charge. My Cable is the law William fellows Chargeth me in the entry of the action with too severall wronges that I haue don to him let his purposse or his end be secret in his mind or verbally exprest what it will yet I must attend to what is written vpon record and I thinke so is the Court and Jury vpon oath the first wronge he chargeth me with is that I have Commited a trespasse in taking hay from of his land in his ocupation but he doth not proue any such thing if the record be serched The other wrong he Chargeth me with is true I haue Claimed his land for which he pays rent for now if I haue damnifyed by my words in that respect the words myt be proued that so I might answere to them and so they must be Judged whether he is damnifyed thereby yea or noe but I suppose there are noe such words or Claime apearing by evidence in the records wether By Confession or testimony from others and I am sure the law admits no new evidence now if there had bin evidence recorded by a person within age it might be sayd there is som evidence though weake but against me there is non at all

and where as it pleased some of the honored Court to say it was forgotten to set damages I hope my purse shall not pay for such omissions, and this may be added further to that, the Court not legally I Conceiue haue set any damages vpon me with out profe of trespass don or slanderous words spoken against his title which Could not haue bin don if it had bin thought vpon, because the Jury was scattered before the Judgment against me was agreed on and recorded"

The following order of the General Court, in May, 1660, relates, no doubt to this judgment of the Court of Assistants: —

"In ans^r to the peticon of Henry Bennet, it is ordered, that the

---

* Edward Rawson Secretary.

petitioner shall haue liberty to cleare his oune innocency before the whole Court, w[ch] if he cann doe, they judge it reason that his fine be remitted, or otherwise that he be dealt wth for his impetuous spirit ag[t] authoritje." (Mass. Col. Records, Vol. IV., Part I., p. 423.)

The "slandering & open traduceing the Court of Ipswich" seems to have occurred in the following "reasons of appeal" by Bennet from the judgment of that Court in September, 1659 (Court Files, Suffolk, No. 351, 3d paper) —

"The reasons of the appeale of henry Bennet from the judgement given agaynst him by Ipswich Court holden September 27 : 1659

The case was betweene William ffellows Tennant to Richard Saltonstall Esquire then Plaintiff now in this action defendant and the sayd henry Bennet is now Plaintiff in this action of appeale in an action of trespasse upon the case for taking the hay of the sayd Defendant off his land to his great Dam̄age by clayming his Land that he pays rent for.

1. The first ground of my appeale is because the Court grants a Judgement & Costs of Court vpon a pretended trespasse done in taking the hay &c and yet no Jury trespasse appeared I have sometimes heard in an action of trespasse that there hath beene but one penny dam̄a[ge] found to prove the trespasse Done. But if noe Dammage certainly no trespasse soe noe ground of action according to the rules & course of Law & Justice as I am able to conceive.

2 Secondly because as I conceave there was not a legall agreement [in] referrence to the Jury; the verdict and the testi[mony] of John Gage the lottlayer which was brought into the Court therefore no just or legall Judgement against mee in this case which things may appeare in the opening of them severally for the verdict as it was given and taken was not agreed vpon by the Jury and so no verdict indeed nor was the Testimony of John Gage receaved as hee gave it or was willing to give it into the Court and vpon which Testimony this way or that way as I conceave the pres[ent] case did depend

3 Thirdly because the Testimony of Robert Roberds improved agaynst me and for whose time Costs were granted to him by the Court is not allowable nor can bee sworne in truth in righteousnesse & in Judgement as I conceave for he sweareth that he knoweth the bounds betweene the sayd ffarme now in the occupation of William fellows & the ffarme now henry Bennetts to the south east-ward was a right line from a wallnut tree then standing neere the now dwelling house of William ffellows to the utmost point of the vpland to the Creeke called Chibactoe Creeke and yet this man only speaks from report or hearesay for he was not presant himselfe when the line which he sweareth he knoweth soe well was layd out.

4 Whereas the verdict or intended verdict of the Jury Depended it seemeth upon the question of the act in laying out the line in question that is to say whether it was done by one Lottlayer yea or noe I thinke it doth or might have fully appeared that it was Done effectually when both the Lottlayers John Gage and Richard Jacob were present & joyned in the act but at the former time which the maior Generall speaketh of in his Testimony there is mention only but of one Lottlayer namely John Gage this therefore is another ground moving me to appeale.

5 John Gage in one of his Testimonys speaketh of an agreement at the first time of their meeting about m^r Wades ffarme that is to say that the line should run from the Wallnut Tree by the poynt of the I [land] and so on. Now all this is nothing Contrary or darke in referrence to what he sweareth in his other Testimony wherein he speaketh & sweareth plainly that this land in question was layd out to m^r Wade as part of his ffarme but he doth darken this agayne in the other Testimony in saying that when m^r Wades ffarme was layd out afterward we altered that line thinking we had power soe to doe, so not knowing whether this might not have some sway in the mindes of the Court I give this my reason that the agreement he speaks of at the first time was not absolute for he so agreed if he had power to doe anything which is not granted making account it might be altered which when there was two Lottlayers & did goe to the place and actually did the worke then they both layd out the Line from the poynt of the Iland the next [w]ay on to the sayd Creeke, which thing the first time they could not perfectly doe at the first time at so great a distance not comming to the place and this agreeth with m^r Wades Testimony.

6 Sixtly Because as I pleaded in Court the Maior Generall is a party for he measured or layd out this parcell of Marsh afterwards to his brother m^r Dudley as part of the three hundred acres wherein they had equall right so he is bound I conceave to make it good to his Brother m^r Dudley if it be Judged to be my ground and this was done by themselves without the Lott-layers.

Henry Bennett did deliuer these reasons vnto me
vpon the first day of the first month 1659.
Samuel Symonds."

The answer to the above Reasons of Appeale is the fourth paper in No. 351.

"The Answere of william fellows tennant to Richard Saltonstall Esqr defd: to the reasons of Henry Bennett pltiff in an action of appeale from the Judgm^t of Ipswich Court 27 7^ber 59 vpon an action of tresspas vpon the case for takeing the s^d ffellows his hay from of his Land to his great damage by claymeing the land he payes rent for

There are two things in the action depending one vpon the other first the trespase in takeing of the hay wch being of les value was less mynded, tho acknowledged in Court at Ipswich by the p^rsent pltiff wch we were then redy to haue proued had it not beene acknowledged, 2 the 2^d^ w^c^h is the principall & vpon w^c^h the trespase dependeth is the title of the Land w^c^h was chiefly intended, w^c^h we haue clearly proued by several wittnesses present at the agreement of the then owners of the Land together with the Lotlayers, in stateing a common bounds betweene the two farmes before either of them was layd out in ꝑticular, w^c^h bounds soe stated and agreed, could not we conceiue be altered by the Lotlayer or Lotlayers (if there weare more (w^c^h cannot be ꝓued) and one of the owners of the land, without consent of the other, as much concerned and by whose consent it was at first agreed, and vpon this poynt at the worst on our part doth the controversy turne for the pltiff hath not ꝓued (as we conceiue) the Land he claymeth to haue beene layd out to him or his predesesour, not soe much as by any after act of the lotlayers; It is true John Gage a lotlayer testifieth this land was Layd out as ꝑt of m^r^ wades farme and he alsoe acknowledgeth vpon oath, that this was an alteratio[n] of the lyne formerly agreed by consent of ꝑtyes, to confirme this testimony is brought m^r^ wades, who it seemes is Ignorant of the bounds, as appeares by his showing them to lye in another place, & causeing a fence to be sett vp diferent from what is now claimed, and moreover the farme was his owne & by him sould to the pltff & without doubt is thereby engaged in honer & honesty to make good his sale (though ꝑhapps not in law) and soe cannot be a competent wittnes in a case wher in he is soe much concerned, and he faileing all the proofe is but one single testimony of gage, who alsoe as appeareth hath forgotten the bounds, by shewing the line to run in another place and causeing a ꝑtition fence to be acordingly sett up / on the other syde we have ꝓued our title to ye land in controversie by consent of the owners of the farmes and lottlayers before the pltiffs farme was layd out, and alsoe by our possesion thereof for many yeares as appeares by the testimonyes of Maior Gen^rll^ Denison John Gage and Robert Roberds

Tho this might be sufisient to haue answered in the case yet least the plt should thinke himself neglected or any stumble at his mistakes we craue liberty to say somwhat to his reasons of appeale if at least we can finde them to the first The Judgmt was not vpon a p^r^tended trespas y^t^ did not appeare;

The matter of fact viz. takeing away of the hay was acknowledged in open Court, whether this was a trespas or not, depended upon the title of the Land, w^c^h was judged for vs by the Court, and thereby our principle damage was repaired, but the pltiff complayneth y^t^ he was not judged to pay more damage (a very just though an unusual reason of appeale and therefore hath taken an efectuall course by aplyeing himselfe to this court w^c^h by the law in 1654 have power acording to the merrit of the fact, to rectifie what is amiss in the formar judgm^t^ without revokeing it to increase damages and heerin we are confident the the justice of this Court will fully answere the pltiffs desire by giveing vs damage for the hay taken away as well as confirme the title of the Land to vs, for the land being ours damage must be given vs for takeing away our hay for we can easily turn the pltiffs argum^t if a trespas done then damage is due It ill becomes the pltif to mention much less to make vse of the omission of the Court wch was caused by there vnseasonable & violent pressing to plead & pduce evidence tho nothing to the purpose, to the offence of ye Court & thereby deferring the juryes verdict to the last day of the week the members of the court being redy to depart to there severall homes

2 his second reason he conceives (and we doubt whether any man else can vnles to scandalize the Court & Jury be thought reasonable) the verdict given in and taken was not agreed by the jury it is a horrible abuse put vpon the Court and Jury [*]of the Court in receiving a verdict from a part of ye Jury or of the Jury in deliuering a verdict to wch they consented not, being all called & present The forman (as is usuall) declared there verdict against wch when some obiected, at the word lotlayer wch they sayd should be lotlayours, the court sent them out to agree, and after some time the whole Jury returneing being called manifested there agreement wch was declared by there foreman in there presents and recorded none of them in the least manifesting any disatisfaction soe ye pltiffs assertio[n] is no less then a gross of the largest sort & exceding Scandalous to the Court The other ꝑt of his complaint is agst the Court that they received not the testimony of John Gage vpon wch his case did depend, doth little concerne vs, The court being able to Justifie there owne acts wch the pltiff soe bouldly traduceth; yet being bound in duty acording to [our] abillity to vindicate the honer of the Court we answere, That wch the pltiff produced Gage to wittnes was y^t the other lottlayer was with him in altering ye bounds first agreed (and this after 4 or 5 days pleading) wch poynt being nothing to ye cause (notwithstanding ye pltiffs conceit) and the witnes not speaking explicetly to it, & being only single ye court we conceive thought it not expedient to admitt oaths to no purpose viz. from a single testimony speakeing vncertaynly to a matter of no concernment; and if psons may be incouraged to appeale because there cause may not be heard acording to ther owne wills (though in this case the court was to admiration patient) there will be noe want of appeales nor reasons of them

3 his 3^d reason is an obiection ags^t the testimony of Robert Roberds was not present when the line of devision was run or the bounds stated, yet he was vpon the farme at that present & was constantly imployed on the farme for dyverse yeares made hay vpon the land in controversye, when m^r wade made hay on the other syde without any clayme made, It is more then heersay, and in a very little tyme such kind of hearsayes must be all the testimonyes we can expect for the bounds of our land, vnles we can prolong the liues of the first layers out, further this testimonye is confirmed by two others

4 to 4th reason the pltiff mistakes or speakes in ye clouds the verdict of the jury not only intended but deliuered depends vpon the

* A few words here are cancelled and now illegible.

legality of the act of the lottlayer, (for it did not appeare to be of more y^{n} one) in layeing out m^{r}. wades line different from the bounds sett betweene the two farmes by the lottlayers [and] consent of ꝑtyes at least [3] months before, wch ye court did determine illegall and soe gave judgment for vs

The obiection y^{t} at the first setting of the bounds there is mention but of one lottlayer, is a new plea therfore not to be admitted, and nothing to the purpose, because the ꝑtyes concerned were present & consented, and moreouer in stead of one lottlayer there weare at that tyme 4 men brought by m^{r} Wade to lay out his farme, and he that came for that end would not come vnfurnished to doe what he intended, & further the pltiff is not ignorant that m^{r} Wade hath testified that the lottlayers, when they came vpon the place tould him his farme could not be layd out till bounds were stated betweene the adioyneing farmes w^{c}h hath beene sayd was then done with consent of ꝑtyes, and his farme not layd out till 3 months after as he confesseth

5 To the 5th reason that because John Gage thought he had power to alter the lyne, therefore the stateing of the bounds at first was not absolute, John Gage thinketh that lotlayers after they haue layd out Land to any man if they see cause may alter it afterward as he expressed himselfe in court & it is possible he might alter the line agreed, vpon that account but we acknowledge not John Gage to be infalible no more then ye pltiff, John Gage testifieth the agreement at first stateing the bounds that the lyne should run from the walnut tree by the poynt of the Island & soe on, y^{t} is the same lyne to be continued to the Creeke as the maior Gen^{rll} expresseth not turne from the poynt the next way to the Creeke, This is the altering of the bounds John Gage witnesseth, w^{c}h you call ꝑfecting by speaking contraryes it being the destruction of the first bounds, if m^{r} Wades testimony agree with this as the pltiff afiermeth, then he yealds the bounds were altered from the first agreement and stateing and ioyneth in this issue, that if the altering of the line agreed by Lotlayers and ꝑtyes conserned be illegal & invalid he yealdeth the cause, he need have sayd no more & might haue spared his six things he calleth reasons

6 To his 6th reason he pleaded and was answered ye maior Gen^{rll} was not concerned in profitt or losse honesty or honer however the land were determined: The whole farme was given to the maior Gen^{rll} & m^{r} Dudley wch they parted between themselues without measureing, but by guesse to there mutuall content without helpe of the lotlayers & we know no offence therein Mr Dudley neare 20 yeares since sould his part of the farme to Mr Gurden by the acre w^{c}h was measured by the lottlayers and acordingly possesed by him, from whom it came to m^{r} Saltonstall a gent. we suppose the maior Gen^{rll} (as many other in ye country) may honner, but cannot imagine how the pltiff should thinke him a ꝑtye in m^{r} Saltonstalls or william fellows case, neither he nor m^{r} Dudley being in the least concerned therein

The justice of the judgm^{t} of the honered court being cleared notwithstanding the indeavours of the pltiff to obscure and traduce the same, we desire this honered court of Assistants to confirme y^e sd $judgm^t$ & give vs further damage for the trespas done, And we shall leaue the appealant to your iustice to be further ꝑseeded with acording to the Laws fol: 2 title appeales Sec: 2 and fol: 36 title maiestrates."

The fifth paper in No. 351 is as follows: —

"The Depositions of Joseph metcalfe william Acie & Richard Swann

We whose names are here under written doe testify being upon the Jury the last Court, held at Ipswich in the Case betwene William ffellows plaintiue & Henry Bennit defendant, Vpon ye request of the said Henry Bennit haueing respect to ye oath we haue taken to act equally in all Cases & to give a Just Verditt we doe testifie to all to whome it may Concerne, that after some Agitation among the Jury we agreed that the Verditt should goe lottlayers, but when we were Come downe into the Court it was read Lottlayer & it seemeth that it was then so recorded but severall of the Jury did then oppose it and further we doe affirme y^t the Verditt was read by o^r foreman Lottlayers before we Came downe & we know none of the Jury that did oppose it at that time.

Joseph Metcalfe
William Acie
Richard Swan

And further being desired by the Court we went up againe, and after some sharp Contest among the Jury, the Court being ready to rise, we went downe againe, and Goodman Gage being present testified that there were lottlayers at the laying out of the ffarme, but whether it were recorded in Court or no we doe not say, & doe not remember any other verditt given in

Joseph Metcalfe
William Acie
Richard Swan

William Acie swares to all that is here exprest, onely he remembereth not y^t they were bidden to goe up by the Court the second time, yet I know that we were there & had a sharp Contest.

Taken vpon oath as it is expressed in this paꝑ according to the severall parts thereof the 5th day of the first month 1659 before me

Samuel Symonds"

[Endorsed] "3 Jurymen's dep"

The following record and two depositions by John Gage are in the sixth paper in No. 351: —

"Att the Court held at Ipswich the 27 of Sept: 1659. William ffellows Tennant to Richard Saltonstall Esqr pltff ags^t Henry Bennett defdt in an action of trespase vpon the case for takeing his hay off his Land to his great Damage by claimeing his Land that he payes rent for, The Jury in this case finde thus, If the act of the Lotlayer in layeing out the land in controversie betweene pltiff & defdt were acording to Law we finde for the defdt If not for the pltiff

The court vpon considderation of the case finde for the pltiff the first Line good & soe the Land & costs of court 28^s 4^d

The defdt: appeales to the next Court of Assistants

This is a true copie as attest Robert Lord clerke.

Henry Bennett in his action haveing appealed stands bound to the treserer of this County in thirty pound to ꝑsecut his appeale at ye next Court of Assistants to efect acording to Law

This is a true copie out of the record as attest

Robert Lord clerke"

"The deposition of John Gage saith that at the first meeting to state the bounds of m^r wades farme & that of m^r Dudleys when the Maior Gen^{rll} Denison was present, It was agreed, the lyne run from the walnutt tree by poynt of ye Iland and soe on, but when m^r wades farme was Layd out afterward we altered that Lyne thinking we had power soe to doe

Sworne in court held at Ipswich 27 (7) 1659

Vera copia as attest Robert Lord clerke"

"The Testimony of John Gage

Testifieth that this Land in controversie betweene William ffellows and Henry Bennett was layd out to m^r wade as part of his farme and his farme was layd out before m^r Dudleyes farme

Sworne in Court held at Ipswich the 27 (7) 1659 Robert Lord clerke

This is a true copie Robert Lord clerke"

The first two papers in No. 351 are as follows: —

"William ffellows bill of costs in the case of Henry Bennett & himselfe

for copies of the records	0– 5 –6
goeing to m^r Symonds house for the Reasons of appeale	0– ~~1~~ –0
for drawing a copy of it	0– ~~1~~ –0
for drawing the answere to his Reasons of appeale	[0– 2 –6*]
for attendance at this court 6 dayes	0–12 –0
	1–02 –0

~~filing papers~~

9 March 1659 ~~allowed E. R. S~~ "

"Bill of costs of William ffellows upon the forfitt of the bond

	£ s d
for copies	0– 5–6
for going to m^r Symonds for to enquire for the Reasons of appeale	0– 1–0
for drawing of a copie of y^m	0– 1–0
for drawing our answere to his reasons	0– 3–6
for our horses & selves 5 dayes apeece	2– 0–0
9 March 1659	2–11–0

Allowed E. R. S."

In the Chamberlain Collection at the Boston Public Library is the following statement by Samuel Symonds: —

"Concerning Bennetts case I say as followeth viz:
That at first, when it was in agitacon in this Court of Assistants, I did not remember that m^r Bradstreet did aske the foreman of ye Jury (after Gage his last Testimony was reade in the Court, which I thinke was vpon the oath he had taken) the question; whether it were lott layer, or lott layers? or that the foreman did answere. But since, considering what was said in Court, & out of Court, about that matter, it is somewhat come to my minde that it was spoken to that effect by m^r Bradstreet, and that the foreman answered to his question: lott layer. And I remember not that any of ye Jury did then speake therevnto. But (by what I observed or can call to remembrance) The Jury did not consult, nor had, or did take any oportunity to consider of Gage his Testimony, before the foreman did so speake./

Samuel Symonds"

There are nine papers relating to this case on file in Essex County Court Papers, Vol. V., Fol. 23.

The first is the bill of costs: —

"[W]ill fellows bill of costs

[ ] entering of the action	10^s–0^d
[ ] wittnes 4 dayes	6–0
[atten]dance 5 dayes	7–6
[atta]chm^t & serueing	3–6
	1–7–0
fileing evedences	0 1–4"

The second paper is the writ: —

"To the marshall of Ipswich or his Deputy

You are required to atach the goods & for want therof the body of Henry Benett & take bond of him to the value of ten pound with sufisient security for his psonall appearance at the next Court held at

Ipswich the last third day of this mo: then & there to answere the complaynt of William ffellows in an action of trespass vpon the case for takeing of hay of his Land as tennant to Rich: Saltingstall Esquire to his great damage by claymeing his land yt he pays rent for & soe make a true returne thereof vnder your hand Dated the 22th of Sept: 1659 By the Court Robert Lord"

[Endorsed] "22 September 1659

Atached a pcell of land broke vp & vnbroke vp wth medowe ioyninge to it contayninge about 8 acres lyeinge betweene Cowe fences next to ye land in ye possession of william fellowes to be responsall accordinge to lawe

p me Edward Browne Marshall"

The third paper is as follows: —

"William Fellows aged about fifty yeares sworne testifieth

That about fourtene yeares since ther being a fence to be made Betwene Mr Saltonstall & Mr Wade: Mr Saltonstall desired this deponent to goe to mr Wade and Goodm: Gage and desire them to shew this deponent ye line now in question ye which accordingly they did: and both of ye parties that is to say Mr: Wade & Goodm Gage: did them Affirme vnto this deponent that ye bounds went by a straight line from ye walnut tree to a black stump: vpon ye Iland four Rod from ye point thereof. by which meanes this deponent was misled to make foure score Rod of fence wth a ditch whereby the owner of ye Land is damnified and also ye tennent and further this deponent testifieth that at ye same time also that they shewed mee ye line that Runes betwene Mr Wade & Mr Saltonstall one the other side of ye farme and did Affirme at ye same time that ye line went from ye walnut tree to ye crotched tree according to which line Mr Wade made his fence

Sworne in Court held at Ipswich 27(7) 1659

Robert Lord clerke"

Fourth paper: —

"The deposition of John Gage

Saith that at the first meetinge to state the bounds of mr Wades farme & that of mr Dudlye when the maior Genall was present, It was agreed the lyne run from the walnut tree by the poynt of the Iland and soe on; but when mr Wades farme was layd out afterward we altered that Line, thinking we had power soe to doe

Sworne in Court held at Ipswich 27(7) 1659

Robert Lord clerke"

Fifth paper: —

"The deposition of Robert Roberts Aged about 40 yeares

Sayth yt he hath knowne the farme now in the occupation of William Fellowes aboue 24 yeares, being imployed vpon the same for dyuers yeares, and that the bounds betwene the sayd farme and the farme now Henry Bennitts to the south eastward was a right line from a walnut tre then standing neere the now dwelling house of william fellows, by the vtmost point of the vpland to the Creeke called Chebaco Creeke, and farther that whiles m^r Dudlye possessed the sayd farme, he hath made hay for him vppon the marsh beyond the sayd point of vpland, to the line wch he perfectly knoweth by a smale percell of dry ground, wch lyeth in the marsh beyond the sayd pointe, and that m^r Wade who was then posessed of the farme now Henry Bennetts at the same time made hay on the other syde of his farme, and could not be ignorant of the improuement made on m^r Dudleys farme yit neuer questyoned or obiected that euer I hard of, all the time I was imployed about the sayd farme wch was about fiue yeares

And farther being at the deuideing the land giuen by the towne of Ipswich to ye maior generall Denison and m^r Dudly y^t pece of land in question fell to m^r Dudly

Sworne in Court held at Ipswich the 27 of Sept: 1659

Robert Lord Clerke"

Sixth paper: —

"The deposition of Jonathan Wade Senr. in the case depending betwene will. fellows plantiff and Henry Benet defendant, Henry Benet chalenging as his land from the place where the stake was sett by the lott layers by the great creeke, and thence to the point of the Eyland, and thence on a strayt line to the plase where the wallnutree stood, this deponent sayth that land was layd out as ꝑt of the farme wch now is the sayd Benets

Sworne in Court held at Ipswich the 27 (7) 1659

Robert Lord Clerke"

Seventh paper: —

"the deposition of Samuell Graues testifyeth that Robert Roberds being asked by the Court how hee knew the line to be a right line and that it run as hee had spoke in his testimony: hee said he was not there present when the line was run but said his master tould him soe

henry bennit afermeth to this:

~~I william Wild can aferme to this~~

Sworne in Court held at Ipswich 27 (7) 1659

Robert Lord Clerke"

Eighth paper: —

"the deposition of John Gage testifyeth that this land in controuercy between william fellowes and henry bennitt was layd out to m^r wade as part of his farm: and his farm was layd out before m^r Dudlyes farm

Sworne in Court held at Ipswich the 27 (7) 1659 Robert Lord Clerke"

Ninth paper: —

"The testimony of Daniel Denison

S^th that he certainly knoweth the bounds betweene the farmes now Henry Beñets and that in the possession of Willm. Fellowes which on that part of the farmes in Controuersy doth run from a walnut tree standing betweene the 2 houses on the sd. farmes upon a right line to Chebockque creek by the utmost point of an Island or upland and that aboue 20 yeares ago while mr Dudley possessed the farme wee cutt the grass and made the hay for seueral yeares without any interruption or claime frō any that I euer heard till seueral yeares after.

Sworne in Court held at Ipswich the 27 of Sept. 1659
By me Robert Lord Clerke"

The record of the judgment of the County Court at Ipswich is as follows: —

"The Court held at Ipswich the 27 of Sept. 1659"

"3. William ffellows tennant to Rich: Saltonstall Esqr. plt: agst Henry Bennett deft in an action of traspase vpon the case for takeing his hay of his land to his great Damage by claymeing [his] Land that he payes rent for. The jury in this case find thus, if the act of the Lotlayer in layeing out the Land in controversie betweene the plt: and defdt were acording to Law we finde for the defdt: if not for the pltiff. The Court vpon consd. of the case finde for the plt: the first Line good and the Land & costs of Court 28s 4d

The defdt appeales to the next Court of Assistants

Henry Bennett stands bound in 30£ to ꝓsecute his appeale at the next Court of Assistants at Boston to effect acording to Law"

The allowance by the Court of Assistants of the "bill of costs of William Fellows upon the forfitt of the bond" shows that Bennett failed to prosecute his appeal to effect, and therefore the judgment of the Court at Ipswich remained good against him, the Court of Assistants, in addition, sentencing him for "slandering and open traduceing the Court of Ipswich."

XXXIII.

[Court Files, Suffolk, March, 1659-60, No. 393, Gooden & Hawkins — 5th paper.]

: 9 March: 1660:

In the case depending betweene Tho Hakins plaintiue and William Gooden vpon ane Apeall from ye Commissioners Court ^ that in case ye Acknoledgement of Tho Hakins vpon Rekord, be a full euidence to proue the Receiuing of ye quantity of fagots, under the word: the: then we find for ye defendant, the former vardet, and cost of Courts: If not then we find for the plaintiue, ye former Judgment void and cost of Courts: the fore man in the name of ye Rest

Richard Callecott

Costs of ye former Court

Attach:	1.8
Ent.	10.8
Witt.	4.6
[filing]	1.6
	18.4

The magistrates hauing considered ye case finde for ye defendant ye Judgment of ye Commissioners Court & Costs of Courts: last being 6s & filing 9 papers

E R S*

NOTE.

This case was an appeal from a Commissioners Court at Boston, 20th. Sept., 1659, where the verdict had been for William Goden, the then plaintiff, and against Thomas Hawkins, the then defendant, the action being for debt.

The other papers in the case are as follows: —

First paper: — "At a Commissionors Court held at Boston the 20th Sept: 1659

Thomas Hawkins owned in Court that when hee had the ffagots home he found they were not merchantable

This is a true coppy compared
with that which is recorded in the
book of Records as attests
Jonath Negus Cleric"

Second paper: — "At a Comissionors Court held at Boston the 20th September 1659

To the Marshall of Boston or his deputy You are required to attach the goods or in want thereof the body of Thomas Hawkins and take bond of him to the value of sigsteene pounds with sufficient surety or sureties for his appearance at the next Comissionors Court to be holden at Boston then and there to answer the complaint of William Goden in an action of the Case for withholding the sum of nine pounds od money due for faggots sold him with due damages, and so make a true returne thereof under your hand dated the 10th 7th mo 1659

p Court Edward Burt

This is a true Copy compared
with the originall as attests
Jonath Negus Cleric

I Thomas Hawkins do bind my selfe heires and executors vnto Richard Waite Marshall in the sum of eighteene pounds vpon condicon that I will appeare at the next Comissioners Court to be held at Boston to answer the complaint of William Goden according to the

* Edward Rawson, Secretary.

tenor of the attachment, and that I will abide the order of the Court and not depart without licence as witnes my hand this 10th 7th 1659

Thomas Hawkins

This is a true Coppy compared with the originall as attests

Jonath Negus Cleric

At a Comissionors Court held at Boston the 20th September 1659

William Goden plaintiffe against Thomas Hawkins in an action of the Case for withholding the sum of nine pounds od money due for ffagots sould him with due damages. The Court found for the plaintiffe nine pounds damage & costs of Court, Thomas Hawkins appealed from the iudgment of the Court to the next Court of Asistants & bound himselfe heires and assigns in the sum of eighteen pounds that he will ꝑsecut the appeale to effect. This is a true Coppy of the Record as attests Jonath Negus Cleric"

Third paper: — "Thomas Hawkins reasons of Appeale from the Commissioners Court held at Boston the 20th of September 1659 in a Case depending betwene William Goden and my self

first wheareas the then plaintif sued mee for faggots sould vnto mee to the vallue of nine pounds od money as appeareth by The Attachment and yet made noe proof of any bargaine made with mee nor deliuering of Any vnto mee according to any such pretended bargaine and therefore its Contrary to lawe equitie and reason to grant a judgment against mee vppon that accoumpt

2 ly whereas sum testifie that William Goden gave bills on mee vnto sum men to pay them for Carting doune faggots to the waters side at Malden sum of which I paied: and I had just reason so to doe hauing had former dealings with him [I] payd his bill and Charged them vnto his accoumpt as I made proof of then by my booke in the Court which I am redie here to show but my paying of his bills doth not proue any such Contract made with mee nor deliuering any such faggots vnto mee thay might bee disposed of vnto whom hee pleased not with standing what I payed him and therfore its an vngrounded Consequenc to proue that I had them: it is true as I then said in Court I had sum faggots of him for which I payd him: but when thay Came whom * vnto my house thay prooued not worth the fraight which most of them lye still in my yard rotting and therfore I refused to haue any more of him which may appeare by one of his owne euidences namly Samuell howard which Came vnto mee with another bill but hee swears that I refused to pay him and whereas the said Goden pade vnto the Carters to Cary faggots for mee: his saying doth not proue it to bee so [ ] thay carted them for him self and hee might doe what hee [p]leased with them if such a practis may bee justified that because a man sayth hee made such a Commodite for a nother let it bee good or bad therfore that man must pay for it that

* Home?

hee saith hee made them for this will admit of strange Consequences Contrary vnto all law and equitie which is the Case here depending and therfore noe reson why I should bee Cast to pay for such faggots. all which hee leaves vnto the determination of this honored Court and Jury

Tho hawkings

I receaued these [rea]sons from thomas Haukins the first of [ ] mo 1659
Anthony Stoddard"

[Endorsed] "Hawkins Reasons of Appeales

Haukins agt
Goodin"

Fourth paper: — "Willm Goodwins answer unto Thomas Hawkins Reasons that whereas Thomas Hawkines saith that when the ffagots were brought home that they were not merchantable his answer is that if he had not liked the fagots he might haue taken as few as he would of them and haue payed him for them; but the fagottes were good till he had used them and when he comes for to pay for them then they are naught."

Sixth paper: — "I James Green aged about 48 yeares testify that William Godine came to mee as he told mee from Thomas Hawkins of Boston and said, that if I would Cart downe some faggots for him, the said Hawkins would pay mee for it, And accordingly I did Cart downe six thousand four hundred & fifty ffagots and the said Hawkins paid mee for the same

Sworn to in Court 20 September 1659
Edw Rawson Commiss"

This is a true Coppy compared with the originall as attests
Jonath Negus Cleric

Seventh paper: — "I Samuell Haward testify that William Godine spake to mee to carry some fagots for Thomas Hawkins to the water side, and accordingly I did cary eight hundred ninety one, and the said Goodine signed mee a bill to the said Hawkins for my pay and he paid it mee, And afterward I carted downe nine hundred eighty eight faggots And the said Goodine signed mee an other Bill for my pay to the said Hawkins, which he refused to pay mee

Sworn vnto in Court 20 September 59
Edw: Rawson Comissioner

This is a true Coppy compared with the originall as attests
Jonath Negus Cleric"

Eighth paper: — "I John Wayte aged about ffourty-two years testify that William Goodine hired mee to cart two hundred of fagots to the waterside for Thomas Hawkins of Boston, which acordingly I did,

Also the said Goodine signed mee a bill to the said Hawkins for my pay, which was acordingly by him acepted & paid mee

Sworn vnto in Court 20 September 1659
Edw: Rawson Comiss

This is a true Coppy compared with the originall as attests
Jonath Negus Cleric"

Ninth paper: — "ffor Mr Hawkins of Boston made by mee William Goodine of Malldin and caried by James Greene of the abouesaid town to the waterside six thousand four hundred and a halfe of faggots

The mark* of James Greene

This is a true Coppy compared with the originall as attests
Jonath Negus Cleric"

Tenth paper: — Willm Goodins Bill of costs at the Comis^rs Court in Boston about Hawkins concern[ing] faggotts

Entering ye Accon	0	10	0
3 wittnesss from Maldon	0	6	0
his owne time & the Attach^t & serving it & finding wittness		4	0
Attendant at Court	0	2	0
	1	2	0

XXXIV.

[Court Files, Suffolk, March, 1659–1660, No. 394, 6th paper.]

in the case betweene Clement Grose plantife and m^r Houchin and m^r williams guardians vnto Isaak and Susana Grose defendants. if the meaning of the courts order † for a third of the whole for the wife be onely for her life the jury finde for the defendant one third and noe more, if the meaning of the aforesaid order be for ever the jury findes reason to revoake the judgment of the former court and finde for the plantife the whole: and for the determination thereof with costs of courts the jury leave it to the honoured court.

Amos Richison forman

The magists. considering of this Speciall virdict declare they cannot find by a third for ye whole is to be vnderstood for life only therefore find for ye plaintiff Costs of courts E. R. S.
9 m^rch 1660.‡

* If there was a mark in the original, the copyist failed to insert it in his copy.

† See second paper.

‡ 1660–1.

NOTE.

This case was an appeal from the judgment of the County Court. (See seventh paper.)

For the earliest stage of the matter involved in this case see Mass. Col. Records, Vol. IV., Part I., p. 231. Division of estate of Edmond Groce, deceased, on petition of Jeremiah Houchin, May 29, 1655. (See also Vol. III., p. 385.)

The second paper in No. 394 is the Court's order referred to and is as follows: —

"At a County Court held at Boston 29th Aprill, 1656.

It was ordered by the Court that Samuell Sheares now Husband to the Relict of Edmond Grosse shall haue the portion of the Sucking Child whose name is John Giuing in Securitie to the Administrators that thay will keepe the said Child and carrie it to England if thay goe carefully bring it vp, and the Gouener and Dept Gouener declared that by A third part for the wife to be ment a third part of the whole

This is A true Copie taken out
of the Courts booke of Records

as attests Edw Rawson Recordr"

The seventh paper is the record of the County Court 29th Jan. 1660–1, as follows: —

"At A County Court held at Boston ye 29th January 1660

Jeremiah Houchin and Nathaniell Williams Gardians to Isack and Susanna Grosse children of the late Edmond Grosse plantiffe against Clement Grosse defendant in an action of the case for keeping possestion of that part of the house by the Dock that was giuen by will vnto the said Isack Grosse with the preuelidges thearevnto beelonging and like wise for keeping possession of the other part of the house that was giuen by will vnto the said Susanna Grosse with the appurtenances thearevnto beelonging according to the will of the deceased Edmond Grosse ^ to yeald vp eather of theire rites allthough legally demanded and dew damages According to Attachement Dated 23th of ye 11 : 1660. After the Attachment and euedences in ye case produced were red committed to the Jury which are on the file the Jury brought in theire verdit *to* A spetiall verdit in the case depending between mr Houching and mr Williams and Clement Grosse wee haue considered as wee are able but find much difficulty and obscurity in it and as wee ar tender of the orphants and that the will of the deceased may bee performed as neare as may bee soe wee are tender concerning the Generall Courts Order and violating of aney just rite and therefore cannot concurr in an absolute verditt but must craue leaue to take liberty for A Spetiall verditt which is this that considering the generall Courts order in impowering the administrators to sell the houses and theire acting accordingly and Clement Grosse his legall purchasing & possessing the same there seemes to vs ground to find for the defendant, but on the other hand considering the Generall Courts after order to the County Court for the settleing of the estate according to the will, if the said order doe revoake the former then there seemes grounds to vs to find for the plantiffe but not haueing suffitient light to conclude vpon eather leaue it to the honored Court to determine. The magists expresse themselues thay judge for the plantiffe the defendant appealed from the judgement to this next Court of Assistance and Clement Grosse and Capt. James Oliuer in open court acknowledge themselues bound joyntly and seuerally in the sume of three hundred pounds to the Tresurer of the Cuntry on the Condition that Clement Grosse shall prosecute this Appeale to effect.

This is a true Copie of y[e] Courts Judgm[t] & bond as Attests

Edward Rawson Recorder"

The other papers in the case are as follows: —

First paper: —Writ of Attachment and return 23–11th mo. 1660 (County Court)

Third paper: — Copy of an order of the General Court, 6th, May, 1657, empowering the administrators of the estate of Edmond Grosse to sell "the two Thirds of the house and land belonging to the children of the said Grose" "to pay his debts." (See Mass. Col. Records, Vol. IV., Part I., p. 295.)

Fourth paper: — Copy of an order of the General Court, 16th October, 1660, on petition of the "guardians to two of the children of the late Edmond Grosse," appointing a commission to audit the accounts and empowering the next County Court "to settle the devision of the sayd estate between the widdow and ye children and as neere as may bee according to the minde of the deceased declared as his will beefore his death and that what land is yet unsold It be reserued for the children and not sold by the Administrators." (Mass. Col. Records, Vol. IV., Part I., p. 448.)

Fifth paper: — Copy of the judgment of the County Court Oct. 28, 1660, in accordance with said order of the General Court. The County Court "doe judge meete to allow of the will of the said Edmond Grosse as it was this Court proved [by] the oathes of Edmond Jackson and Francis Huds[on] and order the same to stand in all respects and that the children haue theire portions according[ly]."

Eighth paper: — Reasons of Appeal by Clement Grose 26 Feb. 1660 from County Court Jan. 1660.

Ninth paper: — Answer to the above Reasons of Appeal.

Tenth paper: — Copy of Deposition of Ann Carter Jan. 30, 1660–1.

Eleventh paper: — Account at County Court Nov. 2'/60.

Twelfth paper: — Bill of Sale.

Thirteenth paper: — Deed.

Fourteenth paper: — Copy of will and probate and of list of debts &c., also of order of the magistrates at Boston May 3 1655 granting administration on the said estate The will is not dated. The testator gives part of his house to his wife for life and after her decease to his daughter Susanna—also other estate.

Fifteenth paper: — Copy of deed and assignment to Clement Grosse of the part of Edmond Grosses house "left to his widdow" — August 14, 1657.

Sixteenth paper: — Copy of deed by the administrators to Clement Grosse Aug. 12, 1657 of the two thirds part of said house.

Seventeenth paper: — Bill of costs.

XXXV.

[From an official copy made by Elisha Cooke, Clerk, about 1716.]

At a Court of Assistants held at Boston 5th March, 1660.*

William Ledra notwithstanding his being banished this Jurisdiction on pain of Death by the Last Court of Assistants in September last, Returned into this Jurisdiction, was Committed to Prison in Order to his Tryal. The General Court in October last by their Order gave him with Nickolson & the Rest of the Quakers libertie to pass for England or else to go out of this Jurisdiction engaging not to Return, which he & they rejected and would not Accept of, Save the said Nicholson & his Wife †: being now brought to the Barr was Indicted by the Name of William Ledra, for not having the fear of God before his Eyes, notwithstanding your being Sentenced by the Last Court of Assistants held at Boston 4th of Septembr. 1660 to Banishment on pain of Death, according to the Laws here established, have Returned into this Jurisdiction in a Rebellious and Seditious Manner contrary to the wholesome Laws of this Country, made for the Preservation of the Peace & wellfare of the same: And in Open Court, on the Reading the Last Court of Assistants Jud[gment ?] against him he acknowledged in open Court that he was [the ?] Person in said Judgment so banished. In answer to what [he ?] sayd he was tendered in open Court if he could produce a [law ?] of England Repugnant to our Law here against Quakers[,]

---

* 1660-1.

† See Mass. Col. Records, Vol. IV., Part I., p. 433.

[he?] should be heard, he sayd in open Court, he owed no Subjectio[n to the] wicked Laws of this Jurisdiction, sayd he [w?]ould not owne [this?] Governour to be his Judge and sayd I have Spoken the truth [ ] you can, on the Governours Question to him why he Intruded [ ] on Us against our Concience, he Answered you know not w[hat?] belongs to Concience & sayd I Shall not hear the Word [of God?] among You and I shall Still owne these you put to death [ ] Quakers to be the Servants of God & sayd with that Spirit [which thou?] callest the Divell do Wee worship God. your Magistrates Do [not?] I owne them no more Subjection than Daniell to Nebuchadnazar, [he?] sayd he knew no hurt in Speaking English then* in Wearing Cloath[es] in a decent manner: and sayd I know your Ministers are deluders & yourselves Murderers and If ever I turn to Such Murderers as you are let all this Company Say I have turned from the God, which is the Salvation of his People & this I will seale with my blood. It was told him he might have his life & be at libertie if he would, he Answered I am willing to dy for it, Saying he Spake the truth. It was sayd do you beleive the Scriptures to be Gods Word, how dare you then Revile Magistrates & Ministers, he sayd it is not Reviling to Speak the truth you are Such as I affirm you to be, was it not the Spirit of Christ breathed in Stephen when he told the People they were Murtherers, he was bid prove himself to be Such an one as Stephen, he sayd We must go where the Lord draws Us, When he was Spoken to to shew any Christian that would divulge his opinion without a call from God especially any New thing he Answered your Ministers say they Preach by Virtue of that Commission Go & teach all Nations he was Answered, where Called, there & then to Preach but not in Turky where Prohibited.

The Indictment being again Read before the Prisoner at the barr, The Jury Considering the Courts Judgment the Prisoners confession brought in their Verdict they found him Guilty.

The Governour in the Name of the Court Pronounced Sentence ag[t]. him That Is You William Ledra are to goe from hence to the place from whence you came & from thence be carried to the place of Execution and there hang till you be dead.

A true Copy As Appears of Record.

Exam[d]. p Elisha Cooke Cler:

[Endorsed] W[m] Leddra his Sentance a true Coppy.

* Than.

At a Court of Assistants held at Boston 5th March. 1660.

William Ledra notwithstanding his being banished this Jurisdiction
on paine of Death by the Last Court of Assistants in September last
Returned into this Jurisdiction, was Committed to Prison in Order
to his Tryal. The Generall Court in October last by their Order
gave him with Nicholson & the Rest of the Quakers liberty to pass
for England or else to go out of this Jurisdiction engaging not to
Return, which he & they rejected and would not Accept of, save
the said Nicholson & his Wife, being now brought to the Barr
was Indicted by the Name of William Ledra, for not having the fear
of God before his Eyes, notwithstanding your being Sentenced by
the Last Court of Assistants held at Boston 4th of Septemb.r 1660.
to Banishment on paine of Death, according to the Laws here
established, have Returned into this Jurisdiction in a Rebellious and
seditious Manner contrary to the wholesome Laws of this Country
Made for the Preservation of the Peace & wellfare of the same.
And in open Court, on the Reading the Last Court of Assistants Judg
against him he acknowledged in open Court that he was
Person in said Judgment so banished. In Answer to what
sayd he was tendered in open Court if he could produce a
of England Repugnant to our Law here against Quakers
should be heard, he sayd in open Court, he owed no subjectio
wicked Laws of this Jurisdiction, sayd he could not owne
Governour to be his Judge and sayd I have spoken the truth
you can, on the Governours Question to him why he Intruded
on Us against our Conscience, he Answered you know not w
belongs to Conscience & sayd I shall not hear the Word
among You And I shall Ever owne those you put to death
Quakers to be the Servants of God & sayd with that Spirit
callest the Divell do Wee worship God. your Magistrates I
owne them no more subjection than Daniell to Nebuchadnazar,
sayd he knew no hurt in Speaking English than in Wearing Clothes
in a decent Manner. and sayd I knew your Ministers are deluders
& your selves Murderers And if ever I turn to such Murderers as you
are let all this Company say I have turned from the God which
is the Salvation of his People & this I will seale with my blood
It was told him he might have his life & be at libertie if he
would, he Answered I am willing to dy for it, saying he spake the
truth, It was sayd do you beleive the Scriptures to be Gods Word,
how dare you then Revile Magistrates & Ministers, he sayd it is not
Reviling to speak the truth you are such as I affirm you to be,
was it not the Spirit of Christ breathed in Stephen when he told
the People they were Murtherers, he was bid prove himselfe to be
such an one as Stephen he sayd We must go where the Lord
draws Us, when he was spoken to to shew any Christian that would

Dwel

divulge his opinion without a call from God especially any New thing he Answered your Ministers say they Preach by Virtue of that Commission Go & teach all Nations he was Answered where Called there & then to Preach but not in Turky where Prohibited.

The Indictment being again Read before the Prisoner at the barr, the Jury Considering the Courts Judgment the Prisoners confession brought in their Verdict they found him Guilty

The Governour in the Name of the Court Pronounced Sentence agt him That is you William Ledra are to goe from hence to the place from whence you came & from thence be carried to the place of Execution and there hang till you be dead.

Vera Copy As Appears of Record.

Exam. p. Elisha Cooke Cler

NOTE.

A certification by Elisha Cooke, Clerk, upon an order of the Superiour Court of Judicature, Nov., 1716, (see Court Files, Suffolk, No. 11150, 1st. paper) leads, by the similarity of form and handwriting, to the opinion that the foregoing copy from the record of the Court of Assistants for March 5, 1660–1, was made at about the year 1716. It would further seem that this book of the records of the Court of Assistants previous to that volume entitled "[S]eccond Booke of Recc[ords] Begunne the 3[d] of March, 1673," printed as Volume I. in this series, was then in existence and in the custody of Elisha Cooke, as clerk of the Court which succeeded the highest judicial Court of the Colony. With the exception of this record of the trial and sentence of William Leddra, copied by Elisha Cooke, no record or official copy of record of the Court of Assistants giving judgment against the Quakers is known to exist. So far as shown by an extended examination of the records and files this copy is also the latest knowledge we have of the lost record. In what connection or for what purpose the copy was made is not known. A sentence by the Court of Assistants of banishment upon pain of death against William Robinson and three other Quakers is cited in the warrant for discharge from prison given above in Fragment XXX.

The earliest record we have relating to William Leddra, the last Quaker sentenced to death and executed, is the following, which is taken from the Essex County Court Record now in the Office of the Clerk of Courts at Salem: —

County Court Record Salem June 1658. "The Court held at Salem the 29 June 1658

* * *

19 William Brend William Lutherway examined why & w[t] they came into these ꝑts to seek a godly seed the lord god sd pase away to New England

* * *

51 The Court being informed of a disorderly meeting of certeyne suspected ꝑsons at the house of Nicolas Phelps of Salem, on the last Lords day in tyme of pullique worship amongst whom there were two strangers William Brend & William Lederay ꝓfessed quakers who then made an escape but afterwards were apprehended brought to Salem Examined by the Court and owneing themselves to be such were sent to the house of corection acording to Law."

The Plymouth Colony Records contain the following entries relating to William Ledra (or Leddra as sometimes written).

Vol. III., p. 176, Oct. 1659. — "Att this Court, William Ledra and Peter Peirson, two of those caled Quakers, whoe haue bine prisoners att Plymouth for some time, were sent for seuerally out of prison, and presented before the Court, whoe were demaunded if they would engage, according to the law, to depart, and to come into this collonie noe more, and pay their fees to the jayler; if soe they might forthwith depart, which they both refused to doe; asperting the law, in agitation about which the said Peter Peirson openly deneyed the humanitie of

Christ; and they, seuerally refusing to answare the law, were returned to the place whence they came."

Vol. III., p. 178, Dec. 1659.—"Att this Court, William Ledra and Peter Peirson, two of those called Quakers, whoe were some time since comītted to prison att Plymouth according to law, as being foraigne Quakers, apeered and were demaunded seuerally whether they would depart the gou^{r}ment in some competent time, viz. two or three dayes, incase wheather and strength were suitable, and that noe vnexpected prouidence in the aforesaid respects did not or should not fall in the way in the interim, and whether it was theire present intentsions, without any sinestery reseruation, directly to depart the gou^{r}ment, with intension (the Lord willing) not to returne into the gou^{r}ment any more; they answared they could not engage to any certaine time to depart the gou^{r}ment; vpon which theire answare they were againe returned to prison, and order was giuen to Mr Southworth and Mr Bradford, that if vpon beter consideration they should or would accept of the conditions of the aforsaid tender of the Court, they are to release them."

Vol. III., p. 184, March 1659–60.—The prisoners appeared again and the same tender was repeated, "to which the said Ledra answared that theire imprisonment was vnjust and illegall; on which the Court made it manifest that theire imprisonment was according to law, both of England and this gou^{r}ment; and as conserning departing the gou^{r}ment, according to the proposition aboue mencioned, hee, the said William Ledra, refused to engage to any certaine time to depart, onely saying, 'Its like if I were att libertie out of prison I might depart in the will of God ere long;' to which was replyed in the Scripture phraise by the Court, that if hee would now resolue (the Lord willing) to depart by such a time, hee might haue his libertie; which hee, the said Ledra, refused, saying hee would not engage to any certaine time."

Peter Peirson made a similar answer and both were returned to prison, but it was arranged that if it should be revealed to either of them that he might depart "hee should send word to the magistrates, and hee may haue his libertie." The following is entered in the margin of the record. "On the seauenteenth day of Aprill, 1660, the said William Ledra and Peter Peirson, engageing to depart as is heer expressed, were released out of prison and departed."

In Vol. 10, No. 265, Massachusetts Archives at the State House, is the following warrant for the arrest of William Leddra. It is dated April 30th., but the year is not given. If the year was 1660 it would seem that Leddra after his release from Plymouth Prison, April 17, 1660, went to Salem in the Massachusetts Colony.

"To the Constable of Salem or his Deputy.

You are hereby Required to take the body of William Leddra, & convey him safely to Boston, there to Appeare before ye Deputy Gouernour, to be further proceeded withall according to Law.

Last: 2mo: Wm Hathorne."

[Endorsed*] "Wm Hawthorns Warrant ag^{t}. Lydra ye Quaker."

* The endorsement is in the handwriting of Edward Rawson, Secretary of the Court of Assistants.

Palfrey (Hist. of New England, Vol. II., p. 480) gives this account of Leddra's subsequent history: —

He was "committed to the House of Correction at Boston. There he refused to work for his food, and, having been repeatedly scourged, was at last dismissed, with the threat of death if he should return. He returned, and was put in prison. On his trial the offer of liberation was made to him, if he would engage to go to England; but he rejected it, saying that he had no business there. He was condemned and executed. 'All that will be Christ's disciples,' he said at the foot of the lader, 'must take up the cross.' The last words heard from his lips were those of the martyr Stephen, 'Lord Jesus, receive my spirit.'"

While Leddra was in prison at Plymouth he sent forth the following letter to the Rulers and People of New England denouncing the persecution of "his brethren," the Quakers, and defending himself and other Quakers for returning to a place from which they had been driven. The original letter formerly belonged to John Holmes, late of Cambridge, deceased. The handwriting and general style of the original, especially the peculiar method of punctuation, resembles so closely that of a similar letter of warning sent by Christopher Holder, at about the same time, to the Governor and Magistrates of the Massachusetts Colony as to render it probable that both were actually written by the same hand.

The manner in which the name of Christopher Holder is written at the close of another letter written from the prison in Boston, 24th. Oct., 1659, given below, indicates that it is not an original signature, but merely descriptive of the person for whom the letter was written; while the name of William Leddra is written at the close of his letter in such a manner as to make it more like an original signature. It would therefore seem most probable that Leddra wrote all the letters. Fac-similes of the three letters, herewith presented, will enable the reader to make the comparison: —

"I wth: many others of my Brethren: haue been often accused by many of ye Rulers: & others of ye People: of New England to haue Walked Contrary to ye Example & practic: of ye servants of God: declared of in Scripture: charginge vs y^{t} we Come into places: where there are laws & Decrees m̃ade ag^{t}: vs: & where we know we shall be persecuted: w^{ch}: thinge. yo^{w}: haue often: declaired (in my hearing) ye serv^{ts}: of x^{t}. did not doe: but when they were persecuted: in one Citty: did flee into another: y^{t} ye serva^{ts}. of x^{t}. often did flee from one place to another: from ye rage of their: enemies: is true: & at other times they did not goe: but were expelled: out of their Coasts: but for yo^{w}: to say they returned not againe: is vtterly falce: & also yor: saying: they went not where they knew they should be p^{r}se-
cuted: in y^{t} yo^{w}: greatly Err: for ye holy Ghost: by w^{ch}:
Acts: [20]: 23: they knew all things: & w^{ch}: brought all things to their
Remembrance: accordinge to y^{e} ꝓmise of x^{t}: witnessed to Paul: y^{t} in every: Citty: bonds & Afflictions abide him: but none of these things moved him: w^{ch}: witness is true: & was & is ye guide &

leader: into all truth: & many times Paul: wth Peter: John & others: wente often to Such places where before they had been: Despitefully vsed: ꝑsecuted & afflicted: & would any speake so often to ye Contrary: but such as neither knowes ye power of God: nor ye scriptures: & to charge vs as Yo^w: haue d[one] when we came againe: amongst yo^w: as if we did acte contrary to y^t saying: of x^t: when yo^w: are p^rsecuted in one Citty: flee unto another: did he Ever say they must not returne againe: Did not [P] say let vs: goe againe: & visitt our Brethren: in Every Citty: where we haue preached ye word of ye lord: & se how they doe: & such as reads ye Acts: may heare: how we had been p^rsecuted: & if there be any who [ ]ly haue been led aside: by this falce & abominable thinge: Soe Comonly reported: in New Engl: (as to Joyne w^th: those: who haue invented it to Cover their Cruelty:) Either to speake evill of ye way of God: or to persecute his people: wth. out searchinge ye scriptures: to se whether it were So: for their Sakes & all others who desires to be informed (y^t they may no longer walke wth Slaunders & w^th: a Lye in their hand) I shall Clear it from ye Scriptures in ye behalfe of ye Truth: though for my Selfe I doe unfaignedly Say: I can w^th: patience beare: w^t: they have done to me to this very houre: & do desire y^t ye lord would not lay it to their charge: For Surely if they knew w^t: they did: they would not doe as they haue done in this thing: Bely ye Ministry of x^t. & lay waste ye Scriptures: as ye sobber Reader: shall heareafter fynd they haue done: But there is a Generation: y^t are soe leavened: w^th: malice: & wickedness y^t though ye truth be declaired never soe plaine: yet will not believe it: but are ready to stopp their Eares: like ye blind p^rsecutors of old: (& if they doe take up Stones to Stone ye publishers of it:) yet still continues their p^rsecution: & Soe become like ye deafe adder: wch. will not heare ye voice^e of ye Charmer: charminge never soe wisely & Such allwayes resisted ye holy ghost: & will neither enter y^m: selfes: nor Suffer y^m: y^t would: but as any Comes preaching ye kingdome of God: wch. is likened to ye least of all seeds: (but ye p^rsecuting: spiritt: canot vnderstand this parrable: neither is it given y^m. to know ye Misterys of Gods kingdome:) they p^rsecute those y^t preach it: as their forefathers did: acts: 4: 1: 3: And as they Spake vnto ye people: ye priests & ye Captaine of ye Temple: Came upon y^m: & laid hands on y^m: & put y^m. in hold till ye next day: ver: 18: & they called y^m: & Comannded y^m: not to Speake at all: nor teach [in the] name of Jesus: But Peter & John answered & said vnto y^m whether it be right in ye Sight of God: to hearken vnto yo^w: more then vnto God: Judge yee: for we canot but speake ye things wch. we have See[n] & heard: & when they had further threaghtened y^m: they let y^m. goe: aft^r. this Peter & John: went vnto their owne Company: & they lifted vp their voices to God wth. one accord sayinge: ver: 29: & now Lor[d] Behold their threatenings: & grant vnto thy Serv^ts: y^t w^th: all boldness: they may speake thy word: Acts: 5: 17: then ye high priest rose vp: & all they y^t were w^th: him: (w^ch: is ye Sect of ye Saduces:) & were fylled w^th: Indignation: & laid their hands on ye Apostles: & Put y^m. in y^e

Comon Prison: ver: 28: & when they were brought before y^m: they asked y^m. saying: did not we st[ ]ightly Comaund yo^w: y^t yo^w: should not teach in this name. & behold yo^w: have fylled Jerusalem: wth. yor: Doctrine: then Peter & ye other Apostles: answered. we ought to obey God rather than men: ver: 40: 41: 42: & when they had: beaten: y^m: they Comaunded y^m: y^t they should not speake in ye Name of Jesus: & let y^m: goe, & they departed from ye p^rsence of ye Councell: Rejoiceinge y^t they were Counted worthy to suffer for his name (they did not flee ye City) but dayly in ye temple & in every house: they Seased not to teach & preach: Jesus x^t.: chap: 6: in those dayes ye number of Desciples: was multiplied: & ye word of God increased & p^rsecution: also increased: for when they had disputeing: wth Steven A man full of ye holy Ghost: they were not able to resiste: ye wisdome & Spiritt: by w^ch: he Spake: then they Suborned: w^ch: Said We haue heard him Speake: blasphemous Words ag^t: Moses & ag^t. God: chap: 8: at y^t. time. there was great p^rsecution: ag^t: ye Church w^ch: was at Jerusalem: & they were all Scatered abroad throughout ye Regions of Judea: & Samaria: Except ye Apostles: mark: ye Apostles: were not yet fled: as for Saul he made havocke of ye Church: Entringe into Every house & hailing men & women comitted y^m. to prison: & therefore they [that] were Scatered abroad: went every where. preachinge ye Word: ver: 14: & when ye Apostles: wch. were at Jerusalem: heard y^t Samaria: had recd: ye word of God: they sent: vnto y^m. Peter & John: & when they had Testified & preached ye Word of ye lord: returned to Jerusalem: where there had been great p^rsecution: ag^t: ye Church: & can yo^w: read these Scriptures: & yet say y^t ye Serv^ts: of x^t: after they were p^rse[cuted] in any place. returned not thither againe: chap: [9:] & Paul after he was Converted: taryed Certaine Dayes w^th: ye desciples: wch were at Damascus: & straightway he preached x^t. in y^e [Sinagogue ?] y^t he is ye Sone of God: & Confounded ye Jewes wch. dwelt at Damascus: provinge y^t this is ye very Christ: & after y^t many dayes were fullfilled: ye Jewes tooke Councell to kill him: but their layinge [in wait?] was knowne: then ye Desciples tooke him by night: & let him downe by ye Wall: in a Basket: & when Saul was come to Jerusalem: he asayed to Joyne him Selfe to ye Desciples: but they were all afraid of him: but Barnabas tooke him: & brought him to ye Apostles: & he was w^th: y^m: coming in & out at Jerusalem: & he spake boldly: in ye name of ye lord Jesus: & disputed ag^t. ye gretians: but they went about to Slay him: wch. when ye Brethren knew: they brought him to Sesaria: & it came to pass: as Peter passed throughout all Quarters: Acts: 11: 2: he came againe to Jerusalem: where he had been: Imprisoned [&] Beaten: & ye Church: had been greatly p^rsecuted: ver: 28: & when it was Signified. by ye Spiritt. y^t there should be a dearth: throughout ye World: ye Desciples: every man according to his Abilitie: Determined to Send releife: vnto ye Brethren: w^ch: dwelt in Judea: w^ch: also they did & sente it by ye hands of Barnabas & Saul: chap: 12: 15:* & Barnabas:

* 12: 25?

& Saul: returned from: Jerusalem (where before they Sought to Slay him) when they had fullfilled their Ministry (let ye hireling: Ministers mind this well:) y^{t} when they had fulfilled their Ministry they departed: & ye p^{r}secuto^{rs}: also may take notice: y^{t} they wente away of their own accord: & after in acts: 13: 4: they being sent forth: by ye holy Ghost: departed & preaching ye Word of God: in divers places: they came to Anteoch: & went into ye Sinagogue [on] ye Sabath: Day: & sat downe & after ye reading of ye law & ye prophets: ye Ruler of ye Sinagogue: Sent vnto y^{m}: Saying: ye Men & Brethren: if yo^{w}: have a Word of Exortation: to ye people Say on: & paul stood vp and said: Men of Israell give audience: So when he had declaired & preached x^{t}. vnto y^{m}: & ye Congregation was broken vp: many of ye Jewes & religious proselites followed Paul: & barnabas who Spea[k]ing. to y^{m}: perswaded y^{m}. to continue in ye grace of God: & ye next Sabath: came allmost ye whole Citty togeather: to heare ye word of God: But when ye Jewes Saw ye Multitude: they were fylled wth: Envy & spake ag[ainst] those things w^{ch}: were Spoken by Paul: contradicting: & blaspheminge: ver: 50: & stired vp ye devoute & honnorable women: & ye Cheeffe men of ye Citty: & raised p^{r}secution ag^{t}: Paul & barnabas: & Expelled y^{m}. out their Coasts: but they shooke of ye Dust of their feett agst: y^{m}: & came to Iconium: acts: 14: where many people beleived: but w^{n}: ye Citty was devided: & an Assault made to vse y^{m}: Despitefully: & to Stone y^{m}. they we[re] aware of it: & fled vnto Listra: & Derbe: & ye regions roundaboute: & there they preached ye Gospell: ver: 19: & there came theither Jewes from Antioch: & Iconium: Who p^{r}swaded ye people: and having stoned Pa[ul] drew him out of ye Citty: Suposinge he had been dead: how be it as ye Desciples: Stood round aboute him: he rose vp & Came into ye Citty: & ye next day departed: wth: barnabas: to Derbe: & when they ha[d] preached ye Gospell to y^{t} Citty they returned againe to Listra: where before he had been stoned: & to Iconium: from Whence they fled vnto Listra: & in returninge did not act Contrary to ye words of x^{t}. where is said. if they p^{r}secute yo^{w}: in one Citty flee vnto another: But where Doth he Say. they must not returne againe: therefore in y^{t} thing ye p^{r}secuto^{rs}: in this generation: may hereafter be Silent: & returned also to antioch: where before they had raised p^{r}secution agst: y^{m}: & Expelled ym: out of their Coasts: confirming: ye Soules of ye Desciples: & exhorting y^{m}. to continue: in ye faith: & y^{t} we must through great tribulation Enter into ye kingdome of God: & not wth:standinge all ye Envy & rage of ye wicked: & all ye Cruell & vnreasonable vsage: of their enemies: they went divers times into ye Cittyes & places where they had been preaching ye word: to strengthen & Confirm ye Soules of those. they had begote through their Ministry: into ye like pretious faith: wth: y^{m}: much more might be said to this thing. but this may satisfie all reasonable people: Seing their accusation: is thus farr clearely proved: to be falce: By ye Scriptu^{rs}: of Truth: & ye Scriptur: fullfilled vpon y^{m}: y^{e} wicked shall be Silente in Darkness: —

The Lip of Truth : shall be Established for Ever :
But a Lying Tongue is but for a Moment : Pro: 12 : 19 :

Wm: Leddra

From ye Prison : Plymouth : this : 19 : of ye 5mo: 59 : "

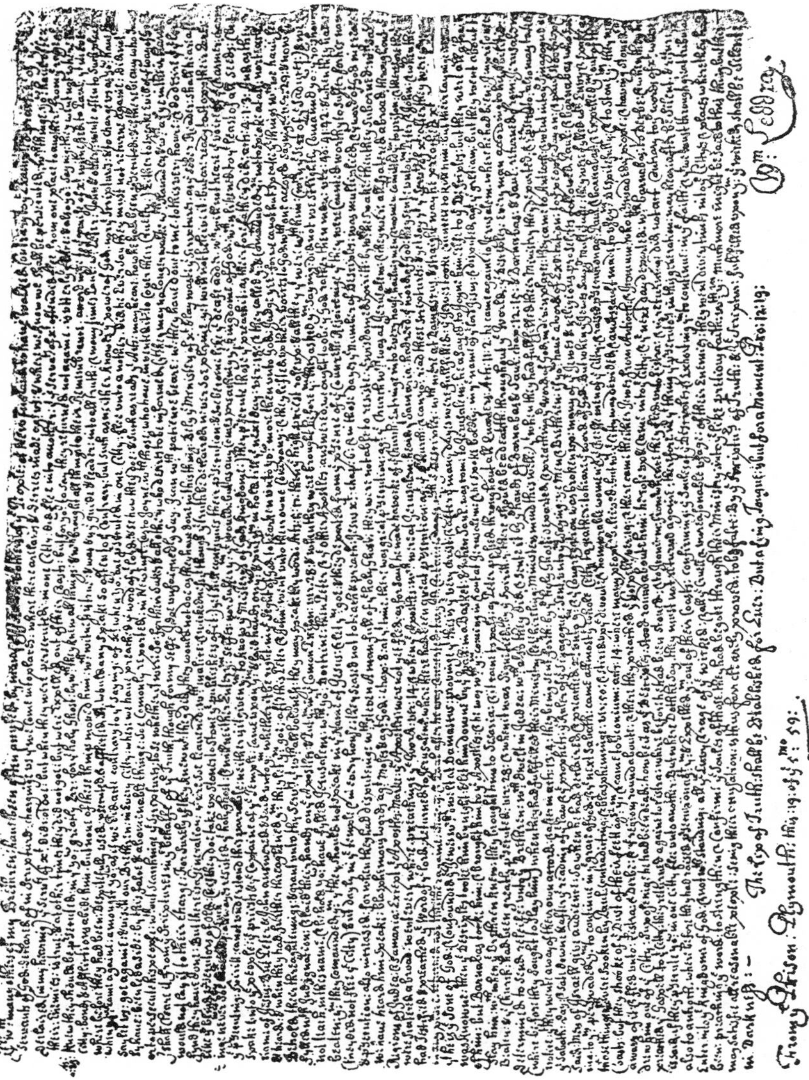

The following is the letter of Christopher Holder. The original is in the Chamberlain Collection at the Boston Public Library: —

" A Warninge From The Spirit of y^e Lord To y^e Gouerno^r: &

Magistrates: & People of the Masathusets Bay: ~

I knowinge: the Terrors of ye lord: aga^t: sine & Transgression: & aga^t: y^t Spirit: y^t leadeth into Rebelion: aga^t, god: am moved by ye lord to warne yo^w: (once more:) who are ye Inhabitants of ye place: above named: both magistrates & people: to lay to hearte & to consider w^t spirit yo^w: haue Joyned wth: come Bringe yor Actions to ye light: that they may be proved: whether they are wrought in God yea or nay: come try yor. selfes: by y^t. wch. gave forth Scriptures: & se whether yo^w: walke vp answerable: to ye Scriptures: wch. yo^w: call yor: Rule: for life & for salvation: nay come but to ye very leter of ye Scripture & try yor practises by it: & se whether it be accordinge to theirs: y^t spake forth ye Scriptures: as they was moved: or accordinge to theirs y^t. ꝑsecuted y^m: y^t spoke in ye name of ye lord as they were moved by y^e. holy Ghost: for in ye Scriptures of Truth: is recorded ye actions of both Spirits: of ye Spirit of God in his Serva^{ts}. & of ye Spirit of ye Divell in his Serva^{ts}. & ye reward y^t both received at ye hand of ye lord: now therefor in Sincerity & Soberness: come & compaire yor. lawes: & actions wth ye law & actions of ye Sa^{ts}. in time of old: & se whether they agree wth: y^m: or whether they will beare yo^w: out: in y^t yo^w: haue already done: & haue decreed to doe for time to come: (as for Instance) w^t. Rule haue yo^w: w^t. presept or presidente: haue yo^w: in ye Scriptures for to prison: whipp cut Eares: & banish vpon paine of death: if they returne: haue yo^w: any Rule from ye Prophets: christ or ye Apostles: for these things: did they ever doe so: did ye Prophets Imprison: any: or did x^t. banish any: or put any mans p^{r}son to death: or did ye Apostles: whip any: now consider: did not those know ye mind of God: & w^t was his will & had not those as greate zeale for ye Gospell: & for ye building vp of ye Church of God: as any can haue in these Dayes: yet they made not vse of such Weapons: as yo^w: doe in these Dayes: Againe had not x^t ye Spirite wth. out measure: & had not he all power comited to him: yet he never vsed this power to prison: dismember: banish & put to death: any mans p^{r}son: Consider from whom then have yo^w: this power: or who is yor. Example: herein: if christ neither any of his Serva^{ts}: never did so: nor never comaunded any to doe so: whose serv^{ts}: are yo^w: are yo^w: not his serva^{ts}: who in all ages: ruled in ye children of disobedience & stured vp ye powers of ye world: to p^{r}secute ye serv^{ts}. of ye lord: to prison y^m. to stone y^m. & to put y^m. to death as in ye Scriptures: yo^w: may se at large: but consider w^t. was ye End of those: did not they receive a Just rewarde: at ye hand of ye Lord: did not they rote did not they perish: is not their names: left on record for a Curse & a reproach & a ꝑpetual shame: vnto this day: & can they y^t. serve ye same spirit: & doe ye same workes: Expecte any beter End if they repente not. Consider this & lay it to hearte: before it be to late: y^t. if it may be: there may be a healinge: of yor Error: & let y^t Suffice wch. hath been allready done: &

now from ye Spiritt of ye lord God : I warne yo^{w}: to beware how yo^{w}: take away : ye life of any man or woman y^{t}. may come amongst yo^{w}: in ye name & feare of ye lord : — For assueredly if yo^{w}: proceed to doe soe : ye feirie Indignation of ye lord will breake forth amongst yo^{w}: yea ye fyer of his wrath shall be kindled in ye midst of yo^{w}: & it will burne as a flame : in yor heartes : woe : & misery : will come vpon yo^{w}: in ye day y^{t} yo^{w}: thinke not of it : even as a theife in ye night. & yo^{w}. shall be snaired & taken for noe man shall be able to deliver him selfe out of his hand : who is arisen to plead wth. all flesh : wth. his sword : & wth. fyre : who will be avenged of all his Enemies : Therefore all of yo^{w}: whom this may concerne : beware how yo^{w}: proceed any further to Defile yor. selfes wth blood Least ye lord give yo^{w}. blood to drinke : for verily know this if yo^{w}. follow y^{t}. spiritt : to ye End wch. hath lead yo^{w}. to Imprison whipe cut Eares & to banish on penalty of death : if they returne : I say if yo^{w}. follow y^{t} spirite : & put any one to death : Wofull & Miserable will yor. conditions be : for when yo^{w}: haue fylled vp ye measure of yor. Iniquityes : then will ye lord breake forth aganst yo^{w}: as a mighty terrible one : who will consume & overturne : all his adversaries : & they shall be all as Dried Stuble in ye flame of fyer : & as chaffe Before ye whirlwind : Consider this & turne unto the lord : Least he Teare ,yo^{w}: in peeces : and make yo^{w}: an abhorringe to all flesh :

This haue I writen as A Warninge : vnto yo^{w}: From ye spirite of ye lord God : who is longe Sufferinge : Towards all men : & wold not y^{t}. any should perish : But y^{t} all might come to ye knowledge of ye truth & be saved : & in this doeinge I shall be cleare of yor: Blood whether yo^{w}: will heare or forbeare : & yo^{w}: shall be left wth out excuse : in ye Dreadfull day of Gods Judgmente :

By A Friend To all y^{t}. loue ye Lord Jesus x^{t}. in Sincerity & Truth.

Rhode Islande the 1st. of y^{e}
7th. moth: 59 : Christopher Holder"

A Warninge From The Spirit of ye Lord To ye Governor & Magistrates: & People of The Masathusets Bay:

I Knowinge: the terrors of ye lord agat sin & transgression: & agat ye spirit: yt leadeth into rebellion: agat god: am moved by ye lord to warne yow: (once more:) who are ye inhabitants of ye place above named: both magistrates & people: to lay to hearte, to consider: wt spirit yow haue joyned wth: come bringe yor actions to ye light: that they may be proued: whither they are wrought in God yea or nay: come try yor selues by ye wch gave forth scriptures: & se whether yow walke up answerable to ye scriptures: wch yow call yor rule for life & for salvation: nay come but to ye very letter of ye scripture & try yor practizes by it: & se whither it be accordinge to theirs: yt spake forth ye scriptures as they was moved: or accordinge to theirs yt persecuted ym yt spoke in ye name of ye lord as they were moved by ye holy Ghost: for in ye scriptures of truth is recorded ye actions of both spirits: of ye spirit of God in his servants & of ye spirit of ye divell in his servants: & ye reward ye both received at ye hand of ye lord: now therefore in sincerity & soberness: come & compaire yor lawes: & actions wth ye law & actions of ye saints in time of old: & se whither they agree wth ym or whither they will beare yow out: in yt yow haue allready done: & haue decreed to doe for time to come: (as for instance) wt rule haue yow: wt president or presidents haue yow: in ye scriptures for to prison: whip: cut eares: & banish upon paine of death: if they returne: haue yow any rule from ye prophets: christ or ye apostles: for these things: did they ever doe so: did ye prophets imprison: any: or did Xt banish any: or put any man's pson to death: or did ye apostles: which any now consider: did not those know ye mind of God: & wt was his will: & had not those as greate zeale for ye gospell: & for ye building up of ye church of God as any can haue in these days: yet they made not use of such weapons: as yow doe in these days: againe: had not Xt ye spirit wthout measure: & had not he all power comitted to him: yet he never used this power to prison: dismember: banish & to death any man's pson: consider from whom then have yow this power: or who is yor example herein: if christ, neither any of his servants never did so: nor never comanded any to doe so: whose servants are yow: are yow not his servants whom all ages: ruled in ye children of disobedience & stirred up ye powers of ye world: to persecute ye servants of ye lord: to prison ym: to stone ym: & to put ym to death as in ye scriptures yow may se at large: but consider wt was ye end of those: did not they receive a just rewarde at ye hand of ye lord: did not they rot: did not they perish: is not their names: left on record for a curse & a reproach & a perpetuall shame: unto this day: & can they yt serve ye same spirit: & doe ye same works: expecte any better end if they repente not: consider this & lay it to hearte: before it be to late: yt if it may be: there may be a healinge of yor error: & let ye sufferinge wch hath been allready done: & now from ye spirit of ye lord God: I warne yow to beware how yow take away ye life of any man or woman yt may come amongst yow in ye name & feare of ye lord: for assuredly if yow proceed to doe so: ye fierce indignation of ye lord will breake forth amongst yow: yea ye fyer of his wrath shall be kindled in ye midst of yow: & it will burne as a flame in yor heartes: woe & misery will come upon yow in ye day yt yow think not of it: even as a theife in ye night & yow shall be taken suddenly for noe man shall be able to deliver him selfe out of his hand: who is arisen to plead wth all flesh: wth his sword & wth fyre: who will be avenged of all his enemies: therefore all of yow whom they may concerne: beware how yow proceed any further to defile yor selfes wth blood least ye lord give yow blood to drinke: for verily know this if yow follow ye spirit to ye end wch hath lead yow to imprison ~~any~~ whipe cut eares & to banish on penalty of death: if they returne: I say if yow follow ye spirit: & put any one to death: wofull & miserable will yor conditions be: for when he overturns: all his adversaries: & they shall be all as dried stuble in ye flame of fyer: & as chaffe before ye whirlwind: consider this & turne unto the lord: least he cease yow in peeces: and make yow an abhorringe to all flesh:

This haue I writen as a Warninge: unto yow: From ye spirite of ye lord God: who is longe sufferinge Towards all men: & would not yt any should perish: but yt all might come to ye knowledge of ye truth & be saved: & in this doeinge I shall be cleare of yor blood whither yow will heare or forbeare: & yow shall be left wthout excuse in ye dreadfull day of Gods judgment:

By: A Freind To all yt loue ye Lord Jesus Xt in sincerity & truth.

Rhode Islande the 1st of ye 7th mo 59:

Christopher Holder

Among the Court Files, Suffolk, is the following letter or petition by Christopher Holder to the Governor and Magistrates, dated at the Prison in Boston, 24th. Oct., 1659. It is numbered 162034^{b}. Some words missing in the original, which is fragmentary and much worn by age, are here supplied conjecturally within brackets.

[" To the] Govern^{r}: [Deputy Govern^{r}. and Magistrates] in place To doe Justice: I ha[ve here stated the] ground & cause as farr as I know [the] Will of God here in: Wherefore I ca[me into Massa]ch-[setts Bay th]is time: for A longe time: it hath [been a] Prophecie: in me: y^{t} when I was Cleare to passe to England [I should go]e To Boston: To seeke fo^{r}: a passage: & S[ee] whether I might be Sufered: To passe to my Native [land] soe heareinge: y^{t} theare was a Shipp: near[ely Rea]dy for to Set Saile for England: it was revealed to me: By y^{e}. Spirte of y^{e}. lord God: y^{t}. now y^{e}. time was come y^{t}. [I must] goe to Boston To Seeke for a passage: Soe as way was made: I set forth from: Rhode Islande: & Came To this Towne: & afte^{r}: y^{t}. I had Set vp my horse: [y^{n} I hye]de On: I inquired fo^{r}. y^{e}. Master of ye Vessell y^{t} was Bound fo^{r}. England: & heareing where he [was] I came to him & asked him fo^{r}. a passage: & after some words had passed betwixt vs: he s^{d}. he would Carry me If he might be Sufered: But Imediately I was apprehended: By a Constable: & Brought befo^{r}. ye Governo^{r}: vnto whom I declaired y^{e}. End of my Cominge: Who Tould me he would not Beleive: a word y^{t}. I said: & after some other words: Comited me to Prisson: By y^{e}. wch. meanes I Remaine in Yo^{r}. Jurisdiction: Otherwise its like I might haue been: By this time: Neare ye Coaste: of Old England: & now I heare: y^{t} there is a Shipp providing fo^{r}. To Goe To Ould England: wch it is like may be ready: wth. in 3: or 4: weeks time: & now the same Remaines wth Me: as it did when I came: y^{t} If I may be sufered: To goe: from hence: a Board of y^{e}. vessell: & Soe to be Transported to Ould England: & now I shall appeall To all y^{t}. feare ye Lord: whether: This y^{t}. I seeke is not reasonable: & may be Granted: wth. out hurte To any man: & If I am deneyed This: whether I am not Amonge Such men: y^{t}. Paul Exh[orted] y^{e}. Church To pray fo^{r}. him to be delivered [fr]om:

24rd: of y^{e}. 8th: moth: 59:

From a [Friend To friends of] y^{e} Truth: Now a Prisoner: in y^{e} Com[mon] Goale [in Boston]
by Name: Christopher: Hold[er]"

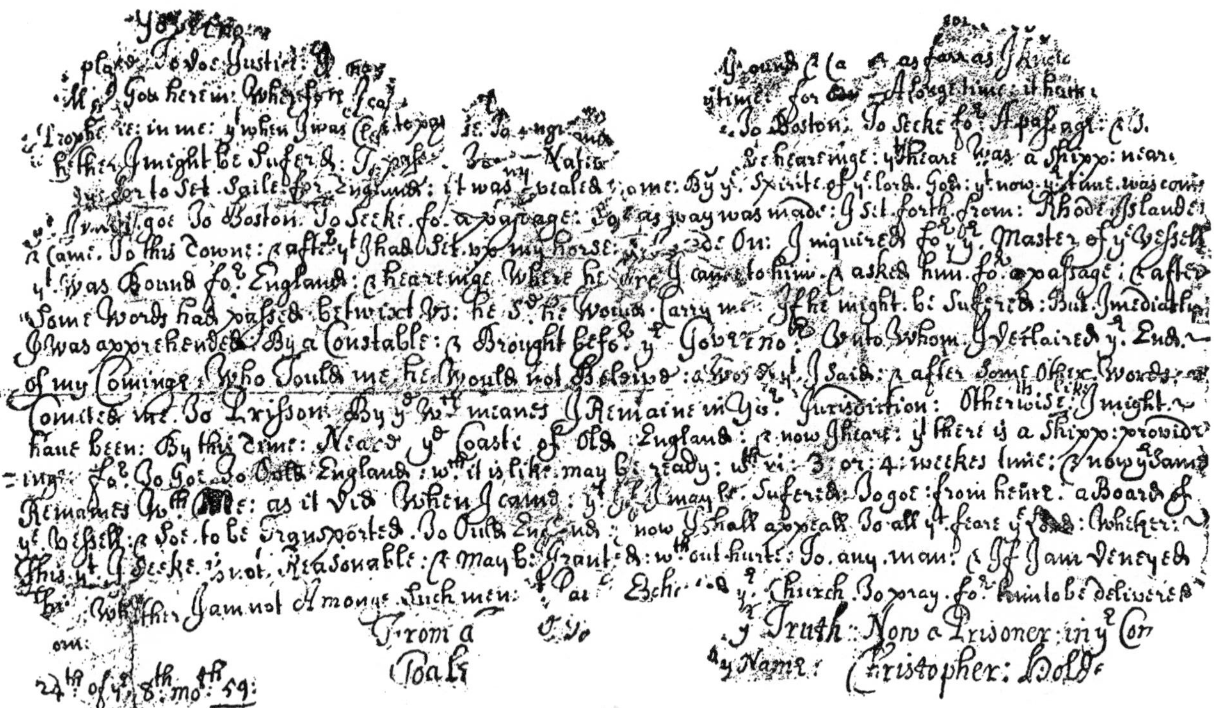
Yo[illegible] ... [illegible]
place To doe Justice: I may ... found [illegible] as far as I kno[w]
M[illegible] God herein: wherefore I ca[n] ... y time: for [illegible] A long time: it hath
Lyeth it: in me: yt when I was clear to goe [illegible] ... to Boston: To seeke for A passage: [illegible]
whether I might be suffered: To passe [illegible] my Native ... hearinge: yt there was a shipp neare
[illegible] for to set saile for England: it was revealed to me: By ye Spirite of ye lord God: yt now ye time was com[e]
yt I must goe To Boston To seeke for a passage: So as way was made: I set forth from: Rhode Island
& came: To this Towne: & after yt I had set up my horse: [illegible] On: I inquired for ye Master of ye vessell
yt was Bound for England: & hearinge where he [illegible] I came to him: & asked him for a passage: & after
Some words had passed betwixt us: he sd he would carry me: If he might be suffered: But Imediatly
I was apprehended: By a Constable: & Brought befor ye Governor: Unto whom I declared ye End
of my Cominge: Who tould me he would not Beleive: a word yt I said: & after Some other words
Comitted me To Prison: By ye wch meanes I Remaine in yr Jurisdiction: Otherwise in likelyhood I might
have been: By this time: Neare ye Coast of Old England: & now I heare: yt there is a shipp: provid
ing: for To Goe To Old England: wch it is like may be ready: within 3 or 4 weekes time: & now ye same
Remaines with Me: as it did when I came: yt I may be suffered To goe: from hence: aBoard of
ye vessell: & soe to be transported To Old England: now I shall appeale To all yt feare ye lord: whether
This yt I seeke is not Reasonable: & may be Granted: without hurte: To any man: & If I am denyed
[illegible] whether I am not Among such men [illegible] ye Church To pray for him to be delivered
From a [illegible] ... ye Truth Now a Prisoner in yr Com[illegible]
Goale ... my Name: Christopher: Holder
24th of ye 8th mo 59:

It was probably in connection with this petition that Christopher Holder by order of the General Court at the October Session, 1659, was sentenced to banishment on pain of death if found "w^{th}in this jurisdiction three dayes after the next shipp now bound from hence to England be departed from this harbor, & betweene this and the shipps departure, with the keeper, at his owne charge, he shall haue liberty one day in a weeke to goe about his business."

An account of William Leddra is given in "A Brief Narration of the Sufferings of the People called Quakers" by Daniel Gould, Rhode Island, 1700; also in "New England Judged" by George Bishop, 1703; and by William Sewel in his "History of the Quakers," 2nd Edition, 1725.

Sewel states (p. 189) that "In the latter part of the fifth month [1658], it came to pass, that William Brend and William Leddra, having been at Salem, came to Newbury, where at the House of one Robert Adams they had conference with the Priest in the Presence of Captain Gerish." Captain Gerish "sent them with a Constable to Salem; where being brought before the Magistrates they were asked whether they were Quakers? To which they answered that they were such as were in Scorn called so." "Some days after they were carried to Boston, where in the next month they were brought into the House of Correction to work there." Here they suffered very great severities fully described by Bishop and by Sewel.

Sewel (p. 263) continues: "William Leddra, who was banished from Boston on pain of Death, was under such Necessity of conscience, that he could not forbear returning thither; where he came about the Conclusion of the foregoing year [1660]; but was soon taken Prisoner, and being fastened to a Log of Wood, was kept Night and Day lockt in Chains, in an open Prison, during a very cold winter." "It was on the 9th. of the first Month of this Year [1661] that he was brought into the Court of Assistants, with his Chains and Log at his Heels." Then follows an account of the trial at the Court of Assistants, which, though apparently exaggerated and unreliable as to the exact character of the proceedings, shows that the prisoner claimed that he was not guilty of any crime under the laws of England and refused to accept liberty upon a promise to go out of the jurisdiction, though willing to go if allowed to without such promise.

Leddra was executed on the 14th. of March 1660–1. "As the Executioner was putting the Halter about his neck, he was heard to say, 'I commit my righteous Cause unto thee O God.' The executioner then being charged to make haste W. Leddra at the turning of the ladder, cried, 'Lord Jesus receive my Spirit;' and so he was turned off, and finished his days."

It seems proper, in justice to Leddra, to give here a letter written by him to his friends from the Prison in Boston the 13th of March, 1660–1, the day before his execution. It certainly exhibits a most gentle, wise and Christian spirit in one who was about to suffer the extreme penalty of the law for a crime of which he evidently felt himself entirely innocent.

The letter is printed by Bishop and also by Gould, and by Sewel: —

"To the Society of the little Flock of Christ, Grace and Peace be Multiplied.

Most dear and inwardly Beloved,

The sweet influences of the Morning-Star, like a Flood distilling into my innocent Habitation, hath so filled me with the joy of the Lord in the Beauty of Holiness, that my Spirit is as if it did not Inhabit a Tabernacle of Clay, but is wholly swallowed up in the Bosom of Eternity, from whence it had its Being.

Alas, alas! What can the Wrath and Spirit of Man, that lusteth to Envy, aggravated by the Heat and Strength of the King of the Locusts, which came out of the Pit, do unto one that is hid in the Secret Places of the Almighty? Or, unto them that are gathered under the Healing Wings of the Prince of Peace? Under whose Armour of Light they shall be able to stand in the Day of Trial, having on the Breast-plate of Righteousness, and the Sword of the Spirit, which is their Weapon of War against Spiritual Wickedness, Principalities and Powers, and the Rulers of the Darkness of this World, both within and without! Oh my Beloved! I have waited as a Dove, at the Windows of the Ark, and have stood still in that Watch, which the Master (without whom I could do nothing) did at his coming reward with fulness of his Love, wherein my Heart did rejoyce, that I might in the Love and Life of God speak a few words to you, sealed with the Spirit of Promise, that the taste thereof might be a Savour of Life to your Life, and a Testimony in you of my Innocent Death: And if I had been altogether Silent, and the Lord had not opened my Mouth unto you, yet he would have opened your Hearts, and there have sealed my Innocency with the Streams of Life, by which we are all Baptized into that Body which is in God, with whom, and in whose Presence there is Life; in which, as you abide, you stand upon the Pillar and Ground of Truth: For the Life being the Truth and the way, go not one step without it, lest you should compass a Mountain in the Wilderness; for, unto every Thing there is a Season. As the Flowing of the Ocean doth fill every Creek and Branch thereof, and then retires again towards its own Being and Fulness, and leaves a Savour behind it; so doth the Life and Vertue of God flow into every one of your Hearts, whom he hath made Partakers of his Divine Nature; and when it withdraws but a little, it leaves a sweet Savour behind it, that many can say, they are made clean through the Word that he hath spoken to them: In which Innocent Condition you may see what you are in the Presence of God, and what you are without him. Therefore, my dear Hearts, let the enjoyment of the Life alone, be your Hope, your Joy and Consolation, and let the Man of God flee those Things that would lead the Mind out of the Cross, for then the Savour of the Life will be buried: And altho' some may speak of Things that they received in the Life, as Experiences; yet the Life being veiled, and the Savour that it left behind washed away by the fresh Floods of Temptation, the Condition that they did enjoy in the Life, boasted of by the airy Thing, will be like the Manna that was gathered Yesterday, without any good Scent or Savour: For, it was only well with the Man while he was in the Life of Innocency; but being driven from the Presence of the Lord into the Earth, What can he boast of? And altho' you know these Things, and (many of you) much more than I can say; yet, for the Love and Zeal I bear to the Truth and Honour of God, and tender Desire of my Soul to those that are Young, that they may read me in that from which I write, to strengthen them against the Wiles of the subtle Serpent that beguiled Eve; I say, Stand in the Watch within, in the Fear of the Lord, which is the very Entrance of Wisdom; and the State where you are ready to receive the Secrets of the Lord: Hunger and Thirst patiently, be not weary, neither doubt; stand still, and cease from thy own Working, and in due time thou shalt enter into the Rest, and thy Eyes shall behold thy Salvation, whose Testimonies are Sure and Righteous altogether: Let them be as a Seal upon thine Arm, and as Jewels about thy Neck, that others may see what the Lord hath done for your Souls: Confess him before Men, yea before his greatest Enemies; Fear not what they can do unto you: Greater is he that is in you, than he that is in the world: For he will cloath you with Humility, and in the Power of his Meekness you shall Reign over all the Rage of your Enemies in the Favour of God; wherein, as you stand in Faith, ye are the Salt of the Earth; for, many seeing your good Works, may glorifie God in the Day of their Visitation. Take heed of receiving that which you saw not in the Light, lest you give ear to the Enemy. Bring all Things to the Light, that they may be proved, whether they be wrought in God; The Love of the World, the Lust of the flesh, and the Lust of the Eye, are without the Light, in the World; therefore possess your Vessels in all Sanctification and Honour, and let your Eye look at the Mark: He that hath called you is Holy: And if there be an Eye that offends, pluck it out, and cast it from you: Let not a Temptation take hold, for if you do, it will keep from the Favour of God, and that will be a sad State; for, without Grace possessed, there is no Assurance of Salvation: By Grace you are saved; and the Witnessing of it is sufficient for you, to which I Commend you all, my Dear Friends, and in it remain,

Your Brother,
William Leddra.

Boston-Gaol, the 13th of the
first Month 1660–61."

XXXVI.

[Court Files, Suffolk, March, 1660–1, No. 386, 8th paper.]

in the case betweene Thomas Gleison plantife and m^r^ Hills and m^r^ Edward Collins executors of the last will of m^r^ Henry Dunster deceased defendants: wee finde for the defendants the judgement of the former court and costs of courts

Amos Richison [for]man

NOTE.

This case appears to have been an appeal by Thomas Gleison to the Court of Assistants at the March Term 1660–1, the above being the verdict on the appeal. The following are the other papers in No. 386: —

First paper: —

"To the Marshall or Constable of Cambridge or his Deputy.

You are required to Attach the goodes, debts, dues or wages of Thomas Gleison in the Hands of Willm Russell, Edward Winship, Thomas Hall, Jn°. Swan; & Richard Cutter, & to secure the same so as to be responsable to the Executors of m^r^ Henry Dunster in an Accon of the case at the next Coun[ty] Court Holden at ~~Cambridge~~ charlstowne, for not performeing the Award of the wor^ll^. Capt. Daniel Gookin & m^r^ Thomas Danforth, with the damages thereby susteined; & so make a true returne hereof vnder yor hands. dat. 14. novem^r^. 1660.

ꝑ Curiam Jn°. Wayte

the 15th. 9th. 1660.

I Have Attached in the Hand of Leift winship. 15^s^.

In the Hand of Wm Russell.

In the Hand of Ri. Cutter. 6^s^.

In the Hand of Tho. Hall 5^s^. 9^d^.

In the Hand of Jn° Swan.

by me Thomas Chesholme Constabl

This is a true coppy taken out of the Court Records. as attests

Thomas Danforth Record^r^."

Second paper: —

"Thomas Glesons Reasons of Appeall from the Scentanc of the County Court; att Charlestown; the 18 (10) 1660 the Exicutors of the will of m^r^ dunster pltff: Thomas Gleson deff^d^: in an action of the case: for not ꝑforminge of an award made by the wp^ll^ Capt. Googin: & m^r^ damforte

1 theare was No Band* in Court: that Gleson Submitted to such award

* Bond.

2ly the Band that was made and after the Court appeared Bound Gleson: & left the exicutors ffree: Neither would the exicutors stand to the award

3ly if the Band be vallid against Gleson: he is lyabl to action [vo]pon the fforfiture of his Band; & not to be Sued for the payment of the award

4ly by the award Gleson was to pay vpon demaund; but no demaund was made:

5ly Gleson leagally tendered payment acording to the award & thearfor no ground for the exicutors to Sue: nor Gleson to be put to Charge of exspence: or Cost of Court

the 25 of the 12 1660 the mark of Tho T Gleson

Receiued the 25th of ye 12th mo.
1660 of Thomas Gleison
By me Thomas Danforth, Rr"

[Endorsed] "Gleisons Reasons
of Appeale"

Third paper: —

"The Answer of Ed. Collins and Jaseph Hills to the Reasons of Tho: Gleezons Appeale.

To the 1 Reason. That there was no Bond in Court that Gleezon Submitted to such Award.

Ansr. 1st The Bond was in the Custodie of the Recorder of the Court, And owned in Court by the defendent without which wee could not well haue proceeded to tryal.

2d. he had repleuied the Corne Attached, but gaue vs no Sumons on it wherevpon to prepare for tryal.

To the 2d R. That the Bond made; bound Gleezon and not the Executors &c.

Ans. There was no need to bind the Executors but onely Gleezon for seueral weighty Reasons.

1 the Exec: had made vp Acco. with Gleezon; Satisfied all his demands to the full as Appeares in the Acco made with him by mr Tho: Broughton and the Executors the 18 of October 1659 which wee pleaded and declared to the Court vpon the tryal.

2 at making vp the Sayd Acco. he was Abated neere ten pounds Sterling, which was declared to the Court and playnly Appears in the Sayd Acco.

3 they then at his request took his own Bond of 20lb. for performance of what after such Acco. and Abatement remayned to be payd and done: as was allso demonstrated to the Court.

4 wee had A Couenant vnder his hand Substanciably witnessed for twelue pounds allowed out of the rent for Certain reparacons which was recited in the Sayd Bond. And Alledged in the Court.

5 Gleezon was bound by lease to reparacon of fences & other things, all which that Bond took in.

6 there was nothing Ambiguous but About fences, reparacons and damages. in which wee lookt for no more then cleer iustice mixt with much fauour shold Afford vs. and was all wee Aymed at in point of proffit in the referring to Arbitracon, other things being before Secured So farr as his Bond could Secure the same.

To the 3d R. That if the Bond be valid against Gleezon he is lyable to Accon on the forfeiture thereof and not to be Sued for the payment of the Award.

Ans. 1. Gleezon was not Sued for the payment of the Award; but for not paying or Satisfying the Award as the Attachment Expresseth.

2. the Bond coms forfeit for not performing the Award, and therefore the pleading and prouing of that is Absolutely necessarie, before we could haue any benefit of the Bond

3 it was our disadvantage the bond was not in Court (though no fault of ours) for on the forfeiture therof we might haue had releif, for our many and great Suffrings for through want therof we had iudgement but for 6lb. of neere 22lb. which otherwise was Cleerly due beside the fences, reparacons and damages which might haue risen to 20 more

4. we shold Sure enough haue pleaded the forfeiture of the Bond if it had then beene in Court And the Attachments were Answerable thervnto.

To the 4th R. By the Award Gleezon was to pay vpon demand. But no demand was made.

Ans. 1. That was pleaded and urged in Court by Gleezon or his Attorney, and by vs fully and playnly Answered to the Satisfaccon of the Court and Jury.

2 we offered proof vpon Oath for the demand before any tender of any thing. but the defendent Seemed to vs and to the Court to own and accept our Testimonie without Oath and So it was Omitted as Superfluous or needless.

To the 5th R. That Gleezon legally tendered payment According to the Award and therfor no ground of Sute against Gleezon, or that Gleezon shold be put to charge of Expence or Costs of Court.

Ans There was no legal tender made by Gleezon

1 because on the demand there was no tender made of any thing.

2 bec: no tender was made til after the Attachment Serued on some Corne at Wooburne.

3 bec: the tender which was after demand and Attachment, was in Cotten cloth, which is not Current pay of the Countrie; it not being of the growth of the Countrie, nor

such as any law of the Countrie makes to be Current pay of the Countrie.

4 it was not refused by m^rs Dunster as Appears by Whitmor and Hubard Gleezons own witnesses but Gleezon wold not leaue it vnless she wold giue him A release or accquittance, whervpon she desired him to deliuer the Cloth to one of the Executors and to take an Accquittance from them.

5 Gleezon forced vs to Enter and prosecute against him Contrary to law, and So put him to Expense and Costs of Court; for by Some irregular or indirect means he repleiued the Corne and did not giue Bond to prosecute wherin wee shold haue been defendents. but only gaue his own Bond to A.ns. the Attachment & so forced vs to be playntiffs, beside & beyond our expectac̄on.

6 Cotton Cloth was menc̄oned when the Award was in hand and vtterly refused by vs, and it was expressed that we shold have as good pay as cold be made monie Excepted.

7 it was well known to all that the lease ingaged Corne or Cattle and that we had Allowed him twelue pounds in the Acc°. out of the Sayd pay, nor did we Imagine the Arbitrators wold think of altering the kind of pay, howeuer for that wee had Allowed him out of the rent for reparac̄ons, which he had not done but neglected to our verie great damage. Considering allso that we had Abated him before neer ten pounds and now about Six pounds more, beside all that might haue been charged on him about fences, reparac̄ons and damages. And were there not A Spirit too too prone to vex the widow and fatherless; Surely this honoured Court wold not haue been troubled with this buisines."

[Endorsed] "m^r Dunsters Executors
Ans^r. to the Reasons
of Tho. Gleezons
Appeale"

Fourth paper: —

"At a Coun[ty] Court held at Charlstowne, decem^r. 18th. 1660.

Mr Joseph Hills & m^r Edward Collins Executors of the last Will of m^r Henry Dunster deceased, p^ls. agst Thomas Gleison sen^r. def^t. for not performeing the Award made by the wor^ll. Capt. Gookin. & m^r Danforth with All just damages, vpon Attachm^t, dated. novem^r. 14th: 1660 The Jury haueing heard the case, do find for the plant^s. six pounds & that m^r Shrimptons receite of 5^t. be legally proved. & costs of Court twenty & two shillings.

This is a true coppy taken out of the Court Records as attests
Thomas Danforth R."

Fifth paper: —

"Wee whose names are Subscribed being chosen Arbitrators, Between the Excecuto^{r}s of Mr Hen: Dunster on the one pte, & Thomas Gleison on the other pte, & haueing heard their respective pleas, do award that in lew of a farr more considerable Sume, y^{t} wee find due from the said Gleison. Hee the s^{d} Gleison shall pay to the said Executors on all demands Six pounds in Currant Country pay, and shall also procure an acquittance from m^{r} Shrimpton for the discharge of five pounds He the said Gleison agreed to pay, & on the paym^{t} of the Said Sumes, the Same to be a finall end of all controversey between the said ptyes, & the Said paym^{t} is to be made by the Said Gleison to Mrs Dunster or her assignes on demand as abovesaid & that this is o^{r} finall award wee do testifie by putting to o^{r} hands, thus 12th. 9th. m^{o}. 1660.

Daniel Gookin
Thomas Danforth.

This is a true Coppy
Extracted out of the Court Records
as attests. Thomas Danforth, Record^{r}"

[Endorsed] "Arbitraccōn
ags^{t} Gleison"

Sixth paper: —

"These p^{r}sents witnes that I Thomas Gleison of menatomy before the first day of decem^{r} next ensueing will pay five pound in good marchantable Wheat at price Currant into menattomy mill. for Henry Dunster or his Assignes witness my hand this 11th. of Augs^{t}.

In p^{r}senc of
George Edcocke
his mark. P
ffrancis whitmore

Thomas Gleison
his marke T

This five pounds I assigne to m^{r} Henry Shrimpton of Boston on the Account of me Henry Dunster
vera Copia Thomas Danforth R."

[On back of paper] "This 11th. of the 10th. 1660:

I do acknowledge to haue receiued in full of this bill at two paym^{ts} by m^{r} Nicholls in Wheat five pounds.

By me Henry Shrimpton
vera Copia. Thomas Danforth Record^{r}"

[Endorsed] "m^{r} shremptons
bill & receite"

Seventh paper: —

"The deposicc̄on of ffrancis Whitmore aged thirty five years, & James Hubbard aged twenty Seven years, or thereab^{ts} Sayth, That ab^{t} Six weeks Since these depon^{ts} were desired by Thom^{s} Gleison to go along wth him to m^{rs} Dunster, and see a parcell of cloath deliue^{d} to her, wch Cloath was cotton cloath, and these deponants did vallew the said cloath to be worth six pounds, as wee the said depon^{ts} did declare o^{r} selves to m^{rs} Dunster, further these depon^{ts} did then Heare the said

Thomas Gleison tender the said six pounds worth of cloath vnto the said m^{rs} Dunster for so much as He was awarded by an Arbitraccon to pay vnto the said m^{rs} Dunster, and if shee had any thing against the said cloath, shee might desire two other men to Judge the worth of the said cloath & Hee would stand to it, yet the said m^{rs} Dunster did refuse to do either, & further saith not.

Sworne in Court. 18. (10) 1660.
Thomas Danforth. R.

further thse depon^{ts}
Testifie m^{rs} Dunster did not refuse to receiue the cotton cloath of Gleison: further Thomas Gleison demanded a discharge, m^{rs} Dunster saith cary it to m^{r} Collins.

This is a true coppy taken out of the Court Records as attesteth.
Thomas Danforth R."

[Endorsed] " ffrancis whitmors
James Hubbards
test."

XXXVII.

[Court Files, Suffolk, March, 1660–1, No. 390, 9th paper.]

in the case betweene Richard Coy plaintife and m^{r} Ezekiell Cheever defendant wee finde the judgement of the former court and costs of courts

Amos Richison forman

Note.

The other papers on file are as follows: —

First paper: —

" Att the Court held at Ipswich the 25 Sept: 1660

Richard Coy Attorny to Samuell Heford pltif agst Ezekiell Cheever in an action of trespas vpon the case for takeing and keepeing possesion of a house w^{c}h was left in his the sd Richards possession by the sayd Samuell Heifer The Jury find for the defendt costs 4 s

The defdt Richard Coy appeales to the next Court of assistants

vera copia as attest Robert Lord cleric "

Second paper: —

" Richard Coye Attorny vnto Samuell Heffer his reasons of appeale from the Court at Ipswich in the cause betwixe himselfe and Mr Ezekiell Cheever vnto the Court of asistanc at boston

ffirst I haue full pouer to make sale of the said house and land as appears by my letter of Attorny

secoundly I neuer did make any sale of the said house and land acording to law nor any posession giuen thirdly acording to that law in pag: 20: the defendent did secretly obtaine posession Without & against my knowledg

forthly: ther is no evidence in Court that this thing they call a sale was before the law tooke plase in (52) therfore I humblely desier I may haue releife in this cause

Richard Coy

February 25: 1660:

I rec^d these ‖reasons‖ of appeale of Richard coy the 27 of Feb: 1660 to be p^r sented to this court

℘ me Robert Lord cleric"

[Endorsed] "Richard Coy
his Reasons of
appeale"

Third paper: —

"Dated 20th december 16[5]1

Be it knowne to all men by this p^r sent that I Samuel Herford of Ipswich doth asigne the disposeing of my house & Land & what I haue [oweing] me, vnto Richard Coy [ ] and alsoe I doe giue Richard Coy full power to come to reckoning & agreement with m^r Bartholomew about ye diferenc[e] that [is] betweene vs, and if they cannot Come to a full agreement, then I doe assigne Richard aforesayd to be my atturney, and to answer [Mr.] Bartholmew at the Court in my bahalfe, and [ ] or sell my house as he [sees] best, In wittness [whereof I h]aue sett too my hand

wittness [Thos Sale] Samuel Herford
Martha Coy [ ]
Martha Coy [ ] oath that this wrighting was the act [& deed of Samuel] Herford made in her presence

May 25, 1660: Daniell Denison
Robert [Lord]"

Fourth paper: —

"Att the Court held at Ipswich the 25 of Sept: 1660 Richard Coy Joseph Armitage & John Leigh acknowledged themselves to stand bound in fiftye pounds to the treaserer of this County vpon condition that the sayd Richard Coy shall ꝓsecute his appeale at the next court of Assistants to efect acording to Law

Vera Copia as attest Robert Lord Cleric"

Fifth paper: —

"[ ] ere to Richard Coy his Resons of appeale from [Cou]rt at Ipswich to the court of Assista[nts]

[ ] We answere Richard Coy had power to [ ] of the house & land in question for Satticefyeing [ ]uell Heifer his debts, by his letter of Atturney but [we deny ?] his letter of atturney gaue him power after he [ ] to sue for it againe, nor hath Samuell Hefer [ ] to the defendant m^r Cheever about it these [ ] & therfor we accompt he is satticefied with [ ]

done nor can we Imagine what reason he [ ] mr Cheever exsept (that seing by the cost & im[provement?] of the ground & the ꝓvidence of god it is now [ ] better then it was then) he should ayme at gayneing [ving] something to himselfe it being then sould [ull] worth, and Samuell never requireing more.

Second we answere It was sould before october 52 [ ] lawfull & will hould good in law and possest [posest] ‖nyne‖ yeares this Spring without any mo[re] [ ] or question about it by Richard Coy or any [ ]ll the atachment came Sept: last and that [ ] Sell it & tooke pay for it appeares by his owne acknow[ledgment] and othe testimonye

Thi[rd] we answere we cant thinke that the pltiff [ ] man, to gaine possession secrettly and against [ ] the house being lockt & haveing corne of [mons] in it, the defdt could not be thought or by [ ] or force to obtaine possesion, but as he afermed [ ]it had the key [ ] to him, (tho it being soe long [ ] doth not remember by whom) the pltiff alsoe [ ] in the Towne could not be Ignorant of mr [ ]er his dwelling in the house & yet did not in all [y]eares ever make soe much as a question or troble [ ] till he served the atachment

[ ] fourth we answere there was evidence in Court [ ] he was dwelling in the house the begining of the [mer] 52 by the defdts afermation & aledging for it [ ] record of his mariage the 18th of november after & the [kn]owledg of his neighbours yt he was dwelling in the [h]ouse before the scoole-house was raysed wch was in [y] 1652 wch some of the court [&] Jury knowing [ ] be soe was saticefaction to court & Jury & spared [ ] calling in of other neighbours and the carpente[rs] [ ] that builded the scoolehouse did repaire [so] yt [ ] before he raised the scoole-house mr Cheever [ ] it, we conceve the pltiff [having] no ground of [ ] this Honored court of our full & iust costs for [ ] sted"

[Endorsed] "Coy papers"

Sixth paper: —

"To the marshall of Ipswich or his deputy you are required to atach the goods & for want therof the body of mr Ezekiell Cheever & take bond of him to the value of eighty pound with sufisient security for his appearance at the next court held at Ipswich the last third day of this month to answere the complaint of Richard Coy Atturney to Samuell Heifer in an action of trespase vpon the case for takeing & keeping possession of a house wch was left in the sd Richards possesion by the sd Samuell Heifer & soe make a true returne therof vnder your hand dated the 20th of Sept: 1660

By the Court Robert Lord

vera copia as
attest Robert Lord cleric"

[On back of paper] "The 20th of Sept: 1660

Attached of the goods of mr Ezekiell Cheever a barne full of Hay & a stack of Hay one acre of Land & 16 sheepe to be responsall acording to the tenor of this attachment & left a sumons at the house

By me Robert Lord marshall

vera copia as attest

Robert Lord cleric"

Seventh paper:—

"William Bartholmew testifieth that some dayes before Samuell Heifers goeing away for England this depone[ ] did atach estate of the sayd Samuell Heifers for a debt d[ ] to this deponent, wch to his best remembrance was the house [ ] question: after wch this deponent meeting with the sayd H[eifer] about weanam when he went last away, he [toled] th[ ]ponent, he had left an atturney to take order for satisfieing the debt aboue mentioned: nameing Richard Coye [ ] deponents best remembrance, some little tyme after [Ric]-hard Coy came to this deponent, and made vp the accompt [and] agreed to pay him tenn pounds for Sam: Heifer & afterward apoynted me to pay six pounds to George Hadley: the wch sixteene poundes I receiued by the apoyntment of the sayd Richard Coy of Mr Robert Payne in a paire of oxen: This deponent further adeth that he haveing ocation to heare discourse about the sale of the house did severall tymes heare Richard Coy acknowledge the sale of itt att Twenty five pounds to this deponents best remembrance

Sworne in Court held at Ipswich the 25 of Sept 1660

p me Robert Lord cleric

Vera Copia Robert Lord cleric"

Eighth paper:—

"Robert Payne testifieth that haueing giuen sixty poun[ ] towards the purchaseing of a house & land for the setting vp a free Scoole in the Towne of Ipswich, and in advizeing with our Eldars about a place most convenient for such a vse, this house and Land now in question was pitcht vpon, it being to be sould I desired mr william Payne to treate with Richard Coye about the price of the same, and after some agitation, Richard Coy did agree to take twenty five pounds for the sayd house and Land, the wch sayd five and twenty pounds I payd acording to his order

Sworne in Court held at Ipswich the 25 of Sept: 1660

p me Robert Lord cleric

vera copia as attest

Robert Lord cleric"

XXXVIII.

[Court Files, Suffolk, March, 1660-1, No. 392, 10th paper.]

in the case betweene William Nickerson plantife & Abraham Busby defendant wee finde for the defendant sixty eighte pounds and a leven pence damage and costs of courts

Amos Richison forman

NOTE.

The following are the other papers on file in this case: —

First paper: —

"To the marshall of the County of Suffolk or his deputy yo^{w} are Required to Attach the goods and for want thereof the body of w^{m} Nicke^{r}son and take bond of him to the value of sixscore pounds wth sufficjent suretje or suretjes for his appearanc at the next County Court to be held at Boston then & there to Answe^{r} the Complaint of Abraham Busby for deteining of a debt of sixty fiue pounds seventeene shilling odd mony as Given to him by a deed of Guift amongst other things by Bridgett Busby his late mother & as Administrato^{r} to the estate and due damages & to make a true returne here of vnder yor hand dated the 11th day of December 1660.

By the Court Jonath Negus

This is A true Copie Compared wth the originall left on file as Attests Edward Rawson Recorder"

[Endorsed] "I haue Attached the dwelling house & Ground & shop of willjam Nicke^{r}son of Boston. this 11$\frac{10}{mo}$ to the value of sixscore pounds

℘ me Rich wayte marshall

This is A true Copie of y^{e} endorsmt as Attests Edw. Rawson Recorde^{r}"

Second paper: —

"Att A County Court 29th January 1660 Abraham Busby plaintiffe ag^{t}. w^{m} Nicke^{r}son. defendant for deteining of a debt of sixty five pounds seventeene shillings odd money as Giuen to him by a deede of Guift amongst other things by Bridgett Busby his late mother & as Administrator to her estate according to Attachment dated 11th decembe^{r} 1660 After the Attachment & other evidences in the Case produced were Read Comitted to the Jury [and are] on file the Jury brought in theire virdict they found for the plaintiffe sixty seven pounds eight shillings and five pence damages and Costs of Court.

The defendant Appealed from this Judgment to the next Court of Assistants This is A true Copie of the Courts Judgment as Attests

Edward Rawson Recorder

Jan^{r}y 1660.

Wm Nicke^{r}son in open Court acknowledged himselfe bound in one hundred & twenty pounds to the Tresure^{r} of the Countey on this

Condicion. that he will prosecute his Appeale to effect. This is A true Copie taken out of the Record[s] as Attests

Edward Rawson Recorde[r]"

Third paper: —

"Resones why I ded Apeale to the Honored Cort of Asestenc as followeth

furst Reason is to shew vnto the Honored Cort that I did not Apeale to take of our Honored gouenor or any of those Honored Judges that hard the Case Befor from Judging in the Case — for I hope that all the Cort to gether will be redie to dwo me Justes according to law for I haue no other Case* yet to Judg otherwise of them

2 Reson that Caused me to Apeale to the Honored Cort was becase I did not know what Abram Busby would plead too And therfor I Could not So fully be prepared to geue Answer to his Complaint Therfor I Intreat The Honored Cort to beare with my weaknes If it dwo apere to be my weaknes for I desier not to wrong any man of ther Just Right nor I would not be wronged my Selfe for vnder Correcktion I Consaiue that The Account that was betwen his mother Breget Busby And me was Satisfied to hur Content: The Reasons foloweth

3 Reson I dwo not find Any Euidenc in Cort that proue me debter to Abram Busby or to his mother sixtie five pound seauenten shillinges odd mony which Abram Busby say was geuen to him in a deed of geft by his Late mother Breget Busby amongest other thinges: for If The deed of geft be Rightly vnderstod vnder correcttion I Consaiue The deed proue the Contrari to that Abram plead for

4 Reason I dwo not find any law that dwo provid any Admenestrator To a deed of geft Therfor by Admenestration Abram dwo not prove me debter to him

5 Reson I find not Any Euedenc in Cort that proue any leagall Afirment geuen And Confermed by his mother Breget Busby to hur sonn Abram Busby to recaiue of willm Nickerson the som of sixtie five pound 17 shillinges odd mony which Abram Busby Charg me Debter to him in his Atachment — which Debte Abram Busby haue not yet proued it Therfor Vnder correction I Consaiue Abram Busby haue don me great wrong to pretend great Debte and damag and haue not proued it. And the law dwo provid that If any shall dwo so to vex And trobell the defendent he shall paie dobell damag to the partie greued As it Apere in the New book pag the: 2 : 7 [ ] branch of that Acte

6 Reason may be this Abram Busby ground his Complaint vpon A deed of geft that was geuen to him by his late mother Breget

* Cause?

Busby And by that deed Abram Busby Charg me debter to him sixtie five pound 17 shillinges odd mony — And as I haue said the deed proue not that which Abram haue Charged me as debter to him But vnder Correcttion the deed Abram plead too proue the Contrarie — for the deed say ther is Twentie foure pound geuen to my Cheldren to be devided amongest them And it is to be paid out of hur goodes And debtes And I was to paie it to my Cheldren Therfor Abram haue wronged me to Charge me debter to him for that which was geuen to my Cheldren

7 Reson may be to shew vnto the Honored Cort And Jeuri that the Accovnt which was betwen my mother in lawe And me is satisfied — for ther is Twentie four pound discovnted by his mothers geft to my Children in hur deed of geft — And for the Remainor of the Accovnt it is satisfied by my wifes sarues to hur father And mother — And it apere this: my wife Cam to boston the furst of march 1657 And my wife did sarues to hur father And mother till the later Ende of August following And then hur father departed this life — And since hur fathers death my wife haue don sarues to hur mother dayly And waching with them in the Night as ther Nessesitie Called for vntell hur mother departed this life: which was in July last: 1660: All which tim my wife did sarues to her father And mother And the tim being somed vp it Contain thre yeares And four months or thear Aboute — And for as much As my wife was dieted At my tabell in that tim she did them sarues Therfor I Charge vpon Account five shillinges a weke And ther Estat was not Charged to hier other help Therfor I may Justly Charg this accovnt for the laborer is worthie of ther hiere — And the accovnt being somed vp Com to forti thre pound for thre years And four month sarues Therfor the debte vpon account is satisfied to his mothers Content

8 But it may be the queston will be Asked why I did not demand satisfacktion of my mother whilst she liued If any such questen shall Arise in the Cort — I Anseuer that my wife vpon a tim since this deed of geft was mad propounded a questen to hur mother — And my wifes questen to hur mother was whether hur mother would leaue hur in debte to Abram — And when hur mother had a lettell Consedred of the questen hur mother did Anseuer that she would not leaue hur in debte to Abram But she would haue me to paie my Cheldren the Twentie four pound that she had geuen them And my wife should haue the rest This was the reson that I did not make any further demand of our mother seeing she was so willing to Alowe me that freely vpon my wifes mosion to hur — And I see nothing yet prodeused in Cort to prove that hur mind was Changed from that which she had promised to my wife — But becase I haue not witness to proue that my mother in law spake such wordes to my wife

as is befor Expressed Therfor I Charg it vpon Accovnt that the Honored Cort And Jeurie may see a Reson Cleare that the Accovnt between my mother in lawe And me was satisfied to hur Content And we know our mother Rested satisfied ther in — Therfor Abram haue don me wrong to prosecute as he haue don against me for Abram know that my wife did the sarues to hur father And mother as I haue Charged And I did tell Abram of it befor master Rason And befor Abram begon this seute.

9 Reson I dwo Intreat the honored Cort to Conseder my Case And to take so much paines to loke ouer the deed of geft And you shall see that my wife haue lese geuen to hur then the other sister haue geuen hur notwithstanding the sarues my wife had don vnto ther father And mother — Therfor ther was great Reason why my mother should Alowe me this that was Remaineng vpon the Accovnt betwen my mother in law And my selfe seeing she had not Consedred it in hur deed of gefte But Abram would forse this out of my hand by lawe And leaue me with out satisfacktion which in my Aprehention is a on Resnabell Act of Abram so to dwo seeing his mother by hur promise had freely geuen it to my wife

10 Reson is This Notwithstanding what I haue aleaged in my Resons If this honored Cort shall be pleased to grant Execusion to Abram Busby to forse the Estat out of my hand And so forse me to prosecut Ann Action to Recouer my Right out of the Estat — I shall loke vpon myself greatly wronged — for vnder Corecttion I Consaiue that The accovnt between my mother in law And me was satisfied to hur Content as haue ben befor Expresed in the other Resones what so Euer Abram Busby or any other for him may aleage to the Contrarie of what I haue wreten yet this is the trewe stat of the Case — As the Reasones of my Apeal subscribed by me

Willm Nickerson : 26 : feb: 1660 :

These Reasons were brought vnto me by y^{e} daughter of w^{m} Nick-e^{r}son y^{e} day & yeere aboue written Edward Rawson Recorde^{r}"

[Endorsed] "Nicholsons Reaso[ ]
of Appeale"

Fourth paper: —

"5 (1) $\frac{60}{61}$ An Anser to the Reasons of william Nickerson giuen ffor this appeale to this Honnord Cort

giuen by Abraham Busby deffet:

The deffendant vpon ꝑrsall of the Reasons giuen by the plantiffe ffindinge them as ffor their number many soe diuers of them longe & tedious by Reason of manny imꝑtinentes Contained in ym wch if he should trouble the Court wth answ vnto would be to Little purpose or satisfactiō in the Case thereffore to avoyd tediousnes the deffendant to the ffirst saith nothinge & to the Rest very breiffly

2dly To the second only this the Attatchment gaue him legall information which the Complaint was & what the (then) deffendant was to ansr vnto & Therefore noe apt Cause of Complaint & ffor that the (now) plantiff saith the accompt was satisfied to Content the deffendant denyes it as yet beinge neuer proued

3dly To the third albeit the summe named by the plantiffe be not so expressed in the deed of gift yet nothinge is more plaine then that the plantiffe was debtor vnto Bridget Busby as appeares by his hand to an accompt passed betweene Bridget Busby and him in her booke and it is as Clear that by the deed of gift the plantiffe is debtor vnto the deffendant to whom all debts fformerly due vnto Bridget Busby are by vertue thereof now due.

4^{thly} To the ffourth if the plantiffe be debto^{r} vnto the deffendant as is already sufficiently proued it is not woorth the while to Contend about the obiectiō made by the plantiffe

5^{ly} To ‖ye‖ ffifth whereas the plantiffe saith he doth not ffind any such a summe ꝑticulorly & legally assigned vnto Abraham Busby: ffor answ therevnto what is said in the third answ might giue Satisffactiō: but to make it Cleare w^{t}hout exceptiō we answ that although such a ꝑticuler summe be not in so many words expressed yet this is w^{t}hout exception (That) that w^{c}h Containes the whole Containes euery ꝑt but the deed of gift bequeathes & Assignes (all) debts accompts &c. fformerly due vnto Brdget Busby & not satisffied vnto her or her order to be and Remaine legally due vnto Abraham Busby: & thereffore this summe or any ꝑt of it, & thereffore the deffendant when (plantiffe) did noe wronge but the now plantiffe doth by his groundles appeale

7^{ly} This Reason affirmes noe more then was said in the second viz that the accompt is satisffied but seeinge it proues as little the deffendant still denyes it: and ffor what is said to proue it the deffendant to avoyd tediousnes ‖fforbeares‖ as iudginge it imꝑtinent to the p^{r}sent Case only ffor w^{t} is said in order to the Twenty ffower powndes giuen to his Children it ‖might haue beene‖ allowed in the accompt to w^{c}h the plaintiffe hath subscribed ~~& yet the ballance accounts to what is Clamed notwithstandinge~~ if he pleased

8^{ly} The eight beinge only a Reforme in Case such a questiō or obiectiō should be made the deffendant for the p^{r}sent makes none such but ‖y^{t}‖ he shall then well Consider of the answ^{r} and in the meane tyme to avoyd tediousnes the deffendant fforbeares and truely affirmes he doth not know that his mother was euer satisffied or did thinke herselffe indebted to her sonne & daughter Nickerson as he alleadges

9ly To nynth it beinge a Request vnto the honnored Court that the Case maie be seriously Considered therein the deffendant humbly ioynes

10ly To the tenth we Conceaue the deffendant [is] not at all to answ it beinge only a discouery how strongly the plantiffe is ꝑswaded of his Case & shall not willingly set downe by any issue that is not to his likinge"

Fifth paper: —

"To all Christian people to whom this pre[sent] writting shall Come Bridget Busby of Boston in [the] County of Suffolke in New England widdow Sendeth Greeti[ng our] Lord God euerlasting know yee that the said [Bri]dgett Busbey being of Good and perfect memory and wthout fraud or deceipt for and In Consideration of the naturall affection that I beare vnto my Sonnes and daughters and also for other Good Causes and Considerations me at present especially mooving Haue Giuen and Graunted and by these presents doe Giue Graunt and Confirme Vnto my Sonne John Busby the some of twenty pounds starling to be pajd vnto him In New England or to his Assignes by the value thereof out of my estate in Goods & debts wch to that end I leaue in the hands & Custody of my Sonne Abraham Busby Also I Giue and Graunt Vnto my daughter Katherine Sauery the some of tenn pounds starling to be paid vnto hir or hir Assignes in New England by the Value thereof out of my estate in [ ] & debts which to that end I leaue in the hands & Custody of my Sonne Abraham Busby both of the aboue named Guifts [to] be pajd wthin thirty moneths after the date of these presents Also I Giue Vnto my daughter Anna Nickerson a truncke & the one halfe deale of all my smale linnen Cloathes and one paire of sheetes and fower diaper napkins and two Couerd stooles and one wrought Cushin and two platters the one to be bigge & the other lesse and two silver spoones & one pillow beere and one great Iron pott and one long tableboard wch is now in hir husbands Custody by way of Loane also I Giue Vnto my daughter Sarah Grout the other halfe deale of all my smale linnen Cloathes and one joinct chest and one paire of sheetes and fower diaper napkins and two Couered stooles and one wrought Cushin & two platters the one bigg and the other lesse and two silver spoones and one pillow beere one feather bed wch is in the chamber the Guifts and Graunts aboue expressed I Giue and Graunt to each of the aboue named persons and to the executors and Assignes of each of them Confirmed from the day of the date hereof foreuer to the propper vse of each of them foreuer freely and quietly wthout any matter of challenge clajme or demand of me the sajd Bridget or any other person or persons whatsoeuer for me in my name by my meanes or procurement and wthout money or any other thing to be therefore pajd or demanded to or for me or any other person or persons whatsoeuer Also I Giue vnto the children of my daughter Anna Nickerson the some of twenty fower pounds to be divided

24 pound geuen to my C[hi]ldren

amongst them and payd by the value thereof out of my estate in Goods & debts wch to that end I leaue in the Custody of my sonne Abraham Busby Also I Giue vnto the children of my daughter Sarah Grout the some of twenty pounds to be divided amongst them and pajd by the value thereof out of my estate in Goods and debts wch to that end I leaue in the Custody of my sonne Abraham Busby to be pajd vnto theire parents for the perticcular vse and behooffe of each of them wthin sixe moneths after the decease of me the sajd Bridgett, And Also I the sajd Bridgett by these presents doe Giue Graunt and Confirme Vnto my sonne Abraham Busby all and singular the Remainder of my Goods estate debts & proppertjes of what value kind condicon quallity and quantitye soeuer the same are ‖be‖ or maybe and in what place or places soeuer the same be shall or maybe found to be aswell in my owne Custody & possession as in the possession hands power and Custody of any other person or persons whatsoeuer and wheresoeuer To Haue and to hold all and singular the Remainder of my estate as aforesaid not formerly Giuen and Confirmed and expressed how much to whome and out of the parts nominated [to] be Given Graunted and pajd vnto him the said Abraham and to the propper vse and behooffe of him his heires execcu[tors] administrators and Assignes foreuer freely and quietly wthout any manner of challange or [de]mand whatsoeuer of me th[ ]sd Bridget or any other person or persons whatsoeuer provided alwayes that the full and free liberty of vse and dis[ ]sement of this Remaynıng part of my estate Given & Graunted vnto my sajd sonne Abraham Busby is Reserved by me to my vse and for my majntenance during my naturall life and a power also to Give Graunt & Confirme A[bove] Guifts if I shall please so to doe and after that so much as may discharge the Costs of my funerall to be performed in a decent manner also I Giue & Graunt vnto my two sonnes in lawe & Willjam Nickerson and John Grout to each of them a peece of Gold of twenty shillings to be deliuered and pajd vnto them by my sajd sonne Abraham on the day of my funerall provided by me also ‖that‖ if any of my sajd sonnes and daughters doe dye before me that then the Guift so Giuen as is aboue expressed shall be vnto the Children of him hir or them so dying and I the sajd Bridgett Busbey haue putt my sajd sonnes & daughters in full and peace able possession of all and euery the prmised Graunts and Guifts warranting it to be pajd vnto them at the tjmes & places sett: by deliuering vp into the hands of my loving freind Mr Robert Saunderson for theire perticular Vse a peece of money Called six pence fixed in the seale hereof. In Wittnes whereof I haue herevnto putt my hand and seale the fowerteenth day of may in the yeare of our Lord one thousand six hundred fiftty & nine

[Margin notes: to be [paid] to [ ] — And the Rema[inder] [ ] — **This deed was not deliuered To Abbram but to Robart Sander[ ] in the behalf of all the [Chil]dren**]

[per]fected in the presence of vs
Robert Saunderson John Hull
Willjam Pearse

the mrke of
Bridget X Busby & a seale

Robe^{r}t Saunde^{r}son and John Hull deposed saith that hauing Subscribed theire names as wittnesses to this deede were present and heard the Same Audibly Read in theire presence to the sajd Bridgett Busby who after it was Read Signed Sealed and deliuered it as hir act and deed and that when she so did to theire best vnderstanding she was of a sound disposing mind and further saith no^{t} taken vpon oath the 2^{d} of the $^{5}_{mo}$ 1660 before me Anthony Stoddard Comission^{r}

[Will]iam Pearse deposed saith that what is aboue written and deposed by Robert Saunde^{r}son and John Hull is the truth and further [ ] that at another time on the last election day he [ ] the deede aboue written to the sajd Bridgett Busby who then again [ ] it to be hir act and deed and further saith not taken vpon oath the 2d of July before me Edward Rawson Comission^{r}

[Entred] & Recorded 5th July 1660

℘ Edward Rawson Recorde^{r}

That this is a true Copie Compard wth y^{t} Copie w^{c}h was Compared wth the originall produced in Court January 1660 & left on file as Attests

Edward Rawson Recorde^{r}."

Sixth paper: —

"Past accomp^{t} wth my mother in law Bridget Busby the 12th day of May 1659 & I am debto^{r} to hir for the some of =113 : 15 : 05

out of wch some my sajd mother pajeth me a legacje given my wife by my deceased father in lawe Nicholas Busby the some of —050 00 00

so that I Remajne debto^{r} vnto my sajd mother the day aboue written the some of —063 15 05

I say ℘ me Willjam Nicke^{r}son

That this is A true Copie taken out of Abraham Busbys booke of accomts signed by the s^{d} Nicke^{r}son & by him ouned in Court to be his hand Compared wth ye sd booke in Court all wch Attests Edward Rawson Recorde^{r}

This is A true Copie Compard wth the Copie on file as Attests Edward Rawson Recorde^{r}"

Seventh paper: —

"Boston In New England 5th July 1660

present ye Govern^{r}
Dep^{t} Goun^{r}
& Recorder

Administration to the estate of Bridget Busby is Graunted to Abraham Busby hir sonne to Administer on the Goods & chattells of the sajd Bridget & to performe the deede made & signed by hir; bearing date 14th of may 1659 as neere as may be.

Edw Rawson Recorde^{r}

This is A true Copie Compard w^{t}h that left on file as Attests

Edward Rawson Recorde^{r}"

Eighth paper: —

"Abraham Busby[s] bill of Costs

To Entring the action	01	00	00
To Attachm[t] & serving it	00	01	06
To Records	00	05	00
To 4 dayes Attendance	00	06	00
To filing 4 pape[r]s	00	00	08
Allowed Edw. Rawson Record[r]	1	12*	2

This is a true Copie Compared w[t]h the original on file as Attests Edw Rawson Record[r]"

Ninth paper: —

"Abram Busby bill of Costs

a bill of Charges

ffor 2 dayes attendance on the court 3[s]:

ffor filing y[e] evidences 10: 1: 8

[All] E. R. S."

The allowance of these bills of costs indicates that the Court of Assistants accepted the verdict of the jury in favor of Abraham Busby given above as Fragment XXXVIII.

XXXIX.

[Mass. Archives, Vol. 60, No. 206.]

Att a Court of Asistants held at Boston y[e] 3[d] Sept. 1661.

Abraham Broune Atturney to Tho. Isaac & Jn[o] Hallet plaintiff ag[t] mathew Armestrong defend[t] in an action of the Case, for deteining & not deliuering vnto the sajd Broune Attourney afore[sd] the Summe of Sixe hundred & odd pounds in money which the Sajd Armestrong received at Jamajca for the Account of the sajd Isack & Hallet, wth other due damages according to Attachm[t] dat. ye 29th January 1660 wch action trjed at the County Court Aprill 1661, The Jury finding for the defend[t] Costs of Court ye magis[ts] refusing the sd virdict it falls in Course to this Court after the Courts Judgm[t] & all other evidences in the Case produced were read Comitted to the Jury & are on file ye Jury brought in their virdict they found for ye defend[nts] Costs of Court the magis[ts] refuse y[e] virdict & so it falls to y[e] Generall Court. This is A true Copie of the Courts Judgment as Attests Edward Rawson Secret[y].

NOTE.

This case, as is shown by the records, started in the County Court, came up to the Court of Assistants, and finally went to the General Court.

---

* So in copy.

The next paper is the order passed by the General Court: —

"In the case of Abraham Broune, of Boston, merchant, atturney to Thomas, Isacke, & John Hallet, merchants, plaintiffs ag^t^ Mathew Armestrong, late master of the good ship called the Willjam & Thomas, defend^t^, coming to this Court by the disagreement betweene the bench & jury, after the Court had duely considered of the Courts judgm^ts^, wth the evidences in the case produced, which are on file, this Court doe judge, declare, & order, as a finall issue of the sajd case, that the sajd Mathew Armestrong, appearing before the Gouevno^r^, or any two magistrates, shall cleare himself, on oath, of all the money he came from Tortoodars, reserving only one fifth part thereof to himself for his care & pajnes in preserving the same; and that on the receipt of the sajd money^s^, the plaintiffe shall giue him a full discharge from all further molestation referring to the moneys by them comitted to the custody of the s͠d Armestrong. And this Court doe order, that in case the s͠d Armestrong shall refuse to cleare himself by his oathe, he shall then pay to the plaintiffs fower hundred pounds, and in case that, by the providence of God, he be prevented of such an oppertunity, then his Suretys shall pay vnto the plaintiffs one hundred & sixty pounds in currant money of this countrey."

Mass. Colony Records, Vol. IV., Part II., p. 49.

There are also some other papers in the Archives relating to it. The case is a good illustration of the procedure in such instances.

XL.

[Mass. Hist. Soc. Misc. Papers, 1628–1691, F. 33.]

At A Court of Asistants held at Boston 3^d^ march 1662.*

Capt: Thomas Clarke plaintiffe agt Capt Wm Dauis &c defend^t^ on Appeale from the County Court at Boston: After the Courts Judg ment Reasons of Appeal & other evidences in the Case produced were read ye parties hauing Joyned Issue in the Case the Jury found for the defend^t^ the confirmation of the Judgm^t^. of the former Court being one hundred thirty & fower pounds together wth thirteene pounds two shillings more wch makes one hundred forty seven pounds two shillings in all & Costs of Court:

Vera copia Attest: Edw: Rawson Secret^y^.

Note.

A rehearing of the case between Capt. Thomas Clarke "and Capt. W^m^. Davis one of the executors ofthe last will & testament ofthe late W^m^. Paddy" was granted by the General Court, June, 1663,

*1662–3.

and judgment was given "for the defendant, capt. Wm Davis, costs of Court." See Mass. Col. Records, Vol. IV., Part II., p. 84. See also below, Fragment, record of 5 March, 1666–7, Clarke v. $Exec^{rs}$. of Paddy.

(Court Files, Suffolk, No. 98507, is a copy of a Deposition given in the County Court.)

Wm Davis aged 45 yeares or thereabouts testifyeth, y^t y^e accott produced by him in Court in y^e Case depending, was p^rsented to y^e said deponent by Capt. Thomas Clarke as an account of y^e stocke in partnership betweene himselfe & Wm Paddy, in the hands of Val: Hill, & by y^e said deponent — receiued as such sworne in Court 28th Janvry 1662 Edw: Rawson $Record^r$

This is a true Copie Compd
with ye Originall As Attests

Edw: Rawson $Record^r$.

(Endorsed)

davis affidavit

XLI.

[Essex County Court Files, Vol. IX., Fol. 65, White $Libell^t$ v. White, Nov., 1663. Also Massachusetts Archives, Vol. 9, No. 43.]

Att A Court of Asistants held at Boston 3^d march 1662*

$Majo^r$ Hauthorne by [his] letter returning a warrant bond & evidence taken before him relating to what Margaret Bennet in behalfe of hir daughter Mary White the wife of Elias White ^ as to his Insufficiency & hir desire of being freed from him that hath nor cannot performe the duty or office of a husband to hir the partjes appeared and after the Court had pervsed the evidence & considered of what they heard from the partjes they declared at present they did not see sufficient ground to separate them but advised them to a more loving & suitable Cohabitation one with the other & that all due phisicall meanes may be vsed. = This is A true Copie taken out of the Courts book of Records as Attests

Edward Rawson $Secret^y$.

NOTE.

The above Fragment of the Court of Assistants record is found in connection with the following copy of a statement to the Court by Elias White and a copy of certain evidence by William Charles and John Codner:

"May it please this Honoured Court I rather desire to Express by writting then by publicke deliuery my Answer to what Willjam Charles and John Codner Inhabitants of marble head haue sworne

---

* 1662–3.

what they haue sworne I doe Ingenuously owne to be the truth. When first I married I thought myself sufficjent: otherwise I neuer would haue entered into that estate: but sithence I am now called before Authority to Answer Insufficjency I doe in Conscience thinke that I am bound in a Case of such weight to declare the truth for the avoyding all further troubles. I doe desire to sattisfy this much Honoured Court that so no Just occasion might be taken against me. I find myself Infirmous not able to performe that office of marriage. What the Cause is I know not. I am fully Contented to be separated if it please this Authority:

Elias White

This is a true Copie compared wth the originall presented to the last Court of Asistants 3 march 1662 & left on file as Attests

Edward Rawson $Secret^{y}$"

"Wee Willjam Charles & John Codner of Marblehead doe hereby certify vnto you^{r} $wo^{r}pp^{s}$ that John Codner & I did aske of Eljas white whither when he lay wth his wife; if there were any motion in him or no; the Said Elias White answered yea fower or five $howe^{r}s$ together but when he turned to hir It was gonn againe Then his wife asked him before vs whither or no he had euer made vse of hir he presently Answered hir no this is a truth as neere as I cann declare.

Taken vpon oath by boath partjes } William Charls
2^{d} $\frac{1}{mo}$ $\frac{62}{63}$ before me } John Codner

Willjam Hawthorne

This is A true Copie Compared wth the originall on file as Attests

Edward Rawson Secretary."

There was also other evidence as to lewd behavior by White's wife. A petition was presented by Margaret Bennet to the General Court, Oct., 1663, on which the following order was passed:

Mass. Records, Vol. IV., Part 2, p. 91, 21 Oct., 1663. "In answer to the petition of Margaret Bennet, in behalf of Mary White, hir daughter, humbly desiring to be sett free from Eljas White, hir husband, for his deficjency, &c., in hir peticon & by witnesses therein exprest & prooved, the Court judgeth it not meete to graunt hir request."

XLII.

[Court Files, Suffolk, March, 1662–3, No. 962, 17th paper.]

Wee find a Speciall verdict. (i e 1 y^{t} m^{r} Broughton ye principal D^{r} to Jno Chickly, made a deed of sale to Richard Cooke & Walter Price, expressing y^{r} in his confidence of y^{r} improveing y^{r} of to Sundry Vses: wherein if by law they are ingaged to sattisfy Jno Chickly his demands wee find for ye s^{d} Chickly if otherwise, y^{n} for ye s^{d} R: Cooke & Price.

5th of march 63. Charles Chadwick

in the nam ofthe rest

The Bench determines that ye plaintiffs are not bound to pay ye defend^t according to his demand & Graunts ye plaintiffs Costs of Courts E R S

NOTE.

It appears by the 10th paper in this case (No. 962) that Thomas Broughton had made an assignment of his estate for the benefit of his creditors (named in a schedule) including John Checkley.* Checkley bringing suit in the County Court at Boston for his whole claim and obtaining judgment and execution, the deed of assignment was set up as a bar to the execution. The question being referred by the General Court to the County Court at Boston † that Court upon special verdict being returned determined, Jan. 27, 1662–3, that "the deede of sale aboue mentioned is no legall barr." The case was thereupon appealed to the next Court of Assistants.

Mass. Records, Vol. IV., Part 2, p. 62, 8 Oct., 1662. "In ans^r to the petition of Mr John Cheeckly, the Court judgeth it meete, as most regular, to refer this peticõn to the determination of that Court, to whom the cognisance ofthe case doeth propperly belong, & that there all partjes concerned haue liberty to speake for themselves."

Same, p. 79, 6 June, 1663. "In ans^r to the petition of John Cheekely, the Court, on reading his peticõn, judge meete to referr the petitioner for remedy against the officer for his defect as the lawe directeth in case that he be defectiue."

Same, p. 107, 18 May, 1664. "In ans^r to the petition of Mr John Cheeckley, the Court judgeth it meete to order, that the secretary renew the executions on the judgments ofthe County Courts ag^t Mr Thomas Broughton, & his proper estate, to & for Mr John Checkley, & to direct the same to the marshall generall, or his deputy, to execute them on the sajd person & his proper estate."

Same, p. 121, 8 Aug., 1664. "In answer to the motion & request of Mr Thomas Broughton, humbly craiving this Courts fav^r that they may haue liberty to come to the publicke ordinances on the Lords days & at other times, & y^t his confinement maybe to some other place, wth Mr Chickleys consent, the Courte grants his request for his attendance on public worship, so he be secured by the keeper, & his credito^r thereby not defrauded; also for his enlargement, so it be wth his credito^rs consent."

Same, p. 138, 19 Oct., 1664. "Mr Broughton, making his suite to this Court that he may be licensed to appeare before the County Court, in Boston, for an oppertunity to haue the benefit of the lawe in favo^r to such debto^rs as are not cabable of paying their credito^rs according to judgment granted ag^t them, itt is ordered, that he haue his liberty

* See Court Files, Suffolk, Nos. 314, 320, 596.

† See Mass. Col. Records, Vol. IV., Part II., pp. 62, 79, 107, 305, 349, 430.

accordingly, being secured by the keeper, & im̄ediately returned from the sajd Court to prison."

Same, p. 305, 23 May, 1666. "In ans[r] to the petic̄on of John Cheekley, this Court, hauing considered & pervsed his petition, and the seuerall particulars therein conteyned, see no cause of complaint in any, except the case w[ch] the petitioner calls a grievance, respecting the manner of levying an execution, wherein a due course of lawe hath not bine attended; & therefore leaues y[e] petitioner to take his remedy against any y[t] did him wrong, in such a way as the lawe provides."

Same, p. 333, 15 May, 1667. "Vpon the comp[lt] of M[r] Broughton, that he is vnder pressure, not being in a capacity to haue his case heard, the Court judgeth it meete to allow him liberty to implead M[r] Checkly at the next County Court; & his keeper shall & is hereby required to bring him fforth, vpon his desire accordingly, he securing him for his returning to prison againe."

Same, p. 430, 19 May, 1669. "In ans[r] to the petition of John Checkly, it is ordered, that Majo[r] Generall Leueret, M[r] Humphrey Davy, & M[r] John Wisewall shall & hereby are appointed & impowred, or any two of them, as com̄issioners, to examiē & adm̄ister oaths to persons Suspected in conceling the estate of the sajd Thomas Broughton; as also that he shall haue the benefit of the lawe which requires sattisfaction by service where estate cannot be found."

Same, p. 349, 9 Oct., 1667. "In the case now before the Court relating to M[r] Thomas Broughton, coming to this Court by petition, ag[t] Jn[o] Cheeckly, defendt, the Court, hauing heard & duely considered of what hath binn alleadged & pleaded in the case by both partjes, see not any reason to alter the judgm[ts] of any ofthe former Courts, & grant the defendt costs of Courts."

Same, p. 405, 23 Oct., 1668. "Att the request of M[r] Thomas Broughton, pleading that he hath been long in prison by virtue of an execution taken out against him by Jn[o] Cheeckley, & that he hath not wherew[th] to satisfy the judgments of the Courts granted ag[t] him, this Court doe grant him the liberty ofthe lawe, that some com̄issioners may be impowred by this Court to take his oath as the law permitts, & vpon the taking his oath, according to the sajd law, he shall be released from prison, & shall sattisfy by service, as the law directs; and that Capt. Gookin & M[r] Danforth be the com̄issioners appointed to take the oath for that end.

I, Thomas Broughton, doe sweare, by the name of the living God, that I haue not disposed of or consealed in any kinde my estate, to the defrauding M[r] John Cheekly of his debt, w[ch] he demandeth of me, & the benefit of the judgm̄ts of the Courts granted ag[t] me; & in testimony hereof, I doe subscribe my name.

Thomas Broughton.

7 November Taken vpon oath, this seventh ofthe 9 m[o], 1668, before vs,

Daniel Gookin,
Tho: Danforth."

XLIII.

[Court Files, Suffolk, No. 532, 1st paper.]

To the Honrd. Court of Assistance

The humble petition of Jnothan Parker Humbley sheweth

That yor: petionrs imprudent and Inconsidrate act haueing Drawne upon him yt severe sentence by the lettor ofthe Law Due to Burglarey — notwithstanding yor petirs: concience condemnes him not as to aney such Intentions as Rendors him Guilty of such a Crime

Yor petir: therefore although the present ap[pea]rance of his offence rendors him altogether unworthey of such a favor Humbley prayeth yt ye Execution of his present Sentence may be suspended till ye next Session of ye Generall Court: hopeinge that his owneinge his ffoley, wth. what may appere to euince that his intentions were not as now they haue apperance to bee, may obtaine fauor from the Hond Genll. Court who haue powre of the Law In there handes

And yor petir. as in duty bound
shall evor pray &c.

Jonathan Parker

In answr to this petition

The Court Judgeth meete to order that ye execution of ye sentence agt ye peticonr shall be Respited till the fifth day after the first Sessions of ye next Genll. Court of Election: & that he bee bound to his Good behauiour wth 2 suretys in one hundred pounds for that time & Also for their deliuering him vp to ye Custody of the law at that time: & ~~his Appearance at the Sd Genll. Court~~

E. R. S.

accordingly in open Court Jnothan Parker as principle mr Richard Parker mr John Pay[ne] & Arthur mason in open Court acknowledged themselves Joinctly & seuerally bound in one hundred pounds a peec on the condition aboue written &c. E. R. S.

NOTE.

In this case Jonathan Parker appears to have been examined on a charge for burglary before Commissioner's Court, bound over to appear before the County Court at Boston, and to have appealed from the sentence of said Court to the Court of Assistants at Boston in March, 1662–3. The above petition apparently relates to the sentence of said Court. The Reasons of Appeal claim as defence that the house was entered by an unlocked door and with no evil intent.

The 5th paper in the case, No. 532, is the order of the General Court June, 1663, annulling the sentence of the Court of Assistants upon the payment to the Treasurer of 40£. See Mass. Col. Records, Vol. IV., Part II., p. 81.

Mass. Records, Vol. IV., Part 2, p. 81, 12 June, 1663. "Att the instant request of Mr Richard Parker, Mr Jno Payne, & Arthur Mason, & in ansr to their peticon, being suretjes for Jonathan Parker, sentenced at the last Court of Assistants for a wicked attempt into the house of Mrs Richards, and into the bed chamber, in the dead of the night, as may fully appeare in the records of that Court, this Court doe graunt to Jonathan Parker, & to his suretjes, the extinguishing of his & their bond for his appearance & yeilding himself to the officer of the country, and do also null the sentence of the sajd Court, provided alwajs the sajd suretjes shall forthwith pay to the Treasurer of the Country forty pounds, tenn pounds whereof shall be pajd in money, & the other into the hands of Capt. Oliuer, to his content."

XLIV.

[Suffolk Registry of Deeds, Vol. IV., p. 14.]

To Edward Michelson marshall Generall or his Deputy. Yow are hereby Required in his Majtys name to levy on the Goods & person of George Hadley to the value of fiue pounds one shilling and sixe pence & deliuer the same wth two shillings for this execution together wth possession of a parcel of Land sued for at Salem Court last according to the seccond diuission or ljne runne to Robert Hazeline & is in sattisfaction of a Judgment Confirmed & Graunted to him by the Court of Assistants sitting at Boston the first of Instant September hereof not to faile Dated at Boston 7th September 1663

By ye Court Edw. Rawson secrety

By virtue hereof I Assigne John Pickard my lawfull deputy for the execution of this warrant this 7. 7th. 1663 Edw. Michelson, marshall Endorst.

The land expressed in this execution was deliuered by Georg hadley vnto Robert Hasseltine I being present as the marshall deputy also Georg Hadley payd the Cost of Court to Robert Hasseltines sattisfaction ꝑ me John Pickard.

Entred & Recorded the 22th of March 1663 at Request of Robt Hasseltine.

ꝑ Edw. Rawson secrety

XLV.

[Court Files, Suffolk, No. 567.]

At a Court of Assistants held at Boston 1st September 1663.

Samuell & Hannah Scarborough sonne & daughter to Jno Scarborough & Mary his then wife, formerly Smith, came into Court & made chojce of Deacon wm Parks to be their Guardian wch ye Court allowed of.

Elijah kenrick & marjah kenrick Sonne & daughter of John kenrick & Anne his wife, formerly Smith came into Court & made chojce of mr Peter Oliuer to be their guar[dian] : wch ye Court allowed of

Allowed E R S

XLVI.

[Court Files, Suffolk, No. 577, 8th paper.]

In ye case betweene Andrew Mansfield & Jno [Hathorne] ye Jury find for ye pt. damages 22£ 10s, & [John] Hathorne to make a publick acknowledgmt. [ ] Court & ye next Court att Ipswich, yt hee [wron]ged ye pl. in charging him wth ye breach [ ] comand in bearing false witness agt. his neig[hbor] wch. if hee refuse to doe, then to pay to [ ] 35li damage & costs of Courts.

Edw. ffle[tcher] for[man]

5 Sept. 1663.*

NOTE.

There are 24 papers in this case which was an action of slander brought against John Hathorne of Lynn first at the County Court at Ipswich and apparently carried to the Court of Assistants.

XLVII.

[Court Files, Suffolk, No. 669, 3d paper.]

Att a Court of Assistants held at Boston the first Day of March 1663 †

Theodor Atkinson plaintiffe agt. John Williams Defendt. in an Action of the Case for not performing the promise to the said Atkinson for the rectifying of Accounts between them and not attending a meeting wch was appoynted by Major Generall Leueret and mr Thomas

* In Rawson's hand. † 1663-4.

Brattle at Liv[t] Turners the 29th Day of December last past, w[ch] the said John Williams did promise and engage to and with the said Theodor Atkinson Sen[r]. That if the said Theodor Atkinson Sen[r] would procure any two men whereu[r] hee pleased Excepting only one man in Boston namely Cap[t]. Oliver to examine all Acc[ts]. & Differences between them y[t] haue been already heard That if there should then appeare any mistakes or Erro[rs] whereby the said Williams hath more giuen him by the award soe called than was iustly Due to him the said Williams hee would abate accordingly. as in the attachm[t] Dated the 31th of December 1663 w[ch] Action was tried in the last County Court in Boston in January Last And comes to this Court for tryall by the Magistrates refusing the Juries verdict: After the Attachm[t] Courts Judgm[t] and evidences in the case produced were read Comitted to y[e] Jury and are on file wth the records of this Court The Jury brought in their verdict they found for the Plaintiffe One hundred and fifty pounds vnles the Defend[t] over haul his Accounts and performe his promise therein to the Plaintiffe by the Last of May next come twelue-month And Cost of Court ffoure pounds sixteen shillings & ten pence.

This is a true Coppie compared wth the originall as Attests

Edw. Rawson Secret.

NOTE.

The 4th paper is the same except that it is attested a true copy from "the Courts book."

The 6th paper is the same & is attested as a "true Copie taken out of the Courts book of Records."

The 8th paper is the same as also the 9th, 10th and 11th.

There are in all seventy-six papers connected with this case, many of them, however, duplicates. They consist of copies of the records of the County Court, of the writs, pleadings and papers in the cases therein, of Reasons of Appeal and answers thereto, of letters, deeds, awards, bonds, agreements, accounts of various sorts, depositions and other matters of evidence. See also below, records of 7 March 1664–5, 7 March 1670–1, 9 June 1671, 5 Sept. 1671, and 12 March 1671–2. (See also Mass. Col. Records, Vol. IV., Part II., pp. 476, 539, 559, 571. See LVI., XC., XCII., CIV.)

XLVIII.

[Court Files, Suffolk, No. 608, 4th paper.]

John Porter sonne of John Porter of Salem being comitted by the order of the County Court at Salem dated the [blank] 1663 for his Abhorred & vnheard of Rebelljous opprobrious vilifying & threatning speeches & carriages ag[t] his naturall parents putting them into frights & his father in feare of his life: swearing he would & Attempting to stabb his brother Contempt of Authority in high & reproachfull speeches & other heinous Crimes The Court on pervsall of the evidences produced ag[t]. him & read and prooved in open Court before his face Judged it meet to sentence him to be (by the marshall Generall wth a sufficjent Guard by him warned) Carrjed on the Lecture Day come sevennight Imediately after the lecture to the Gallows & there cause him to be made to stand on ye ladder by the executioner wth a Roape about his necke for one hower & then brought back & tjed to the great Gunne & whipt seuerely wth thirty nine stripes & then returned & comitted to the house of Correction. there to remajne & kept closely & safely to work according to the orders of the house & that he be not thence releast by any Authority vnlesse the Court of Assistants or Generall Court & that the keeper or m[r] of the house of Correction suffer neither his father or mother or any other person whatsoeuer to releaue him wth any other diet than the orders of that house provides & that he pay as a fine to the Country the some of two hundred pounds & stands Comitted till he performe the sentenc: voted: 4th march 1663.

E. R. S.

NOTE.

The first paper in this case shows that the above is a record of the Court of Assistants, 4th of March 1663–4. It is as follows:

"At a County Court Held at Salem 24: 9[mo]: 1663 John Porter Jun[r]. being complayned of to this Court for Rebellious & abusiue cariages & speeches to his parents, and there being seuerall euedences produced against him, the Court vpon examination of ye matter, see cause to comitt the said Porter to the Goale at Boston & there to remayn vntill the Court of Assistants next, to whome he is referred for further tryall.

This is a true copie taken out of Salem Courte Records per me
Hillyard Veren Cleric"

The second paper in the case is a Deposition recounting threats made by the offender; the third is the Warrant of Commitment to the prison in Boston; the fourth is the sentence imposed as it appears in the record, and the fifth is a note of instances of abusive conduct, "Rebelljous opprobrious vilifying & threatning speeches and carriages" and "other heinous Crimes," between October 20 1662 and June 10 1663, as testified to and proved.

See also Mass. Col. Records, Vol. IV., Part II., pp. 137, 146, 177, 195, 196, 210, 216, 217, 227, 251.

XLIX.

[Court Files, Suffolk, No. 746, 6th paper.]

Att A Court of Asistants held at Boston the 6th of September 1664

Benjamin Ward plaintiff agt Roger Kelly defendt. in an action coming for trjall to this Court by the magists. refusing the virdict of the Jury at the last County Court in July = after the Attachment & other euidences wth the virdict of the Jury were read Comitted to this Jury & are on file wth the reccords of this Court they brought in their virdict they found ffor the defendant Costs of Courts fo[ur] pounds fiueteen shillings & ffower pence:

This is A true Copie taken out of ye Courts booke of Records as Attests Edward Rawson Recorder

Vera Copia Attests Edw: Rawson Recorder

Note.

The 12th paper is the same as above except it is attested as follows, — "This is a true Coppy Compared with the originall on file as Attests Edw: Rawson Secrety.

Vera Copia Attests Edw. Rawson Secrety."

This case like many others came up to the Court of Assistants by reason of "the Magistrates refusing the verdict of the jury" in the lower Court.

It was an action on the case in the County Court, Ward v. Kelly, for "Inperiously & illegally withholding & improving & imploying without order his Catch called the Hope," and Kelly as appears by the return on the writ was committed to prison.

There are forty-two papers in all in this group variously connected with the litigation.

The first paper is a copy of the writ and the return by the Marshall in the case in the County Court — Ward v. Kelly.

The second, third and fourth are copies of the writ, etc., in other cases connected therewith. The fifth, seventh, eighth, ninth, tenth and eleventh are copies of various records of the County Court.

The thirteenth, fifteenth and seventeenth are copies of Reasons of Appeal and answers thereto.

The fourteenth, sixteenth, eighteenth to twenty-third, twenty-fifth, twenty-sixth and fortieth are copies of various papers connected with the history of the Ketch and the litigation.

The twenty-fourth and the twenty-seventh to the forty-second are copies of various depositions.

L.

[Court Files, Suffolk, No. 1372, 8th paper.]

Att a court of Assistants held at Boston ye 6th of Septembr 1664

Jno Redman Attorney for ye town of Hampton plaintiff agt: Nathll: Boulter Defendt: in an accon of Appeale from ye judgmt of ye last county Court att Salisbury: The accon being called, pltff: not appearing being three times called was non suted, ye defendt: being also absent wth ye plaintif, ye court judg it meet to order yt this accon. should bee contineued to ye next Court of Assistants & then to bee heard: The plaintiff only paying ye defendent costs, & ye defendent to bee sumoned accordingly:

That this is a true copie taken out of ye courts booke of records, Attests Edward Rawson secret,

This is a true Copie of ye copie now on file wth Salisbury Court records 1675 as attests Tho: Bradbury recr.

NOTE.

Court Files, Suffolk, No. 1372, contains sixty-two papers. The eighth is given above; the eleventh is a copy of the record of the Court of Assistants March 7 1664–5, which contains the conclusion of this case, involving the title to one hundred acres of land in the town of Hampton. See below, LV.

The first paper is a copy of the writ in this case to appear and answer in the action of Appeal at the Court of Assistants to be held in March 1664.

The remaining papers consist of copies of writs, pleadings, Court Records, Town Records, Statements and testimony, depositions, the original laying out of the town, bonds, deeds, grants, bills of cost, etc. A few are connected with some later litigation as to the same tract.

LI.

[Court Files, Suffolk, No. 644, 3d paper.]

In the Case depending betwene Wm: Salter plentife & Wm Clements deft. wee find a spechall verdict, viz: if the aresting of a prisoner in the prison make him a prisoner of charge to him for whos accompt hee is last arrested according to law, then wee find for the plentiffe, damiges thirtie shillings, and cost of Court, if otherwise then wee find for the deft: Cost of Courts, which wee leaue to the worspll. Bench to determin

John Paine forman Jury

NOTE.

This case of Salter v. Clements was an appeal to the Court of Assistants, Sept. 1664, from a Commissioner's Court at Boston, August 17, 1664, when the judgment was for the defendant Clements, the action being for the plaintiff's "dietting & lodging Mounseir Laborn, being the said Clements prisoner."

The first paper in the group is a copy of the writ returnable to the Commissioner's Court; the second a copy of the record of that Court; the third the original verdict as given above; and the fourth is the reasons of appeal in an earlier case connected with this.

The matter of the two Frenchmen Laborne and Laremett gave rise to much litigation and various proceedings. See further, Court Files, Suffolk, No. 826, Salter v. Woodmansey, and Mass. Col. Rec., IV., Part II., p. 89.

Mass. Col. Rec., IV., Part II., p. 89—The prisoners Alex^r. Laborne & Wm Laremitt Frenchmen to be maintaind by those "whose prisoners they were or are" Oct. 1663. Also order on certain questions by the prison keeper. Also—"In the case now depending betweene Wm Salter & John Woodmansy" as to "diet for two Frenchmen coming to this Court by reason of disagreement of bench & jury in the Court of Asistants" the Court find for the said Salter 17^s 6^d & costs "Granted May 64" Also order 27 May 1663 that these prisoners committed for Sr. Thos. Temple and while prisoners arrested on private accounts be released at end of this session from "commitment, by virtue of the councils act"

Ib., p. 136—Order as to payment for Laborne expenses by Mr. Woodmansey and by Sr Thos. Temple—Oct. 1664—

Ib., p. 106— May 1664—Wm Salter allowed costs in Mr Woodmanseys Case—22^s 10^d

Ib., p. 340—May 1667—order reversing all "judgments of former courts"—

Ib., p. 353, Oct. 1667—order in explanation of above order—

LII.

[Suffolk Registry of Deeds, Vol. IV., p. XV.]

To Edward Michelson marshall Generall or his Deputy.

Yo^w are hereby required in his Maj^tys name to Levy on the goods & person of Capt Richard Walderne to value of forty pounds fiueteene shillings & two pence & deliuer the same to Israel Wight wth two shillings for this execution, and is in sattisfaction of a Judgment granted him for so much by the Court of Asistants held at Boston 6th of September 1664 hereof not to faile.

Dated at Boston 10th Septembe^r 1664.

By the Court Edward Rawson secret^y

The 20 of 7 1664. By Virtue hereof I Assigne Christopher Palmer my lawfull Deputy for the execution of this warrant

Edward Michelson marshall genll.

Endors^t on a paper Annext

Thomas Wiggins Ju^r & John Stannion sworne to Apprize goods & lands this 25 of (9) 64. Porthmouth

By me Richard Cutt Commission^r

Vnderwritt This execution was Levied vpon a peece of Pasture land at Douer about two acres & a halfe butting on the South South east side on the land of Job Clemens. on the East North East on the land of Tho. Beard on the west south west vpon the majne streete of Douer prized at three pounds fiveteene shillings & vpon a parcell of vpland & meadow beginning at the lower most South east ljne of m^r Wiggin his farme and running vp fiueteene rod from high-water marks vpon the sajd line & from thence by a direct line to the mouth of walls creeke this land butts on the north west side upon the riuer. of exeter on the south east side vpon the land of m^r Andrew Wiggins prized at thirty pounds & vpon two hundred acres of vpland adjoyning to the other tract of vpland and meadow lying two hundred rod along by the great bay. & one hundred and sixty rod. by the ljne of m^r Andrew Wiggin his farme prized at tenn pounds and possession given to Israel Wight of the same in sattisfaction for this execution. & the charges of levying the same on the twentieth 8^ber. 1664. by me. Christophe^r Palmer marshall gen Deputy.

The aboue sajd lands were prized at the prizes aboue sajd by us.

Tho. Wiggin. John Stanion

Entred & Recorded at Request of Israel Wight 5th December 1664

p Edward Rawson Record.

NOTE.

This case of Wight v. Walderne began in the County Court held at Salisbury and came finally to the Court of Assistants. In Court Files, Suffolk, No. 764, the first paper is a copy of the writ, which sets out the grounds of the action, and is as follows: —

To the Marshall of Hampton or his Deputy

You are hereby required in his Maties name to attach ye goods or for want y^r of ye body of Capt Richd Waldern & take bond of him to ye value of fifty pounds, with sufficienty surety suretyes for his appearance at ye next County Court to be held at Salisbury ye 2^d tuesday of the p^resent mo^th then & there to answer ye Complaint of Israel Weight in an acco͞n of ye case for with holding ye estate of ye s^d Israel Weight ye wch estate was Co͞mitted to or receiued by ye sd Capt Waldern for

ye use & in ye behalfe of ye s^d Israell Weight, in ye time whilst ye s^d Capt Waldern was guardjan for y^e s^d Israel Weight & for just damage & so make a true returne here of under yor hand Dated y^e 5th of y^e 2^d 1664 per Curiã

Sam[ll] Dalton

This is a true Copie Compd with y^e Originall As Attests Tho: Bradbury rec

Vera Copia Attests Edw: Rawson Secreet

$5:2^{mo}:64$

By virtue hereof I doe assigne Tho: Read my Lawfull Deputy to serue this Attachm̃t according to y^e tennor thereof

By me Abraham Drak Marshall
Vera Copia Attests Tho: Bradbury rec
Vera Copia Attests Edw: Rawson Secreet

This attachm̃^{t} was serued upon y^e Lands & boults belonging to Capt $Rich^d$ Waldern Lying in Quamscott Pattent this present day of Aprill being y^e 6th 1664

Per me Tho: Read Marshalls Deputy
This is a true Copie Per me Tho Bradbury rec
Vera Copia Attests Edw Rawson Secrey

Endorsed. the first Attachment of Land & bolts

Only fragments of the record in the Court of Assistants are to be found.

The second paper in No. 764 is a copy of the original execution issued out of the Court of Assistants; and the tenth is a copy of the "apprizement." These are not repeated here, as they appear in full in the copy above from the Registry of Deeds. The case gave rise to other litigation.

LIII.

[Court Files, Suffolk, No. 26760.]

Beleiffe Gridley of Boston yow are Indicted by the name of Beleiffe Gridley for not hauing the feare of God before your eyes & Instigated by the divill did on or about the 17th of August Rayle agt & Revile yor naturall father by Calling him Ljar & Drunckard & holding vp yor fist agt him & most Diabollically Cursing [yourself] & wishing you might be damned in hell if you did not burne your fathers house that night wth other desperate & diabollicall speeches as by the euidences against yow will & may appeare. Contrary to the peace of our Soueraigne Lord the king his Crowne & dignity & the knowne wholesome lawes of this Jurisdiction here established.*

Wee ffind this bill and leaue it to
the farther triall of this honered Cooart
Edward Porter
in the behalfe of the rest

† The prisoner pleaded not Guilty
sajd he would be trjed by the Jury.

[Court Files, Suffolk, No. 649.]

Jurys Verdict in the Case of Beleue Gridly

Wee find him Guiltie of many diabolicall expressions and Cursing him self in a high nature as allso reuiling and vnnatturally reproching his father by Calling of him lyer and drunkerd and drunken sot as allso Lifting vpp his fist against him with horible wishes Against him self if hee did not burne his fathers house about his ears: allso reproching the name of god by profaine swering as allso vnnatturall kicking his sister vppon the belly to her great hazzard and dainger: Vnherd of wickednesses in this place but according to the Indictment and euidences wee doe not find him Guiltie of the breach of any Cappitall Law and wee Leaue him to the farther sentenc ofthe honoured bench

Richard Cooke in the
behalf of the rest

[9]: September 1664

~~Considering ofthe Heynousnes of his Crime~~

The Court Judgeth it meete to sentenc him for his Reviling & vnnaturall reproaching his father & his horrible Cursing himself to be whipt wth thirty fiue stripes seuerely to be layd on & to stand on the pillory on the next lecture day presently after lecture for one whole hower wth a paper fixt on his breast by the Marshall Generall his hands bound down to [ye] pillory wth this Inscription in Capitol letters

This is for Reviling & vnnaturall reproaching of his naturall father & most desparate Cursing of himself.

E R S‡

* To here is in Rawson's hand.

† This is in Rawson's hand.

‡ This paper is endorsed in Rawsons' hand, "Virdict of ye Jury agt Beleife Gridley"

LIV.

[Court Files, Suffolk, No. 651.]

In Ans[r] to the petition of Sarah Helwis & on pervsall ofthe oathes of Richard Hoskins & Elisabeth Browne Affirming that Edward Helwis late a priuate souldjer in the Tower, now serjant to a foot Company in Ireland was lawfully married to the aboue mentioned Sarah daughter to m[r] Willjam Hauthorne of Salem in New England. and that since the sajd Helwis marrjed another woeman (although his former wife Sarah Haythorne is yet liuing) and wth in these two years last past he had a child by the woeman he last marrjed which the sajd Helwis owned to them and that both the woman. which he last marrjed & child which he had by hir are at this time both liuing at Westminster as is testified by Walter Littelton one ofthe masters in chancery the 7th day of Aprill 1663. Refference thereto being had may Amply appeare

The Court Judgeth it meete to declare that the sajd Sarah Helwis is at liberty to marry wth any other man & is freed from hir former husband. 9: Septemb 1664 E. R. S.

LV.

[Court Files, Suffolk, No. 1372, 11th paper.]

Att a court of Assistants held at Boston 7th of March 1664*

The accõn of y[e] town of Hampton: John Redman in their behalfe plaint[f]: Ag[t]: Nath[ll]: Boulter Defend[t]: entred att y[e] last court of Assistants in Septemb[r] & contineued by order of this Court† came now to be tried by consent of parties proued on y[e] oathes of Jn[o] Samborn & Jn[o]: Redman vide: oath on file Aftér y[e] Courts Judgment resons of Appeale & other evidences in ye case produced were read cõmitted to ye Jurie & are on file wth ye records of this Court The Jurie brought in their verdict: they found for ye defendent, confirming ye former Courts Judgm[t] & costs of Courts fower pound three shillings & two pence.

This is a true Copie taken out of ye Courts book of records as attests Edward Rawson Secret

This is a true Copie of y[e] Copie now on file wth Salisbury Court Records (75) as attests Tho: Bradbury rec[r].

---

*1664–5.

†See above record of 6 Sept. 1664.

LVI.

[Court Files, Suffolk, No. 669, 12th paper and 17th paper.]

Att a Court of Asistants held at Boston 7th march 1664. Theoder Atkinson plaintiffe against Capt. John Willjams defendt. in ^ action of Appeale from the Judgment of the County Court in october last or November After the Courts Judgment & euidences in the Case produced wth the reasons of Appeale were read Comitted to the Jury & are on file wth the reccords of this Court the Jury brought in their virdict they found for the defendant seeing no cause to alter the former Judgment but confirme it wth Costs of Courts three pounds nineteen shillings & eight pence.

This is A true Copie taken out ofthe Courts booke of Records. as Attests Edw. Rawson Secret.

NOTE.

See above, XLVII., record of 1 March 1663–4. See also XC., XCII., CIV.

LVII.

[Court Files, Suffolk, No. 670.]

This Court being informed by Josiah Converse Constable of Wooborne that wthin a few days there hath beene two seuerall Generall Towne meetings in wooborn & at each meeting chojce hath binn made of select men & Constables differing one from ye other & objections agt either chojce hath binn made wch this Court sees not Cause to Inquire into but knowing how much it Concernes the peace of the Country that the Inhabitants of each Toune studdy & pursue ye ways of peace & loue This Court Judgeth it necessary to Advise that the present Constable Josiah Converse forthwith warne a due & full meeting of all persons quallified as the law directs to proceed to make a due & legall Chojce of Constables at least & select men: the former chojces being lajd aside yt so loue & peace may Continue amongst yew. not doubting of yor Readines herein to complie & Remajne

Your very lo: frends

Boston 10 march 1664 E. R. S.

Voted: In ye name & by order of ye Court of Assistants.

To: Josiah Convers Constable of wooborne to be Comunicated to ye Inhabitants of wooborn at their next Generall Toune meeting

LVIII.

[Court Files, Suffolk, No. 722, 6th paper.]

Att A Court of Asistants held at Boston 5th September 1665

Tho. Deane Atturney to Silvester Deane plaintiffe agt Theoder Atkinson defendt in an action tried at the last County Court & yt comes to this Court for trjall = After the Courts Judgment & all euidences in the Case produced were read Comitted to the Jury & are on file wth the reccords of this Court the Jury brought in their virdict they found for the defendt. the plaintiffs replevying the warehouse to be null & yt ye sd warehouse attached by the defendant shall remajne in the Custody of the law to answer the Judgment of the next County Court or other Court according to the Comon Course of lawe wth Costs of Courts. This is A true Copie as attests Edw: Rawson Recorder.

Vera Copia Attests Edw. Rawson Recorder.

Note.

The 3d paper in No. 722 is a copy of the judgment of the County Court referred to above and is as follows:

"At a Countie Court held at Boston 25th July 1665 Thomas Deane Atturney to Silvester Deane Plantiff agast. Theodore Atkinson defendt in a Replevin dated 12th march 1665, after ye Replevine was read with ye euidence in ye Case produced wch remaines on fyle wth ye Records of this Court ye Jury found for ye Plaintiff Costs of Court, the Magist. Refused ye verdict & so it falls to ye Court of Assistants in Course.

This is a true Copie taken out of ye Courts Records

As Attests Edw. Rawson Recordr."

The 5th paper in No. 722 is a copy of the writ of replevin with the return and bond. The return on the writ is as follows: —

"I have replevied the Goods debts houses or other estate of Silvester Deane to the value of fower score pounds whither in the hands of Thomas Deane Atturney of ye sd Silvester Deane or otherwise now Attached by Theoder Atkinson senr of Boston this 12 of May 1665. Per me Richrd Wayte marshall."

The remaining twenty-three papers consist of copies of writs and returns, records of the County Court at Boston, reasons of appeal, and answers to the same, bonds, letters, accounts, depositions, and other papers relating to this case of Deane v. Atkinson.

LIX.

[Court Files, Suffolk, No. 815, 5th paper.]

"To Edward Michelson Marshall Generall or his deputy Yo^{w} are hereby Required in his Majestjes name to Deliuer quiet & peaceable [possession] unto Thomas Diar ‖Atturney to ye Towne‖ of Weimouth ‖& in their behalfe‖ of the thirty sixe acres of land being [now] possessed by James Louill of sajd Weimouth and also levy on the goods of the sajd James Louill to the value of fower pounds nine shillings & fower [pence] & deliuer the same to the sajd Thomas Diar Atturney aforesajd together wth 2^{s} for [ ] in satisfaction of a Judgment Granted him by the Court of Assistants [ ] the 5th of September last 1665 ag^{t} the sajd James Louill hereof [fail not] Dated at Boston the 12th of May 1666.

By ye Court Edw. Rawson Sec^{y}."

NOTE.

See below for review of this case, writ dated Aug. 26 1667, No. 815, 6th paper.

(6th paper) "To Thomas Dier of Waymouth

You are in his majesties name required to appeare as a Selectman of the towne of waymouth & in the sayd tounes behalfe at the next Court of assistants to be held at boston vpon the third day of September next then and there to answer the Complaint of James Louell in an action of Review to the vallue of fifty pounds of an appeale and Judgment thereon giuen at a Court of Assistants that was held at boston vpon the fifth day of September in the yeare 1665 which sayd action was betweene Thomas Dyer as Attorney to the Selectmen of the Towne of Waymouth and in ye Sayd Townes behalfe as plaintife and James Lovell defendant and hereof you are not to fayle at your perill Dated this 26 day of August 1667

By the Court Daniell Cushing"

There are in all forty-three papers in group No. 815, touching this case of Dyer Attorney to the town of Weymouth v. Lovell, made up of copies of records of the County Court in Boston, writs and returns thereon, summonses, reasons of appeal and answers to the same, of records of town meetings in every month, orders of the town laying out lots therein, town records, deeds, records of the General Court, and numerous depositions.

Mass. Records, Vol. IV., Part 2, p. 375, 27 May 1668.

"In the case of James Louel, plaintiff, ag^{t} Thomas Dyar, defendt, & the selectmen of Weymouth, coming to this Court by the sajd Lovel his peticon, after the Court had heard & considered all the euidences in the case produced, they found for the defendt, Thomas Dyar, confirmation of the judgments of the former Courts of Asistants, and order the marshall generall forthwith to giue him, the sajd Dyar, againe full & peaceable possession of the sajd thirty sixe acres of land, wth the costs of this Court for hearing the case five pounds, fifty shillings for each house, & grant the defendt thirty eight shillings & eight pence."

LX.

[From the County Court Papers (Exeter, N.H.), 1681–2, folio 229, now deposited in the State Archives at Concord, N.H.]

To Edward Michelson. M^r^shall Generall or his dep^ty^ These req^r^ you in his Majs^ties^ Name to Levy by way of Execution on the Goods or person of Capt. Wm Davis (that undert[ooke] & engaged the charges wth damages recorded ag^t^ J^no^ Kenniston in behalf of Capt. Thomas Clarke & Mr. Paddy's Interest) the sume of Nine Pounds, fourteen shillings & six pence & deliver the same wth two shillings for this execution to phillip Lewis in behalf of himself. Nathaniel [ffryer] & Henry Langstar & is in satisfaction of a Judgement granted y^m^ for so much by ye Court of Assistants, held at Boston the 7th of September 1665.

By ye Court Edward Rawson, Secrty

Vera Copia out of ye records of ye quat^ly^. Court held in Portsmouth 7th Decemb 1680.*

LXI.

[From the Chamberlain Collection at the Boston Public Library.]

Deliuerance french the daughter of Thomas Chubb & wife of J^no^ french is Indicted by the name of Deliuerance french for not having the feare of God before hir Eyes: & Instigated by the Divill hath in hir husbands absenc ‖he living‖ comitted Adultery & broken hir marriage couenant & hath had a base child since hir husbands departure ‖as Appeares by hir oune confession‖: Contrary to the peace of our Soueraigne Lord the King his croune & dignity: & the wholesome lawes of this Jurisdiction in this case provided as Appeare in law book page 8:†

---

* See Mass. Col. Records, Vol. IV., Part II., pp. 84, 447, 455.

† This is in the handwriting of Edward Rawson.

We find this bill against Deliũance ffrench wife of John ffrench
James Euerill in the name of the rest

Wee finde the sd prisoner not Guilty of the inditem[t]:
John Saffin in the name of the Rest:

[Endorsed by Secretary Rawson] Deliũnc french[s] Indictm[t]
Sept. 65. Ent.

LXII.

[Essex County Court Files, Vol. XIV., Fol. 112, "Godfrey *v.* Elah, June, 1669."]

Att A Court of Asistants held at Boston 6th march 1665.*

John Godfrey being bound ouer to this Court by the County Court in January last in Boston on the Complaint & accusation of Job Tyler & John Rimington on suspition of witchcraft, the said Job Tyler & John Rimington being also bound ouer to prosecute against the sajd John Godfrey sumons for wittnesses being granted out & many appeared Edw: yeomans Robert Swanne Mathias Butten willjam Symons & John Rimmington deposed in Court that whateuer euidence either of them shall give into the Grandjury in relation to John Godfrey shall be the truth, whole truth, & nothing but the truth, & divers others wth them being sworne in Court before & against the prisoner wch are on file John Godfrey being brought to the barr it was declared that the Grand Jury had found him guilty & putting him on tryall for his life = The Jury was impannelled the sajd John Godfrey holding vp his hand at the barre, he was Indicted by the name of John Godfrey of Newbery for not having the feare of God before yo[r] eyes did or haue Consulted wth a familiar spirit, & being instigated by the divill haue donne much hurt & mischeife by seuerall acts of witchcraft to the bodjes & goods of seuerall persons as by seuerall evidences may appeare contrary to the peace of ou[r] Soueraigne Lord the King his Crowne & dignity and the wholesome lawes of this Jurisdiction. To which he pleaded not guilty & referred himself for his triall to God & the Country: The seuerall euidences produced against the prisoner being read Comitted to the Jury & remajne on file wth the reccords of this Court the Jury brought in their virdict i.e. wee finde him not to haue the feare of God in his heart he haue made himself ^ to vs. being suspitiously Guilty of witchcraft. but not legally

* 1665–6.

guilty. according to lawe & euidence wee haue receaved = y^{s} virdict was accepted & party discharged =

It is ordered that the Treasurer of the Country dischardg the charge of the [witnesses] in the Case of John Godfry to value of sixe days allowanc per each witnes & make it vp to y^{t} value: only the two prosecutors Job Tyler & Jno Rimington shall be allowed for eleuen dayes a peece two shillings per each day a peece & that the said John Godfrey discharge the Costs of the trjall to the Treasurer of the Country & stands Comitted till he performe this order & then to be dischardged. That this is A true Copie taken out of the Court of Asistants reccords Attests Edw. Rawson Secret.

[This paper is endorsed "Godfrey ag^{t} Elah in the action of Slander."]

NOTE.

On the same paper with the Court of Assistants record 6 March 1665–6, Essex County Court Files, Vol. XIV., folio 112, is a copy of a sentence of the County Court at Boston Jan. 28, 1667–8 against John Godfrey on complaint for stealing.

The case in which the paper appears is a complaint of John Godfrey against Daniel Elah "in an action of defamation for reporting that he ye said Godfery, was seene at Ipswich, & at Salisbury, at the same time viz: the first daye of the last Salisbury Court," the writ of attachment being dated "10: 4mo 1669" There is also in the case a copy of the sentence against Godfrey by the County Court at Salisbury 13: 2^{d}. m^{o}. 1669 for "his wicked & most pernicious subborning witnesses," etc. Also copy from the record of that court that "John Godfery did own in Court y^{t} his dwelling or vsuall aboade is at one ffrancis Skerries in Salem." There are also copies of record of the County Court at Ipswich showing that Godfrey had been convicted of drunkenness and of cursing. There are several depositions, some testifying that Godfrey was seen at Salisbury and some that he was seen at Ipswich on the same day.

The writ, records and depositions here mentioned, 1665–6, and the warrants to constables of Haverhill and Andover to summon witnesses to Court of Assistants in Boston on the first Tuesday in March 1665–6, are given in full in this note.

"At a county Court held at Salem the 29: June 1669, John Godfery plt: agast: Daniell Elah deft: in an action of defamation &c: accor: to atach^{t}: da: 10: 4: 69 the Jury find for the deft: costs of Court: 39^{s}–6^{d}." The following are the papers on file in this case:—

First paper:—

"To the marshall of Salem or his deputy or the constable of Hauerill or his deputy

You are required in his majesties name to atach the body or goods of Daniell Elah, & take bond of him to the value of one hundred pounds with sufficient security for his apearance at the next County Court held at Salem the last tuesday of this instant month then & there to answer the complaint of John Godfery in an action of defamation, for reporting, that he ye said Godfery, was seene at Ipswich, & at Salisbury, at the same time viz: the first daye of the last Salisbury Court & heare of make returne dated: 10: 4mo 1669

ꝑ the Court Hilliard Veren."

[On the back]

"This ataichment sarved on a[bout] ten akeres of vpland and medo liuen [lying ?] with thin fines [fence ?] by the sid of the great pond a bout to myeles frome the twon [town ?] as all so on the body and band taken for his a perenes

by me Thomas Whittier Constabell of hauerell the 14 of Juen 1669"

Second paper: —

"Att the Court held at Ipswich this 30 of march 1669 John Godfry vpon his presentmt. for being Drunke It being proved is fined ten shillings and to pay costs & fees

Vera copia out of the Record taken the 28 of June 1669 ꝑ me Robert Lord Cleric.

Att the Court held at Ipswich the 30 of march 1669 John Godfry vpon his presentmt. of this Court for curssing speeches, which confest is fined ten shillings & to pay fees of Court

Vera copia out of the Record taken the 28 of June 1669

ꝑ me Robert Lord Cleric."

Third paper: —

"Att ye County Court held at Salisbury ye 13: 2d mo. 69. John Godfrey for his wicked & most ꝑnicious subborning witnesses to ye ꝑverting of Justice both by himselfe & others by his instigating of them: sometimes by hindring ꝑsons from giueing evidence & sometimes to giue false evidence as doth fully appeare by many testimonies now on file wth this Courts records: This Court for these horrible & destructiue crimes doth sentence him to pay one hundered pound as a fine to ye County & to stand vpon ye pillerie ye space of one hower wth this inscription written in Cappitall letters vpon a paper fastned vpon him: viz: in these words: (John Godfrey for subborning witnesses) & this is to bee putt in Execution vpon ye next lecture day at Salisbury neare ye meeting house & hee is vtterly disabled frō giueing euidence in any case hereafter: vnles hee bee restored by Authority: & to pay costs & to stand cōmitted to prison vntill this sentence bee ꝑformed in all respects:

This is a true Copie out of ye Courts booke of Records

as attests Tho: Bradbury rec."

Fourth paper: —

"Daniel Elas bill of Cost in the case of John Godfray that he cals Defamation or Slandor

for eight sum̃onses and taking them out at the Clarks	00–02– 0
for goeing to Salisbery to tak out records and seruing witnes 2 dais and on witnes sworn	00–03– 0
for goeing to boston for witnes and records four dais	00–06– 0
for 2 dais goeing to serue witneses at Ipswich	00–04– 0
for records taken out	00–04– 6
for 3 witneses sworn before m^{r} bradstrets worship	00–03– 0
for 3 witnes sworn before m^{r} Simons his worship	00–03– 0
for 2 witneses sworn before the worshipful magor Dineson	00–02– 0
for myne owne atendans 5 dais	00–10– 0
for one witnes sworn before the ~~Gou^{r}nours Honour~~	~~00–01– 0~~
	01:17: 6
filing euedences	00:02:00
	01:19: 6"

Fifth paper: —

"Att ye County Court held att Salisbury ye 13th: 2^{d} m^{o} 69 John Godfery did own in Court y^{t} his dwelling or vsuall aboade is at one ffrancis Skerries in Salem: —

This is a true Copie out of ye Courts booke of records as attests

Tho: Brradbury rec."

Sixth paper: —

"The Depocisions of Andrew Grele & Abraham Whiticker whoe Testifieth and saith that wee heard Daniell Ela say that John Godfrey was seine at Ipswich and at Salusbuery at both places at on time the furst day of Salusbuery Court last past as he heard at Ipswich

taken vpon oath 15.4.69

before mee Simon Bradstreet,"

On the back is written in Bradstreet's hand "ffor the Clerke of the Court att Salem"

Seventh paper: —

"Att A County Court held at Boston the 28th of January 1667. John Godfrey being bound ouer to this Court to answer for his stealing of beavar skinns and a beavar Cap and other things out of m^{r} Edmond Dounes his warehouse belonging to Stephen Serjant the said Steven Sarjant being also bound ouer to prosecute against him = the partjes appeared the said Godfrey desired the liberty of a Jury wch was granted him = and After the mittimus and the euidences in the case produced were read comitted to the Jury and are remayning on file with the reccords of this Court the Jury brought in theire virdict they found him guilty of the fact lajd to his charge i : e stealing seven beavar skinns and a beavar Cap and a shirt. The Court sentenct him to pay treble damages i.e. three pounds ten shillings in tenn pounds of the beavar wth the Cap returned. so that he is to make good eight pounds and that he pay a fine to the County of five pounds or be whipt wth fiueteen stripes dischardging the fees of the Court standing comitted till the sentence be performed. John Godfry Appealed from the sentenc of this Court to the next Court of Asistants and for want of security was returned to the prison againe.

That what is aboue written is a true Copie of the Courts Judgment or sentenc against John Godfrey taken out of the County Courts booke of Reccords

Attests Edward Rawson Recorder"

[On the same paper is the Judgment of the Court of Assistants 6 March, 1665, given above.]

Eighth paper: —

"Abiell Som̄erby aged 28 yeares

This deponent testifyeth that he being at Salsbery Court heard James Ordway & one or two more say that they would haue bin bound for John Godfry If the Judge of the Court had not said, if he were gone ~~into the farthest part of Newengland~~ we would haue him brought back againe in Chaynes or Irons. and John Godfry was pleading with the Court to take his owne bond for his appeal in Buttons action, and he would haue all his writings fetcht, and they should be left in the Courts hands. and the Judg of the Court made answer. wee shall not take a thousand pound bond in this c[ase] then the voyce of the people that stood by was that there should be no bond taken for him [which] did discourag those that was intended to be bound for him

Abiel Som̄erby

Peter Godfry aged 38 yers can euidence all aboue written

Peter Godfry

James Ordway aged about 45 years testifyeth to all abouesaid. & further saith that he intended to be bound for him freely but the matter was made so odious by the Court that afterward John Godfry offered twenty pounds to him to be bound but he would not. & further this deponent saith that the Judg of the Court said, he did beleiue that no man will haue the face to appeare in this case to be bound for him

James Ordway

Sworne before me by James Ordway
June 21 1669

Daniel Denison"

Ninth paper: —

"The deposision of John Griffing aged 28 yeares testifieth & saith that being at the hous of Stephen Swett of Newbery the last winter was twelue month I did then and their see John Godfray goeing towards newbery meting hous at which tyme John Godfray was in boston prison as I was informed by John Godfray himself ‖ about 2 months after ‖ I doe further testifie that I saw John Godfray the first night of Salsbery Court last at the hous of John Seaurans at Salsbery and many tyms mor at the sam Court other days and further that John Godfray told me this deponent that he was not at Ipswich any tym that weke of the Court at Salsbery I further testifie that about seauen years agoe the last winter John Godfray and this deponent went ouer meraymak riuer on the ice to goe to And[ouer] Godfray on fote and this deponent on hors back and the hors was as good a one as aure he rid on and when I was at goodman Geag his feild I saw John Godfray in the same feild a letel befor me this deponent but when I had rid a letel furder not sein Godfray nor any track at al and it was at a tym when their had falen a midlin snow ouer night and not seing him nor his steps I rune my hors al the way to And[ouer]; and the first hous I cam into at And[over] was goodman rusts hous and when I cam in I see John Godfray siting in the corner and goode rust told me that he had bene their so long as that a maid that was in the hous had maid cleane a kettel and hung on peas and pork to boyle for Godfray and the peas and pork was ready to boyl and the maid was skiming the ketel.

taken vpon oath. 22.4.69 before mee

Simon Bradstreete"

Tenth paper: —

"The deposition of Susana Roper aged about 5[3] saith that the second tewsday of Aprill last standing at the dore of my owne house I saw John Godfry goeing along in the street toward Rowley my two daughters being present & one of them speaking & saying ther is Godfry he turned his face towards the dore & I spake to my daughters & sayd I wonder Godfry was heere now being Salsbury Court daye and the reason I tooke the more notice of him was because I heard he was to be at Salsbury Court this being about the middle of the affternoon that day

Taken vpon oath June 24th 1669

before me Samuel Symonds"

Eleventh paper: —

"The deposition of Robert Lord Marshall aged about 37 yeres

This deponent testifieth that I being at Salsbery Courte to waight vpon the worshipfull m^r Symonds saw John Godfry at Salsber[y] in Cornitt Sevorances hous about twelve of the clocke the first day of the Courte: & so euery day of the Court ocasionally & [lefte] the sd Godfry ther at Salsbery at the end of the Courte when we came home: & further saith not:

Sworne before me

June 24, 69 Daniel Denison"

Twelfth paper: —

"The deposision of Rob[t] Pike aged 52 year or ther about

This deponent sayth y[t] att ye last County Court held att Salusbury he see John Godfry att the house of goodman[s] Severanc in Salsbury and in the forenoon of that day being tusday he the sd Godfry and this deponent had a long discours to gather vpon the head of the stayrs at ye sd Severanc his hous conserning an action which this deponent had against the sd Godfry in which this deponent ꝑmised the sd. Godfry not to enter it: if the sd Godfry woold do w[t] the sd deponent desired him to do: (but he did it not) and therfor this deponent entered his action att noon to save dubl entry having wayted for his answer all the fore noone also farther testifys that he saw the sd Godfry ther every day of the sd Court and when the Court ended and farther sayth not

Deposed in the p[r]senc god whom I cale to wittnes to the truth therof this 15 of y[e]: 4: m[o] 1669

by me Rob[t] Pike Comiss." *

Thirteenth paper: —

"Elizabeth buton aged 47 yers or their about saith about 4 or 5 wekes after Salsbery Court last my daughter Saray being in the hous and it being a rayne tyme she and I sat together in a bed by the fire sid about twelue or one a clok their was a great noys about the hous which this deponent tok to be the catel but when she was a wak she saw a shap of a man and sit in a great chare and being a great fire nere the bed and nere the chare within a yard and a half I saw Godfray siting and I would faine a struck him but could not put forth my hand and I did what I could to wak the maid that was in bed with me but could not for I could neither speak nor stire and thus he contenewed for the spas of tow ours I se him three or four tyms but as son as I had com to setel myself in the bed he vanashed away to my aprehension for he went strangly out and the dore was fast and when I ris in the mornin I went to the dore and it was fast bolted the tyme I saw Godfry was about 12 or one of the clock in the night.

taken vpon oath. 22.4.69.

before mee Simon Bradstreet"

Fourteenth paper: —

"The Depos[it]ion of Edward Cleark who saith that I heard Daniel Eli say that John Godfre was at Ipswich and at Salisburi boath at one tim the first day of Salisburi Court as he heard and further saith not

Edward Clarke

Sworne in Court at Salem 30: 4: 69

atestes Hilliard Veren Cleri[s]"

---

* This paper is wholly in the handwriting of Robert Pike.

Fifteenth paper: —

"The deposition of D[a]nill M[a]ning aged about 21 yeares

This deponant testifieth comeing along in the street nere our hous [I saw?] John Godfry comeing from Rowley words goeing into the Town: The [ ] day after goody Archer was Buryed about eleven or twelve of the [clock?]. The sd Godfry pased close by mee in the street: The same [ ] Goody Roper & hir daughters told me at night they saw Go[dfry] By their hous towards Rowly in the after none: & further sai[th not]

Taken upon oath before me

June 28 1669 Daniel De[nison]"

Sixteenth paper: —

"The deposition of Sarah Roper & Elizabeth Roper

saith that vpon the middle of the afternoone on the second Tewsday of Aprill last we saw John Godfry goeing along the street toward Rowley & one of vs speakeing there is Godfry the sd Godfry turned his face towards the dore toward vs standing att our ffathers dore

Taken vpon oath June 24th. 1669

before me Samuel Symonds"

Court Files, Suffolk, Nos. 723 and 724, are Venires, Boston and Dorchester for Grand Jury and Jury of Trials at Court of Assistants at Boston, March 7, 1665–6.

Court Files, Suffolk, No. 725.

First paper: —

"Y^{ou} are hereby Required in his Majestjes name to [sum]mon & require mathias Button & sarah his daughter Edward yeomans & his wife Abraham whitacre & Elisabeth his wife Robert swan & Elisabeth his wife Abigaile Remington wife to John Rimington & John their sonne Joseph Johnson & the wife of w^{m} Holdrige Ephrajm Dauis willjam symons samuell symons & mary the wife of willjam Neaffe all of Hauerill to make their seuerall appearances before the next Court of Asistan^{ts} to be held at Boston on the first tuesday in march next at eight of the clock in the morning then & there to give in their particular & seuerall euidences what they know of & concerning John Godfry of Nubery being a witch or of any act of witchcraft done by him he being bound ouer to that Court in order to his triall on the Complaint of Job Tyler & John Rimington making y^{r} returne hereof to the Secretary at or before the time prefixed hereof yo^{u} are no^{t} to faile dated in Boston the 6th of february 1665

By order of the County Court sitting in Boston 4th febr. 1665.

Edw: Rawson Secre^{ty}"

[On the back is written.]

"Thi^{s} warent wa^{s} serued vpon each perticular person Acording to the tennor of it arest sarah butten and [ ] liues not in Hauerhill

by me George Browne Constable of Hauerhill."

Second paper : —

" To the Constable of Andiuer

You are hereby Required in his Majestjes name to sumon & require mr ffrancis Deane & Nathan Parker both of Andiuer to make their personall appearances before the next Court of asistants to be held in Boston on the first tuesday in march next then & there to give in their euidences what they know of & Concerning John Godfry of Newbery being [a] witch or of any act of witchcraft donn by him [ ] bound ouer to that Court in order to his trjall on the Co[mplaint] of Job Tyler & John Rimington making your Returne to the Secretary at or before the time prefixed hereof you are not to faile Dated in Boston the 6th of february 1665

By order of the County Court sitting in Boston 5th febr. '65

Edw Rawson Secrety"

[On the back is written.]

" this warant was servd apon mr dane and nathan parker the 22 of the 12 month 65

by me Tho Johnson Constabel"

Seventh paper : —

" the testimony of Nathan Parker 44 years

John godfry Cam in to my hous and discosinge of Jobe tiler godfry said that he Could aford to blowe on tiler and not leaue him worth a grat

Deposd in Court 7 march 65 E R S."

Twelfth paper : —

" I Joseph Johnson of hauerill being about 27 yers of age went two Joh remintons and ther was John godfree and good man buten and I herd John godfree say that if John remintons son was a man as hee was a boy it had bin worser for him

Sworne In Court 7 March 65

As Attests E R S."

Thirteenth paper : —

" The Deposition of willm Howard Aged about 56 yeeres

[ ] Deponant witneseth that about 26 yeers agoue he goeing vpon [New]bery plaine towards hampton he ther spoak with a man that was following of Cattle, who sayd he had bin m̃ spencers prentice & his time was then out (or neer out) & he then discovered that he wanted a servis : & this Deponant did then Contract with yt pty to serue him for a Considerable time (but how longe yt time was this Deponant haue forgott) But he doth rememƀ that he did give him a peece of money in part of payment & as this Deponant doth suppose he did then wright the agreement : wch sd ꝑson was like John godfery & as I suppose he [di]d ‖then‖ name himself by that name : & further this Deponant sayth not

[sw]orne In Court 7 March 65 E R S"

Fourteenth paper: —

"The Depocishon of John Reminton

This deponant Testifieth that I herd John Godfry saie to my father that if he drived the Cattell vp the wods to winter then my ffather shod say and haue cas to repent that he did drive them vp and thes words he said in a great rage and Pashon and of [ ] this my father and I did drive vpe the cattell and I for the most part did tend them: and about the midell of Desember last as I was a coming home from the cattell about a Mille from them: then the Hors I rid on begun to start and snort and the Dog that was with me begun to whine and cry and it still I Mad a shift to sit on the horse still for a matter of a quarter of a mill and then I smelt a sweet smill like seder and presently I lockt vp in to the swamp and I se a crow come to wards me flying and percht vpon a tre against mee and she lock at me and the horse and Doge and it had a veary great and quicke Ie and it had a veary great bill and then the sd crow flew of that tre to a nother after mee then I begune to mistrust and thinke it was no crow and thought if it was not a crow it could not hurt my soule though it hurt my body and Horse and as I was a thinkeing thus to my selfe the hors I was vpon fell down [v]pon on sid in pain growne vpon my lege and as sone as I [ ] the Horse was fallen then the crowe came and flewe Round me severall times as if she would lite vpon mee but she ~~should~~ did not Tuche me then the hors ris and went about fower Rod and then stod still and I lay on the ground still and was not abell to follow hime for the Present then when I came a litell [be]tter to my selfe I mad a shift to cripe on my hands and ‖knes‖ the hors and the crowe scre[ ]d and made a noise like a catt and the hollowing of a man then I gott vpon the hors and went on then the crowe apeared to me sometimes a great Crow and sometimes like a littell burd and soe continued with mee about a Mill and a halfe furder and she flewe vpon the doge and bete hime to the last all this whill after I fell withe the horse I was tacken veary sicke and thought I should haue died tell such time the crow left me and then the doge mad on me and rejoyest very much after the crow left vs: and then the Second day *fowling* I being at home John Godfry cam to my fathers hous in a great Rage and aske of me how I did and I toulled hime prety well only I was lame withe the hors falling on me too days befor then said Godfry every Cockating boy must rid I unhorst on boy tother day I will unhors the shortly ‖to‖ if the Rids my Hors then said I I am not abell to carre vettols vpon my back then said Godfry tis a sorre hors cannot carre his ow provendar then said Godfry to me John if the hads ben a man as the wast a boy the hads died on the spott whar the gott the fall then said my Mother to godfry howe canest the tell that thar is non but god can tell that and except the be more then a ordnary man the canest not tell that then godfry bed my mother hould her tungue he knew what he sed better then she and said I say agen had he bin [a man] as he was a boy he had died on the spott whare he fell."

[In the margin is written.]

"Godfry saith that he know^{s} not y^{t} he sajd if he had bin a man [as he was a] boy he had died y^{t} he had knowledge of [ ] ye boy

E R S

y^{s} was đđ in on his oath in y^{s} Cour^{t} 7 : March 16 [ ] S."

"The Depocishon of Abigell Reminton

This Deponant Testifi[eth] that John godfry came to our Hous the beginning of winter and said to my husban that if he drove the Cattell vp to the wods to winter then my Husban should haue cas to say and repente that he did drive them vp and thes words he said in a great rage and Pashon then after this the Second day after my son John was lame with the fall of the hors vpon hime John Godfry came to my hous and asked my son John how he did in a veary great Rage and John mad answer prety well only he was lame with the hors falling on hime too days before then sd godfry eveary Cockating boy must rid I vnhorst on boy tother day and I will vnhors the shortle to if the Rids my hors then said John I ame not abell to carrey my vettels on my back then said Godfry tis a sorre hors cannot Carre his own provendar then said Godfry to John : John if the hads ben a man as the wast a boy the hads died on the Spot whar the gott the fall Then said I to godfry how canst the tell that: thar is non but god can tell that: and except the best mor then a ordnary man the canst not tell that then Godfry bed me hould my tungue he knew better what he sed then I : and said : I say againe had he bine a man as he was a boy he had died on the spot whar he fell.

Abigall Remintun her marke"

"The deposiscion of mathias Button

This deponant testifieth comeing into the house of John Reminton tow dayes after that John Reminton son being hurt with a fall of a hors : seeing him ly in the chimny corner asking him how he did his answer was to me that he had a fall of a hors : which hurt his leg godfre being thar mad answer and said to John and saide if thou hadst ben a man thou hadst dyed upon the spot whar he fell but seing he was a boy he scaped the horse thes words was spoken by John godfrey tow or [three] times ouer : this was deliuered in by Mathias Button on his oath tooke in Court 7 March 1665

E R S"

There are fourteen papers in No. 725 but no record of the Court of Assistants appears among them.

See also LXIII., Chandler *v.* Tyler and LXXVII., Godfrey *v.* Remington and wife.

Court Files, Suffolk, No. 28949, Tiler *v.* Godfrey is a mutilated fragment.

LXIII.

[Mass. Archives, Vol. 39, Fol. 238.]

Att A Court of Asistants held at Boston the 6th of march 1665*

Thomas Chandler plaintiffe agt Job Tyler Defendt in an action of appeale from the Judgment of the County Court at Cambridge. After the Attachment Courts Judgment Reasons of Appeale & other euidences in the Case produced were read Comitted to the Jury & remajne on file wth the Reccords of this Court the Jury brought in their virdict they found for the Defendt Confirmation of the former Judgment & Costs of Courts — the magistrates Refused this virdict & so it falls to the Generall Court in Case — That this is A true Copie taken out of the Courts book of Reccords Attests

Edw: Rawson Secrety.

Note.

[This case was an appeal from the County Court at Cambridge Oct. 3, 1665. The General Court, at the May Session, 1667, confirmed the judgment of the County Court. See Mass. Col. Records, IV., Part II., p. 340.]

Mass. Records, Vol. IV., Part 2, p. 326, 10 Oct. 1666.

"In answer to the petition of Job Tyler, of Roxbury, humbly desiring the favour of this Court to grant him a hearing of his case betweene him & Thomas Chandler, the Court, considering of his peticon, in regard of the shortnes of the Courts continuance in this present session, it is ordered, that the peticoner haue his cause heard at the next Court of Election, & that in the interim, Thomas Chandler haue Notice thereof, & by order from the secretary be oblidged to attend the issuing thereof, provided that the peticoner then bring the case."

Same, p. 340, 15 May 1667. "In the case now depending betweene Job Tyler & Thomas Chandler, coming to this Court by reason of disagreement betweene bench & jury at the Court of Asistants, the Court, hauing heard all the euidences & pleas of both partjes, & duely considered thereof, confirme the judgment of the County Court held at Cambridge, October 3d, 1665, i.e. forty three pounds, & two pounds eight & sixpence costs; the payment made by the plaintiff, in prt of ye purchase, thirty eight pounds, to be returned him by ye defendt in kind & bill, for thirty pounds giuen by the plaintiff, to be returned & made null, costs of ye Court & fower pounds seuenteen & six penc."

Same, p. 351, 9 Oct. 1667. "In answer to the information & request of Job Tyler, the Court judgeth it meete to grant him liberty to try any action or actions he hath agt Thomas Chandler in any of our County Courts, in forma pauperis, till he hath brought them to their legall issue."

---

*1665–6.

Same, p. 387, 27 May, 1668. "In answer to the petition of Job Tyler, the Court, having pervsed his petition & other writings, declare that the case should propperly haue gonne to the Court of Asistants, wch being neglected in its season, yet a hearing there may best satisfy the persons concerned, & doe therefore referr the peticoner thither"

See also LXII.

LXIV.

[Court Files, Suffolk, No. 730, 7th paper.]

I[n th]e Action of Apells James Evrell plaintif against Mr Symon Bradstret [Esq.] defendant we find for the defend[ant] Cos of Courts (or confirmation of the [former Judg]ment

[Blank space]

In the Action of Apels Jams Evrell plaintif against Mr Symon Bradstret Esq. we find for the defendant we a bat of the former Judgment all but 30li which is to be paid ‖in a months time‖ in Current money of New England [by] the plaintif to the defendant ‖with Cost of Corts‖ & so the defendant to deliver in all morg[ag] b[on]ds or bills & to discharge all debts & dues concerning this case [from the] first deling to the paiment of the money with Costs of Courts

Note.

These two verdicts were written on the same paper which was sealed up and directed "To the Honorable Court now sitting at Boston." It appears from the other papers in the case, No. 730, that these two actions of appeal related to the same subject matter and were tried together at the session of the Court of Assistants in March 1665–6. The question at issue was whether certain payments on account of a mortgage given by Everell to Bradstreet amounted to full satisfaction of the debt. At the Suffolk County Court, Oct. 1665, Everell bringing an action against Bradstreet for "withholding his mortgage being satisfied," judgment was rendered "for the defendant Costs of Court." The plaintiff, Everell, appealed to the Court of Assistants, and it is to this appeal, no doubt, that the first of the two verdicts at the Court of Assistants refers. The other verdict at the Court of Assistants appears, in the same way, to refer to an action at the same Suffolk County Court by Bradstreet against Everell for "debt upon the case for breach of covenant or obligation conteyned in a writing or conditionall bill of sale bearing date 5th. June, 1652, &c." The judgment in this action at the County Court was for the defendant, Bradstreet, "eighty nine pounds fiue shillings damage & costs of court" being the judgment abated by the Court of Assistants to 30li with costs of courts.

The following records of the General Court relate to this case: —
Mass. Col. Records, Vol. IV., Part II., p. 326 — Oct. 1666.

"In ansr to the peticon of James Euerell, the Court judgeth it meete to refer his declaration, now in Court, wth his peticon, to the consideration of such a meeting of a Generall Court, for answer, as shall intervene betweene this & the next Generall Court of Election, (in case there be any,) or otherwise to the said next Generall Court of Election."

Same, p. 349 — Oct. 1667.

"In the case now depending betweene James Euerell, plaintiffe, by peticon to this Court, & Mr Symon Bradstreet, defendant, this Court, hauing heard & spent much tjme in examination of the accounts & debate of the case, doe find for the plaintiffe the sume of thirty five pounds fiue shillings & sixe pence in money, & costs of this Court, twelve pounds twelve shillings & eight pence."

Same, p. 376 — May 1668.

"In ansr to the peticon of Mr Symon Bradstreet, the Court judgeth it meete to grant him a hearing ofthe case between himself & James Euerell, at the next sessions of this Court, on the first Wednesday after the begining of yt session, & notice to be given to the defendant accordingly."

No further proceedings appear on record, and we may infer therefrom that the case was settled by agreement between the parties.

The judgment in this action was for the plaintiff, Bradstreet, "eighty nine pounds fiue shillings damage & costs of court." The consideration named in the mortgage deed was 150£ while the mortgage was conditioned upon the payment of 57£ 10s in the following March, 65£ in March 1653–4 and 72£ 10s in March 1654–5 making the sum of 195£ to be paid in all.

Everell in his plea, at the County Court, Oct. 1665, argues his case as follows "It is very considerable in the case that the obligation puteth a very sufficient advance vpon the money to call it no worse to put 45£ interest vpon 150£ [for] two yeares and nine moneths the which seems much more then the lawe allowes. especially considering that 122£ is to be pajd in one yeare and nine months. much more vnreasonable seemes it that yet the mortgage should remajne when 40£ of the money is taken of in a weekes time." To this Bradstreet answers, 31 Oct. 1665, as appears by the 4th paper in the case, which is a copy of the answer certified by Edward Rawson, Recorder: "I deny I lent him the money; but bought an Anuity for three yeares for the some of one hundred & fifty pounds in money as Appeares by the bill of sajle or mortgage:" As to the 40£ paid back "in a week's time" not being needed by Everell Bradstreet claims that it was taken by agreement as part payment of the first instalment, and that there then remained 17$^{£}$ 10^{s} of that instalment to be paid in March, 1652–3, "which yet he fayled to pay: the next payment that I could receiue of him (notwthstanding all my calling vpon him) to mind his engagement was 8$^{£}$ (1) (4) 55. more then a yeare after the last payment should haue binn made. if Goodm̄. Everill will not owne this the most that can be made of it is that I had 40$^{£}$ of his in my hands from 13th: 4th. 52 till the 1th of march after (for then that & 17$^{£}$ 10^{s} more was due for wch. I am to allow as the lawe provides." Bradstreet acknowledges to have received in all 196$^{£}$: 17 : 10. including the 40$^{£}$. "If he alleadges any more to be payd he must prooue it for I know not of one shilling more, & hope the Court & Jury will consider the damage which I haue received for want of my money at the dayes & time according to agreement & the inconvenience & losse by receiving my money in such smale & broken somes as I could get it of him, & that so many yeares after it was due & giue me such satisfoction as the lawe allowes & reason requires in such a case; for I can truely say that considering the trouble I haue been put unto the many disapointments I haue mett withall & sufferings in my name, occasioned by his causeles speeches & reproaches, I had much better haue throwne a great part of my money into the sea, then to haue had anything to doe wth the plaintiffe."

The 17th and last paper in the case is Everell's "bill of charges" apparently upon the trial of the cause at the General Court, and is as follows: —

James Everills bill of Charges

for so much paide Mr Brodstrete by order of the Courte of asistant be side the 30^{lb} for dammeg and allso for his Charges and Cost 3^{lb}: 19^{s}: 8^{d}: in : 19 : 1 : 65 :	33^{lb} : 19^{s} : 8^{d}:
for my oune Charges at the County Courte in 65: and [for the Court] of asistants for enterring the Action [and] for my rittings and my on time in both Courtes	4^{lb}: 9 : 8
for my son maunings attendance on the Courtes 7 dayes	00 : 10 : 6
for my Petishon to the generall Court	00 : 10 : 0
for my Ritting to master Rawson	00 : 15 : 0
to M^{r} [Brow]ne for Rittings	00 : 10 : 0
to M^{r} [name illegible] for Rittings	00 : 03 : 6
for my oun attending at the generall Court 3 sessions 10 dayes	00 : 15 : 0
for [N]ickelise Phillips as a witnes on day	00 : 01 : 6
	41^{lb} : 14^{s} : 10^{d}

with my being alowed for being with out my [money] to this day my allowance according to [the cu]stom in the Country and order of Court

The other papers in No. 730, not here given, are copies of various matters in the County Court — records, pleadings, depositions, etc.

LXV.

[Suffolk Court Files, No. 726, 4th paper.]

"To the Hon[ble
The Petition of John Gifford [
H[umbl]y shewing [
obtained judgment the [last
to ye vallue of [1047 ?] pounds [
to Ex[ ]te ye sayd estate of [
which came to more by Sun [
exsicution amounted to [
: ward [ ] by Capt Breedo[n
is left remediless not [
[ ] all lyeing vnder [
according to Law. And that [
Carried out of his Studdy [
great C[once]rnment to you [
your petior not b[
himself, the Est[
favor ofthis hon[
desirous to [
be prevented
March : 7 : 65/66 :
In Ansr to this [petition
persons concerned [
ye Court would hear [
[ ] on 9th Instant [

NOTE.

This mutilated fragment is an original petition to the Court of Assistants, and the answer of the Court thereto, as clearly appears from internal evidence. In No. 726 there are three other papers connected with the controversy between Gifford and Breedon, all original depositions; one as follows : —

(Court Files, Suffolk, No. 726, third paper.)

"The Deposition of Richard Walker aged 55 years or thereabouts : Saith, That being Chosen to Apprize the Estate of Mr. John Giffard to answer a Judgment granted by the Court to Capt Thomas Breedon, and being Sworne therevnto I went with Thomas Joye to the Iron works where Mr. Giffard dwells, and came there on Tuisday the 20th, of February, and Stayed till Wednesday a little before Sonne Sett before Robert Knight came; whome Mr. Giffard had Chosen to joyne with vs in the said apprizall, on Thursd[ay] morning being ye 22th of Februry, This Deponent and Robert Knight viewed the Furnis Damme Howses & other Estate presented to vs; wee agreed on the price and value of all except the Furnis the Damme, the Land, & the Dwelling house, The difference between vs was very great, namely for the Dam, Robert Knight valued at two hundred and Fifty pounds, and I the Said Walker at One hundre[d] and ten pounds, The said Knight valued ye Fernace and vtensalls at Eight hundred pounds, and I the Said Walker at Three hundred and fifty pounds The, Dwelling howse, by the said Knight was valued at two hundred pounds and I the said Walker at One hundred & forty pounds, The Land that was bought of Leift. Richard Cooke and Goodm̃: Kilcup as they Said about 260 Acres the said Knight valued at 40 lbs ℘ acre, wch. came vnto Fiue hundred & twenty pounds, and I the said Walker valued it at Two hundred & Thirty pounds, which difference in the Said Foure things, To say the Furnis Dam the Land and Dwelling howse, I the said Richard Walker and the said Knight declared vnto Thomas Joye, [ ] was Chosen for the Country, Then on Fryday morning being the 23d day wee looked over ye pap[er] where the said things was written the day before, and propounded the said Difference to the said Joye in order to an Issue, The said Joye said, that as yet he had done nothing, and that he was vpon his Oath, and for the Country, and that he could not goe blindfould about it the Land being covered with Snow and alsoe the Damm and alsoe about the foundac̃on of the Furnis I the said Walker said I knew the Land very well and the said Knight said he did ye Same, The Said Joye said that he did not know it, and ~~and~~ before he prized it he must See it and alsoe the Damm, and other words to the same effect, wherevpon wee all three concluded to doo nothing, and with the consent of the said Knight and Joye I toare the paper And they both desired mee to declare the Same to the marshall and Company and Soe I did, and Said that wee left things as wee found them,

Taken vpon Oath the 6th of the
first m° 166$\frac{5}{6}$ before Tho. Clarke Comss "

(Endorsed)
"166⅚
Capt. Walker [Copied]"

(Also Endorsed)
"To Mr Edw Rawson
Recorder deliuer"

The first paper is the deposition of Thomas Joy "chosen from the country to prize the estate of Mr John Gifford"; the second, the depositions of Jno Hawks and Francis Huchison; to the same general effect as the one here printed.

Nothing further has been found touching the case.

LXVI.

[Court Files, Suffolk, No. 828, 4th paper.]

Att A Court of Assistants held at Boston the 4th September **1666.**

Tho. Kellond & Edmond Doune of Boston Merchants p^{lts}. ag^{t}. Wm Greenough defendant in an action of Appeale from the Judgment of the last County Court at Boston = After the Attachm^{t} Courts Judgmt Reasons of Appeale & other euidences in the Case produced were read Comitted to y^{e} Jury & remajne on file wth the Reccords of this Court the Jury brought in their virdict they found for the plaintiffs three eights of the ballanc payable in bills of exchange & Costs of Court: ‖ ye magists refused ye virdict & so it falls to ye Genl Court in case: ‖

This is a true Copie of the Courts Judgm^{t} as Attests

Edw: Rawson Secret.

NOTE.

Mass. Records, Vol. IV., Part 2, p. 349, 9 Oct. 1667.

"In the case of Wm Greenough, plaintiffe, ag^{t} Thomas Kellond & Edmond Dounes, defendt, coming to this Court by the magis^{ts} in the Court of Asistants last refusing the virdict of the jury, the Court, on a full hearing & pervsall of the euidences in the case produced, find for the Sajd Wm Greenough, plaintiffe, reuersing the former judgm^{t} ag^{t} sd Greenough, & grant him costs of Courts."

See also LXXVI.

LXVII.

[Court Files, Suffolk, No. 754, 3^{d} paper.]

Att A Court of Assistants held at Boston the 4th Septem. 16[66]

Jno Saffin of Boston merchant plaintiff agt. Edward Ting of Boston merchant in an action of Appeale from the Judgm^{t} of the last County Court in Boston After the Courts Judgm^{t} Reasons of Appeale & other Euidences in the Case produced were read Comitted to the Jury & are on file wth the Records of this Court the Jury brought in their virdict they found for y^{e} plaintiff one hundred forty two pounds damage payable one third mony one third goods & ye other third provisions & Costs of Court = This is A true Copie of the Courts Judgm^{t} as Attests

Edw. Rawson Secret^{y}.

[Upon a hearing of this case, on petition of Tyng plaintiff ag[t]. Saffyn, defendant, the General Court, Oct. 1666, found for the defendant. See Mass. Col. Records, Vol. IV., Part II., p. 321, below.]

NOTE.

The first paper in 754 is a writ of attachment dated July 18, 1666, against "Edward Tyng merchant in ye behalfe ofhimselfe & Comp[a] concerned in a certaine Voyage, with y[e] vessell called y[e] James & John Richord Hickes Master, bound for y[e] Isle of Sables in ye yeare 1664, and take bond of him to y[e] value of three hundred pounds with sufficient surety or suretyes for his appearance at y[e] next Countie Court holden at Boston then & there to Answ[r] y[e] Complaint of Jn[o] Saffine in an action of y[e] case, for Detaining from, depriving him y[e] sd Saffin of, & Contrary to Law, & without his Consent Disposing his third p[art] of y[e] aforesd vessell, in y[e] yeare aforesaid, with Due Damages."

By the 34th paper in No. 754 it appears that Tyng presented a petition to the General Court as to the judgment of the Court of Assistants, and that on the 13th of October, 1666, "the magistrates declare they see no Cause to alter the Court of Assistants Judgm[t] but Grant the defendant* the Costs of this Court & order the present plaintiff to pay forty shillings for y[e] hearing of the Cose"

The Deputies consent thereto "provided the sum̃e mentioned in the Judgment of the Court of Assistants be reduced to one hundred pounds, to be payd to m[r] Edw: Tynge & Company" To this the magistrates "consent not;" but "15. 8[mo]. 66 This voated by y[e] whole Court on the affirmative as the Deputys voted it: i e: 100. & costs [& charge]

Edw. Rawson Secret[y]"

Mass. Records, Vol. IV., Part 2, p. 321, 10 Oct. 1666.

"In the case of M[r] Edward Tyng, plaintiffe, by petic̄on, ag[t] M[r]. John Saffyn, defendt. After the Court had heard the petic̄on, pervsed the Court of Asistants last judgment, & all other euidences in the case produced, the Court found for the defendant one hundred pounds damage, & y[t] the plantif pay forty shillings for the Courts hearing the case, & costs of this Court seuen shillings & sixpence."

There are thirty-six papers in No. 754. Those not given here are copies of records of the County Court, writs, pleadings and other matters therein, and of records of the General Court — numerous depositions, etc.

---

*Saffin.

LXVIII.

[Court Files, Suffolk, No. 764, 7th paper.]

Att A Court of Assistants held at Boston 4th September 1666

Capt. Richard Walderne plaintiffe agt Xtopher Palmer defendant in an action that comes to this Court by the magists. refusing the virdict of the Jury at the last County Court at Salisbury After the Attachment & other euidences in the Case produced wth ye virdict of the Jury were read comitted to ye Jury & are on file wth the Reccords of this Court the Jury brought in their virdict they found for the defendant Costs of Courts. The magists. refused ye virdict & so it falls to the Generall Court in Case =

This is A true Copie of the Courts Judgmt as Attests

Edw: Rawson Secrety.

NOTE.

This case came to the Court of Assistants from the County Court at Salisbury April 10, 1666, where the verdict of the jury (for the defendant) was refused by that Court. The action was for an "irregularity" in levying an execution, the officer levying on land although the execution was only expressed for "goods & persön." At the General Court, in Oct., 1666, the case was determined in favor of the plaintiff. See Mass. Col. Records Vol. IV, Part II, p. 321.

Mass. Records, Vol. IV, pt. 2, p 321 10 Oct. 1666.

"In the case of Capt. Richard Walderne, plaintiff, agt Xtopher Palmer, defendt, coming to this Court by the benchs refusing the virdict of the Jury at the Court of Asistants, &c., the Court hauing heard & read the virdict of the jury, & all euidences in the case produced, the Court finds for the plaintiffe three pounds damage, & the grasse he had, & costs of Courts, fowerteen pounds seventene shillings & fowerpence.*

In the case now before the Court, betweene Xtopher Palmer & Edward Colcord, coming to this Courts cognizance by reason ^ disagreement betweene the bench & jury at the Court of Asistants, the Court, on the hearing of the case, & perusall of all euidences produced in the same, doe finde for Edward Colcord costs of Court, confirmg the the virdict of the jury at the Court of Asistants, & the judgment of the Court at Salisbury, who found for the sajd Colcord the meadow sued for, & costs of ye Court.†

In ye case of Christopher Palmer, being bound ouer to the Court of Asistants wth his oune consent, to answer his criminall offence in irregular proceedings as deputy to the marshall generall, in extending an execution for Israell Wight, & by the Court of Asistants referred to this Court for a determination, the sajd Palmer making default by his non appearance at

In margin

* "Courts judgmt in Capt Walerns case agt Xtopher Palmer. Jno Redman, atturney for Palmer."

† "Courts judgmt in Palmer agt Colcords case Jo. Redman, atturney for Palmer, appeared."

this Court, being three times called, & it being cleared to the Court that sum̄ons issued out for his appearance at this Court, which Capt. Waldern, on his oath, affirmed he deliuered to the sajd Palmers wife, the Court finds that the sajd Palmer hath forfeited his bond of one hundred pounds, together wth his surety, which is to be estreated to the Tresurer accordingly, out of which the Tresurer is to pay vnto Capt. Richard Walderne sixe pounds eleven shillings, as his costs in prosecution, &c."*

Same p. 337, 15 May, 1667.

"In ans^r to the petition of Christopher Palmer, humbly desiring the favo^r of this Court to remitt him the forfeiture of his bond, the Court judgeth it meete to remitt the forfeiture thereof to fiue pounds, he paying it speedily."

The fifth paper in No. 764 is a copy of the judgment of the Court at Salisbury April 10, 1666, "Capt. Richard Waldern Plaintiff aga^st. Christo: Palmer Defend^t in an action of ye Case, for Irreguler & Illegall proceeding about an execution granted to Israel Weight at a Court of Assistants ye 6th of Sept: 1664 whereby ye said Capt. Waldern is much Damnifyed in grasse & hay vpon some land at Sandy point nere Exiter River. The Jury finde for ye defend^t Costs of Court ye Court consents not with ye Jury, & so it falls to ye Court of Assistants by Law"

The second paper in No. 764 is a copy of the execution on the judgment of the Court of Assistants 6th of Sept. 1664 directed to the Marshall General who assigns Christopher Palmer as his Deputy.

It appears by the pleas in the case that the principal "irregularity" charged was that the officer levied on land although the execution was only expressed for "goods & person."

The twelfth paper is a "summons" to "Christopher Palmer of Hampton" to give his attendance at the Generall Court "on ye 11th of october next" (1666).

Signed "By the Court Edward Rawson Secret^y."

The sixteenth paper is the judgment of the General Court Oct. 24, 1666, declaring a forfeiture of his bond by Christopher Palmer for default in not appearing though summoned.

See below CVII, record of 21 May 1672, case of Edward Colcord

---

LXIX.

[Court Files, Suffolk, No. 744^a, 1st paper.]

Att A Court of Assistants held at Boston the 4th September 1666.

After a full hearing & considering of both the Courts Judgment at Cambridge & what Tho Gold & Tho Osborne could say for themselues The Court Judgeth it meete to confirme the sajd Courts Judgment abating the sajd Tho. Gold & Tho. Osborne forty shillings a peece of their fine, &

In margin

* "Courts judgm^t ag^t Xtopher Palmer in ye Criminall case."

"Capt. Waldernes costs 6^li 11^s"

for their Contempt of the order of the Gen[1] Court doe Sentenc them to stand Comitted to prison in Boston till the Generall Court shall take further order therein.

This is A true Copie taken out of the Courts Records as Attests

Edw. Rawson, Secret.

Endorsed "Court of Assistants Judgm[t] 4 Sept. 1666 ag[t] the Annabaptists."

NOTE.

Second paper in No. 744[a] "To Thomas Gold Edward Drincker Jn[o] George W[m] Turner & Thomas Osborne yow & every of you are hereby required in his Majestjes name to make yo[r] personall appearance before the Generall Court Sitting in Boston on twenty one day of this Instant Moneth: to give an Answer for your schismatticall practises in rending yo[r]selues from the Comunion of the churches of christ here (as is informed) notw[th]standing the Court of Assistants in September last prohibiting you from persisting in such scandalous & sinfull Courses & that at nine of the clock in the morning hereof you & euery of you are not to faile dated in Boston this 20[th] of october 1665 By order of Court Edw. Rawson, Secret[y].
For the Constables of Boston &
Charles = Towne, you are hereby
required in his maj'[ts] name to execut
this warrant & make yo[r] Returne
hereof to y[e] Court accordingly
Per order Edw. Rawson Secret[y]."

Endorsed — "I haue Sumons Edward Drinker & William Turner to apeare at the Generall Court to morrow being the 21th of october at nine in the morning By me Nathaniell Bishop Constable of Boston this 20 of october 65"

"I have sommenst thos pursons that live in Charlstown bi mee John Smith

"21 $\frac{8}{mo}$ 1665 Connstabell"

Tho Gold Edw: Drincker W[m] Turner & Jn[o] George appeared before the Court & y[t] W[m] Turner in Ans[r] to y[e] [quest.] whither they had met together on ye Lords days & week dayes as a church [since] y[e] Court of Assistants Affirmed he had being bound in Conscience [thereto] Tho Gold affirmed ye same Edw. Drincker sajd he had mett [on] days but not on Lords dayes. Jn[o] Georg sajd he had mett according to his duty &c. E. R. S."

Third paper in No. 744[a]

"Iff the honord Court please wee have A word or two further to say In answer to our Charges First ffor our Gathering together and practise wee have already Given in our Grounds which wee Judge were according to Scripture.

Secondly Wee humbly Conceive the Pattent Gives us leave for soe doeing, and as his Majesty hath explained in his letter to the generall Court, saying that the principall end and foundation of that Charter was and is the fredom and liberty of conscience.

Thirdly Wee Conceive the Law of the Colony doth not deny it to us though with some Provisoes added which soe farr as wee failed of Attending unto wee humbly Crave Pardon, or Submitt to the Penalty of the law therein. this paper was owned by Edw. Drincker Tho Gold Wm Turner Tho Osborne & J^n°^ George: particularly to be their act which was deliuered in by Edw. Drincker & on his & their request was publickly Read in Gen^ll^ Court as Attests Edw. Rawson Secret^y^.

24 october 1665

In Answer to o^r^ Summons as touching schismaticall Rending from Churches. all of us except two were never Joyned to any Church here, and therefore could not Rend from them and as for those two they are willing there Case May Bee heard By Comp^ent Judges chosen by either Parties and are willing to see any irregularity which the Lord by any such helps shall discover to them and shall desire to fall und^r^ the same according to God. This as the other part aboue was at the same time in open Gen^ll^ Court both Read & by the sd partjes owned: as Attests

24 october 1665 Edw. Rawson, Secret^y^.

on proposall of the Qu: to Thomas Goold & Company whether by Competent Judges they intended the: neighbour chhs: they answerd (i. e.) Thomas Goold that he intended the ch: should choose some, & [Hims:] others. & in case that He could be convinced by any thing propounded that he was in an error in his practise for wch the Court dealt with him, he should readily submitt thereto. It being replyed y^t^ ye rules required submission to an orderly conclusion, The said Goold returned as before''

Fourth paper in No. 744^a^

"Wee Whose names are under written doe humbly beeseech this honored Court that they will be pleased to lett ous haue A hearing in A Case of Appeale from the County Court held at Cambridge the 17th of 2nd mo: 1666, or at least be pleased to appoint ous A sett time when wee shall attend this honored Court by reason the time of the yeare requires our diligence for the preservation of the fruits of the earth And wee shall remaine yours to serue you in the Lord

Tho: Gold
Tho: Osborne
John: George''

Court Files, Suffolk, No. 787.

"I Samuel Ward do attest that the presentm^t^ given in the last octob. Court ag^t^ Thomas Goold & company therein menc̄oned, whereto my name is put downe as a witnes is the truth, & nothing else, according to my best knowledge & observation.

2. 2. 1667. Samuel Ward.

2. 2. 67. attested on oath in Court. By Sam[l]. Ward.
as attests. Th: Danforth Recorder.
Vera Copia Th. D. R."

See also Court Files, Suffolk, No. 317.

Mass. Records, Vol. IV, pt. 2 p. 290, 11 Oct. 1665.

"Whereas, at the last Court of Assistants, Thomas Gold & his company, sundry of them, were openly convicted of a schismatticall rending from the comunion of the churches heere, & setting vp a publick meetinge in opposition to the ordinances of Christ here publicly excercised, & were solemnly charged not to persist in such their pernitious practises, yet this notw[th]standing, (as this Court is informed,) they doe still persist in contemning the authority here established, it is therefore ordered, that the aforesajd Gold & company be sumoned before this Court to give an account of such their irregular practises, together w[th] their celebrating the Lords Supper by an excommunicat person.

Warrant issued out accordingly.

The partie appeared. After a due hearing what they had to say, the Court proceeded. Whereas Thomas Gold, W[m] Turner, Edward Drincker, Thomas Osborne, & Jn[o] George, being summoned before the last Court of Asistants, held at Boston in September last, were legally convicted of a schismatticall opposition to the churches of Christ here setled, & of prophaning the holy appointments of Christ, &, in speciall, the Sacrements of baptisme & the Lords Supper, by administring the same to persons vnder censure of an approoved church among us, & presuming, as a couert of theise their irreligious & pernicious practises, to declare themselves to be a church of Christ,—

On consideration whereof, the Court solemnly admonished the sajd persons of their great euill in attempting, wth so high a hand, to polute & prophane Gods holy ordinances, they being not only privates, but also some of them excommunicate persons, that haue intermedled in the administration of those ordinances, that are propper only to office trust. And also, the sajd Court solemnly charged them that, for the future, they desist from such their meeting & irreligious practises, as they would answer the contrary at their perrill. And whereas Thomas Gold, W[m] Turner, Thomas Osborne, Edward Drincker, & Jn[o] George were sumoned before this Court, & by their oune acknowledgment doe stand convicted of non observation & submission unto the abouesajd sentence & charge of the Court of Asistants, professing their resolution yet further to proceed in such their irregular practises, thereby as well contemning the authority & lawes here established for the maintenance of godlines & honesty, as continuing in the prophanation of Gods holy ordinances. This Court, taking the premisses into their serious consideration, doe judge meete to declare, that the sajd Gold & company are no orderly church assembly, and that they stand justly conuicted of high presumption against the Lord & his holy appointments, as also the peace of this gouernment, against which this Courte doeth account themselues bound to God, to his trueth, & his churches heere planted, to beare their testimony, and doe therefore sentence the sajd Gold, Osborne,

Drincker, Turner, & George, such of them as are freemen, to be disfranchised, & all of them, vpon conviction before any one magistrate or Court of their further proceeding herein, to be comitted to prison vntill the Generall Court shall take further order wth them.*

Zeckaryah Roads, being in Court when they were proceeding ag^t^ Thō Gold & company, saying in Court that the Court had not to doe wth matters of religion, for wch he was comitted, being sent for, acknouledging his fault, & declaring he was sorry he had given them any offence, &c.,—

The Court, hauing considered of Zekariah Roads answer, given in referring to those expressions of his wch were offensive to the Court, judge meete, vpon his acknoulegement already made, to discharge him the Court, the Gouerno^r^ giving him an admonition for his sajd offence."

Same p. 316, 11 September, 1666.

"This Court, on a due & full hearing of Thomas Gold & Thomas Osborne, standing comitted by virtue of an order of the Generall Court October, 1665, for their schismatticall & irregular practises ag^t^ the publick worshjp of God, in opposition to the order & peace of the churches of Christ here setled, the prohibition of the sajd Court notwithstanding, doe order, that on the sajd Thō Gold & Thō Osborne paying their fines according to the sentence of the last Court of Asistants, & fees of Court, they shall be discharged the prison. It is hereby also further ordered, that the order of the Court of October, 1665, referring to the sajd schismatticall assembly, shall & hereby is declared to stand in full force in relation to the sajd assembly, & all such as are members thereof."†

Same, p. 373, 27 May 1668.

"Whereas Thomas Gold & company haue been complajned of, & stand conuicted in this Court of setting vp an vnlawfull assembly, wch they call a church of Christ, as may fully appear by seuerall orders of this Court, whereof they haue been admonished, warned, & required to desist from their offenciue & presumptuous practizes, yet haue declared their resolution to continue therein,—

And whereas the councill assembled in March last did, for their further conuiction, appoint a meeting of diuerse elders, & require the sajd persons to attend the sajd meeting, wch was held here in Boston, wth a great concourse of people, the effect whereof hath not been preualent wth them as wee could haue desired,—

This Court, being sencible of their duty to God & the country, & being desirous that their proceedings in this great cause might be cleare & regular, doe order, that the sajd Gold & company be required to appeare before this Court on the seuenth instant, at eight in the morning, that the Court may vnderstand from themselues, whither, vpon the meanes vsed, or other considerations, they haue altered their former declared resolution, & are willing to desist from their former offenciue practize, that accordingly a meete & effectuall remedy may be applyed to so daingerous a malady & ye secretary to issue out accordingly.

In margin

*"Courts testimony & order ag^t^ ye Annabaptists."

†"Courts Sentence ag^t^ ye Annabap^ts^."

Att the tjme Thomas Gold, Wm Turner, & John Farnham, being sum̄oned, made their appearanc, & after the Court had heard what they had to say for themselues, proceeded: Whereas Thomas Gold, Willjam Turner, & Jno Farnham, Senr, obstinate & turbulent Annabaptists, haue some time since combined themselues wth others in a pretended church estate, wthout the knowledge or approbation of the authority here established, as the law requires, to the great greife & offence of the godly orthordox, some of themselues, excommunicated from the churches to which they formerly belonged, haue also constituted among themselues officer or officers to carry on all administrations in their pretended church society, contrary also to the lawe in that case provided, vizt, that such officers should be able, pious, & orthodox, ffor which irregularitjes they haue been convented before seuerall Courts & about two yeares since were enjoyned by this Court to desist from the sajd practise, & to returne to our allowed church assembljes, wch they haue not the least attended, the council in March last, desirous (after long forbearance) to vse the vtmost meanes to convince & reduce them, intreated the asistance of diuers elders, who, in the meeting house at Boston, did publickly endeavour the same: this Court, considering wth how great pertinacy & presumption the sajd Thomas Gold & company had continued their schismattical assembling together, (the order of this Court notwthstanding) judged it necessary to convent the said Thomas Gold, Willjam Turner, & John Farnam, Sen̄, before them, that, from themselues, the Court might vnderstand what effect the endeavo^{rs} of the sajd elders had taken wth them, where the sajd persons did in open Court assert their former practise to haue been according to the mind of God, and that nothing that they had heard convinced them to the contrary, which practise (being also otherwise circumstanced, wth making infaunt baptisme a nullitje, & thereby making vs all to be vnbaptized persons, & so consequently no regular churches, ministry, or ordinances, and also renouncing all our churches as being so bad & corrupt that they are not fitt to be held com̄union wth, denying to submitt to the government of Christ in the church, & enterteyning of those that are vnder church censure, thereby making the discipline of Christ in his churches to be of none effect, & manifestly tending to the disturbance & destruction of these churches, the wch practise of theires, vpon examination before the Court, they professe themselues still resolued to adhere vnto; all wch to allow, would be the setting vp a free schoole for seduction into wayes of error, & casting off the government of Christ Jesus, in his oune appointments, wth a high hand, & opening a doore for all sortes of abominations to come in among us, to the disturbance not only of our eclesiasticall enjoyments, but also contempt of our civil order & the authority here established) doeth manifestly threaten the dissolution & ruine both of the peace & order of the churches & the authority of this government, wch our duty to God & the country doth obleige vs to prevent, by vsing the most compassionate effectual meanes to atteyne the same; all wch considering, together wth the danger of disseminating their errors, & encouraging p^{r}sumptuous irregularitjes by their example, should they continue in this jurisdiction, this Court doe judge it necessary that they be remooued to some other part of this country or elsewhere; and accordingly doeth order, that the sajd Thomas Gold, Willjam Turner, & John Farnam, Señ, doe, before the twentjeth of July next, remooue themselues out of this jurisdiction; and that if, after the sajd twentjeth of July, the sajd Thomas Gold, Willjam Turner, & John Farnam, Señ, or either of them, be found in any part of this jurisdiction, w^th^out licence first had & obteyned from this Court or the council, he or they shall forthwith be app^r^hended & cōmitted to prison, by warrant from any magistrate, there to remajne, w^th^out bayle or majne-prise, vntill he or they shall give sufficjent security to the Governo^r^ or any magistrate iṁediately to depart the jurisdiction, & not to returne as abouesajd.

And all constables & other officers are required to be ffaithfull & diligent in the execution of this sentence. And it is further ordered, that the keepers of all prisons whereto the sajd Thō Gold, Willjam Turner, & John Farnam, Señ, or any of them, shall be cōmitted, shall not permitt any resort of company of more than two at one time to any ofthe sajd persons; and though wee might expect that our indulgence till the twentieth of July might prevajle wth them to refreine their offenciue practises during the tjme permitted them to continue amongst us, yet our experience of their high, obstinate, & presumptuous carriages doth engage vs to prohibit them any further meeting together on the Lords dayes, or vpon any other dayes, vpon pretence of their church estate, or for the administration or exercies of any pretended eclesiasticall functions, as, dispensation of the seales, or preaching, wherein if they shall be taken offending, they shall be imprisoned till the tenth of July next, & then left at their liberty w^th^in tenn dayes to depart the jurisdiction vpon poenalty as abouesajd.

Whereas Thō Gold is cōmitted to prison in the county of Midlesex, by the last Court of Asistants, for non payment of a fine imposed, this Court, hauing past a censure on him & others, judgeth it meet, after the sentence of this Court is published this day after the lecture to them, that the sajd Gold shall be declared to be dischardged from his imprisonment in Midlesex as to his fine, that so he may haue tjme to prepare & submitt to the judgment of this Court.''

Same, p. 404, 23 Oct. 1668. ''Itt is ordered, that the sentence of this Court in May last past ag^t^ the turbulent Annabaptists be sent to the presse by the secretary.''

Same, p. 413, 7 November 1668.

''In ans^r^ to the petition of seuerall inhabitants of Boston & Charls Toune, humbly desiring the Courts favour to Thō Gold, Wm Turner, & Jno Farneham, &c., as in peticōn wch is on file appeares, the Court hauing considered & pervsed ye peticōn, doe finde many reproachfull expressions against the Court & their proceedings wch are not true, and hauing charity towards many of ye peticōners, that haue been mislead by some others cōmiserating the restreint of the persons, not knowing, or at least not duely considering, the righteousnes & necessity of the Courts proceeding as they did, all which is euident in the reccords of this Court, doe order, that Capt. Edw. Hutchinson, Capt. James Olliuer, Richard Way, Thō Grubb, W^m^

Howard, Randal Nicholls, Solomon Phipps, & James Cary be sent for to appeare before this Court on 22 instant, to answer what shall be objected ag^t^ them referring thereto. Warrants issued out accordingly. & Capt. James Olliuer, Randall Nicholls, Rich. Way, Benj: Negus, Wm Howard, & Solomon Phips, & Thō Grubb, &c, appeared, & on their hearing of the peticon, in open Geñ Court, they presented a peticon, vnder their hands, expressing their sorrow for giving the Court such just ground of offenc, wch ye Court accepted of; & it then appearing to ye Court that Benjamin Suitzer & Joshua Atwater were ye cheife promoters of the sajd peticon, & had gonne from house to house to get hands to it, the Court sent for them; they appearing, the Court hauing heard what they had to say for themselues, they refusing to discouer the first contriuer thereof, finding them to haue been very active in promoting so scandalous & reproachfull a peticon, of wch they were fully convict, judge meet to beare testimony ag^t^ their proceedings, & doe censure the sajd Benjamin Switzer to be admonished, & pay the sum̄e of tenn pounds as a fine, and that Joshua Atwater be alike admonished, & pay as a fine ye sum̄e of five pounds for his offence."*

Same, p. 414, 7 November, 1668.

"In ans^r^ to the peticon of Jno Farnam, Señ, the Court judgeth it meete to grant him his liberty from prison at present, vpon the promise he hath made to attend duly vpon the publick ordinances of God, in the solemne assembljes allowed by the lawes of this jurisdiction, euery Lords day twice, except the prouidence of God some way disable or hinder him, provided always that the sajd Farnam doe refreine himself from disorderly meetings, set vp contrary to law; and if the sajd Farnham be prooved guilty of that offenc, the former sentenc of banishment & imprisonment shall remaine in force ag^t^ him."

Same, p. 427, 19 May, 1669.

"Whereas Edward Drincker, of Boston, being legally returned by the constables of Charls Toune, for assembling wth the schismatticall assembly of Annabaptists at Thomas Golds house on the Lords day the 7th of March last, according to the sentenc of the Generall Court, October 11th, 1665, was com̄itted to prison vntill the Generall Court, & was further admonished of the euill of such a turbulent practise, thereby open opposition & disturbance being given to the lawes & authority here orderly established, and doe order his present release; and in case he be againe convicted of the like offence wth the sajd company, to be com̄itted to prison by any magistrate or Court that shall haue proper cognisance thereof, vntill the Generall Court or councill shall give further order."

See below CI, record of the 5th March 1671–2, case of John Russell.

In margin

* "Many inhabitants of Boston & Charls Toune scandalous peticon in favo^r^ of ye Annabaptists."

"Seueral sent for"

"Their acknouledgm^t^."

"Ye 2 principall actiue promoters, Benj Switzer, 10^li^, & Josh. Atwater 5, & admonished.

LXX.

[Essex County Court Files, Vol. XII, Fol. 94. "Craford et ux. *v*. Ashby, June, 1667."]

Att A Court of Assistants Called by the Governo^r^ & magistrates & held at Boston for trjall of Edith Crafford now in prison on suspition of burning a house at Salem. & bound ouer from the County Court at Ipswich in order to hir further trjall 18th of october 1666:

The County Courts Judgment of Jpswich being read the Court proceeded & an Indictment was made & given to the Grand Jury & was = Edith Craford wife to mordecay Craford of Salem marriner: you are Indicted by the name of Edith Craford for not hauing the feare of God before your eyes & being Instigated by the devill did wittingly willingly & feloniously fire the dwelling house lately your husbands in Salem & more lately belonging to & in possession of Capt. Thomas Sauage or Anthony Ashby at or upon the tenth day of September last as by the euidences will & may appeare & all this Contrary to the peace of our Soveraigne Lord the King his croune & dignity. & the wholesome lawes of this Jurisdiction in that case made & prouided. = The Grand Jury returnd. wee finde cause to bring this woeman to further triall Jno Allen in the name of the Grand Jury: = On which the prisoner was sent for & brought to the barr & the Indictment as aboue publickly read She holding vp hir hand at the barr pleaded not guilty. being Askt whom she would be trjed by sajd by God & the Country: making no exception against any of the Jury Impannelled & sworne. = The Euidences in the Case also produced by the aboue mentioned Anthony Ashby that prosecuted against hir being read Co͠mitted to the Jury & are remayning on file wth the reccords of this Court the Jury brought in their virdict i: e: In the Case of Edith Craford now prisoner at the barr The Jury hauing thoroughly scanned the Indictment & vejwed the euidences finde hir not guilty of burning the house for which she is now on hir trjall = Rich. Collecot wth the Consent of the whole Jury = on the Courts ꝑvsall thereof she was dischardged. That this is a true Copie of the triall & Courts Judgment Attests Edward Rawson Secret.

[Endorsed] "Edith Crafords Indictm^t^ Courts Judm^t^ &c."

NOTE.

Suffolk Files Nos. 756 to 760 — Venires, Dorchester, Roxbury, Charlestown, Boston, Watertown and Dedham — for a "Speciall Court of Assistants Called to Assemble & Sitt in Boston on the 18th Instant at eight of the clock in the morning" (October 1666)

Suffolk Files No. 762 — First paper Petition dated Oct. 11, 1666, of Edus* Craford (accused of setting fire to a dwelling house at Salem and in prison awaiting the action of the General Court) that the General Court may appoint a time for her trial — In answer to this petition the magistrates appoint her trial to be "on the next fifth day" "at ye Court of Assistants then to be holden."

The second paper is a portion of the Indictment.

The fourteenth paper is as follows; —

"In the Case of Edith Crafford now prisoner at the Barr the Jurey hauing thorowly scaned the Inditement and vewed the euidences finde her not guilty of Burning the house for which shee is now on her trieall Per Richard Callicott with the consent of the whole Jurey"

There are fifteen papers in No. 762. Those not given here are various depositions attested by Edward Rawson Secretary.

LXXI.

[Court Files, Suffolk, No. 780.]

Att A Court of Asistants held at Boston ye 5th march 1666/7

Walter Burke plaintiff agt. michael white defendt in an action of Appeale from the Judgment of the last County Court in Boston: After the Attachmt Courts Judgmt Reasons of Appeale & other euidences in the Case produced were read Comitted to the Jury & are remayning on file wth the Reccords of this Court the Jury brought in their virdict they found for the defendt Confirmation of the former Judgmt. & costs of Courts = The magists. Refused this virdict & so it falls to ye next Generall Court in Case &c. That this ^ A true Copie taken out of the Courts booke of Reccords Attests Edw: Rawson Secrety.

Note.

At the General Court, May, 1667, the case was determined in favor of the defendant. See Mass. Col. Records Vol. IV, Part II, p. 341.

Mass. Records, Vol. IV, pt. 2, p. 341, 15 May, 1667.

"The whole Court mett together voted, that Mr Peter Lidget, as suerty for Michael White, in January last County Court, where judgmt passed for ye sd White, is no further bound, but dischardged.

In the case coming to this Court for its trjall, by the magists in the Court of Asistants last refusing the virdict of the jury in the case of Walter Burke, plaintiffe, agt Michael White, defendt, after the Court had heard the atachmt & euidences in the case produced read, & which are on file, the Court found for the defendt costs of Courts."

---

* Edith?

LXXII.

[Court Files, Suffolk, No. 846, 3^d paper.]

Att a Court of Assistants held at Boston the 5th march 1666/7

Peleg Sanford plaintiffe agt. Edmund Gibbon defend^t in an action of Appeale from the judgm^t of the County Court in Boston, in October last, after the attachm^t Courts judgmt reasons of Appeale, and euidences in the case produced were read Committed to the Jury, and remaine on file wth the Records of this Court, the Jury brought in their virdict they found for the defend^t, confirmation of the former judgmt i. e. Two hundred sixty six pounds, thirteene shillings fowre pence damage or that the defend^t render and giue vnto the plaintiffe a just and true Account of thirty two thousand Pounds of Sugar wch hee the defend^t owned to bee in his hands in Bills and sugars for the plaintiffs account, &c: and Costs of Courts fowre pounds six shillings six pence: This is a true Copie taken out of the Courts booke of Assistants as Attests,*

[Fourth paper in No. 846]

"To the hon[ble] Court of Asistants now siting in Boston this 11. 7mo. 1667

The humble petiti[on] of Edward Hutchinson being a prisoner — humbly sheweth

That whereas Edm[u]nd Gibon comensed an action in the Countie Court in October last ag^t Peleg Sanford and judgm^t given ag^t s^d Sanford from wch Judgme[nt] he appealed to the next Court of Asistants. And for the psecuteing of the appeale Edward Hutchinson was bound wth Peleg Sanford t[o] the treasurer of the countie in 500£ the s^d Sanford should psecute his appeale at the next Court of Asistants to effect. as by the s^d Judgment apears. ye s^d Sanford did acordingly psente his appeale to effect. at ye next Court of Asistants. wch I humbly conceaue frees my bond I being bound for noe thing else for him as by ye bonde apears. the s^d Court of Asistants confirmed ye Judgement of the Countie Court wch Judgment I here wth psent. and acording to ye Judgem^t of Court the s^d Sanford did forth wth render and giue to ye s^d Gibon a true & Just aco^t of 32^m pounds of Suger. and upward. wch he had receiued and was stil standing out in bills in Barbados. wth ye pteculers of whome receiued and

* This attestation is not signed.

who was stil debters. and alsoe deliuered to m^{r} Rawson a true Copie of the same aco^{t}, and tooke his oath to ye truth of it before ye maj^{r} General. as also did ye witnesses to ye truth of ye Coppy wch I humbly conceiue was al y^{t} was sued for, and al y^{t} ye Courts Judgment required. so I humbly conceiue there could not legally goe out any execution, and yet ye secritary hath granted out execution, not onely ag^{t}. s^{d} Sanford but yor petitioner who now lyes in prison vpon it. making him selfe a iudge of ye Justnes of ye aco^{t}. and yet neuer herde or see ye euedenses Sanford was able to ꝑduse for ye proueing of it. and also iudges y^{t} my selfe was liable as well as Sanford to Execution. and whereas y^{e} Judgm^{t} requirs the s^{d} Sanford should onely giue the aco^{t} to Gibon & y^{t} wth in ten daies. yet y^{e} s^{d} Sanford did leaue a copey of y^{e} same ac$^{t}_{o}$ wth y^{e} secretary atested vpon oath as before & required him to record it, & ꝑfered him his fee for it y^{t} soe he might see y^{t} y^{e} Judgement was satisfied. But if Sanford had not satisfied the Courts Judgem^{t}, wch he did. I humbly conceiue I am not as suertie liable to this execution. ye most y^{t} can come to me is but ye forfiture of my bond, wch must be first legally ꝑued & ꝑsecuted before I can be damnified. And 2 ly if I had bene suertie for the action, wch I was not but an other, the law for suerties frees them alsoe if it be not extended wth in amonth after Judgm^{t} as by the law apears.

Yo^{r} petitioner therefore (being as I humbly conceiue vniustly imprisoned. and being as I conceiue in this Courts power to declaire there sence of there owne Judgm^{t}) humbly prais this Court for releife ag^{t}. such an vniust and illegal imprisonment. And yor petitioner shal alwaies pray as in duty bound".

[Ninth paper in No. 846]

"The humble peticione of Edmund Gibbon to ye honor^{d} Court now Siting [in] Boston humbly Sheweth

That whare as yor petitioner hath bine much kronged and impouerisht by peleg Sanford by his detayning of an Estate of yor petitioners to ye value of 800£ sterling yor petitioner was Constrayned Contrary to his practis or desiare to Commence an Actione against ye Sayd Sanford and not being Capable at present to Legally proue any more then 32000£ of Sugers in ye sayd Sanfords hands therefore Could obtaine judgment for noe more, yet not withstanding I haue obtayned two Judgments against hime with much labor to my self and great trouble to ye honored Courts yet he indeuors to defraud mee of my Just right ofe there verdits by Tendering a fraudulent Acount there by to ꝑvent Accicutione soe that I am still in ye dark now ye humble request of youre peticioner is yt this honored Court would be pleased to giue Such Order yt Excicutione may be granted hime, for soe much monyes as is Mentioned in ye Verdits or else such an Acount as is there Expressed yt soe I may Either haue my Sugers or money

9 Mrch 66

This peticon being shewne to ye Gourno^r & magists 9th march 66 & also acquainting them wth mr Sandfords oath &c to prevent Execution they exprest declard yt. that not being brought to ye Court I ought to Issue out ye execution agt Sanford & his Surety*

E R S."

[On back of paper]

"Gibbons petition
Mr Usher
Mr Hull
Mr Bratle
Capt Dauis
Mr. Lidgett
Mr. Tyng
Mr: Stoddard
Mr: Bridgham. 8."

NOTE.

The General Court, Oct. 1667, passed the following order relating probably to this case — "In answer to the petition of Capt. Edward Hutchinson, & on consideration of his pleas & allegations on the lawe, title Suretjes, it is hereby ordered & declared, that the sajd Hutchinson shall & hereby is released from his imprisonment, & that his bond of fiue hundred pounds for Peleg Sandfords abiding the order of the Court of Asistants doeth & shall stand in force agt the said Hutchinson till the Courts judgm̄t be sattisfied, or the principall surrendered into the custody of the prison keeper." Supposing this order to relate to the judgment in the case between Sanford and Gibbon, it would show that the verdict in the Court of Assistants "for the defendant" was meant for Gibbon, the defendant on the appeal; and that by the word "defendant" used further on in the verdict was meant Sanford, the defendant at the County Court. See Mass. Col. Records Vol. IV, Part II, p. 350.

In margin
*"Gour
Capt Gook[in]
Mr Symonds
Mr Danforth
Mr. Hauthorn"

The second and eleventh papers in No. 846 are as follows

"To Edward Michelson Marshall Generall or his deputie Yow are hereby required in his maj^{ties} name to leuie by way of Execution on y^{e} goods estaite or person of Peleg Sanford or in defect there of one y^{e} goods estaite or person of Capt Edward Hutchinson his suertie, y^{e} Some of 271$^{£}$ & deliuer y^{e} same wth 2^{s} for this execution to Edmond Gibbon, & is in satisfaction of a iudgement granted & confirmed to y^{e} sd Gibon for soe much damage & cost by y^{e} court of Assistants held at Boston y^{e} 5th Instant, it being in defect of y^{e} sd Sandford not giueing in a iust and true aco^{t} of 32^{m} pounds of sugor wch ye said Sanford owne to be in his hands in bills & sugor for ye sd Gibons aco^{t} as in the Said iudgment is exsprest here of yow are not to faile dated in Boston this 23 march 1666. By ye Court Edward Rawson Secret.

This execution hath bene seueral times demanded of Capt Edward Hutchinson at his house & at his farme & he denying to produce or shew any estaite or goods to answer ye execution his body was arested and comited to prison this 10. 7^{m}. 67

Edward Micheson Marshal Genl.

This a true Coppie giuen me by Marshal Mitison

atests William Salter"

"In Answer to the pet. of Capt. Edward Hutchinson & on Consideration of his pleas & Allegations on the law Tit. Suretyes, It is hereby ordered & declared that the s^{d} Hutchenson shall & heareby is released from his Imprisonment & that his bond of 500 pounds for Peleg Sanfords abidinge the order of the Court of Assistants doth & shall stand in force agaynst the sd Hutchenson till the Courts Judgment be satisfyed or the principall surendered Into the Custody of the prison keeper the deputyes haue past this desireing the Consent of o^{r} Honord magis^{ts} hereto

William Torrey Cleric

31 (8) 1667

Consented to by ye magis^{ts}

Edw. Rawson Secrety"

The other papers in No. 846 are as follows: —

First paper:— Copy of Writ of Attachment and return 4 — 7th. mo. 1666 (County Court)

Fifth paper:— Petition by Edward Hutchinson to the General Court 9 — 8th. mo. 1667

Sixth paper:— Statement by Jer. Howchine, Comiss. Sept. 20th. 1667.

Seventh paper:— Declaration by Edward Hutchinson to the General Court 1 — 9th. mo. 1667

Eighth paper:— Apprizement of land of Capt. Edward Hutchinson. 25 Oct. 1667

Tenth paper:— Votes in the General Court 26 Oct. 1667 on the petition and complaint of Capt. Edward Hutchinson.

Twelfth paper:— Copy of deposition of Ephraim Turner 16 March 1666

Thirteenth and fourteenth papers are copies of accounts of Peleg Sanford 1663–1664

The fifteenth, sixteenth, seventeenth and eighteenth papers are depositions.

LXXIII.

[Court Files, Suffolk, No. 965, 3d paper.]

Att a Court of Assistants held at Boston: 5 march 1666/7

Capt: Thomas Clarke plt: agt: Capt: William Dauis & Capt.: Thomas Willet Executors to the last will & testament of the late William Paddy Merchant defendts in an Action of Appeale from the judgment of the last County Court in Boston After the Attachment Courts Judgment Reasons of Appeale & Euidences in the Case produced were read Committed to the jury & are on file wth the Reccords of this Court, The jury brought in their virdict they found for the defendt Costs of Courts

This is a true Copie of the Court of Assistants judgment. As Attests Edw: Rawson Secret.

NOTE.

In a case between Capt. Thomas Clarke, plaintiff, and Capt. Thomas Willet & Capt. Wm. Davis, executors to the last will of Mr. Paddy, defendants, the General Court, May 1670, gave judgment for the defendants. See Mass. Col. Records Vol. IV, Part II, pp. 427, 447, 455.

There are sixteen papers in No. 965. They consist of copies of the records of the County Court, of summons, of Reasons of Appeal and answers thereto, of will, agreement, declaration, accounts, record of the General Court, bill of charges, etc. (See also above XL record of March 3, 1662–3 Clarke & Davis &c.)

LXXIV.

[Court Files, Suffolk, No. 823, 2d paper.]

Att A Court of Assistants held at Boston 5th march 1666/7

Capt James Pendleton Agent & Atturney to Capt Brjan Pendleton plaintiff agt Nathaniel Boulter defendt in an Action of Appeale from the Judgment of the last County Court at Hampton — After the Attachment Courts Judgment reasons of appeale & euidences in the case produced were read Comitted to ye Jury & are on file wth the reccords of this Court the Jury brought in their virdict they found for the plaintiff reuersion of the former Judgment & fifty pounds eighteen shillings one penny dam̃age & Costs of Courts fower pounds eight shillings — This is a true Copie of the Courts Judgment as Attests

Edward Rawson Secrety.

NOTE.

The above judgment of the Court of Assistants was reversed by the following order of the General Court in May 1668:—

"In the case of Nathaniel Boulter, plaintiff, ag[t] Capt. James Pendleton, agent & atturney ffor Capt. Brjan Pendleton, defendt., com̄ing to this Court by petition, after the Court had heard the euidences in the case produced they found for the plaintiff the som̄e of ffifty fiue pounds sixe shillings one penny damage, being the reuersion of the judgment of the Court of Asistants, fifth of March, 1667, wth costs of Courts, & damage, & hearing of the case, in all thirty fower pounds one shilling[s] & nine pence." See Mass. Col. Records Vol. IV, Part II, p. 376.

Fourth paper in No. 823 "To Edward Michelson marshall Gen[l] & his deputy

Yo[w] are hereby required in his Maj[ts] name to levy on the goods estate & person of Nathaniel Boulter to value of fower pounds eight shillings & deliuer the same wth two shillings for this execution to Capt James Pendleton Atturney to Capt Brjan Pendleton & is in sattisfaction of a Judgment granted him for so much by the Court of Assistants Sitting in Boston this [fifth] hereof not to fajle Dated in Boston [ ] of march 1666/7

By the Court Edw. Rawson Secret[y].

(Endorsed) this execusyon is leuied vpon y[e] hous and land of nathanill Bolter and prised by John Samborn and william fifeld of hampton and deliurd in possesion to Captain Pendleton acording to y[e] tener hear of

By mee Abraham Perkins marshall Gen̄ Deputy

y[e] 9th Aprill 1667

Recd in Court 13 Sept 1667 E R S"

Thirteenth paper in No. 823 "We find a Speciall Verditt

we find pt of a mill mortgaged by Boulter to Pendleton as security for a debt of about 50[li] on condition ye sd Some be pd ½ in August 1664 y[e] other ½ y[e] last of march 1665 before y[e] last of w[ch] payment fell due y[e] said mill was caried away if by law this mortgage so lost answeres y[e] debt we find for y[e] P[lt]. Returne of ye execution 55[li] 7[s] if not we find for the Deffnt cost of Court Vpon the Consideration of this speciall virdict the Court finds for the defendant Costs of Court."

Mass. Records Vol. IV, pt. 2, p. 350, 9 Oct. 1667.

"In answer to the petition of Nathaniel Boulter, humbly desiring the favo[r] of this Court to grant him a hearing of his case betweene him & Capt. James Pendleton, &c, in regard the persons liue so remote that seasonable notice cannot be given to the parties to come to this Court before it be too late, it is ordered, there be a hearing of this case on the 3[d] day of the first weeke after the next election day, the petitioner giving Capt. Pendleton seasonable notice ag[t] that time, & bringing the whole case to this Court."

Same, p. 376, 27 May, 1668.

"In the case of Nathaniell Boulter, plaintiff, ag[t] Capt. James Pendleton, agent & atturney ffor Capt. Brjan Pendleton, defendt, com̄ing to this

Court by petition, after the Court had heard the euidences in the case produced they found for the plaintiff the Some ffifty fiue pounds sixe shillings one penny damage, being the reuersion of the judgment of the Court of Asistants, fifth of March, 1667, wth costs of Courts, & damage & hearing of the case, in all thirty fower pounds one shillings & nine pence." *

The remaining eleven papers in No. 823 consists of copies of writ, reasons of appeal, deed, letters of attorney, account, depositions and bill of costs.

LXXV.

[Court Files, Suffolk, No. 791, 4th paper.]

Arthur Mason of Boston in the County of Suffolk in New England Bisket Baker

Yo^{w} are Indicted by the name of Arthur Mason for not having the feare of God before you^{r} eyes did on or about the 19th of January last in the dwelling house of Thomas Kellond mercht. being Instigated by the Divill maliciously & treasonably vtter & expresse treasonable words against our Soueraigne Lord the King in saying (that yow being as Constable sent to Apprehend certaine persons then at John Vialls a publick house of enterteinment in the breach of the lawes) not only sayd yow would haue Ap^{r}-hended them all had yow found them there but if the king himself had been there you would haue donne the like by him. and this contrary to yor Allegiance & contrary to the peace of our Soueraigne Lord the King his Crowne & dignity & the wholesome lawes of this Jurisdiction.

~~we of the Grand Jury, vpon the pervsall of the euidences that were giuen into vs, find not the Bill [6th] 1 mo. 1666/7 William Park in the name of the Jury.~~

we of the Grand Jury find by euidence that those words conserning the king mentioned in this Bill of inditement were spoken by Arthur masson this 8 (1) $\frac{66}{7}$. William Park

in the name and Consent of the Jury

Note.

The question whether these words found by the grand jury were treasonable was referred to the General Court as appears by the following order by that Court at its May session 1667:—

The Court, hauing considered the accusation & euidences ag^{t} Arthur Mason, doe find that the words spoken by him & found by the grand jury,

---

In margin

*Courts judgm^{t} in Boulters Case —	55	6	1
Costs & dam.	29	1	9
Hearing Case	5	0	0
	89	7	10

were rash, insolent, & highly offensiue, yet, forasmuch as his accuser & witnesses in the case doe all cleare him from any overt act or evill intended against the kings most excellent maj^{t}y, they doe not see cause to proceed ag^{t} him as a capitoll offender, but doe sentenc him to be admonished in a solemne manner by the Governo^{r}. See Mass. Col. Records Vol. IV, Part II, p. 340.

Court Files, Suffolk, No. 791, 5th paper Arthur Mason accused of treason —

"S^{r} I haue receyued a writing jā. $^{day}_{20.}$ 66/7 subscribed wth yor name, where in Arthur Mason is accused of Treason. these are to acquaint ||signifie to|| you that I expect you ∧ Come vnto my house at three of the clocke this ~~after instnt~~ twosday being 22th instant to oblige yo^{r}selfe to prosecute the charge against him ∧ the next Co^{r}t of asistants to be held in march next

Bosto: 22. 11: 66/7 } R. B. G:
about 11. clock. } True Copye Sent by Sergt
Wayte."

Sixth paper in No. 791 — "Being required by the Hon:^{ble} Court of Assistance to giue in euidence concerning Mr Arthur Mason as to what words I heard him then speake relating to the kings maiesty our dread Soueraigne I did heare him say that if the king himselfe had bin there he would haue done as much & more but as to the former part of the discourse he can not safely say any thing to take his oath of it. but did then conceaue that Mr Mason meant it as in the execution of his office & not otherwise. T. Temple.

Taken vpon oath the 6 of march 1666/7

before Jno: Leverett Asist.

Owned in Court 8th march 1666/7 E R. S."

The third paper in No. 791 is a deposition by Nicholas Paige made at the same time as the above before John Leverett and "ouned in Court 8th march 1666/7" also "ouned in Generall Court 22 May 1667"

The first paper in No. 791 is a summons to witnesses to appear "forthwith" and give evidence before the General Court, dated May 22, 1667.

The second paper in No. 791 is the plea by Mason in his own defence in which he claims that the words were only spoken "in heate of discourse in the execution of my office" & without malice or guilt. At the end of this plea is entered "This was publickly Read 22 May 1667 & owned by Arthur Mason to be his defence & proclamation was againe made y^{t} any y^{t} had ought to testify ag^{t} Arthur Mason in behalf of his maj^{ty}. they should be heard = Edw. Rawson Secret^{y}."

See below XCI, case of Arthur Mason, 14 June 1671.

LXXVI.

[Court Files, Suffolk, No. 828, 8th. & 9th. papers.]

[Eighth paper in No. 828] "Att A Court of Asistants held at Boston 3d September 1667.

Wm Greenough plaint agt Edmond Doune & Tho: Kellond defendt in an action of Appeale from the Judgment of the last County Court in Boston. = After the Courts Judgment Reasons of Appeale & euidences in the Case produced were read Comitted to the Jury & remajne on file wth the reccords of this Court: the Jury brought in their virdict they found for the defendant one hundred & twelue pounds dam̃age (& the former Judgment to be reuersed) in the same specie as before & Costs of Courts || The magists refused ye virdict & so it falls to ye Genl Court in Case ||

This is a true Copie taken out of the Courts reccords as Attests

Edw: Rawson Secret."

[Ninth paper in No. 828] "Att A Court of Assistants held at Boston 3d September 1667

Wm Greenough plaintiffe agt Tho Kellond defendt in an action of Appeale from the Judgmt of the last County Court at Boston. = After the Courts Judgmt Reasons of Appeale & euidences in the Case produced were read Comitted to ye Jury & remajne on file wth the reccords of this Court the Jury brought in their virdict they found for the defendt Confirmation of the former Judgment & Costs of Courts in the same specie as before the magists refused the virdict & so it falls to ye Generall Court in Case

This is a true Copie taken out of the Courts Reccords as Attests. per Edw: Rawson Secret."

NOTE.

Thirty seventh paper in No. 828

"In the Case now dependinge betweene William Greenough plt. agaynst Thomas Kellond deffendt., Com̃inge to the Cognizance of this Court by reason of disagreement of Bench & Jury at the last Court of Assistants, the deputyes on a full hearing of the Case & the evidences therein, doe find for the sd Kellond vizt. the Confirmation of the Judgment of the County Court held at Boston the 30th. of July 1667, only the terme of six monthes therein exprest & allowed, for the sd Greenough to bring in his accounts is to begin, from the date hereof & the sd accounts to be giuen In, either to the next Court of Assistants, or to any County Court at Boston, which shal be within the sd Terme with refference to the Consent of or Honord magists. hereto

William Torrey Cleric.

25 (8) 1667

Consented to by the magists Edw. Rawson Secrety"

Mass. Records, Vol. IV, pt. 2, p. 349, 9 Oct. 1667

"In the case of Wm. Greenough, plaintiffe, ag[t] Thomas Kellond & Edmond Dounes, defendt, coming to this Court by the magis[ts] in the Court of Asistants last refusing the virdict of the jury, the Court, on a full hearing & pervsall of the euidences in the case produced, find for the sajd W[m] Greenough, plaintiffe, reuersing the former judgm[t] ag[t] sd Greenough, & grant him costs of Courts"

There are thirty seven papers in No. 828. Those not given here are copies of records of the County Court at Boston, writs, pleadings and other matters therein, letters, accounts, numerous depositions, etc. (See also above LXVI, record of the 4 Sept. 1666, Kellond &c. ag[t] Greenough)

LXXVII.

[Mass. Archives Vol. 15 B. No. 236. Godfry ag[t]. Remington, 3 Sept. 1667.]

"Att A Court of Asistants held at Boston the 3[d] September 1667

Jn[o] Godfry plaintiff ag[t] Jn[o] Remington defend[t] in an accon of Appeale from the Judgm[t] of Salisbury Court After the Courts Judgm[t] Reasons of Appeale & euidences in the Case produced were read comitted to y[e] Jury & remajnes on file wth the Reccords of this Court: the Jury brought in their virdict they found for y[e] defend[t] Confirmation of the former Judgm[t] & Costs of Courts. ||the magis[ts] refused the virdict & so it falls to ye Generall Court in Case &c.|| This is A true Copie of this Courts Judgm[t] as Attests Edw. Rawson Secret[y]."

NOTE.

By the next paper it appears that the General Court confirmed the judgment of Salisbury Court. See Mass. Col. Records Vol. IV, Part II, p. 349.

By the other papers it appears that the action was brought by "John Godfery plaintiffe against John Remington and Abigall his wife def[t] in an Action of the Case for denying and refusing to resigne and yeald vp unto the sajd John Godfery possession of a house and seuerall lands in hauerill as is at large expressed in a deed of mortgage w[ch] is due vnto the sajd John Godfery vpon the forfeiture of the sajd mortgage"

Mass. Records, Vol. IV, Part 2, p. 349, 9 Oct. 1667.

"In the case now depending betweene John Godfrey, pl[t], ag[t] Jn[o] Rimington & Abigaile, his wife, defendts, coming to this Court by disagreement of the bench, at at the last Court of Asistants, from y[e] virdict of the jury, the Court on a full hearing of the case, doe finde for the defendt confirmation of the judgment of the last County Court at Salisbury."

(See also above LXII, record of the 6 March 1665–6, case of John Godfrey)

LXXVIII.

[Court Files, Suffolk, No. 814, 2d paper.]

Jn° Simple yow are Indicted by the name of John Simple of Charles Towne for not hauing the feare of God before your eyes & being Instigated by the divil did on or about the 13th of March last past Attempt & comitt a Rape on the body of Sarah Bursly a Girle of thirteen yeares of Age as by the euidences may Appeare Contrary to the peace of our Soueraigne Lord the King his Crowne & dignity & the wholesome lawes of this Jurisdiction in such Case made & prouided

Wee find this Bill that John Simpull Comitted a rape on the body of Sarah Burshly, and leaue him to the Court for his further triall

James Euere[ll] in the name of the rest.

Wee find him guilty of an Attempt vppon the body of Sarah Bursley and a rape comitted

Tho: Deane in the name of ye rest

NOTE.

This case was tried at the Court of Assistants Sept. 3, 1667 as appears by the depositions in the case

The other papers in No. 814 are as follows:

First paper:— Warrant to take into custody the body of John Simple, 14 Mar. 1666–7.

Third paper:— Deposition of Abigaell Chadwell, 3 Sept. 1667.

Fourth paper:— Deposition by Mary Spreague, 3 Sept. 1667

Fifth paper:— The Examination of John Simple and Sarah Bursley, March 1666–7 also a statement by Goodwife Ketle, senior &c. as to examining the body of Sarah Bursly. The Judgment of the Court does not appear.

LXXIX.

[Court Files, Suffolk, No. 821, 2d, 3d, 11th and 12th papers.]

[Second paper].— Bethjah Bullojne wife of John Bullojne is indicted by the name of Bethjah Bullojne for not having the feare of God before hir eyes & being Instigated by the divill did in or about the last weeke in December last lye in bed wth Peter Turpin & Comitt Adultery wth him the sajd Turpin as by the euidences may fully Appeare Contrary to the peace of our Soueraigne Lord ye King his Croune & dignity & the wholesome lawes of this Jurisdiction in that Case made & provided.

Wee find this bill and leaue hir to
furder tryall James Euerell
in the name of the rest

We find her guilty of lieing in bed with Peter Turpin Tho: Deane foreman.

On further going out ye Jury returned a speciall virdict i e If by lawe Bethjah Bullojne lying in bed wth Peter Turpin be adultery wee find her Guilty: If by lawe Bethjah Bullojne lying in bed wth Peter Turpin be not adultery wee find her not guilty

Tho: Deane foreman.

[Third paper].— Elisabeth Hudson wife of Nathaniel Hudson is Indicted by the name of Elisabeth Hudson for not hauing the feare of God before her eyes & being Instigated by the divil did in or about the last weeke in December last lye in bed wth Peter Turpin & Comitt Adultery wth him ye sd Turpin as by the euidences may fully Appeare Contrary to the peace of our Soueraigne Lord ye King his Crowne & dignity & the wholesome lawes of this Jurisdiccon in that case made & prouided.
We find this Bill and leaue hir to
furder tryall James Euerell
in the name of the rest

Wee find her guilty of lieing in bed with Peter Turpin

Tho: Deane in
ye name of ye rest.

[Eleventh paper] A Speciall verditt

If by law, Elizabeth Hudsons lieinge in Bed with Peter Turpin be Aultery we find her Guilty

If by law, Elizabeth Hudsons lieinge in Bed with Peter Turpin be not adultery we find her not guilty

Tho: Deane foreman

A Speciall verditt

If by law Betthia Bullines lieinge in Bed with Peter Turpin be Adultery we find her guilty

If by law Bethia Bullines lieinge in Bed with Peter Turpin be not Adultery we find her not guilty Tho: Deane foreman.

[Twelfth paper] Elisabeth Hudson &c the Court sentenceth yow to be by the marshall Generall or his order on ye next lecture day presently after the lecture carried to the Gallowes & there by y^e^ executioner set on the ladder & wth a Roape about $y^{o}r$ neck to stand on the Gallowes one halfe hower & then brought downe & brought to the market place & be seuerly whipt wth tenn stripes or pay the sume of tenn pounds standing comitted till y^{e} sentence be performed E R S

11 Sept 67 voted & published

The like sentenc in Bethyah Bullojnes Case &c.

11 $Septemb^{r}$ 1667 voted Per E R S

NOTE.

[First paper] "Yo^{w} are in his ma^{tyes} name required to take into yor custody Elizabeth y^{e} wife of nathaniel Hudson & Bethiah y^{e} wife of m^{r} Bull[en] it is for suspicion of Adultery and yo^{w} are them safely to keepe till further order Dat. 29. 5. 1667

To th keeper of the Prison in Boston" Ri. Bellingham Govr

[Fourth paper] "To Edw: Creek & deborah his wife & Tho Shepard: Yow & euery of yow are hereby required in his Maj^{tys} name $forthw^{th}$ to giue your personall appearances at the Court of Assistants now sitting & give in your euidences in the case of Elisabeth Hudson & Bethyah Bulloyne now on tryall here of they are not to faile

Dated in Boston this 3^{d} September 1667

By the Court

Edw. Rawson $Secret^{y}$.

To marshall Genl. Edward michelson or his deputy who are alike required to execute this warrant & make returne to ye Court.

By vertue Hearof I Assigne Returne Waitt my Lawfull Deputy to execute this warrant

Edward michelsone

(Endorsed) By vertue of this warrant I haue sumend Edw: Creeke & Deborah his wife & Tho: Shepard to apeare forthwith before the honored Court of Assistance now Sitting in Boston

This 3^{d} $Septemb^{r}$ 1667. Byme Returne Wayte Marsh: Generals deputy"

The other papers in No. 821 not here given are as follows:

Fifth paper:— Bond for the appearance of Elizabeth Hudson and Bethiah Bullen at the Court of Assistants 3 Sept. 1667

The sixth, seventh, eighth, ninth, tenth and thirteenth papers are depositions.

LXXX.

[Court Files, Suffolk, No. 955, 1st paper.]

Att a Court of Assistants held at Boston ye first of September 1668.

Joseph Davis plaint: against Capt. Walter Barefoot defendt in an accon yt comes to this Court by ye Magistrates refuseing the verdict of ye Jurie at ye last County Court at Salisbury, After the Juries verdict, & evidences in ye case produced were read comitted to ye Jurie & remayne on file wth ye records of this Court The Jurie brought in their verdict, they found for ye defendent costs of Court, forty shillings & fower pence: [Valld]

This is a true copie of ye Court of Assistants Juddgmt

as attests Edw: Rawson Secret.

This is a true Copie: now on
file, as attests: Tho: Bradbury recr.

NOTE.

There are fifteen papers in No. 955. The remaining papers are copies of the records of the County Court at Hampton and at Salisbury, of writ of attachment, of execution, of bills of costs and various depositions. They seem to be connected with some later litigation.

LXXXI.

[Court Files, Suffolk, No. 906, 2d paper.]

Franck Negro is Indicted by ye name of ffr: Negro for conspiracy: aiding or assisting John Pottell in his escape out of ye prison in Boston ye 8th of Decembr last. the said Pottell being comitted in order to his tryall for murdering of ye Cooke of ye Ship Golden Fox.

[On the reverse] wee the Grand Jurie doe not find ffrank negro: guilty of the fact according vnto this bill of Inditement

Hugh Mason with the consent of the Rest

Boston the 2 (1) 1668.*

NOTE.

First paper in 906 Warrant to summon witnesses to appear "before the Court of Assistants now sitting in Boston to give in their evidence in a case depending relating to Franck Negro" dated 2d March 1668.

The remaining paper in No. 906 is the examination of Franck Negro by Richard Bellingham, Govr., also examinations of William Pollard, Thomas Sexton and others.

*2 March 1668–9.

LXXXII.

[Court Files, Suffolk, No. 912.]

To the honored Court of asistants Siting att boston 9 march $\frac{68}{69}$

Your humble petitioner hauing with more serious Consideration waied many vnsutabell expressions of mine in somthings that were to high for mee to haue been soe bould in put in to Reasons of appeell presented to this honored Court desier humbly to Cast my selfe down to your honors feet as in all humility I am bound beeseeching your honors high Clemency to pas by what you may in wisdom and fatherly compassion towards mee and my poore wife and distressed family who haue beene of latte vnder many troubells fears and opresing temptations which I forbear to mention to your honors Soe wee shall as in bounden duty pray for your honors high hapines in this World and in the World to Come life everlasting

Your honors in all humbell Submission to be Comanded to my power

John hoare *

Owned by ye sd Hoare 9th march 68:†
being read to him.

The Court is willing ffurther to trye him. & accepts of this his acknowledgment ordering that he be seriously admonish^t^ by the Gou^r^no^r^ in open Court: that he take warning y^t^ he neuer more Appeare in such a reproachfull way ag^t^ Courts & ye officers thereof:

Edward Rawson Secret

(Endorsed) "m^r^ Hoare [his] acknowledg^t^ publish^t^"

Note.

The reasons of appeal referred to, in the petition are the 3^d^ and 4th papers in Suffolk Court Files, No. 904.

The fourth paper is certified to, as Rec^d^ 24 Febr. 1668‡ as John Hoares Reasons from Thomas Wyborns hand"

The other (the third paper) is certified to, as follows: "This paper called by Mr Jno Hoare to be his further Reasons I rec^d^: 25 Febr. 1668 as Attests Edw. Rawson Record^r^"

In these Reasons of Appeal it was claimed that the proceedings were contrary to the Charter & that the Clerk was not sworn &c.

Mass. Records, Vol. IV, pt. 2, p. 291, 11 Oct. 1665.

"In answer to the peticon or remonstrance of John Hoare, the Court, finding that seuerall of the magistrates, & some others, are impeached for not doing justice, & other complaints of a very high nature, doe therefore

* The petition is in the same hand as the signature.
† 1668-9.
‡ 1668-9.

order, that a hearing be granted to the peticõner, & that due notice be given to the complaynant to appeare to make good his seuerall charges, or otherwise to give answer for the same. Notice was giuen accordingly to the sajd Hoare; and the sajd John Hoare appearing in Court, his peticõn or remonstrance being read, wth such euidences as he produced, the Court proceeded as followeth:—

Whereas John Hoare, of Concord, hath presented to this Court a petition or remonstranc, wherein he complaines of great wrongs & injurjes he hath susteyned as his brothers agent, by reason he could not obteyne justice in some of our Courts of judicature in seuerall actions depending betweene himself, as agent, & Leiut. Richard Cooke, of Boston, the Court, having affoorded him large liberty & oppertunity to make good his charges, & hauing heard all his allegations, together wth such witnesses as were produced to prooue the same, & duely weighed the case, doe judge his complaints to be groundless & vnjust, & his offences to be of a very high nature, tending not only to the dishoñor of God, but to the scandall & reproach of seuerall of our Courts, hoñored magistrates, & officers of Court. That due witnes maybe borne against such sinfull practises, & the gouernment of this jurisdiction, vnder his majestjes royall charter, may be vpheld & majntajned, this Court doeth order, that the sajd Hoare shall find suertjes, bound in one hundred pounds, for his good behavior during the Courts pleasure, & that henceforth he shall be disabled to plead any cases but his oune in this jurisdiction, & also that he pay as a fine the sume of fifty pounds for such his miscarriages, & be imprisoned till it be pajd, or security given for the same. Whereas John Hoare, contrary to the expresse order of the Court, hath w[th]draune himself from the Court before his sentence was declared, the secretary is appointed by the Court to send for him, & require the performance of the sentence of this Court to all intents & purposes therein contejned."

Same, p. 301, 23 May, 1666.

"In answer to the peticõn of John Hoare, humbly desiring the favour of this Court to release him of his bonds of good behaviour, & to make such abatement of his fine as their wisdomes shall judge meete,—

The Court judgeth it meete, & orders, the peticoner be released his bonds of good behavio[r], & that twenty pounds of his fine be abated him."

Same, p. 387, 27 May 1668.

"In ans[r] to the petition of Alice, the wife of John Hoare of Concord, the Court judgeth it meete, on the petitioners sattisfying & paying in to the Treasurer to his content the sume of tenn pounds, to abate the remajnder of hir husbands fine yet remayning, & vnpajd."

LXXXIII.

[Court Files, Suffolk, No. 914.]

The Court now assembled, taking notice of ye great damage y[t] do daily happen to ye townehouse in Boston by neglect of seasonable reparation, according to ye order of ye Gen[ll] Court requiring ye Select men of y[t]

Towne to see y^t ye same be done. Do herby order y^t ye Select men do take care y^t ye order of ye Gen^ll Court be attended. & ye said house repayrd befor ye next Court of Electiõ. on Penalty of 20£.

9th march 68 * By ye Court of Asistants

Edw. Rawson Secret^y

NOTE.

Mass. Records, Vol. IV, pt. 2, p. 351, 9 Oct. 1667.

"For the necessary, full, & suiteable repaire of the Toune or Court House in Boston, founded by the late Capt. Robert Keayne, it is ordered by this Court, that the selectmen of Boston shall & hereby are desired & impowred as a comittee to see to & order the same wth all convenient speede, the chardge whereof is to be borne & defrajed the one clere halfe by the Tresurer of the country, one fowerth part thereof by the Tresurer of ye county of Suffolke, & the other fourth part by the Tresurer of the toune of Boston"

Same, p. 466, 12 Oct. 1670.

"The Court, being informed & finding that the toune house is very much wanting of repajre, & by reason thereof is very dangerous, judge meete to appoint Mr Thomas Danforth, Mr Anthony Stoddard, & Mr Willjam Parkes, a comittee to vejw the same, & make report to this Court of what they judge most necessary is to be don for the so repayring thereof, as all danger may be prevented, & the house preserved."

Same, p. 486, 31 May 1671.

"It is ordered, that Capt. John Allen, Mr Wm Stiltson, in behalfe of the country, Capt. Foster & Mr Wm Parks for the county of Suffolke, & the selectmen of Boston for & in behalfe of the toune of Boston, shall & hereby are appointed & impowred a comittee effectually & speedily, by a firme whole wall to the bottom of the braces, wth bricke or stone, to repaire the court or townehouse, that so all inconveniencjes by rotting the timber, &c, be prevented. The charges thereof, by bill charged on the Tresurer of the country for the cleere half thereof, on the Tresurer of the country, on the Tresusrr for ye county of Suffolke for one fowerth part, & on the Tresurer for the toune of Boston for the other fourth part thereof, shall be defrayed & discharged accordingly."

LXXXIV.

[Court Files, Suffolk, No. 964, 4th paper.]

Att a Court of Assistants held at Boston the 7th: September 1669.

Edmond Angier plt: against William Bordman defendant in an Action that comes to this Court for its tryall by the magistrates refusing the virdict of the jury at the last County Court at Charls-Towne, After the Attachment juries virdict & Euidences in the Case produced were read Com-

* 1668–9?.

mitted to the jury & remaine on file with the Reccords of this Court, The jury found for the defend^{t} Costs of Courts. The magistrates refused this virdict: & soe it falls to the Generall Court in Case.

This is a true Copie of the Court of Assistants judgment. As Attests Edw. Rawson Secret:

NOTE.

It appears by a copy of the Judgment of the County Court, which is the second paper in this case, that the parties were "Mr Edmond Angier," plaintiff, and William Bordman "Administrator to the Estate of Stephen Day, deceased," defendant —

Second paper in No. 964

"Att a Countie Court held at Charls-Towne June: 15: 1669.

Mr Edmond Angier plt. against William Bordman defend^{t} Administrato^{r} to the Estate of Stephen Day deceased in an Action of Reuiew for a debt of about fowre pounds due to the sajd Edmond Angeir vpon account in his Booke according to Attachment dated June the 5th. 1669, both parties appeared & joyned issues in the Case, The jury haueing heard & Considered their seuerall pleas & alligations in the Case with the Euidences therof on file brought in their virdict, finding for the defend^{t} Costs of Court, —

The magistrates Comparing the virdict of the jury with the Euidences presented by the plaintiffe, ||ye magists|| doe refuse this virdict of the jury

vera Copia Thomas Danforth Record^{r}

vera Copia Attest^{r} ℘ Edw Rawson Secrety"

Mass. Archives Vol. 39 No. 375

"Att A Court of Asistants held at Boston 7 September 1669

Edmund Angier plaintiff ag^{t} w^{m} Bordman defend^{t} in an Accon that comes to this Court for its trjall by the magis^{ts}. refusing the virdict of the Jury at the last County Court at Charls Toune. After the Attachment Jurys virdict & euidences in the Case produced were read Comitted to the Jury & remajne on file wth the Reccords of this Court — the Jury found for the defend^{t} Costs of Courts — The magis^{ts} Refused this virdict & so it falls to the Generall Court in Case &c.

This is A true Copie taken out of the Courts booke of Reccords as Attests

Edw. Rawson Secret^{y}.

on the motion of m^{r} Angier who thrō. his defect of hearing at the Court of Asistants of ye latter part of ye reccord & being Ignorant of his duty to give sumons to ye defend^{t} at ye last sessions of the Generall Court & the Generall Court hauing many occasions the accon wth others proceeded not for want of Sumons: now earnestly desiring the Case may be heard & issued at this Court — The magis^{ts}. Judge meet to order the Secretary to Issue out warrants to the defend^{t} to Appeare personally at this Court on 16th day of this Instant for the Issue of the sajd Case. the magis^{ts} haue past this their brethren the deputjes hereto Consenting: Edw. Rawson secret^{y}.

Consented to by the Deputyes

William Torrey Cleric."

Mass. Records, Vol. IV, pt. 2, p. 454, 31 May, 1670.

"In the case of Edmond Angier, pl^{t}, ag^{t} Wm Boardman, administrato^{r} to Stephen Day, the Court, after a full hearing of both partjes, finde for the defend^{t} costs of Courts."

The remaining fourteen papers in No. 964 are copies of the record of the County Court at Cambridge, of record of the General Court, writ of attachment, accounts, bonds and depositions.

LXXXV.

[Mass. Archives, Vol. 39, No. 366.]

Att A Court of Asistants held at Boston 7th 7^{ber} 1669

Patrick Jeanison was Indicted &c. After the euidences in the Case produced were read comitted to the Jury & remajne on file: the Jury brought in their virdict: i e they found Pattrick Jeannison to be guilty of abusing the body of Grace Roberts named in the Indictment so as he brake or peir[ced] hir body by vncleane act or actions — The magist^{ts} Consent to & Concurr wth the Jury in the virdict but finding the Crime is Capitoll & that the lawe provides only for a Rape of one aboue te[nn] yeares & the first law declares for want of law to be referd & determined by ye Generall Court & ye word of God — Judg meete to referr the prisoner together wth the euidence to the Generall Court.

This is A true Copie taken out of the Courts Records Edw: Rawson Secret^{y}.

Question: whither Carnall copulation wth a child vnder tenn yeares of Age be not [ ] as Capital as a Rape on ye body of one aboue tenn yeares —This Question is comended to the deputjes for their resolution:

Edw: Rawson Secret^{y}

NOTE.

(Mass. Archives, Vol. 39, No. 367) "Quest. what shall be his punishment that hath had Carnall Copulation wth a child under 8 yeares. The reason of the Question is that It seemeth not to be a lesse offence wth one of 8 yeares then wth one aboue tenn yeares wch the lawe provides for, and in Capitoll Cases when there is no postive law: the Generall Court must determine what the law is — The magist^{ts} haue past this for their brethren the deputjes Resolution in ye 1st place:

15 October 1669: Edw: Rawson Secret^{y}

ffor resolution of this question the deputyes Conceive that such a person ought to be punished with some grevious punishment or hono^rd magis^ts. Consenting hereto

William Torrey Cleric
Consented to by ye magist^ts. Edw: Rawson Secret^y."

(Mass. Archives, Vol. 39, No. 365) "fforamuch as Carnall Copulation with a woman child under the age of ten yeares is a more haynous sin then with one of more yeares as beinge more Inhumane & vnnaturall in it selfe & also more perilous to the life & welbeinge of the child, It is therefore ordered by this Court & the Authoritie thereof, that whosoever he be that shall comitt or haue Carnall Copulation with any such child vnder ten yeares old & be legally Convict thereof, he shalbe put to death. The Deputyes haue past this wth refference to the Consent of o^r Hono^rd magis^ts hereto

13th. 8th. 1669 William Torrey Cleric

Consented to by ye magis^ts

Edw. Rawson Secret^y."

(For the above order see Mass. Records, Vol. IV, pt. 2, p. 437.)

LXXXVI.

[Court Files, Suffolk, No. 1009, 6th paper.]

Att A Court of Asistants held at Boston 1st m[arch 1669–70] James Pecker plantiffe ag^t m^r Symon Bradstreet & m^r Edward T[yng] defend^t in an Action of Appeale from the Judgment of the last County Court at Salem = After the Attachment Courts Judgment Reasons of Appeale & euidences in the Case produced were read Comitted to the Jury & remajne on file wth the Reccords [ ] Court the Jury brought in their virdict they found for [the] defendants Confirmation of the former Judgment & Cos[ts of] Courts. This virdict the magis^ts refused. This is a true Copie taken out of ye Court of Asis[tants] booke of Reccords as Attests Edw: Rawson Secret^y.

(Indorsed) "Court Asist Judg^t m^rch 1670 inter Pecker & m^r Bradstr[eet]"

Note.

Mass. Records, Vol. IV, pt. 2, p. 455, 31 May 1670.

"In the case depending betweene James Pecker, plaintiff, at the last Court of Asistants, against Mr Symon Bradstreet & Mr Edward Tyng, defend^ts, in an action of appeale from the judgment of the last County Court at Salem, coming to this Court by reason of the Magists refusing the virdict of the jury at the last Court of Asistants, the Court, on a hearing of the case, & pervsall of all the euidences, doe finde for the defendants twenty pounds in money, & costs of Courts, reuersing the judgment of the County Court at Salem.''

It appears that the judgment of the Salem Court had been for eighty pounds.

By the seventh paper in this case (No. 1009) it appears that upon the case going to the General Court by the Court of Assistants refusing the verdict of the jury the Deputies found for "Mr Symon Bradstreet & Mr Edward Tynge tw[enty pounds] in money & costs of Courts reversinge the Judgm^t^ [of the] Court of Salem"* The Magistrates "consent not hereto but judge meet that ye plaintiffe pay [†] defendants [&] Costs of Courts"

"25 3 mo 1670 Voted as ye dep^ts^ ‡ agreed it i e for 20^£^ only & costs &c Per ye whole Court E R S."

There are nine papers in No. 1009. Those not given here are the Reasons of appeal and various depositions.

LXXXVII.

[Court Files, Suffolk, No. 1022, 2nd paper.]

Att A Court of Asistants held at Boston 1st march 1669.

Mr Paul Parker plantiff on Appeale from the Judgment of the last County Court in Boston = After the Courts Judgment reasons of Appeale & euidences in the case produced were read Comitted to the Jury & remajne on file wth the reccords of this Court the Jury brought in their virdict they found the Appellant Convict of twice playing passage but not for any certeine sum̄e of mony = The magists refused the virdict, and Ordered that his bonds be Continued, or yt he give sufficient security for his appearance at the Generall Court on twelfth of may next and yt he abide ye Judgmt of ye Court & be of Good behauiour in ye meane time or else to stand Comitted till the Generall Court. This is a true Copie of the Courts Judgment as Attests Edw. Rawson Secrety.

NOTE.

Mass. Records, Vol. IV, pt. 2, p. 453, 31 May 1670.

"Paul Parker appearing before the Court, & being by his owne confession convicted of being a gemester at dice, & sundry demonstrations given of his being a very ill example to the youth of the place, this Court doe sentence him to pay as a fine to the country tenn pounds, & yt he be

---

* Which appears to have been for 80£.

† 80£.

‡ Deputies.

bound, w[th] two sufficjent suretjes, in two hundred pounds sterling for his good behaviour & observance of the lawes against that vnlawfull practise, vnlesse he depart the Colony w[th]in one moneth, & not to retourne againe w[th]out licence first had & obteyned from the Governo[r] or council."

There are in all eighteen papers in No. 1022. They consist of copies of records of the General Court, of warrant, of reasons of appeal and answers thereto, bonds, the examination of Paul Parker and numerous depositions.

LXXXVIII.

[Mass. Archives, Vol. 9, No. 57.]

A Question putt to y[e] Generall Courtt* for Resolution A man Haveing Buried his first wife whether itt be lawfull for him to marrie with Her y[t] was his first wiues naturall sister.

This Question is Ans[r]d on the negative their Brethren the Deputies hereto consenting.

13 May 1670 Edw Rawson Secret[y]

Consented to by the Deputyes

William Torrey Cleric.

NOTE.

Mass. Records, Vol. IV, pt. 2, p. 454, 31 May 1670.

"In ans[r] to the quaestion, whither it be lawfull for a man that hath buried his first wife to marry wth hir that was his first wiues natturall sister, the Court resolves it on the negative."

LXXXIX.

[Court Files, Suffolk, No. 988, 2nd. paper.]

To the much honered The Governer Deputie Governer & Magestrats of the honered Court of Assistance now assembled at Boston Sept. 8: 1670: The Petition of William Stacey: Humbly Sheweth:

That Satan haueing filled his heart & layed a temptation before him, his corrupt nater was redy to imbrace it And therefore he Doe & must owne the sentence of the honered Court to be just upon him & according to his merit, the which may justly stop his mouth: for ever craueing any favour from the sayd honered Court, In abateing or aquiting any part of his sentence: But becase his poore parents & masters family (wch are giltless) are afflicted by the remain[d]er of his suffering, Therefore if your poore Supplyant (an abject) may implore your honers favours to permit

* By the Court of Assistants?

the bagg* of his iniguity to be taken off, viz the rope about his neck Dureing the Courts pleasure) it would be a great reviveing to his sayd parents and present master & famylie: wch if a poore contemptable person may obtaine It would deeply oblige him vnto your honers & vnto the lord for you, That haue made you instrumentall for his humbling: & he hope for ever a reclamation from any horrid vice: Not Daring further to presume, but in all subjection your sayd supplyant doth hum‸ly submitt & remaine

Your honers in all obedience

Willm̄ Stacy

8 of September 1670

In Answer hereto It is ordered that the Secretary send ouer to ye Constable of Charls Towne the Copie of this Courts sentenc ag^t^ Wm Stacey & Requires him from this Court to see that It be performed in all respects & y^t^ on his neglect of wearing his Roape on the outside of his cloath^s^ to take him & seuerely whip him according to Lawe

By the Court Edw. Rawson Secret^y^.

NOTE.

The first paper in No. 988 is a‸certificate in favor of "William Stasy" by his "master and dame" and others.

The Petition of William Stacey appears to be in the handwriting of William Howard.

XC.

[Court Files, Suffolk, No. 1276, 14th and 92nd papers.]

[Fourteenth paper in No. 1276]

Att A Court of Asistants held at Boston ye 7th march 1670.†

Theoder Atkinson Plantiffe against John willjams defendant in an Action of the Case vppon a revejw of an action Comenct by the sajd Atkinson agt the sajd willjams at a County Court held at Boston in Jaunary 1663 for not performing his promise to the sajd Atkinson for the rectifying of accounts betweene them and not attending a meeting which [was] appointed by major Generall John Leueret & m^r^ Thomas Bratle for that purpose &c as may further Appeare by the Attachment to the County Court dated 31th tenth month 1663 reffereence thereto being had wch sajd action Came to the Court of Asistants following according to Course of law by the magis^ts^ refusing the Jurjes virdict which sajd Court of Asistants found for

* Badge?
† 1670–1.

the plaintiffe one hundred & fifty pounds vnless the defendant ouer haule his Accounts & performe his promise therein to the plantiff by the last of m[ay next] come twelue months & Costs of Courts foure pounds sixteen shillings & tenn pence as Appeares by a Copy of the sajd Judgment vnder the Recorders hand wth due damages according to Attachment dated 27 of february 1670. After the Attachment & euidences in the Case produced were read Comitted to the jury: The Court by Consent of partyes referring the ouer hauling the accompts betweene them the sajd Atkinson & willjams extending to the time that Capt willjams hath given the sajd Atkinson credit for in the Account presented & in Court begining in 1656: to m^{r} John Joyliffe Capt. Thomas Lake & Capt Laurence Hamond m^{r} John Joyliffe to Appoint time & place and after their thorough examinations of what each party Can produce before them; to make their returne of what they Can finde to this Court on the eighth of June next either jointly or severally the plantiffe & defendant mutually engaging each to other to pay the ballance of the account as the Court shall state it and the pa[rtyes] to Attend the Auditors = Att y^{e} sajd Adjournm^{t} 8th June 1671: the Auditors m^{r} J[ ] Capt Thomas Lake & Capt Laurence Hamond brought in their returne which [after the] Court & Jury had pervsed & Considered wth the Euidences in the Case [produced] brought in their virdict they found a speciall virdict: i: e if the returne [of the] Audit Appointed by the Honoured Court (wth Consentt of plantiff & defendant) being [added] to what the Honoured major Generall Leueret & m^{r} Bratle did before, doe amount [to] a full performance of the defendants promise; for the ouer hauling & rectifying of Accomp[ts] or be equivolent thereto then wee finde for the plantiff one hundred ninety & foure pounds thirteen shillings & tenn pence in money to be payd to the plaintiffe on Accompt of Errors & particulars not prooved by the defendant to be due vnto him according to the Accompts examined by the Auditt & Costs of Courts If otherwise then for the plantiffe foure hund[red] pounds in money except the defendant shall attend the ouerhauleing & rectifying accompts wth [the] plaintiffe to effect (according to his promise) wth in three months wth Costs of Courts which [we] leaue to the Honoured Courts determination on the pervsall of this virdict the magis^{ts} finde for the plaintiffe one hundred ninety foure pounds thirteen & tenn p[ence] damage in money & Costs of Courts twenty three pounds two & five pence that this is A true Copie of the entry of the action, order for Auditting Accom[pt] & Courts Judgment therevpon, taken out of the Courts booke of Reccords is Attes[ed] by Edward Rawson Secret.

The ninety-second paper in this case (No. 1276 Court Files, Suffolk) is the Special Verdict and judgment of the Court of Assistants, 9 June 1671, and is as follows:—

In y[e] Case depending betweene Theod[r] Atkinson plt. & Capt[n]. Jn[o] Williams Defft.

The Juery findes a speciall Verdict, Vizt. If the returne of the Auditt appointed by the hono[r]d Court (with consent of plt. and Deft.) being added to what the hono[r]d Maj[r] Gen[ll]. Leveritt and m[r] Bratle did before, doe amount to a full performance of the Defts. promise for the overhaleing and rectifying of accompts or be equivolent thereto then wee finde for the plt. one hundred ninety and foure pounds thirteene shillings and ten pence in money, to be p[d] to the plt. on accompt of Erro[rs] and perticulers not proved by the defft to be due unto him, according to the accompts examined by the Auditt and Costs of Courts; If otherwise, then for the plt. ffoure hundred pounds in money except the Deft shall attend the overhaleing and rectifying accompts with the plt. to effect (according to his promise) within three monthes, with Costs of Courts, which wee leave to the determination of the hono[r]d Court

This virdict Given in by y[e] foreman of y[e] Jury in y[e] name of the whole 9 June 1671: Per Edw: Rawson Secret.

on the pervsall of this virdict the magists find for y[e] plantiff one hundred ninety fower pounds thirteen shillings & ten pence damag in money & Costs of Courts

9 June 1671 as Attests Edw: Rawson Secret.

Note.

The ninth paper in No. 1276 is as follows:—

"To Edward Mitchelson, Marshall Generall or his Deputy

Yo[w] are required in his Majtys name by way of Execuc̄on to levy on the goods or estate of Cap[t] John Williams in mony the Sum̄e of two hundred seventeen pounds sixteen shillings & three pence or in defect thereof on his person & deliver the same with two Shillings for this Execuc̄on to Theodor Atkinson Sen[r]. & is in Satisfaction of a judgment granted him by the last Court of Assistants held at Boston in March last & on Adjournment 8th. June last for soe much. hereof you are not to faile. Dated in Boston 6th. July, 1671.

By the Court Edward Rawson Secret.

Vera Copia Attest[r] per Edward Rawson Secret.

Copia Vera per Is[a]: Addington Cler.

Underwritt,

Seized the Warehouse & Workhouse with yard & what other of the Estate may Satisfy this Execucon & is to lye for the Security of the same all the land belonging to the house &c: this 12. $\frac{6}{mo}$ 71.

By Mee Edward Mitchelson Marshall Gen[l].

Endorst,

M[r] Peter Brackett & Samuell Sendall were sworn to apprize the Estate of Captain John Williams now resident in Boston

before mee Richard Parker Comiss[r].

13 $\frac{7}{mo}$ 1671.

Sept. 13, 1671,

Samuell Sendall & Peter Brackett being chosen by Marshall Mitchelson & Theodor Atkinson & sworn to apprize an Estate of Cap[t]. John Williams being shewed by Marshall Mitchelson an house with yard & out houses over & against the house of Hudson Leverett & being Ordered by the sd. Mitchelson to apprize soe much thereof as amounts to the Summe of two hundred & seventeen pounds sixteen Shillings three pence & two Shillings for the Execucon & about fifty Shillings for serving Wee doe judge that Theodor Atkinson shall haue the warehouse & workhouse & all the lands belonging to the great house, as also the corner Shop opposite unto John Morse his Shop & the Sellar under that Shop as witness o[r] hands the day & yeare above written, being by vertue of an Execution granted to Theodor Atkinson.

Peter Brackett
Samuel S Sendall
his marke.

I haue Seized the workhouse & warehouse with the lands belonging or about the great house; as also the corner Shop opposite to John Morses Shop with the Sellar under the Shop to Satisfy an Execucon of two hundred Seventeen pounds Sixteen shillings & three pence with the charges of the Execucon & being prized I delivered the same unto Theodor Atkinson this 13 of $\frac{7}{mo}$ 1671, & is in full of this Execucon. Edward Mitchelson Marshall Gen[ll].

That this is a true Coppie of the apprizement Marshalls return &c. Attests Edward Rawson Secret.

Copia Vera Attest[r]. per Is[a]: Addington Cler."

There are in all ninety seven papers in No. 1276. They consist of copies of the records of the General Court and of the County Court, of the writs, of reasons of appeal and answers thereto, of bonds, letters, depositions, bills of costs and verdict. (See XLVII, LVI, XCII, CIV.) (See also Mass. Col. Records, Vol. IV., Part II., pp. 476, 539, 559 & 571.) (See also Mass. Hist[l]. Soc[y]. Miss[s]. Papers 1628–1691, fol. 57 & 58.) (See also Mass. Hist[l]. Soc[y]. Letters & Papers 1632–1678, fol. 104).

XCI.

[Mass. Archives, Vol. 10, No. 57.]

To the hono^rd^ Court of Assistants now sitting in Boston The petition of Arthur Mason humbly sheweth

That whereas yor Suplyant was the last yeare Justly sentenced by this hono^r^d Court unto disfranchisem^t^, ffor his sinfull, passionate, and vnadvised wordes and behavio^r^, before the ffirst Church of Christ in Boston, and to their great offence, contrary to the duty wch God requires of him vi^zt^ to walke inoffenciwely towards all, especially towards the Church of God, ffor all wch yor Suplyant hath beene, and desires still to bee vnfeignedly sorrowfull, hopeing (through grace assisting) to manifest my sincere repentance to all, by a more inoffencive conversation towards all,

May it therefore please this hono^r^d Court, soe far to Compassionate yor poore Suplyant, as to release him from that sentence of disfranchisem^t^, and to restore him to his former Liberty as a ffreeman of this Collony, which I shall by Gods helpe endeavo^r^ better to improove, to the glory of God, and the service of the Countrey, And yor petitioner shall euer pray:

14th June 1671:

The Court in Ans^r^ to this Request the Court Judgeth it meete to restore him to his former liberty taking of his disfranchisment accordingly

as Attests Edw: Rawson Secret^y^

(See Court Files, Suffolk, No. 162088 and No. 986. See LXXV.)

XCII.

[Court Files, Suffolk, No. 1276, 16th paper.]

At a Court of Asistants held at Boston the 5th Septemb^r^. 1671.

John Williams plaintiffe against Theodor Atkinson sen^r^. Defend^t^. in an acc̄on of reveiw of the acc̄on tryed at the last Court of Assistants according to Attachm^t^. Dated. 29th. June. 1671. After the Attachment Courts judgment & Evidences in the case produced were read comitted to the Jury & remaine on file with the Records of this Court the Jury brought in theire verdict they founde for the plaintiffe two hundred Eighty five pounds five shillings & ten pence damage & costs of Courts. The Magistrates refused this verdict.

That this ^ a true Coppie taken out of the Courts records.

Attests Edward Rawson Secret.

Copia Vera Attest^r^

ꝑ: Is^a^. Addington Cler.

Note.

The eighteenth paper is a copy of the Judgment of the General Court Oct. 8, 1672, the case coming to that Court by reason of the refusal of the verdict by the Court of Assistants, Sept. 5, 1671. The judgment is for the plaintiff John Williams. See also below, record of 12 March 1671–2.

XCIII.

[Court Files, Suffolk, No. 2997, 8th paper.]

Att A Court of Assistants held at Boston the 5th. of September 1671.

In Answer to the peticõn of Hugh Clarke and Elizabeth Buckminster It is ordered that Thomas Gardiner & mr John Peirpont shall & hereby are Appointed a Comittee to lay out the peticonr hir Just thirds as the law directs &c: That this is A true copie of the Courts Order and Ansr to Hugh Clarke & Elizabeth Buckminsters peticon taken out of the Courts Reccords Attests Edw Rawson Secret.

XCIV.

[Court Files, Suffolk, No. 1290, 7th paper.]

At a Court of Assistants held at Boston 5th. Septemb 1671

Capta. Wm. Davis Attourny to Cornelius Stenwick plaintiffe against ffathergon Dinely Defendt. in an action of Appeale from the judgmt. of the County Court in Boston. After the attachment the Courts judgment, Reasons of Appeale & Evidences in the case produced were read comitted to the jury & are remaining on file with the Records of this Court The Jury brought in theire Verdict. a Speciall Verdict i: e: in case the great blots or blurrs on the bill in question being mostly in the place of the Testimonies Subscription will make it voide in law notwithstanding a possitive witness to the bill affirming the Subscription of the Debtor & other Testimony affirming the owning the Debt, then wee finde for the Defendant costs of Courts; But in case such blot as aforesaide will not nullify the saide bill in law then wee finde for the plaintiffe one hundred forty one pounds Eight Shillings in Country pay & costs of Courts. The Magestrates on perusall of this Verdict findes for the plaintiffe one hundred forty one pounds Eight Shillings in currant Country pay & costs of Courts four pounds thirteen Shillings & nine pence = This Verdict is to stand Entred from ye 5th. March 167½. according to law.

That this is a True Coppie taken out of the Courts booke of Records Attests Edw: Rawson Secret.

This is a true Coppie As Attests Isaac Addington Cler.

Endorsed. "Courts of Assistants judgment 1672"

NOTE.

[See below, record of 2 Sept. 1673. See also Suffolk County Court Record Oct. 1672, p. 83. John Dinely's Adm^{r}. against Steenwick. This County Court Record is at the Boston Athenæm.]

The third paper in No. 1290 is as follows:—

"To Edward Micheson Marshall Generall.
[ ] require you in his ma^{ts}. name to levy by way of Execucon on the goods & [ ] of the late John Dinely in the hands of ffathergone Dinely Administrator to ye estate of the said John Dinely Deceased in Current Country pay to the value of one hundred forty one pounds Eight shillings & in money foure pounds thirteene shillings and Nyne pence as costs & Deliuer the same i: e: one hundred fforty sixe pounds one shilling and Nyne pence with two shillings for this Execution to Capt. Willam Davis Attorny of Cornelius Stenwicke & is in satisfacon of a Judgm^{t} granted the sd Stenwicke the 5th of September last and according to lawe stands Entred from the 4th. of March 1671. the said Dauis hauing given Security to respond &c. as the law directs hereof you are not to faile Dated in Boston 3^{d} of May 1672. By the Court Edward Rawson Secret.

vnder writ I haue Seazed the land Expressed by the prizers both parcells & these men to prize the same & haue deliuered the same to willm Dauis by virtue of this Execucon.

m^{r} Peter Bracket & John Conney were sworne to prize the goods of Jno. Dinely Deceased according to the Courts Judgm^{t}. & knowledge Before me Richd. Parker Comisio^{r}

That what is above written is a true Coppie of the Execution appriz^{ers} oath &c. attests Edward Rawson Secre^{t}

Endorsed & annexed.

Wee whose names are here vnder written being chosen by Marshall Mitcheson and Capt Wm Dauis to apprise the Estate of Jno. Dinely late of Virginia Deceased by virtue of an Execution granted the 3^{d}. of May 1672 vnto Capt Dauis attorny of Cornelius Stenwicke of New Yorke there being presented to vs a piece of land abutting vpon the Street where the prison is between the Dwelling house of Richard Critchly & the dwelling house of m^{r} Samuell Legg. wch. is Sixty one foote vpon a line running South fforty one foote & a halfe facing to the Street west & one hundred & fifteene foote bounded vpon Richard Critchlies house & land East & one hundred foote vpon the land of ffathergone Dinely's South Provided Richard Critchly is to enjoy as is Expressed in his Deed During his naturall life only fiueteene foote & a halfe fronte on the Street North from Critchlyes house and fifty two foote in length backwards bearing the same breadth of fifteen foote & a halfe all the way without disturbance or molestation all which lands as it is bounded & Staked wee haue apprized at ffoure score pounds. Moreouer wee being showed a peece of pasture land of Jno. Dinelyes above sd lying at the West end of Boston adjoyning to the pasture lands of Deacon Jacob Elliot & next to ye Sea in quantity two acres bee it more or less being betweene the above sd John Dinely & his Brother ffathergone Dinely this two Acres being equally diuided between them two, wee haue apprized the one halfe to bee worth twenty fiue pounds vnto which apprizment of Eighty & twenty fiue pounds wch is in all one hundred & fiue pounds wee haue hereunto set our hands this 3^{d} Day of July 1672

Peter Bracket Jno Conney

I haue according to the Execution & in the presence of m^{r} Nicholas Page & Robert Howard one parcell of ground in the towne and also one Acre more in the Com̃on in the presence of Theodor Atkinson & James Meeres all wch being Seazed by Execution & prized by the above persons I haue Deliuered to William Dauis as Attorny vnto Cornelius Stenwicke as appeares by Execution I say deliuered by mee the 15th. 5th: 1672

Edward Micheson Marshall generall.

That this alsoe is a true Coppie of the Aprizm^{t} & the Marshalls Act there vpon being Compared with the Originall on file

Attests Edward Rawson Secret

This is a true Coppie as Attests

Isaac Addington Cler."

XCV.

[Court Files, Suffolk, No. 1050, 2^{d} paper.]

Wee the Grandjury vnto the honoured court of Assistants in the case com̃itted vnto vs concerning Samuell the son of William an Indian wee doe find him vehemently & suspitiously guilty of attempting to ravish the wife of Daniell Bacon Senr. of Cambridge, & further leave him to the Honoured Court. Boston this 5th (7^{ber}) 1671 James Euerell fore man

"To the Constable of Cambr̃ or ||Watertoune or|| his Deputy.

In his Maties name you are required to app^{r}hend the body of Samuel, Indian, Sonne of W^{m}. Natick, Indian, & bring him before some of ye Mag^{tes} to answ^{r} for assaulting the wife of Daniel Bacon in the highway neere her dwelling house the last night in ye evening time, & attempting to ravish her. you are not to faile hereof at yor pill. & make a true return. Dat. 31. 6. 71.

you are to warn as witnesses
Jno. Whitney, Sonne of Jonathan Whitney
& Jno. Jackson Senr. to appeare also.

Daniel Gookin
Thomas Danforth.

In case he be fled. you are to pursue
him with horse & man & to press
such help as you need.

Watterton Constable put in
By me Dan: Gookin"

(From the Chamberlain Collection)

XCVI.

[Court Files, Suffolk, No. 1052, 9th paper.]

Wee the Grand Jury for our Soueraigne Lord the King doe Indict Phillip Read of Concord Chirurgeon or practitioner in Phisick: for not having the feare of God before his eyes & being Instigated by the divill did Sometime in may last Blaspheme the holy name of christ & also on a motion then & there made to pray to God for his wife then sick blaspemously Cursed bidding the divill take yow & yor prayer. Contrary to the peace of our Soueraigne Lord the King his Crowne & dignity the lawes of God & of this land title Blasphemy: & doe find this to be a true bill. James Euerell fore man

Boston this 5th. 7br. 1671

XCVII.

[Court Files, Suffolk, No. 1137, 7th paper.]

Wheras there came in to the port of pascataway; about six weekes since a ship called [Lenham of burthen] about 80 or 90 tunne mand wth Dutch men; which ship and company being suspected by the Authority vpon the place to be questionable & so much the Rather because the Skiper & company had contracted a sale for the Shipp & furniture in a pri[vie] way & manner at a smal valew whervpon the magistrates vpon the place Informed the Goūnr & magistrates att Boston & seasd the sails of ye said ship vntill the matter should be further examined; whervpon the skiper being sike others of the company appeared at Boston before the Counsel who being examined & the matter Inquired into The Counsel do find yt; the said ship belongs to a person in Amsterdam & yt none abord ye ship haue a legall powre to sell [ye sd] ship & therefore doe Judge that : the sale of the shipp to mr Greenland & his Company is null & voyd, and that if the skipper & company haue a desire for the releefe of their nessecitys to sue for their wages they may proceed in A legal way to recour the same. Past 11 Sept. 1671: E. R. S.

XCVIII.

[From the "County Court Papers (Exeter, N. H.) 1674–1677, Folio 333," now deposited in the State Archives at Concord, N. H.]

Att a Court of Assistants Held att Boston 5th. March 1671.

Walter Barefoot Being Bound over by the County Court last in Boston* to Appear att this Court to Answer what should be layd agt. Him for

* See Court Files, Suffolk, No. 1066.

his profane Swearing: the Court having Considered of the Evidence ꝓduced against him doe sentence him to pay for His prophaine & Horrid Oathes: twenty shillings fine: and itt [Appearing] to this Court that there is just Cause to [ ] thatt he left his wife & two Children in England. Doe sentence him forthwith to Return to England by the first ship. on penaly of the Law. ⁝ the payment of Twenty pounds as ye Law Directs or thatt he Departt this Jurisdiction, yt hee is & shall bee Debared from Henceforth to practise Chirurgery or physicke in any partt of this Jurisdiction, on penalty of ten pounds for Every Acte he puts forth in Either of those sciences: thatt During his Abod in this Jurisdiction Hee put in Security for 50lb apeece & his owne hand for 100lb thatt he [live of] Good Behaviour. And Abstaine from [Mris] Hiltons House att Exeter especially her Company. In Answer to his petition the Court ordered thatt his owne Bond Bee taken.

That this is A true Copie taken out of the Court Records & yt Bond was Given & taken accordingly

Attest. Edward Rawson. Secre'ty

XCIX.

[Court Files, Suffolk, No. 1104, 4th paper.]

Att A Court of Asistants held at Boston the 5th march 1671.*

John Richards Atturney to Capt. wm meade & mr Ralph Ingram of London plaintiffe against Ephrajm Turner defendant in an action of Appeale from the Judgment of the last County Court in Boston After the Attachmt Courts Judgment & Reasons of Appeale & other euidences in the Case produced were read Comitted to the Jury & remayning on file wth the Reccords of this Court the Jury brought in their virdict they found for the plantiffe reversion of the former Judgment & tenn pounds sixteen shillings starling mony of England & Costs of Courts fiuety five shillings. This is A true Copie taken out of the Courts booke of Reccords as Attests Edward Rawson Secrety.

C.

[Court Files, Suffolk, No. 1316, 1st paper.]

At a Court of Assistants held at Boston 5 March 1671.†

John Godfrey Plt. against Matthias Button Deft. In an Action of Appeal from the Judgmt. of the Last County Court in Hampton after the Attachmt. Courts Judgmt. Reasons of Appeal & Evidences in the Case pro-

---

* 1671–2.

† 1671–2.

duced were read Comitted to the Jury which remain on File with the Records of this Court The Jury brought in their Verdict they find for the Pl[t]. If Buttons Acquittance be good in Law the reversion of the former Judgm[t]. and two Hundred thirty Eight pounds two shillings Damage and Costs of Courts If otherwise they find for the Pl[t]. one hundred Thirty one pounds damage and Costs of Courts The Court on Consideration of the Jury's Verdict in Relation to John Godfrey and Matthias Button do declare for John Godfrey agreeing with the Jury in the last part of their Verdict finding for John Godfrey one hundred thirty Eight pounds Damage & Costs of Courts.

Execution issued out 13th March 1671/2 which in its Compleation was returned 28 July 74 and is on Execution file as ℘ return ——	A True Copy as appears of record — Exam[d]. ℘ Benj[a]. Rolfe Cler —

A True Copy Exam[d]. ℘ Mitchel Sewall Cler —

NOTE.

Mass. Records, Vol. IV, pt. 2, p. 406, 23 Oct., 1668.

"In ans[r] to the peticon of Mathias Button, complaining ag[t] John Godfrey, the Court judgeth it meete to referr the peticoner to his course of lawe by action at the County Court of that shire, & is admitted, sub forma pauperis, to whos justice the case is referred."

CI.

[Mass. Archives, Vol. 10, No. 229.]

Att A Court of Asistants held at Boston 5th march 167½

John Russell of Woborne being bound ouer to this Court by the County Court last at Charls Towne to Answer for his renouncing Comunion wth the church of Christ there; whereof he is a member & Joyning himselfe wth the schismatticall church of Annabaptists & taking office power amongst them &c he appeared before the Court & acknowledged that after many strivings in his owne spirit he did Joyne himself wth those called Annabaptists & tho vnder the sence of his owne weaknes being prest & ouercome by them did accept of & become a Teaching officer to them, & that he had exercised officiall power amongst them the society or meeting of Annabaptists* so much declared against by the Generall Court whereof Thomas Gold is a pretended officer and that he the sajd Russell refusing also to promise for

* See above, record of 4th. Sept. 1666, case of Thos. Gold &c.

after times to refrajne frequenting the aforesajd disallowed meeting This Court hath therefore vpon Consideration of the sajd Russell pernitious practises & obstinat profession to persist therein haue Adjudged him to be Comitted to the prison at Cambridg there to remajne wthout bajle or mainprise till the Generall Court take further order therein vnless in the meane tjme he doe engage by solemne promise to some tuo of the magistrates of midlesex to desist from his Irregular scandalous practises & Attend the publick worship of God on the Lords dayes in the place where he liues which he refusing to performe warrant Issued out for his Comittment Accordingly. That this is A true Copy taken out of the Courts booke of Reccords:

Attests Edward Rawson Secret^{y}

[The next paper is another copy of the same sentence]

CII.

[Mass. Hist. Soc.^{y}, Miss^{s} Papers, 1628–1691, Fol. 59 No. 3.]

S shipping goods upon B to be deliuered to R beyond the sea the sd R paying freight and the sd B upon his arrival at the port tendering the sd goods to R and ye sd R refusing to meddle wth ye sd goods and to pay freight whether the sd B can recouer his freight for the sd goods of the sd S the sd goods being left in a safe hand by good advice by the sd B or whether sd B ought not to haue satisfied himselfe for his freight out of the sd goods without molesting the sd S: Resolued vpon the 12 of march 71/2 to be put to the Genl Court for Resolution as Attests

Edw: Rawson Secret^{y}

(Indorsed) "Quest a^{s} to ye case of S.. & Edw^{ds}."

Mass. Records, Vol. IV, pt. 2, p. 516, 15 May, 1672.

[Question stated as above] "This question agreed upon to be put to the Generall Court for resolution by ye Court of Asistants last. This Court resolues it thus: That S. is not liable to pay freight vnto B., but B. to sattisfy himself for the freight out of the goods."

CIII.

[Court Files, Suffolk, No. 1099.]

John Russell, Senr., being presented by the Grand Jury att the Court att Charles Towne 19. day of Decr. 71 & from thence comeing ||bound|| to this Court, the sd. Russell being called owned the sd present^{t}. & in particular his departing out of the Congregac̃on of Obourne att the administrac̄on of the ordinance of baptisme of a child or children & because thereof, & y^{t} hee had ioyned himselfe to y^{t} sismaticall society or meeting of Anibaptists soe much declared ag̃st by the gen^{r}all Court whereof Tho: Gold* is a pretended officer & y^{t} hee the sd Russell hath taken office power on him there, refuseing also to promise for after tymes to refraine frequenting the aforesd disallowed meeting. This Court hath therefore vpon considerac̄on of the sd Russells pernicious practises & obstinate profession to persist therein, haue adiudged him to be comitted to prison att Cambridge there to remaine wthout bayle or maineprize till the gen^{r}all Court take further order therein vnles in the meane tyme hee doe ingage by solemne promise to some 2 of the magistrates of myddlesex to desist from his irregular scandellous practises & attend the publ. worshipp of god on ye Lords dayes In the place where he liues — past this 12th of March 1671

as Attests Edward Rawson Secret^{y}.

CIV.

[Court Files, Suffolk, No. 1276, 31st paper.]

Theodore: Atkinson Senio^{r} Apealing to this Court from the Judgment of the last County Court at Boston for Baratry & vexatious sueing Capt. Williams : The Court haue heard the case & do ~~determine~~ ||Judge|| that the said Atkinson: hath dealt ~~weakly~~ inconsideratley ||& Iregulerly|| to prosecute the said Williams: in a case wch hath beene so offten Issued ~~& after a promise made by him in open court as some do Remember to aquess in the last conclusion of ye court of assistants & therefore do hereby inhibitt & disable the said Atkinson to sue the said Williams in any matter of Accts betwene y^{m} in any Court within this Jurisdiction~~: and doe order that he bee admonished to cary it peacabley wth all men & attend his particular calling wth diligence herafter ~~& so paying the fees of Court he is relesed~~ & ye fine laid vpon him at ye County Court ~~the taking of it~~ is suspended vntill this Court take further order.

past 12 m^{r}ch 1671† Per E. R. S.

Note.

Among the papers in this case are the arguments of plaintiff and defendant. See also above, records of March 1, 1663–4, 7 March 1664/5, 7 March 1670–1, 9 June 1671, 5. Sept. 1671. See Suffolk County Court Record 30 Jan. 1671–2 p. 18. Atkinson fined 10£ & fees of Court for a vexatious suit against Williams.

---

* See above, record of 4 Sept., 1666, as to case of Thomas Gold &c.

† 1671–2.

[Suffolk County Court Record, Boston, 30 Jan. 1671–2, page 18.]

Atkinson agst. Wms.

"Theoder Atkinson Senr. plantiff against Capt. John Williams Defend^t. according to Attachm^t Dated the 24th of January 1670. The Cour^t (haueing considered the Attachm^t with what was produc^d & proue^d. in Court against the plantiff Theoder Atkinson) doe Judge that as there was no ground of Action, soe it was a vexatiose suite contrary to ye Law title baratry & therefore fine him ten pounds fine to the County & fees of Court standing comitted till the Sentance be perform^d. Theoder Atkinson appealed from this Sentance to the next Court of Assistants & the s^d. Theo: Atkinson in ten pounds & Peter Brackett & Tho: Matson sen^r. in fiue pounds apeice acknowledged themselves bound to the Tresurer of ye County of Suffolk on condicoñ that the said Atkinson shall prosecute his appeale from the Sentance of this Court to ye next Court of Assistants to efect & in ye meane tyme bee of good behauior.

Appeald".

CV.

[Court Files, Suffolk, No 1173, 4th paper.]

1672* March the 5th

The Returne of the Grand-Jury in the Case of the indian Called twenty rod

the grandjury fynde twenty rod guilty of rauishing an Indian Girle about 9 yeares of age

John Sherman with the ffull Consent of the rest of the sayd Jury

[Court Files, Suffolk, No. 1173, 5th paper.]

"The Jurys verdit concerning ye Indian Called twenty rod, The Jury finds y^t if all ye circumstances in this case doth amount to one evidence, then ye Girles testimony makes it two & soe we[illegible]de twenty rode Indian guilty according to Indictment. The circumstances y[illegible] wee meane are as followeth viz first his being in ye place or neare it. 2^{ly} his not denying ye fact when accused before Maior Hathorne. but excuseing him selfe y^t if he did it, he was in drink. 3^{ly} noe other person being found neare ye place but ye Indian before specified. & he alledging noe other person to cleare him selfe.

Joshua Tidd
foreman

The bench Judges the Euidence Good & so [he] is found Guilty.

E. R. S.

[Court Files, Suffolk, No. 1173, 7th paper.]

Twenty Rod Indian Indited for a Rape vpon the Body of Bety ~~one of the praying~~ indians ~~vnder~~ about nine yeares of age ~~the Court doth sen-~~

---

* 1671–2.

is found guilty & the Court sentence him to bee sold for his life to some of the Cariba Islands & if he returne into this Jurisdiction againe to be put to death

16. may 72. past & pronounct E R S

CVI.

[Mass. Archives, Vol. 106, No. 200(2).]

Henry Greeneland appearing before this court and being legally convicted of many high misdemeano^rs i. e. endeavouring to disturb his ma^ties Goverm̃ent here setled, revileing the Courts of justice and the mag^ts. in base & vnworthy termes and making quarrels & contentions among the People, in a very perfidious manner, with profane swearing & curseing, Is sentenced to pay a fine of 20^li. in money and to depart the limits of this Jurisdic̃on within two months next comeing, & not to returne againe, without the license of the Generall Court or Councill, On penalty of being severely whipt 30 stripes, & to pay a fine of 100^li. and not to be admitted hereafter to be a surety or Attorney in any legall process, and to stand comitted, vntill the fine of 20^li be sattisfied.

In Court of Assistants 21 — 3 — 1672.

Voted affirmatively as Attests
Edward Rawson Secret^y

NOTE.

Mass. Records, Vol. IV, pt. 2, p. 555, 7 May, 1673.

"As to the acco^t presented to this Court in relation to expences & charges in seizing Henry Greenland by Mr Edw̄ Rushworth, amounting to fower pounds, the Court reffers the determination thereof to the County Court at Yorke, who is to order the payment of what is due as the law directs."

Same, p. 557, same date.

"In ans^r to the petition of seuerall inhabitants of Douer, Portsmouth, &c, on behalfe of Henry Greenland, & for his liberty, the Court sees no cause to grant their request."

"In ans^r to the petition of Mary Greenland, it is ordered by this Court, that Henry Greenland haue liberty to returne into this jurisdiction, & abide here vntill the first of September next, for the disposing his estate & remooving his family, prouided he doe in other respects observe the order of the Court of Asistants, and depart after the tjme expired."

CVII.

[Mass. Archives, Vol. 106, No. 202(2) continued.]

Edward Colcord for his reviling of Authority is referred to the next County Court in Yorkshire where he comitted ye fact to Ans^r for his so doing and that he Give in his bond in forty pounds to ye Treasurer of the Country yt he be of Good behaviour till the sajd Court shall haue heard & determined ye Case & yt ^ Appeare at ye sd Court & Abide their sentence that the Secretary send a Copie of ye Judgmt wth y[e] euidence in Court now Ag[t] him to the Clarke of y[t] Court that so his Case may be duely heard & determined as euidences shall then make it out ag[t] him

Past by y[e] Court Edw Rawson Secret[y].

Edw. Colcord in open Court acknowledged himself his heires bound in forty pounds to Rich Russell esq[r] Treas[r] that he will Appeare at the next County Court to be held in Yorkshire and Ans[r] what shall be lajd to his charge for reviling Authority and Abide ye sentence of y[t] Court & in the meane time to be of good behaviour

21: may 1672 E R S

NOTE.

Mass. Records, Vol. III, p. 66, 6 May, 1646.

"In ans[r] to the peticon of Edward Colcord & John Moulton for releife ag[nt] y[e] vnaequall stinting of the comons at Hampton, itts referred to M[r] Samuell Dudley, Edward Rawson, M[r] W[m] Payne, & M[r] Carlton, & they haue power hereby to examine witnesses on oath, & search into all the distractions there; making reporte of w[t] they shall doe or find in the p[r]mises to y[e] next sitting of this Court. By both."

Same, p. 253, 14 Oct., 1651.

"In answer to a petition p[r]ferd by seuerall of the inhabitants of Hampton, for releife in respect of vnjust molestation from some persons there pretendinge power for what they doe from M[r] Batchelo[r], its ordred, that whatsoeuer goods or landes haue ben taken away from any of the inhabitants of Hampton, afforesd, by Edward Colcord or Joh- Sanbourne, vppon pretence of beinge authorized by M[r]. Batchelo[r], either with or without execution, shalbe returned to them from whom it was taken, & the execution to be cald in & no more to be graunted vntill there appeare sufficyent power from M[r] Batchelo[r] to recouer the same, to the County Courts, either of Salisbury or Hampton."

Same, p. 347, 15 May, 1654.

"The Court having receiued seuerall informations of many gross & abusive cariages of Edward Colcord in a seeming way of fraude, which, if proued as is tendred, ought to be duely & timely wittnessed agaynst, & meet punishm[t] inflicted, & bec̃ this Court would not be wanting in the vse of all due meanes for the discouery of such vile practises, it is ordered, that the secritary shall forthw[th] graunt out atatchm[t] ag[t] the s̄d Edward Colcord, in the some of fifty pounds, binding him to be responsall to the next County Court at Hampton, for such his miscariages as is w[th]in mentioned, & shalbe then prved agaynst him for that end. This Court doth hereby appoynt & impower the recorder for the County Court at Hampton, by warrent, to send for all such p[r]tyes as haue profered to proue the within mentioned abuses of Edward Colcord, & such other as he shalbe informed off can come in & testifie ag[t] him, and that Court to make returne to the next Court of Asistants of what they shall find, that so justice may be administered in case that Court cannot reach to due punishment."

Same, p. 395, 23 May 1655.

"Forasmuch as this Court is informed there is some wittnesses in Colcords case that were not allowed their charges, it is ordered, that it shalbe in the libertie of Salsbury Court to satisfie such wittnesses charges out of the fowre pounds thirteen shillings, in M[r] Stanions hands, as a fine to the country, which yet is not payd in."

Same, p. 414, 22 May, 1655. The above order not having been "attended by reason no notice hath bin giuen of the Courts pleasure hearin, it is therefore ordered that the like liberty shalbe graunted to the next Court at Hampton" &c.

Mass. Records, Vol. IV, pt. 2, p. 11, 22 May, 1661.

"In ans[r] to the petition of seuerall inhabitants of Hampton, compalyning ag[t] Edward Colcord for scandalous living by cheating & cousening, vilefyng magistrates, &c, as in ye sd peticõn is exprest, the Court judgeth it meete to referr the examination of the complaint to the County Court at Hampton, & if by due proofe found to be true, they are impowred to punish him according to his demeritts."

Same, p. 50, 7 May, 1662.

"The Court doeth order, that Edward Colcott, be sent for, by warrant from the secretary, & comitted to the house of correction in Boston, there to remajne, according to the sentence of Hampton Court, vntill he have giuen bond to the value of fifty pounds for his good behaviour."

"This Court doeth order, that what moneys or goods doeth yet remajne in Robert Marshalls hands yet vnpajd to Edward Colcott, according to contract, in exchang of the horses, shall be pajd by the sajd Marshall to Xtopher Palmer, or allowed in part of the judgm[t] of this Court graunted to the sajd Marshall."

Same, p. 67, 8 Oct., 1662.

"It was voted by the whole Court, that Henry Roby, constable of Hampton, for his vnfaithfulnes in not duely attending his warrant in bringing Edward Colcord to prison, both in March or Aprill, & now shall loose his chardges & beare it himselfe."

Same, p. 68, 8 Oct., 1662.

"Whereas Edward Colcot was sentenced by the County Court at Hampton, in October last, to be sent & put into the house of correction at Boston, & not be dischardged thence till he gaue sufficjent bond for his good behauiour, the constable neglecting his duty in putting him in to the house of correction, and, by the subtilty of sajd Edward Colcord, bond was given for his good behauiour, & the other part not yet performed, the Generall Court, in May last, ordered, that the sajd Colcord should, by warrant from the secretary, be brought into the house of correction, according to sajd Hamptons Courts sentence. The Court hauing put it to the question whether the sentence of the Generall Court in May last shall be nulled, the

Court resolved it on the negative, & ordered, that after the sajd Colcot haue suffered in the house of correction, he shall be dischardged the prison forthwith, and Henry Roby, constable of Hampton, for his neglect, shall loose all his chardges for bringing the sajd Colcot to Boston, both formerly & now, & beare it himself. Voted by ye whole Court."

CVIII.

[Court Files, Suffolk, No. 1132, 1st paper.]

In an action of the Case depending betweene Henry Dering Atturney to Mr John Fletcher & John Eaton & Benj: Collins Defendts. the Jury finds for the defendants a confirmation of the former Judgmt & Costs of Courts

NOTE.

By the second paper in this case it appears that this was on appeal to the Court of Assistants from a judgment of the Norfolk County Court in April 1672.

CIX.

[Court Files, Suffolk, No. 1135, 5th paper.]

In ye Case Depending Between Henry Ashdon Appealt. and James Jarret Defendant ye Jurie finds for ye Appealant Reuersion of ye former Judgement and Costs of Courts

NOTE.

By the other papers in the case it appears that this was an appeal to the Court of Assistants from a judgment of a Commissioners Court at Boston Aug. 6 1672.

CX.

[Court Files, Suffolk, No. 1142, 12th paper.]

In ye Case Depending Between Henry Harris: Appealt and Thomas Edsill Defendant ye Jurie finds for ye Appealant Reuersion of ye former Judgmt and ten pounds to bee paid According to Couenant and Cost of Courts

NOTE.

[This was probably on an appeal to the Court of Assistants, Sept. 3, 1672, see the following execution]

The second paper in No. 1142 is as follows:— "To Edward Mitchelson Marshall Generall

These require yow in his Majtys name to levy by way of execution on Thomas Edcell his Goods & estate the sume of twelue pounds fower shillings & seven penc: in mony [six] pounds fower shillings & seven pence fower pounds in English Goods & forty shillings in [merchantable provission]: & deliuer the seuerall sumes in specie [being] twelue pounds fower & seven penc in ye whole, wth two shillings for this execution to Henry Harris & is in sattisfaction of a Judgment Granted him by the Court of Asistants sitting in Boston 3^{d} Instant heere of yo^{w} are not to faile making your returne as the law directs. Dated in Boston the 10th Septemb^{r} 1672.

By the Court Edward Rawson Secret^{y}."

[Court Files, Suffolk, No. 1143, 1st paper]

"To Edward Mitchelson marshall Generall

These require you in his Maj^{ties} name to levy by way of execution on Thomas Edsell his Goods or estate nine shillings as mony & as Costs in mony forty five shillings & fower pence in all fivety fower shillings & fower pence & deliuer the same wth two shillings for this execution to Richard Trauis or Peter Golding his Atturney and is in sattisfaction of a Judgment Granted him by the Court of Assistants sitting in Boston 3^{d} Instant here of yo^{w} are not to faile & make yor returne as ye law directs. Dated in Boston 10th of September 1672.

By the Court Edw: Rawson Secret^{y}."

CXI.

[Middlesex County Court Files, Oct., 1674, Bridge *v.* Edsell.]

To Edward Mitchelson Marshall Generall

" These require yo^{w} in his Maj^{tys} name to levy by way of Execution on Thomas Edcell his Goods & estate the some of twelve pounds fower shillings & seven pence; in mony, sixe pounds fower shillings & seuen pence; in English Goods fower pounds; & in merchantable provissions forty shillings wch makes the summe of Twelve pounds fower shillings & seven pence & deliuer the same wth two shillings for this execution to Henry Harris or Peeter Golding his Atturney & is in sattisfaction of a Judgment Granted him for so much by the Court of Asistants sitting in Boston the 3^{d} Instant heere of yo^{w} are not to faile & make yor returne as the law directs dated in Boston 10th of September 1672.

By the Court Edward Rawson Secret^{y}.

This is a true Copy Compared
wth the originall on file Attests

Edw: Rawson Secret^{y}.

This execution was demanded on Thomas Edcell at his house. no Goods no^{r} mony produced his person was comitted to prison this 17th 7mo. 1672.

Edward Mitchelson marshall

That this is A true Copie of Thomas Edcells Comittm^t^. by the marshall in Ans^r^ to this execution & wth ye originall left on file

Attests Edward Rawson Secret^y^."

(Middlesex County Court Record, p. 102) (Pulsifers Copy)

"At a County Court held at Cambridge Octob. 6th 1674

Mathew Bridge assignee of Peter Golding p^l^. ag^t^ Thomas Edzell Deff^t^. In an acc̄on of Debt of six pounds due by bill, according to Attachm^t^. dat. Sep^t^. 8th. 1674. Both partyes appeared & Joyned issues in the case, the Jury haueing heard their severall pleas, & evidences in the case, brought in their verdict, finding for the plant. damages six pounds, & costs of Court Twenty one shillings. & foure pence,

Execuc̄c̄on granted for this Judgem^t^. Octob. 26, 1674 per Thomas Danforth Recorder"

CXII.

[Court Files, Suffolk, No. 1139.]

Boston Sept. 3. 1672

wee the Grand Jurie do indite Samuell Judkins (iff Indian Testymony be valid) to be guilty of great incivillity with Sarah the Indian squaw. The Court declares ye Case not triable at this Court & therefore refer it to ye next County Court [ ] the suertyes of ye delinq^t^ declared in open Court y^t^ their bonds should continue & y^e^ [case] is to be remitted by ye Secretary according.

Item wee Indite Humphrey and the other Indian to haue bene in comp with the Indian lately found dead, and so farr guilty of murder as to leave them to further Tryall for their lives.

Item wee Indite Edward Rolph guilty of having two wives at one & the same tyme.

Hugh Mason with the consent of the rest.

The sd Edward Rolph acknowledged in Court 7. 7^ber^ 1672 y^t^ he was married here to Francis Corwithen widdow the first of march 1671/2 as Attests Edw. Rawson Secret^y^.

The Jury finds the said Rolph not guilty of the abovesaid Indictment

Thomas Fitch: forman in the name of the rest

Humphrey Indian yow are Indicted by the name of Humphrey an Indian for not having the feare of God before yor eyes & being Instigated by the divill did murder (wth Pabatucloh an other Indian sinc run away on or about the third day of July last) Pabatuchouh an Indian found the next day of sd July dead on Boston necke beaten & bruised about the head: Contrary to y[e] peace of our soueraign*

NOTE.

No. 1134 Court Files, Suffolk, consists of two papers one a warrant for commitment of Humphrey the Indian, and the other an inquisition on the body of "Paugatowhen found dead vpon Boston neck," 4-5-1672, also an examination before Edward Tyng of Humphrey the Indian —

No. 25945 Court Files, Suffolk, is the original bill of indictment and the finding of the Jury — as follows — It is without date

"Humphery, you are Indicted by the name of Humphery, an indian for not haueing the feare of God before your eyes and beeing Instigated by the divell, did on or about the third day of July last with Paupachokow an other indian (who present[ly] fled) murder Sam. Paba[t]ough an indian on Boston neck beeing ther found dead lying in the watter his head bruised & body beaten. Contrary to the peace of our Soueraigne Lord the king his Crowne & dignity the lawes of God & of this Jurisdiction.

The Jury finds the said Houmphery
not Guilty"

CXIII.

[Mass. Hist. Soc[y]. Misc[s]. Papers 1628-1691, F. 62, No. 2.]

To this honered Cort

The humble petistion of Rebeckah turel humbl sheweth that whereas the honered Cort of asistance on a jornment the last July was twelue was plesed to sentanc your pore petistioner to depart this jurisdiction and to goe to uergenne to her husband: your pore petistioner is all wayes redy in obedyenc to your honers sentanc to goe and for want of where withall to tranc port her self and letel child is faine to ly in pris son and cannot goe unleas she goes to be sould for a saruant and that will in all like ly hod make my condistione wors then it is there fore your pore and humble petistioner with submistion to your honers dus humble craue your honers to prescribe soome way where by I may haue a soeply for my trans portation and I shall goe along with m[r] bolard hoe is now bound to uergenne: and this shall oblige your pore petistioner as bound in duty euer to pra for your honers helth and prosperitie

Rebeckah turell

7th Sept. 1672

* This paragraph is in handwriting of Edward Rawson.

In answer to this petition the Court orders the Tresurer Rich Russell to discharge the passage of the petitioner to Virginea: yt is vtterly vnable to pay any thing hirself & yt it be donn forthwith yt so the Country may be freed from further charge

Edw: Rawson Secrety

CXIV.

[Court Files, Suffolk, No. 1163, 3d paper.]

Att A Court of Asistants on Adjourmt from ye 3d of Septembr to the 8th october 1672

Allexander wood master of a fishing shallop Complayning agt John Chantry. master of the Ketch trueloue & his Company for Running downe his shallop Riding of [agt] Cape Cod. by reason whereof two men were lost wth the shallop & ye fish. the sajd master wth difficulty saued & this being done 12 September last between 7 & 8 of the clocke in the night; The Court after hearing of the partjes concerned & pervsing the euidences produced wch are on file sentenced the sajd master Jno Chantry Jno Mellons Junr Hugh Perins Henry James Joseph williams negro Joseph Wing Joseph Rawlings & Saml Eaton marriners of the sd ketch severally to be admonished refferring the partjes damnified thereby to their legall advantages & that they pay the fees of Court

origi: E. R. S.

CXV.

[Court Files, Suffolk, No. 1148, 6th paper.]

The hvmble petition [of] Edward Nailer vnto ye Honored Governer Deputy Governer & ye Rest of ye honord C[our]t of Assistants now Sitting in Boston.

Youre Aflicted & distresed petitioner Entreats begs & beseeches yr honors fauor yt whereas I Am Indebted vnto severill Gentlemen of this Towne, & yr honors having banished me Tenn Milles ofe this Towne soe yt I Am not in A Capassity to Compley wth Aney of my Crediters Nither Am I in A Capassity to fitt my selfe for A Voyage to sea: wherefore I hvmbley beg yr honors fauor yt I may haue Liberty for to dispach my Business & Compley wth my Crediters: wch I hope I may doe: if I haue Liberty to walke ye towne: wth in two or three monthes at furthest dewring wch Time I hope I may procewer Security yt I shall not in ye Least Iniewer my wives person or famely I Likewise beg y[t] I may haue my Childeren: my Bookes & all my wrightings & my Estate delivered me y[t] soe I may y[e] better Compley w[th] my Crediters & y[r] petitioner shall Eauer pray

Edward Naylor

In Ans[r] to this petition The Court Judgeth it meet to grant the peticone[rs] his request ||ie.|| libe[r]ty for two months to dispatch his busines & Comply w[th] his Credito[rs] in Boston during y[t] time he Carrying it Innoffenciuely & Enter into bond to the Secre[ty] in 500£ himself & 250£ a peec his suretyes that he shall be of Good behauior during his aboad in y[t] time in Boston towards all persons ||especially his late wife|| and doe further order that y[e] secretary deliuer vp all y[e] sajd Naylo[rs] books & pape[rs] left wth him by orde[r] of this Court by the marshall Generall to Capt Edward Hutchinson & Cap[t] Thomas Lake who after pervsall thereof are to deliuer the same so much as belongs to y[e] sajd Naylor to him. past this by y[e] Court of Asist[ts] 11th of octobe[r] 1672

E R S

NOTE.

[See below, record of Sept. 11, 1673, CXXVIII, Petition of John Wheelwright and answer of the Court as to said Edward Naylor.]

The first paper in No. 1148 is as follows:

"To the Constable of Boston:

These require you in his maj[tys] name forthwith to sumon & Require mary Read Hanna Allen. mary litle John Howen Israell Bowen & Anni his wife John Russell Alice Carpenter Elisa shute Elisabeth Harrendine m[rs] Jemima Bisse Georg Henly Jabez Salter Anna Keene John Seely John Anniball Susanna Crosse Hanna Hilman Dorcas wooddey John Brooking & Elisabeth his wife to make their Seuerall Appearances before the Court of Asistants now sitting in Court this 7 Instant to Give in their seu[r]ll euidences or ouning what they have Given in ag[t] Edward Naylor w[ch] is now on hearing & not to faile dated in Boston. 7 September 1672

By y[e] Court Edw. Rawson Secre[ty]."

[On the back is written.]

"I have Summonsed according to y[e] Tenor ||of this Sumons|| Mary Little Susanah Cross Hanah Hilman Dorcas Woody: Jabez Eaten, John Hawen, John Aniball John Russell, Israell Bowin & Ann his wife: Elizabeth Shute is Sick. Jabez Salter, but y[e] rest I cannot find:"

The second paper in No. 1148 is as follows:

"To the Constable of Boston

These Require you in his maj[tys] name forthwith to sumon & Require Xtophe[r] Lauson. Thomas Briggs mary Turill & Elisabeth walte[rs] ||mary

Litle & mrs moulder|| to make their Appearance before the Court of Asistants now sitting at Boston to Give in their euidences ag^{t} Edward Naylor now depending hereof make y^{r} returne speedily wthout faile dated in Boston: the 7 Sep^{t} 1672: By ye Cour^{t} Edw: Rawson Secre^{ty}

I haue Sumoned and required Thomas Briggs Mary Turen: Elizabeth Walter Mary Little & Mrs Moulder To appeare at Court according To this war^{t} and haue made Inquiry for Xtoph^{r} Lawson but Canot find him

Richd Wharton Cons^{tle}

Sepr. 7 1672"

"John Anibal as a further addition to his testimony sworne saith. y^{t} Jabez Salter came and asked me who was in ye shop of widow Thomases (wch now Mason ye ioyner hath) I answered I could not tel, but he asked me to go goe wth him & he would see: & I said I thought it best to keepe to my worke, then he went to wilm Godfrey & tould him & he went & fecht a candle & he [and] ye neger woman went & looked in & see who it was. & I asked godfrey who they were & he said he was loth to tel me but bed me ges & I gest m^{r} Nailer & Mary More & he said I gest right. I hereing too talkeing in ye shop an houer before y^{t} & continued talking all ye while & some tims laughing: & next morning Godfrey came to me & wisht I had stayed a little longer & I should haue had as much wine as I would drinke, & I s^{d}. how comes y^{t}, & he s^{d}. M^{r}. Naler came & carryed me into his wineseler & gaue me as much as I would drinke. & I further testify y^{t} I haue often sene Mary More & m^{r} Nailer at ye widow Thomases howse together

taken vpon oath 2^{d} febr^{y}. 1671 before vs

Edward Hutchinson }
Thomas Clarke } Commissioners

Own^{d} in Court vpon the oath taken

[From the Chamberlain Collection]

CXVI.

[Court Files, Suffolk, No. 1257, 1st paper.]

To the Honorable County Court now sitting in Boston

The humble petition of Edward Bant on the behalf of himself and the rest of the Company belonging vnto the ship called the Little Barkley being five men in number

Humbly sheweth

That they your Hono^{rs} petitioners with the sd. ship were taken about Eighty Leagues East & by north from the Capes of Virginia by A prize formerly taken by Captn. Cornelius Lincoint Cōmander of A ship belonging to Flushing called in English the Cōmonwealth. And the next day following the Comander of the sd prize went on board the said Barkley intending to have taken out her goods to put them on board his own vessell. whilst wee your petit^rs. were on board his vessell as prisoners close in the hold. And then the English Company remaining on board the sd Barkley surprised them the sd Comãnder & his Company & sailed away wth them And about six houres after your petitioners together with the other English men belonging to the aforesd. prize (when in the possession of the English) made an Insurrection and tooke the ship by violence from the Dutch men and have brought her into the harbour at Puscataqua with eight Dutch men prisoners in her & her Goods & Loading secured in the wearhouse of m^r Nathaniell ffryer.

Whervpon your Hono^rs. serious wise Consideration of the premesies your petitioners humbly pray your hon^rs be pleased to order what salvage they shall have out of the said ship & Cargo now in Puscataqua & that with all Expedition that may be because they are all Strangers & willing to returne to their hoames and lying here vpon great Charges haveing nothing but what they borrow & cloathes on their backs

And as in duty bound they shall pray for your prosperity &c.

8th may 1673 Att ye Court of Asistants on adjourn^nt

In Answ^r to the petition of Edward Bant in behalfe of himself & fower seamen The Court Judgeth it meet to order that m^r Nathaniel ffryer allow & pay the sum̃e of fiueteene pounds for their salvage taking their receipts for the same

past Edw: Rawson Secret^y.

CXVII.

[Court Files, Suffolk, No. 1257, 4th paper.]

To the Hono^able. the Deputy Goven^r. and Majest^es Now assembled in Court —

Hen: King.

Humbly Recommendeth to yor worships Candid Consideration his present Case and Condition, hoping to obtaine yor worships Juditious approbation therein, to ye end and intent that all persons Concerned and Related to ye ship providence of falmouth wch was taken by a dutch ship of warr on ye 4th instant about 40 Leagues short of ye Capes of Virginia, and Retaken again by ye means and directions of yor Suppliant who Requests y^t yor worships will please to Grant order that yor petition^r. and these other Seamen belonging to ye said ship, who were assistant in Retaking her may haue their wages According to Agreem^t^. from ye time of their being shipt till ye said ship providence wth her Loading was brought into pascataqua Riv^r^. and there put into ye Custody of m̄^r^ Nathan^ll^ ffryer, who is ye Correspondant of one of ye owners of said ship wth her Cargo where she is to Continue till ord^rs^. from Authority or instructions from ye proprieters.

And yor Petition^r^ shall
Ever Pray ——

Boston 30th april 1673.

Att A Court of Assistants held at Boston on Adjourm^t^ 8th may 1673.

In Ans^r^. to the petition of Henry King in behalfe of himselfe & the sixe seamen according to their Portlidge bill Given into this Court wth their declaration the Court Judgeth it meete to Grant & order that m^r^ Nathaniell ffryer pay them their seuerall wages he taking their receipts for the same

past by ye Court as Attests Edward Rawson Secre^t^.

NOTE.

[See Suffolk County Court Record April 1673 p. 127 Petition of Henry King &c.]

[Suffolk County Court Record 29 April 1673, page 127]

Court Order About Ship Providence

"In Answer to the petitions presented to this Court by Henry King & Edward Prant [sic] who lately brought into the River of piscataquay the Ship Providence of ffalmoth, whereof saide King was Mate in a Voiadge from England to Virginia in which Voiadge they were surprized by a Dutch man of Warr & by the Petition^rs^. & Company rescued out of theire hands who haue since surrendred the saide Ship & her lading into the hands of m^r^. Nathaniell ffryer for the securing of & looking after both in behalfe of the owners. This Court doe order & empower m^r^. Elias Stileman & m^r^. Henry Deering together with said ffryer or any two of them to take a perticuler Acco^t^. of ye state of saide Ship & to Inventory the Goods brought in by & belonging to her & to make provition for the securing of both for the right Owners, making a return thereof to the present Dep^t^. Govr. by the seventh of May next: And the saide ffryer is further ordered to disburs't for the Company arrived in the saide Ship what maybee for the Supply of theire present necessities & alsoe order that hee take care that the 8 Dutchmen brought in prison^rs^. in the saide Ship bee forthwith brought to Boston before Authority to bee disposed of as the matter may require & for the other part's of the Peticons touching Salvage or Wages the Court refers them to the Councell at theire next meeting.

These Petition's were sent for & delivered into the Councill at theire Sitting."

[Court Files, Suffolk, No. 1257]
Second paper: —
"To Wm Salter keeper of the prison.

These Require you in his majtys name to take into yor Custody Wm Forrest now in chaines & him securely & safely keepe in order to his tryall for felloniously & pirattically wth others seizing ye ship Antonio on the high seas & forcing Mr Jno Tarry the master thereof wth others in ye long boate to sea &c hereof you are not to faile dated in Boston 30 octobr 1673

By ordr of ye Court of Assistants Edw. Rawson Secret."

Third paper: —
"To Wm Salter keeper of the prison.

These Require you in his majtys name to take into yor Custody the person of Alexandr Wilson & him very securely & safely keepe in order to his tryall for his wth others felloniously & pirattically seizing the ship Antonio on the high seas & forcing Mr John Tarry the master thereof wth others into ye long boat to sea &c hereof you are not to faile dated in Boston 30th october 1673.

By order of the Court of Assistants Edw Rawson Secret.

To Wm Salter keeper of the prison.

These Require you in his majtys name to take into yor Custody Jno. Smith & him very securely & safely keepe in order to his tryall for his wth others felloniously & pirattically seizing the shipp Antonio on the high seas & forcing Mr John Tarry the master thereof wth others into the long boate to sea &c hereof you are not to faile dated in Boston 30th october 1673

By order of the Court of Assistants Edw. Rawson Secret."

Fifth paper: —
"To the Honed Governer and Court of Asistance
The Humble Petition of Allwin Child

Sheweth that A shipe Called the St Anthony was Consigned vnto your petitionor from Lisbon vnder the Comand of John Farry and in his voyge About one hundred and ten Leages from Lisbon the seamen of sd shipe mutined Against the sd Commander and turned himselfe his Supercargo Mate and Boy out of sd shipe in to the Boate to shift for them selves and Ran Away wth the shipe Some of the men soe Runing Away being at presant vnder conviction in this prison and three others haveing bin tacken at Plimouth in order to bee also Brought to Answare for theire misdimeniors before the Authouritey of this Coliney, But did theare Breacke Prisen and escaped vnto the Goverment of Road Island at which place they are Apprehended. and the sd Farry is Liquise now ARived there wth Another shipe Consigned allsoe to your petitioner & is there detained to prosicute the Aboue sd offenders

Your Petitionor in Behalfe of the Imployers humbly Craues yt your Honrs would Be-pleased to tacke such Coarse that the sd escaped prisonors may bee sent for to this place to Answare there fact According to Law the

Evidences Against them Being partly heare All Readey and the Comandor being allso Bound to this place soe that his stay theare will bee verey preduditiall to the voyge of sd shipe & Imployers the shipe Requiering A spedey dispatch

& hee shall Pray

Endorsed. Allwin Childs peticõn to Gou^r^n^r^ & Magis^ts^ in Court of Asistants 24 october 1673."

Sixth paper: —

"At a County Court held at Boston Aprill: 29th. 1673.

In answer to the petitions presented to this Court by Henry King & Edward Bant who lately brought into the River of Piscataquay the Ship Providence of falmoth, whereof said King was Mate in a Voiadge from England to Virginia in which Voiadge they were surprized by a Dutch man of War & by the Petition^rs^ & Company rescued out of theire hands: who haue since Surrendred the said Ship & her loading into the hand's of m^r^. nathaniell ffryer for the Securing & looking after both in behalfe of the Own^rs^.

This Court doe Order & Empower m^r^. Elias Stileman & m^r^. Henry Deering together with saide ffryer or any two of them to take a particuler Acco^t^. of the state of saide Ship & to Inventory the Goods brought in by & belonging to her & to make provition for the Securing of both for the right Own^rs^. making a return thereof to the present Dep^t^. Govr. by the 7th. of May next, and the saide ffryer is further ordered to disburst for the Company arrived in the saide Ship what may bee for the Supply of theire present necessities & also order that hee take care that the 8 dutch men brought in prison^rs^. in the saide Ship bee forthwith brought to Boston before Authority to bee disposed of as the matter may require & for the other parts' of the Petition's touching Salvage or wages

The Court refers them to the Counsell at theire next meeting./.

Copia Vera. ꝑ: Isaac Addington Cler"

Seventh paper: —

"To the Hon^rble^ ye Gouernour and Magistrates Assembled in Boston.

The humble request of Thomas Raddon is that whereas the authority of this Jurisdictiõ hath taken care to secure the shipe Providence of fallmouth in old England wich was brought into piscataway by serprisall and the Cargo in her whereof I ye s^d^ Thomas Raddon was shiped master ꝑ ye owners to performe A voige to Virgin^a^ and frõ thence home againe for wch Care I doe in ye behalfe of my selfe and owners, returne humble and hearty thanks to y^r^ worship^es^

And whereas the providence of God soe ordering that I am now come my selfe my humble request is that y^r^ worship^es^, would bee pleased to giue ord^r^ that ye s^d^ shipe and Goods may bee speedily deliuered vnto y^r^ petitio^r^ that soe I may (wth Gods blessing) proceed in my intended voige for the benifit of my imployers, according to my obligation and y^r^ petitio^r^ shall euer pray for y^r^ worship^s^ prosperity

Tho: Raddon

In Boston this 10th
of June 1673

This was presented to the Hono^{rble} Jno Leueret Esqr Gou^{r} the 11th of June 1673. as Attests Edward Rawson

The Gou^{r}no^{r} & Magistrates hauving pervsed the Cirtifficats & finding that Tho: Raddon aboue being now Arrived wth part of ye Company that was tooke out of hir was the master of the sajd ship Prouidence ordered the Secretary to signify to m^{r} Nathaniell fryer that they Advise him to deliuer the sajd ship & what was in hir to the sajd Tho: Raddan master for the vse & benefitt of the owners he dischareging the charges formerly advised to: as Attests Edw: Rawson Secre^{t}.''

Eighth paper: —

''To John Amenseene

You are req^{r} in his Maj^{tis} Name to take on bord yor sloope m^{r} John Johnson Steeresman that was brought in to this Riuer piscattaque: by ye prouidence of fallmouth and him to transport unto Boston there to appeare befor ye worpll: Jno Leueritt esq^{r} Dep^{tis} Gou^{r} of ye Massatusitts Collony & Counsell to giue in his testimony how & by w^{t} means he was taken in s^{d} ship after she was taken by ye dutch: & to be disposed of as they in their wisdoms shall se cause. hereof fale not & this shalbe yor sufficient war^{t}.

Da: in piscattaque Riuer ye 28: Apr: 1673

℘ Elias Stileman Comsr.

There is ord^{r} taken for pay for his passage & prouisions by ye way

℘ Elias Stileman Comsr.''

Ninth paper: —

''Know all men by theise presents that I Thomas Raddan of Plimouth in ye County of Devonsh^{r}. marrine^{r} & Comand^{r} of the ship Prouidence of falmouth doe firmely bind myself heires exeecuto^{rs} administrators and Assignes in the some of five hundred pounds sterling money of England to Richard Russell Tresure^{r} for the Massachusets Jurisdiction in New England & to his successors the sajd sume of five hundred pounds sterling to be payd unto the sajd Richard Russell Tresurer aforesajd or to the Tresurer for the time being on all demands as wittness my hand & seale this eleventh day of September 1673.//

The Condition of this obligation is such that if the aboue Bounden Thomas Raddan his heires executors administrators or Assignes or any or either of them shall from time to time and at all times & places respond & Answer what shall be layd to his charge or be prooved against him either for not doing his duty as he ought & might in sufficiently seazing & securing of w^{m} forrest pretended master of the ship of Portingall Called Antonjo wch ye sajd forrest in a fellonious & piratticall way seized on ye high seas & took from one Terriff master thereof & forcing the sd Terriff his mate & merchant in ye long boate to depart not being heard of or if by any of the owners or others Concerned in sd ship Antonio or hir Goods shall in any Court or Courts of this Jurisdicon be prooved to haue any hand in vndue

Countenancing ye sd forrest & Concealing his escape & also answer all such Just damages so prooved & Recouered in any of our Courts by any of the owners or others Concerned then ^ obligation to be voyd or els to be & remajne in full force & virtue Tho: Raddon: —

Signed Sealed & deliuered
in the presenc of us after y^e
interlin^g the words ye sd forrest
Edward Rawson
william needom."

Seal

Tenth paper: —

"A Declaracon of some Occurrents that happened us in our late Voiadge from falmoth intended for Virginia in the Ship Providence of falmoth.

Añño 167⅔. Thomas Radden Comander.

About the 12th. November 1672 wee Sailed from falmoth in the aforesaid Ship to Plimouth for convoy & there lay till the 15th. January following when wee sailed under convoy with a fleete of about .90. sail our convoy went with us about 80 Leagues to the westward of Silly then with about ten Sail more wee parted from the fleet & were making the best Emprouement of winde and weather to gaine our port till the 4th. aprill following when wee between the houres of four & six in the morning saw a Sail upon our weather quarter wee made what sail wee could, hee giving us chaze in about two houres hee came up with us, showed us Dutch colours comanded us by ye See & to strike our Topsaile & ancient; wee seeing of him to bee a man of War of force could make noe resistance against him did accordingly; then the Capt. himselfe came aboard of us with twelue Dutch men more showed us his Comission Signed by the Prince of Orange for the taking of English Ships; the Capt: was named Cornelius Linquoint & comanded the Ship in English called the Comonwealth of 20 peice of Ordnance then hee tooke our master merchant & ten Seamen more out of our Ship & left seven of us aboard & soe went aboard his man of war againe & ordered the Dutch Steeresman whome hee left with Eleven Dutchmen more on board of our Shipe to Steere after the man of War & in case wee should bee parted by weather to Saile with our Ship to the Groyne in Galecia as the saide Steeresman informed mee; the same night following wee lost the man of War, the saide Capt. having told mee that if wee kept Company while the next morning hee would take the goods out of our Ship on board the man of war & giue us our own Ship againe but having lost Company of him in the night wee bore up the helme to the Eastward intending for the Groyne as the Steereman informed mee, having plied too & againe 6 dayes hoping to meete with the man of war againe. two dayes after wee bore up wee saw a Sail which made towards us, being about 3. leagues from us between six & eight oclock in the Evening they came up with us & hailed us asking whence wee were. The Dutch Steeresman standing with a laden pistoll presented to my breast comanded mee to answer them in those word's hee should dictate to mee bid mee answer them of falmoth & to tell them wee came from Petuxine River in Virginia & if they wanted any thing if they would hoise out theire Boate & Come aboard wee would Supply them upon which they hoised out theire Boat & the Master Merchant Mate Doctor & two Seamen came on board in the Boate & after they had Entred our Ship the Dutch men Surprised them & sent three Dutch men on board theire Ship & the Ship staid by us all the night next morning the Dutchmen intending to goe on board com̄anded the saide Ship's boate on board who came accordingly & the Dutch Skipper went on board the aforesaide Ship intending to take out her goods & put on board of our Ship as hee saide, in order whereunto hee tooke the merchant along with him, about halfe an hour after the saide Ship made sail & steered to the westward wee in our Ship making Sail followed them between two & three houres & finding wee could not come up with her left our chaze & stood to the Eastward againe. there being five Englishmen belonging to the saide Ship prisoners in our Ship's hole. about six houres after the same day wee English men that were at liberty by writing to them in the hole conspired together with them to lett them come up & soe to rush all out together upon the Dutch men & if wee could Subdue them to rescue our Selues & Ship, which accordingly with god's blessing wee Effected without any loss of life or shedding of blood & soe intended to New England being afraide to goe for Virginia, leaste wee should meete the man of War againe & being unable to carry the Ship home for England & after Eleven dayes lying at Sea by reason of ffoggy weather & contrary windes wee arrived at Piscataquay in New England aforesaide being 23th Aprill: 1673.

Henry King; Matt
John Champion B[oswin?]

Att A Court of Asistants held at Boston on $Adjourm^{t}$ 8th may 73 Henry king John Champyn & John Sennet deposed in open court that this declaration is y^{e} trueth the whole trueth & nothing but the trueth as Attests

Edward Rawson $Secre^{t}$.

Portlidge bill of Wages due to the Company belonging to saide Ship Providence is as followeth.

	£	s	d
Henry King Mate at: 55^{s} ꝑ m̄°. 4 m̄°. 5 dayes - - - -	11:	9:	2
John Champyn Boatswaine 36^{s} ꝑ m̄°. 4 m̄°.½ 5^{d}. - -	8:	6:	2
John Jorey Carpenter: at: $3^{£}$ ꝑ m̄°. 4 m̄°.½ - - - - -	13:	10:	0
John Sennett. at: 28s ꝑ m̄°. 3 m̄°. 5 dayes - - - - -	04:	08:	6
John Burley. at: 28s ꝑ m̄°. 4 m̄°. 5 dayes - - - - -	05:	16:	6
sick George Taylor at: 28s ꝑ m̄°. 3 m̄°.½ - - - - - - -	04:	18:	0
aboard Richard Gross at: 20s ꝑ m̄°. 4 m̄°. 5 dayes - - - - -	04:	03:	4
£ s d 52—11—8	£ 52:	11:	8

8th may 1673

It is ordered that the seamen aboue shall be allowed & payd their Seuerall wages (according to their Portlidge bill here given in:) by m^{r} feyer he taking their receipts of the seuerall seamen

as Attests = Edward Rawson $Secre^{t}$."

No. 1257 — Eleventh paper: —

"Lett it bee knowne to all kings princis and potentates in Chrisondom and to all those that it may Concerne how that upon the 21th day of aprill 1673 before the Riuer of Virginia haue taken and ouer Mastered Vnder the Comition of his highness my lord prince william the third of Oringe, taken a Cetch Called decgens Coming from Boston out of new england goeing to y[e] Riuer of Virginia whearof was skiper John Cox which ketch I was intended for to burne or to sinck but after seuerall Considerations I doe giue y[e] Same ketch and all that belongs vnto her freely and liberaly vnto y[e] honorable Cap[t]. Thomas Raddon and m[r] Joseph Hix whoo both likewise weare taken by mee to haue and to hold as their owne Ketch and to dispose thereof to their owne Content Signed by mee in the ship Called [Stanswelovarn] at sea the 22th day of Aprill 1673/

Cornelious Delincourt

stierman	Jop Cornelisse
stierman	pieter gerrits
bootswan	thomas severs
Constapel	antoni fero
[seaman?]	jacob wall

I the under written doe acknowledge that this aboue Mentioned act is done and signed in the presence of my officers and signed by them before Skiper Cox Master of the aboue Mentioned ketch dated as aboue,

Copia Vera Cornelious Delincourt

[g v sib]ermyen."

Twelfth paper: —

"A Declaration of some Occurents that happened to us in our late Voiadge from London in the Ship Barkely of the saide port Nicholas Prynne Cōmand[r] intended for Virginia.

Ann[o]. 1672/3.

On the twelfth Aprill 1673 being in saide Ship about the Lattitude of the Capes of Virginia about 80 Leagues distant wee saw a sail towards Evening & being in want of provition seeing her to bee a fly boate made towards her & came up with her about Eight oclock & hailed them asking them of whence theire Ship they answered of falmoth, wee askt them from whence they came they answered from Virginia & called mee by my Name & asked mee how I did. wee askt them what place they loaded at they answered in Petuxin River wee told them wee wanted some provitions they answered us if wee would hoise out our Boate & come on board they would spare us water or other provitions what they could in order thereunto wee did soe & I being desired by the Master & Merchant to goe on board with the Boate to Endeavor to gett what provitions I could; our Merchant who was owner also desired mee to stay & hee & the Doctor would goe with mee as soon as they had Sealed theire Letter's our master not having ended his writing the marchant desired him to goe on board with us also & to finish his letter there & accordingly with three more Seamen wee went on board saide Ship & when wee came there founde severall Dutchmen on board who had the cōmand of her they having lately taken her from the English the

Ship was called the Providence belonging to falmoth Thomas Radden having been lately master of her; the saide Dutchmen Surprized six of us & kept us prisoners & sent one of our Company with three Dutchmen on board our Shipe who lay by us till the next morning then the Dutch Comãnder comãnded our Ship's Boate to come on board his Shipe againe which accordingly they did hee promising our Merchant to take out our goods & to giue us our Ship againe in order whereunto hee provided one hogshead of bread to haue given us as hee saide & tooke our Merchant with him & went on board our Ship & about halfe an hour after our Ship made Sail & Steered to the westward; & then the Dutchmen put us who formerly belonged to her down into the hole & made sail after the saide Ship for about two houres & seeing they could not come up with her, stood on theire course againe to the Eastward & by receiving advice from those English men that were at liberty wee combined together for them to make way for our coñing up & soe to rush out upon the Dutch men at once & to Subdue them for the rescuing of our Selves & Ship which with gods blessing wee Effected without loss of life or blood shed to any & then agreed among our Selves to come away with saide Ship to New England which accordingly wee did and after Eleven dayes passadge by reason of contrary winds & ffoggy weather arrived in Piscataquay River on the 23th Aprill: 1673.

Edw. Bant matt
John Russell
Jonas Lewis

Att A Court of Asistants on Adjournmt the 8th may 1673 Edw. Bant John Russell & Jonas Lewis deposed in Court that hauing subscribed their names to this declaration that it was ye truth the whole truth & nothing but the truth: as Attests

Edward Rawson Secret."

[The thirteenth paper is in Dutch, the eleventh paper being a translation.]

Fourteenth paper: —

"Boston in new England

Wee whose names are under written doe here testifie that Thomas Raddon of plymo in old England, was shiped master of ye Providence of fallmouth to performe a voige to virginia and that wee were shipt by the sd Thomas Raddon on the sd shipe providence as wittness our hands this 10th of June 1673

Geo: Deacon
John M* May
John I* Gipson
Robertt Raddon
Geo: Taylor
Joseph Crayse
William Baker

*His mark.

11th June 1673

The subscribers doe further Add yt. ye ship Providenc aboue mentiond was the same ship yt Henry King was mate of & was taken to ye Eastward of ye Cape of Vir^inia by Cornelljus de ljnquort Dutchman: & brought in as wee find by the sajd mate & some of ye Company to Piscataqua Riuer in Aprill last deposed before Jno. Leueret Esqr Gour the`day aboue sajd = Attests Edw. Rawson secret."

Fifteenth paper: —

"Newport one Road Island

The Examinations of William forist marinr taken the 20day 8 mo 1673

the foresd forist beinge Examined acknowlegeth that he was owne of that mutinous Company that Raised Reb^lion in the shipe Called the saint Anthony vpon the Coaste of portingall one hundred and tenn leags from lands and theire wt others did depriue John Tarry master of his power giuen to him: leagelly to Gouern: the: aforesd: shipe: but Denies that he had a hand in forsinge him ouer boarde: or those that wente wt him: but sd he and them might haue Continued longer in the aforesd shipe, but owned that he wt others did deprive him the sd John Tarry the Gouerment and ordring the aforesd ^hipe and beinge asked Conserninge theire further prosedings,: owned that he wt others brought the aforesd shipe Called the Sainte Antony: in to pascattaqa Riuer in new Ingland wheire he the sd forrist was then the Reputed master: whoe vndertooke to be owne (to witt the [Cheefest]) that managede and disposed of most or all the aforsd ships Cargoe tell by some meanes of fallinge out amonge them selfes was Discouered vpon wch the sd william forrist mad an E^cape for a time tell he was aprehendend at new plimoth in new Ingland wheire he acknowlegeth he lately Escaped out of his magistise Gale at new plimoth as aforesd

and further being Examined owned (to witt william forist:) That John Tarry and the suprocargoe ware the persons that had trew Right to Gouerne order and dispose of the aboue sd shipe and Cargoe:, which he the aforesd william forrist & Com[pany] vnjust[ly] Depriued: them: of taken before vs

Nicholas Easton Gour

William C^ddington. Dt gour"

Seventeenth paper: —

"It was my Chance to be in Lesbon & wanting A woage I shiped my slefe A board of a portungall built ship Mr Orchard Comander but some five dayes After it plesed ye Almyty God to take him out of ye woarld & when yt wee was Agoing to bury him I heard The men yt was in ye boate to helpe Rowe him ouer ye water for ye portugeses would not suffer us to bury him in Lesbone say yt thay would haue A ship Are longe but I did not know how not then & some one day thay went into ye house for thay Could open ye Locke of ye Haches when thay plesed & drawed wine of ye Marchantes & soe sate doune to geather to drinke & I being near thay not deming of it I heard them say yt thay would pay it all at once & Liquise yt thay would Rune away with ye ship soe I disclosed it to ye Master & ye Marchant for our Marchant had [Gone] another Master which was Cat. Haddockes second Mate which was then Comander of An Engles ship Lying in Lesbone Reuer John Terry by Name soe thay tooke three of them & put them in presone at Lesbone it was ye boatswane & two men more but by Resone y^{t} one willam forrest which was Aboard y^{t} Gaue ye suprecarco M^{tr} John Pane fare words ye super Cargo would not sufer him to be put in the preson but y^{t} hee should Goe ye woage & because thay Could note Geete another Carpenter thay would not put ye Carpenter in to preson but y^{t} hee should Goe ye woage Lyquise soe ye Master John Terry shiped tree men more in there Roomes which ware Engles m[en] Edmun Cooke & John smith & After wards hee shiped two duchmen there names I know not & wee ware bound for newfoundland for a sacke but when wee had bene about A weake at sea these two men namly willam forrest & John peket ye Carpenter perswaded ye other two Engles men Edmun Cooke & John smith & one other Engles which was a board & ye two duch men to surprise ye Master ye suprecargo ye Mate A portungall boy & I & soe to Rune away with ye ship And waching thare Oppertunity when ye ye Master and ye marchant was a slepe in ye Roundhouse ye Mate A Riting in ye Cabing & I was at helme ye Carpenter Came into ye sterege & Cauled ye Edmun Cooke & John smith out of thare Cabing whare thay ware a slepe & soe thay went forward togeather into y^{e} for Casell & inmeadly thay Came Aft agane ye tow duchmen & willam forrest ye Carpenter & Edmun Cooke John smith & ye other Engles man soe ye two duchmen & y^{t} Engles man y^{t} is not named Came into ye sterege ye other fower wente up upon ye Quarter Decke & surprised ye Master & ye Marchant where thay ware a slepe in ye Round house & ye other three sayed to me y^{t} if I did ofter to ster I was a dead man soe ye mate hering y^{t} in ye Cabin where he was a Riting salied out of ye Cabing in to ye sterege soe thay tooke hould of him & throed him upon his back & soe held him & would not suffer him to ster soe I Rune doune ye scutell which was in ye sterege & hede my slefe amounge ye sayles betweene deckes for I heard ye Master & ye Marchant Cry out most petifully soe I thought to my slife y^{t} when thare pasone was over y^{t} I mite perswade them to saue my Life soe thay bo[und] ye Master & ye Marchant & Carryed them forward upon ye forcastell but presenly after thay Loused them agane us put them in to ye Greate Cabing all togeather & would suffer but one to Come upon ye deck at a time ye Master & ye Marchant profered them y^{t} if thay would thay would take a drame of ye botell & set doune & drinke frinds & y^{t} all things should be forgoting but thay would not Exsept of there profer soe I went upon ye deck & desyred them y^{t} thay would be plesed to Lend us a sayle for thay tould us y^{t} thay would hoyst out ye boate & Giue us some prowisones & tourne us to shift for our sleus soe wee desyred to beare up ye helme for to put us As neare ye Land as thay Could [soe] some two howers soe thay Gaue in to ye boate All nessesaryes As prowisons wood water & Lequers with a sayle & Mast & ores A Grapnall & Grapnall Rope sayle nedles twine & [yarne] for to mend ye sayle soe will forrest walking upon ye Quater deck with a backe swoard in his hand Commanded ye baat to be hoysted out & all those forenamed nessesarys to be put in to her with a Compas Quadrant & a plat & soe Comanded ye Master ye Marchant ye Mate & ye portuges boy in to ye boate John Tooley & Allexsander would haue gone in to ye boate with them but they would not suffer us to goe [ ] Master sayed [ ] Asked them [ ] yt thay would kepe us but they would not harking unto them & would not Let us goe

John Tooley gave in this upon examination as a true Narrative of the transaction in the ship Anthony when she was surprised by forest & Pickard &c: he the sayd Tooley being of the age of twenty yeres or thereabouts Before us

John Leverett Gor
Edward Tyng
William Stoughton

John Terry not being present when this was spoken by John Toolly before the Gourno r Mr Ting Mr Staughton & major Clarke on 17 jnst 73 being Asked whither what John Toolly had declared was the truth the sajd Terry Ansed he acknowledged the same to be ye truth: as Attests

Edward Rawson Secret

19 November 1673

prst	Mr Russell	Mr Staughton
y Gour	Mr Danforth	Mr Clarke
Capt. Gookin	Mr Tynge	

This Examination of John Toolly being read in the Councill wth the Acknowledgment of ye master John Terry yt it was the Truth The Councill ordered his discharge from further attendance & yt the Secretary Give him the signification thereof to the sajd John Toolly as Attests Edw: Rawson S.

The Examination of Jno Tooly marriner of ship St. Anthony.
what is your name
Jno Tooly borne nere norwich
He saith that he was at Helme when ye Rising was
how long was it after you came to sea
Ansr about a weeke
who rise first or the manner of their Rising
ye Carpenter hauing a hand spike in his hand Called to forrest who wth the 2 dutchmen Came forward off wth Cooke &c."

Eighteenth paper: —

"The examination of John Johnson steeresman of the frigott commonwealth Capt. Cornelius Lincourt Comr:

Decemr the 15 their stile they came out of ffflushing in ye aboue sd ffrigott with 20 gunns & ninety six men & boys bound from flushing to the Canarie Island, & in their way they took a londoner bound from malaga laden with fruite which they sent to the Groyne & the men they putt on shore at the canaries, from the canaries we sailed to the Cape de Verd Islands, & from thence to Barbados where they tooke a small ffrench sloope,

& from thence we sailed to the Capes of Virginia & in our way we mett with the Prouidence of Famouth, which ship we tooke on y^e: 15 day of Aprill ours stile in the latitude of the capes about 30 leagues to y^e: Eastward: it being a stormy night they driue away under a maine course to the northward for 2 days afterward the ^ stood in againe to the capes but could not see their frigott, so then we stood away for y^e: Groine, & mett with a small londoner bound for Virginia, who came abord on vs for water, & we tooke the men being 5: & putt y^m in to the hold, then he y^t was master of the ship went on board the Londoner & three men with him, whome the Londoner carried away, so then we followed them but could not over take him, so the night following the English that were upon Decke conspireing with them in the hold, in the morneing they tooke the ship from us & brought us to Piscataqua.

Taken in Boston 5: May. 1673 before
John Leverett Dep. Go^r."

Nineteenth paper: —

"The deposicuns of John Johnson aged 48 yeeres steeresman & Henry Harris aged aboute 24 yeers:

These depon^ts testifie & say that they these depon^ts together with seuerall other seamen belonging unto ffushing vnd^r ye comand of Capt. Cornelius Lincort Comand^r. of ye shipp [Elandtweluaers] in English ye Comonwelth by vertue of a Comisson from his highness the prince of orange we came vp with the prouidence of ffallmouth (who was bound to Virginia) in the Latitude of 36: & 40: & tooke her wch when taken these depon^ts. & ten more were put on bord her to Keepe & secure her and after wee had been on bord some hours in ye night wee Lost our owne shipp & saw them no more & aboute seuen dayes after wee came up with a Londoner & thinking to take him foure of our company went on bord in ye night but neuer returned & ye next day after the English that belonged to the s^d ship providence & som of the other ship before menconed that wee had on bord wth us prisoners rose and retooke her & suppressed us & haue brought s^d shipp & us into piscattay Riuer.

Gr^t Island ye 26th Aprill 1673 taken upon oath by ye persons aboue named before me

Elias Stileman Coms^r."

(See Mass. Records Vol. IV, pt. 2, p. 573)

CXVIII.

[Court Files, Suffolk, No. 1195.]

John Redman Marshall Gen^ll his Deputy his Bill of charges in apprehending & bringing to Boston Cap^tn. Walter Barefoot by virtue of A warrant vnder the hand of m^r Edw: Rawson Secretary.

for Twenty one dayes time from the 18.th day of Aprill vntill the 11th day of May, for himself & his horse at 6s per day is money	6 : 6 : 0
for one man & horse from Hampton to Dover for aid 3 dayes - - - - - - - - - - - - - - -	0 : 18 : 0
for one & hors more on ye 6th day of May -	0 : 6 : 0
	7 : 10 : 0
more in February 5s - - - - - - - - - - - - - - - - - -	7 : 15 : 0

Allowed by ye Court of Assistants in yr chamber: 10 May 1673: for ye Treasurer to pay in mony

Edw: Rawson Secrety.

NOTE.

Mass. Records Vol. IV, pt. 2, p. 529, 15 May 1672.

"In ansr to the peticon of Walter Barefoot, the Court judgeth it not meet to grant his request."

Same, p. 557, 7 May 1673.

"In ansr to the certifficat or request of seuerall inhabitants of Douer, &c, on behalfe of Walter Barefoot, the person petitioned for not standing rectus in curia, the Court sees no cause to grant their request."

CXIX.

[Court Files, Suffolk, No. 1197, 1st paper.]

To the honoured Governor Deputy Gour & Assistants now Seting in Boston.

The humble petition of the Company of men belonging to the ship William & John of Lime; William Osborne lately deseased Comander, humbly sheweth, that whereas it has pleased almighty god by his prouidence to depriue vs of our Master by death where by wee are left without guide or warontable order in the concenements of our former intended voyage, & alsoe without prouissions & other neessarys belonging to such a ship; & being generally or for the moste parte not able to helpe our selues for want of money to defraye our Charges in this place beside the debts that sume of vs haue made since wee came here; doe humbly in treate your honours to take into your concideration how wee may bee releued, wee being in your honours power & not capassitated to helpe our selues, nor dare wee or if ||wee|| dared are wee able to proceed the voyage, the instructions concerneing ||which|| dyeing with our Mastr: therefore wee intreate that some order may bee taken for the payment of our wages, that soe wee may repaire to our natiue Country or elce where that may bee for the Comfort of our selues, & those belonging to vs, that thereby wee & them may as in duety bound pray for your honours posperity

George Squier Bo||a||tson
Andrew Edmonstoun Carpinter
Gregory Maple Cooke
Richard Sweett his meat
Edward Gregory
Richard Bacon
Thomes Trickey
Charles Ceape
Robert Cox
William: Baker:

Boston, 16 may, 1673.

In Ans^r^ to the peticons of Thomas Orchard mate & the Seamen of the ship [W^m^] & John: of lyme: on ye miscarriage of ye late Wm Osborne master thereof the Gou^r^n^r^ & Assistants advised the mate & Seamen to keepe to the ship and to proceed in Some vojage for the best advantage of ye oune^rs^ & to Gett home as soone as they may.

Edw. Rawson Secret^y^.

NOTE.

[The second paper in this case, No. 1197, is a petition by the Mate of said ship to the General Court.]

Second paper:

"To the Hono^rd^: Governo^r^. Deputy Governo^r^. & the rest of the Hono^rd^. Magestrates assembled in Generall Court in Boston.

The Petition of Thomas Orchard Mate of the Ship William & John of Lime in England.

Humbly Sheweth

Whereas the lord by his late awfull Providence hath taken away William Osborn Master of the saide Ship, by drowning: Who by Charter party had indented with some Merchants in England to make a Voiadge with saide Ship upon ffright for Virginia & soe for England & had taken up in Mony of the said ffreighto^rs^. upon the bottom of the Ship for fitting her for the saide Voiadge to the vallue of two hundred pounds: in the proceeding on which Voiadge by reason of contrary windes & bad weather o^r^. time of being at Sea was soe long that wee were Streightned for provisions & had received much damage in o^r^ Mast's soe were forced to come away for New England; since when some considerable time being spent in repairing o^r^. Ship & fitting her for saide Voiadge the Company declaring theire unwillingness to proceede by reason of the Season of the yeare the Master & Company some few dayes before his death had a treaty about laying up the Ship till the 10th or 20th of august next & to bee out of pay & victualls till that time. now there being neither Charter party nor orders to the saide Master to bee founde & I not knowing how to act as to proceeding on o^r. intended Voiadge or for the Securing the saide Ship for the Owners

My humble request to yor. hono^rs. therefore in that yor. Hono^rs. would bee pleased to appoint some meete persons to take an acco^t. of the state of saide Ship & of her Store, that soe both may bee secured for her owners & Emploiers."

CXX.

[Court Files, Suffolk, No. 1290, 12th paper.]

Att A Court of Assistants held at Boston the 2^d September 1673

Fathergon Dinely administrator to the estate of Jno Dinely deceased plantiff against the estate of Cornelius Stenwicke in the hands of Capt w^m Dauis in an action of Appeale from the Judgment of the County Court at Boston in July last* After the Attachment Courts Judgment Reasons of Appeale & Euidences in the case produced were read comitted to the Jury & are on file wth the Reccords of this Court the Jury brought in their virdict they found for the Appellant Reuersion of the former Judgment wth the land in Controuersy & Costs of Courts fowre pounds ten shillings & two pence this stands entred from march next. That this is A true Copie taken out of the Courts booke of Reccords Attests Edward Rawson secre^t

To Edward Mitchelson Marshall Generall or his deputy

These require you in his majesty' name by way of execution to execute the Judgment aboue written in all respects & deliuer the same wth two shillings for this execution to Fathergon Dinely administrator aforesajd & is in sattisfaction of ye aboue sajd Judgment granted him by the Court of Assistants sitting in Boston as abouesajd making Returne hereof as ye law directs & not faile dated in Boston 6th october 1673.

By ye Court Edw. Rawson Secret^y

Execut. Issued out 23 m^rch 73 E R S

Note.

The thirty-fifth paper in No. 1290 is as follows: —

"In the Case of fathergon Dinely Apealeant and Cap^n william Davis Attorney to Cornelius Stenwicke Deffendant the Jury finds for the Apealant Reversion of the former Judgment with the lands in Controuersy & Cost of Courts

Jonas Clarke in
the name of the rest"

[See above, XCIV, record of 5 Sept. 1671]

---

*See Suffolk County Court Record, July 1673, p. 149, and Oct. 1672 p. 83.

[Suffolk County Court Record, 29 Oct. 1672, page 83.]

Dinely conta. Steenwick

"Fathergon Dinely admr. to the Estate of John Dinely late of Boston deceased plaint. against the good's Debt's or estate of Cornelius Steenwick, in the hand's of Capta. William Davis, or wherever else it may bee founde, the saide Capta. Davis being Attourny to the saide Steenwick Defendt. in an Accon of Reveiw of a judgmt. entred the last Court of Assistant's in March last past, but the saide Accon was tried at the Court of Assistant's in September last past, wherein saide Capta. Davis was as Attourny to saide Cornelius Steenwick plaint. against the Estate of saide John Dinely deceased; which is greatly to the damage of the plaint & other due damages according to Attachmt. Dat. August 29th. 1672. after the Attachmt. & Evidences in the case produced were read comitted to the Jury & are on file with the Record's of this Court. The jury brought in theire Verdict as followeth The jury findes for the plaint that the Defendant shall deliver up to the plaintiffe whatever was Levied by Execucon which was the Estate of John Dinely & now in the hand's of Capta. William Davis attourny to Cornelius Steenwick or to pay the plaintiffe two hundred pound's in Mony & Cost's of Court, The Defendant appealed to the next Court of Assistant's, & the saide Capta. William Davis as principall in four hundred pound's & Mr Nicholas Page & John Vsher as Sureties in two hundred pound's apeice acknowledged themselves in open Court jointly & severally bound to the Treasuror. of the County of Suffolke & party concerned on condicon that the saide Capta. Davis shall prosecute his appeale from the judgmant of this Court at the next Court of Assistant's to Effect."

[Suffolk County Court Record, 29 July 1673, page 149.]

Dinely agst. Steenwick

"Fathergon Dinely admr. to the Estate of John Dinely deceased plaint. against the goods or estate of Cornelius Steenwick of New Yorke in the hands of Capt. Wm. Davis or wherever it may bee founde Defendt. in an accon of reveiw of a judgmt. the Sd. Davis (as hee was Attourny aforesaide) obteined agst. the Sd. Dinely as hee was admr. to John Dinely aforesaide deceased at the County Court held at Boston in Aprill last which accon was for illegally seizing apprizing & making division of a house & land that the aforesaide John Dinely was never legally possessed of noe division haveing ever been made between the Sd. John & ffathergon Dinely in the Sd. house & land but after the death of John Dinely ffathergon Dinely's brother as admr. to the deceased his Estate was legally possessed of the Sd. house & land & hath fully Satisfied for them as may more fully appeare by ffathergon Dinely his Accoumpt given unto & accepted of by the County Court with all due damages according to Attachmt. Dat: July. 16th. 1673.

After the Attachmt. & Evidences in the case produced were read comitted to the Jury & remaine on file with the Records of this Court The Jury brought in theire Verdict & founde for the Defendt. costs of Court. The plaint. appealed from the judgment of this Court to the next Court of Assistants & the Sd. ffathergon Dinely as principall in three hundred & twenty pounds & John Sandys & James Meares as Sureties in one hundred & sixty pounds apeice acknowledged themselves

Appeale

respectiuely bound to the Treasuro^r^. of the County of Suffolke & party concerned on condicon that the S^d^. ffathergon Dinely Should prosecute his appeal from the judgement of this Court at the next Court of Assistants to Effect."

CXXI.

[Middlesex County Court Files, Oct. 1673.]

At A Court of Assistants held at Bo[ston 2^d^ Septemb^r^.] 1673. John Clarke plaintiffe [ag^t^ Joseph Bartlett defend^t^] in an Action of Appeale fr[om the Judgment of the] County Court at Cambridge [After the Attachment Courts] Judgment & Reasons of Appeale [were read. The Defendant] pleading as a barr for a no[nsuite that the Appellants] hand was not to the Reasons [of Appeale as the law] requires

The Court declar[ed the plantiff was non]suted & Granted the Defendant [Costs of Courts: of y^s^ Court] nineteene shilling & six penc [ ]

This is a true Coppy of the Courts [ ]

This is a true Coppy exam [ ]

7 8. 73

The following is another copy of the same record.

[At A] Court of Assistants held at Boston 2^d^ Septemb^r^ 1673. [John C]larke plantiff ag^t^. Joseph Bartlett Defend^t^. in [an Ac]tion of Appeale from the Judgment of the County [Court] at Cambridge: After the Attachment Courts Judgment [& Reas]ons of Appeale were read The Defendant pleading [as a] barr for a non suite that the Appellants hand was [not to] the. Reasons of Appeale as the law requires The Court [declar]ed the plantiff was non suited & Granted the defend^t^ [Costs of] Courts: of y^s^ Court nineteen shillings & six penc.

[ ] A true Copie taken out of the Courts Reccords

Attests Edw: Rawson Secret^y^.

NOTE.

Middlesex County Court Record, p. 56 (Pulsifers Copy)

"Joseph Bartlet p^l^. ag^t^ Jno. Clarke def^t^. In an accon of the case, for pulling downe a frame of his, taking away the timber thereof, and carijng away about a load of barque all done vpon the land of the said Bartlett, lying within Cambr. bounds, bounded vpon Hugh Clarke east, Noah Wiswall South, and the highway West & Hugh Clarke aforesaid North, and for damages thereby susteyned to ye vallue of sixteen pounds, according to attachm^t^ dated. dat. 25. 1st. m^o^. 1673. Both partyes appeared and Joyned issue in the case, and after a full hearing of their pleas & evidences as they were by them presented in Court. the Jury brought in their verdict, finding for the Plant. damages nine pounds, & costs of Court, one pound fourteen shillings & two pence *

The Deft appealeth.

John Clarke as principle, & Hugh Clarke as surety do acknowledge themselves to stand bound Joyntly & severally to the Trer of the Coun̄, in ten pounds a peece, by them to be forfeited & payd. The condic̄c̄on of this Recogniscance is that the said John Clarke shall prossecute this his Appeale at the next Court of Assistants to effect as the law requireth and that he shall abide the order of the Court therein and not depart without license."

At the County Court at Cambridge Oct. 7, 1673, "in an action of the case upon the forfeiture of a bond, for not prosecuting his appeale" from the above judgment the defendant Clarke refused to join issue and appealed to the next Court of Assistants "

CXXII.

[Essex County Court Files, Vol. XX, F. 87.]

Att A Court of Assistants held at Boston 2d Septembe^r^ 1673

Henry Leonard plantiff agt Andrew† makfashion partner wth John Ramsdall &c. defendts in an Action of Appeale from the Judgment of the last County Court at Ipswich. After the Attachment Courts Judgment Reasons of Appeale & euidence in the Case produced were read Comtted to the Jury and remajne on file wth the Reccords of this Court the Jury brought in their virdict they found for ye defendt Confirmation of the former Judgment: only abateing twenty one pounds sixteen shillings & sixe pence finding for ye plaintiff ye Costs of ys Court = so yt execution is only to Issue out of ys Court for one hundred & one pounds eleuen shillings & sixe pence wth Costs of Ipswich Court fower pounds [eight shillings] & fower pence = That this is a true Copie taken out of the Courts Reccords Attests Edward Rawson Secrety

NOTE.

The following is the record of the judgment from which the appeal was taken: —

Ipswich County Court Records 1666–1682.

"The Court held at Ipswich the 25 of march 1673"

"(3) Ambrose makefashon ptner with John Ramsdell & by his order or Atturnye plt. agst. Henry Lennard deft. in an action of debt of 143£ according to attachmt. the attachmt & other evidences pduced were read comitted to the Jury & are on file The Jury found for the plt: damages 143£ 8s & costs of Court

---

In margin, * "At a County Court held at Cambridge Aprill 1. 1673"
† Error of the original for Ambrose.

mr Lenard desireing the court to take the considderation of the apparent equity of his cause after the verdict of the Jury agst. him to pay vnto Ambrose Makfashon & John Ramsdell 143£ 8s damage and costs and haveing heard the ꝑtyes on both sydes cannot but Judge the sd. Leonard to be very much damnified in respect of the measure of the loades of cōles wch by agreemt should have beene 12 quarters the loade wheras by suficient testimony it appeares the coale cart would not hold above sixty eight bushells The court therefore doe Judge meet to abate of the said verdict 20£ and doe acordingly give Judgment against the said Leonard & for the sd. Ambrose mackfashon & John Ramsdell 123£ 8s damages & costs of court 4£ 8s 4d

The deft. appeales to the next court of Asistants at Boston

Henry Leonard acknowledged himselfe stand bound. to the tresurer of the county in the sum̄ 300£ and Ensigne Thomas Chandler & Anthony Carrell acknowledged themselues to stand bound to the tresurer in the sum̄ of 300£ The condition is that the sayd Henry Leonard shall ꝓsecute his appeale from the Judgmt of this Court att the next Court of assistants at Boston to efect acording to law''

CXXIII.

[Middlesex Files, Lawton *v.* Bonner, April 1683.]

''At a Speciall Court* held at Boston August 26th. 1672.

Henry Lawton plaint. against John Bonner Defendant in an Ac̄c̄on of the case for that hee the saide Bonner doth withold & vnjustly detaine from him, the saide Lawton, his part of the whole Effect's produce & profit, whether in goods' or servants' & an Accot of a voiadge or voiadges made with the Catch Recovery for his one & severall men theire accot. with him in Company from Boston to Virginia & from thence to Barbado's & from thence backe againe to Virginia & from thence for England; & alsoe for that the saide Bonner hath neglected & refused as hee was master to saile wth. the saide Catch from Liverpool & other places according to the order of the saide Loaton as merchant according to Agreement; but on the contrary the saide Bonner hath made many vnreasonable delaies, loosing many faire oppertunities of winde & weather, & at last in a wilfull & clandestine manner ran or went away with the aforesaide Catch from the port of Dublin in Ireland & left him—the saide Lawton — there behinde contrary to his will & order: & finally for that the saide Bonner since his arrivall in New England hath disposed of the saide Lawton's good's & chest & wearing apparrell & writing's according to the saide Bonners will & pleasure, still refuseing to deliver or give him saide Lawton an accot. thereof. with all due dam̄ages according to Attachment Dat: August: 21th. 1672. After the Attachmt. & Evidences in the case produced were read com̄itted to the

* See * in margin of pages 247 and 248.

* jury & are on file with the Record's of the Court of Assistance; The jury brought in theire verdict they finde for the plaintiffe that the Defendant deliver vnto the plaintiffe his quarter part of the Catch Recovery in good order & repaire with one quarter part of all her appurtenances; & deliver alsoe to the plaintiffe his four servants viz[t]. ffrancis Sciddall, ffrancis Stafford, John Hoakesy & James Jarrett; & alsoe doe give a true accompt vpon Oath & the produce thereof of a parcell of Tobacco, porke, Tarr & pease; which the plaint. shipped vpon the saide Catch in Virginia for Barbado's & consigned to the Defend[t]. & per bill of lading; & alsoe that the Defend[t]. pay vnto the plaintiffe fifty pounds in mony for the dam̃age susteined in leaving of him behinde in Ireland with Cost's of Court. The premises to bee done & performed by the Defend[t]. vnto the plaintiffe within thirty daies next ensuing; or else that the Defend[t]. pay vnto the plaintiffe two hundred twenty eight pound's in mony with Costs of Court.

This is a true Coppie As Attest's

Isaac Addington Cler."

NOTE.

There is also another copy of the same judgment, attested by Freegrace Bendall, Clerk, which differs from the other in the heading, which in this copy is as follows: — "At A Speciall Court held at Boston Agust 26th. 1672 called at the Request of Henry Lawton marchant"

This copy has also in the margin "Execuc̃on Issued for 236[li]. 14 money Sept. 30. 1672.

[The writ is dated August 21 1672 & returned same date.]

There is also on file the following execution: —

"To the Marshall of the County of Suffolk or his Deputy

These require you in his Majesties Name to Levy by way of Execuc̃on upon the good's Estate or person of John Bonner in mony, to the vallue of two hundred thirty six pound's fourteen shilling's & deliver the same with two shillings for this Execuc̃on unto Henry Lawton, and is in satisfaction of a judgment granted him for soe much at a Speciall Court held at Boston on the Twenty sixth day of August 1672. & hereof you are not to faile. Dat. in Boston September the 30th 1672.

By the Court

Isaac Addington Cler.

This is a true Coppie as Attest's Isaac Addington Cler."

[Endorsed] "I haue Extended this Execuc̃on on the other side upon the person of John Bonner this first of October and haue com̃itted him to prison for the want of mony to the vallue of two hundred thirty six pounds' sixteen shillings according to Execuc̃on.

Per mee Rich: Wayte Marshall.

This is a true Coppie as Attests Isaac Addington Cler."

"Att A Speciall Court held at Boston August 26th. 1672 Called at the request of Henry Lawton mercht.

Henry Lawton Plantiff Contra John Bonner Defendt. according to Attachment July 21th. 1672 —

After the Attachment & euidences in the case produced were read Comitted to the Jury & are on file wth. the Reccords of the Court of Assistants the Jury brought in their virdict. They find for the plantiffe that the defendant deliuer vnto the plantiffe his quarter part of the Catch Recouery in good order & repajre, wth one quarter part of all hir Appurtenances & deliuer also to the plantiff his fower servants vizt. ffrancis Sciddall ffrancis Stafford John Hokesy & James Jarrot, & also doe give a true accompt vpon oath & the produce thereof of a parcell of Tobacco, Porke, tarr & pease; which the plantiff shipped vpon the sajd Catch in Virginia for Barbadoes & consigned to the defendant as per bill of lading & also that the defendant pay vnto the plantiffe fiuety pounds in mony for the Damages susteyned in leaving him behind in Ireland wth. Costs of Court. The premisses to be donne & performed by the defendant vnto the plantiffe wthin thirty dayes next ensuing: or else that the defendant pay vnto the plantiffe two hundred twenty eight pounds in mony wth Costs of Court.

This is a true Copie as Attests Isaac Addington Cler:

That this is a true Copie Compared wth. the originall on file Attests Edward Rawson Secrety."

[In the margin of the above is the following]
"Present Richard Bellingham Esqr Govr.
John Leueret Esqr. Dept Govr.
Edward Tyng Esqr. Asistant.
Jurymen Sworne
Mr Symon Lynde.
James Whetcombe.
Joseph Dudson.
Nathaniel Greene.
Xtopher Clarke
Antho: Checkley.
Samuel Scarlet.
Augustin Lyndon.
Wm. Parkes.
John Stebbyn.
Thomas Tyleston.
Enoch Wisewall"

It appears by the record of the County Court (Middlesex) that in April 1673 Henry Lawton brought an action against John Bonner for detaining certain goods to the value of two hundred and ninety two pounds. The defendant refused to join issue and appealed to the next Court of Assistants. At the same Court Lawton brought an action against Bonner for "neglecting his duty as master" of a "Ketch" to the damage of said Lawton about 50£. The defendant refused to join issue and appealed to the next Court of Assistants. Also at the same Court Lawton brought another action against Bonner for carying away a chest &c. to the value of about 25£. Also another action for debt of 23£ 19s 1d. Verdict was rendered for the plaintiff in each case and the defendant appealed to the next Court of Assistants.

Mass. Records, Vol. IV, pt. 2, p. 541, 11 Oct. 1672.

"In ansr to the petition of John Bonner, the Court judgeth it meete to grant the petitioner a revejw of his case at the next County Court to be held at Boston"

Same, Vol. V, p. 9, 27 May, 1674. "In ansr to the petition of Henry Lauton, the Court declares the peticoner hauing had sundry accons refferring to this case, wherein he hath been sometimes plt & sometimes deffendt in seuerall Courts, & justice don him according to law and euidence prescribed, that it is in his oune liberty to implead any person or persons that haue perverted justice by false testimony in any Court of justice, as the law hath fully prouided."

See below Jury's verdict & Attaint of Jury at Court of Assistants Sept. 2 1673 (Suffolk Files).

Court Files, Suffolk, No. 1221, thirteenth paper.

"Att A Court of Assistants held at Boston 2d September 1673.

John Bonner plantiffe against Henry Lawton defendant in an action of Appeale from the Judgment of the County Court in Cambridge as to the chest of cloaths. After the Attachment Courts Judgment reasons of appeale and euidences in the case produced were read comitted to the Jury & remayne on file with the reccords of this Court the Jury brought in their virdict they found for the deffendant Confirmation of the former Judgement & Costs of Courts: The plantiff in open Court declared he did attaynt the Jury. And accordingly the sajd John Bonner Richard Cooke & Humphry Hodges acknowledged themselues Joyntly & Seuerally bound in fiuety pounds apeece to Richard Russell Esqr Tresurer of the Country and to the partys concerned that they shall & will prosecute their Attaynder at the next Court of Assistants to effect & abide the order of the Court as the law directs.

That what is aboue written is a true Copie of the Jurjes virdict: and the aboue mentioned plantiff John Bonner his Attaint of the Jury & his suertjes bond for the prosecution thereof taken out of the Courts booke of Reccords

Attests Edward Rawson Secrety."

CXXIV.

[Court Files, Suffolk, No. 1341, 7th paper.]

At a Court of Assistants held at Boston 2d. September 1673.

Benjamin Gibbs & Henry Lawton plaintiffs. against John Bonner Defendt in an action of Appeale from the Judgment of the last County

Court in Boston*: = After the Attachment Courts Judgment reasons of Appeale & Evidences in the case produced were read comitted to the Jury & are on file wth. the Records of this Court. The Jury brought in theire Verdict they found for the Defendant confirmation of the former Judgment & costs of Courts = 3[lbs] = 1[s] = 6[d] = The plaintiff[s]. desired the bond might bee chancered† The Court on hearing of both parties declared they chancered the bond with all damages to One hundred pounds mony for the plaintiff[s]. to pay or that they deliver possession of the house & land and in other respects performe the Award.

That this is a true Coppie taken out of the Courts booke of Records Attests Edward Rawson Secret.

Copia Vera Attest[r]. Is[a]. Addington Cler.

[Court Files, Suffolk, No. 162121.]

"Jn[o] Bonne[r] Bill of Cost in y[e] forfeture of y[e] Bond y[e] Case of [292£] of Goodes in y[e] first Action Ag[t] Henry Lawton://

Imp[rs]. To Coppies of Records of M[r] Addington	00:	04:	00
To y[e] Entring y[e] Appeale p[d] to M[r] D[a]nford	00:	02:	00
To two Wittnesses one Day	00:	04:	00
To: 3 Dayes Attendance	00:	06:	00
To Entring the Action	00:	10:	00
To 11 Dayes Attendance at y[e] Courtt of Assistance	00:	16:	06
To Records of M[r] Danford	00:	[04:]	06
To filing papers: 14	00	02	4
	2	9	4

E T. Allowed E R S.
E R.

[Endorsed] "Bonn[er] Costs
as to y[e] bond"
[ ]

[Suffolk County Court Records, 29 July 1673, page 148.]

Bonner ag[st]. Gibbs &[a].

"John Bonner plaint. against Benj[a]. Gibbs & Henry Lawton Defend[ts]. in an accon of the case for breach or non performance of theire bond or Engagement in one hundred pounds apiece bound jointly & Severally made at a County Court held at Boston the 29[th]. of October 1672. by theire not performing of an Award under the

* See Suffolk County Court Record July 1673 p. 148.

† In the margin is the following entry "at y[e]ire Adjou[r]. 30 — 8 mo. 73"

hands & Seales of mr. John Joyliffe mr. Peter lidget & mr. Thomas Deane bearing date the twentieth of January 1672. relateing thereunto wth. other due damages according to Attachmt. Dat. july 24. 1673. After the Attachmt. & Evidences in the case produced were read comitted to the Jury & remaine on file with the Records of this Court.

The Jury brought in theire Verdict & founde for the plaint. two hundred pounds the forfiture of the bond & costs of Court. the Defendt. Benjamin Gibbs' appealed from the judgment of this Court to the next Court of Assistants & the Sd. Benja. Gibbs as principall in four hundred pounds & mr. John Saffine & mr. Richard Wharton as Sureties in two hundred pounds apeice acknowledged themselves respectively bound to the Treasuror. of the County of Suffolke & party concerned on condicon that the Sd. Benja. Gibbs should prosecute his appeale from the judgment of this Court at the next Court of Assistants to Effect."

Appeale

CXXV.

[Court Files, Suffolk, No. 1234, 11th paper.]

In ye case betwene the Executrs of Thomas Bishop plantife and mr Stoughton Attorny of Richard Saltonstall Esquir defendant ye Jury finde ^ spetjall verdict vizt: if the Euidence to [prove] A dett of 150£: with the plantifes acknowledgment of a dett yt was due: ye possession of the house & lande of ye defendants: with the agrement of the [hands] of Artickils and bonds compared be good Euidence in Law to [prove] the bond sued for with out the oath of those witnessing the bonds then we find for ye defendant Confirmatjone of ye former judgment & Cost of Courts. If not for the plantife Reuersyone of ye former Judgment & Cost of Courts.

The magistrates finde for the defendt wth Costs of Courts as Attests E. R. S.

Note.

This case was an appeal to the Court of Assistants from a judgment of the County Court at Boston July 29 1673 in favor of Richard Saltonstall and against the Executors of Thomas Bishop for 300£ sterling "according to bond."

CXXVI.

[Court Files, Suffolk, No. 1245, 23d paper.]

Inter Tho. Miller & Robert Risco: defend the Jury [on a second going out] brought in their virdict they found for the defendant Confirmation of the former Judgmt & Costs of Courts = dd in open court Attests E R S 4 Sept 73

NOTE.

This was an appeal from a judgment of the County Court at Boston, July 29 1673 in favor of the defendant Robert Brisco — The action was for breach of covenants.

CXXVII.

[Court Files, Suffolk, No. 1230, 2d leaf.]

Srs.

The Reuerend mr Woodbridge of yor Toun hath made complaint unto this Court that having for some tyme spent his labour in ye ministry of the word amongst you there hath been due recompence made unto him for the same some part of what he conceaves due to him being yet behind. Now although the proper cognisance of this matter belongs unto yor County Court, yet because of the Addresse made unto us & that we might prevent further trouble, we have thought good to recom̃end this matter unto your speedy consideration to doe what in equity you are bound therein, that what yet remaines unpayd to mr Woodbridge may be levied & delivered to him: we judge you will very well consult your own credit & doe that wch may tend to pe[ace] & composure of matters amongst you, if you bee not over difficult or strait handed in yor Allowance to mr Woodbridge for his paines past. However we determine not in a case unheard from each party, but only move you to doe of yorselues what is right, otherwise if mr Woodbridges complaint yet continue, we have declared that his remedy according to lawe lies wth yor County Court where it must be issued: not els at present:

Boston 4 Sept. 1673 By ye Court of Assistants
Edw. Rawson Secrey

Suprscription,
To our loving neighbors & friends
Mr Anthony Somersby & the
rest of the Selectmen for Newbury
to be Communicated to the Towne.
dd.

[See Mass. Colony Records Vol. IV, pt. 2, pp. 487, 521, & 549.]

CXXVIII.

[Mass. Archives, Vol. 9, No. 63.]

To ye honrd Court of Assistants now Assembled

The humble petition of John Wheelwright Humbly Sheweth

That where as ye honrd Courte hath seene just reason to grant my Dauter Nanny A diuorse from ye greiuous oppressions of Edward Nailer

Sometimes her husband, vpon his breach of ye marriage couen^t^ for wch I desire to be thankfull to god, & also to ye hon^rd^ Court; And also did appoint two persons to looke ouer ye writeings then vnder ye seasure of the Courts order, & deliuer to Nailer thos wch conserned him, wch was accordingly donne so farre as I vnderstand, & I did then humbly conceive y^t^ ye other papers & books was to be deliuered to my dauter, but it being not exprest in ye order were sealed vp till aduise could be had of ye Court of Assistants, wch was taken last march, but still they ley sealed & noe thing donne & for what reason Nailer best knows.

My humble request therefore is y^t^ ye papers & books may be deliuered to my dauter that they may be by her opened & made vse of according to ye Intendment as I apprehend of ye first order. haueing ocation at p^r^sent for some writeings about her land y^t^ was her husband Nannys & otherwise. & yor petitioner shall pray as in duty bound.

John Wheelwright

11th of September 1673

In Ans^r^ to this petition the Court doe order y^t^ all the bookes writtings & papers belonging to m^rs^ Nanne the late wife of Edward Naylor y^t^ are in the hands of Capt Edw Hutchinson & Capt Tho: Lake to whom they were Comitted be forthwith deliuered to the sajd m^r^s nanne or hir order =

By y^e^ Court Edw Rawson Secret^y^

NOTE.

Mass. Records, Vol. IV, pt. 2, p. 549, 23 Oct., 1672.

"In ans^r^ to the petition of Edward Naylor, Q. Whether Edward Naylor shall, vppon good security given to the Secretary to the Court of Asistants for the good behauiour towards all persons, in speciall towards his late wife, be released from his bannishment from Boston, & w^th^in twenty miles thereof: The Court resolves this quaestion on the affirmative. Whither Edward Naylor shall haue deliuered to him all the estate propperly & legally belonging to him, together wth his bookes & papers: This quaest. is resolved on the affirmative. Whither Edward Naylor shall haue his children to dispose of according as he shall see meet for their further good: This question is resolved on the affirmative, provided the sajd Naylor give good security to the County Court next in Boston, that the children be well educated & provided for according to his abillity: & this is also resolued on the affirmative."

See also above record of 11 Oct. 1672.

CXXIX.

[Mass. Archives, Vol. 135, No. 16.]

Wee the Grand Jury for the Massachusets Jurisdiction in New England doe present & Indict Vnice Cole of Hampton [now] widdow for not hauing the feare of God before hir eyes and being Instigated by the Divill did on the 24th of Nouember in the yeare 1662 and since [enter] into Couenant wth the divill and then & since haue had familiarity wth the Divill Contrary to the peace of our Soueraigne [Lord] the King his Crowne & dignity, the lawes of God & of this Jurisdiction

[Endorsed]

Wee finde this Bill thus farr yt she hath had familliarity with the Deuill and put her vpon further Triall

William Alford in the name of the rest of the Jury

[Mass. Archives, Vol. 135, opposite to No. 16.]

In ye case of vnis cole now prisoner att ye Bar — not Legally guilty acording to Inditement butt Just ground of vehement suspissyon of her haueing had famillyarryty with the deuill

Jonas Clarke in the name of the rest

[Court Files, Suffolk, No. 1228, tenth paper.]

This is to Certify all whom it may conserne ordinary keepers of ys Jurisdic̃on: that the persons here vnder expressed haue theire seurll. Creditts on the Tresurer who is to sattisfy them theire seurll. expences to ye seurll. values here expressed: as being ye remajnder of wt was Allowed them for theire time expended in wittnessing agt Eunice Cole on triall for witchcraft

as To Thomas Coleman & his wife	14s : 00d
To Goodwife Hobs	07 : 00
To Widdow wedg woode	15 : 08
	1 : 16 : 8

By the Court Edw. Rawson Secrety.

NOTE.

[There are a number of depns. in the case of Unice Cole (No. 1228) attested by Edwd. Rawson Secretary Sept. 1673.]

(Mass. Archives, Vol. 135, No. 10.)

"To the marshall of ye County of Norfolk or his deputy

Yow are hereby required in his majestjes name to sumon forthwith & [alike] require Abraham Perkins Senr & mary his wife Abraham Drake Alexander Dunum Bridget Clyfford Sarah Clyfford John Mason & Ann [Smith] & Ann Huggins Elizabeth Shaw & Mary Perkins ye wife of Jacob Perkins of Hampton & Ephraim Winsley of Salisbury to make their Appeareances before the Court of Asistants sitting in Boston on the first tuesday in September next to give in their seuerall euidences agt Vnice Cole [then] & there to be tryed being in Custody for having familiarity wth the divill: hereof they & you are not to faile at yor perrill making yor returne hereof to the Court or secretary at or before the 1st of September next

Dated in Boston this 5th of August 1673

By the Court Edward Rawson Secret^{y}.

I haue serued this warrant vpon Abraham Perkins Senr Alexander Dennum Mary Perkins Senr Bridgett Clifford & Sarah Clifford John Mason Ann Smith & Ann Huggins Mary Perkins the wife of Jacob Perkins & Elizabeth Shaw of Hampton & Ephraim Winsley of Salisbury to make their Apperance att the next Court of Assistant according to the tennor of this warrañt & required them to Attend Accordingly this

17: 6 mo 1673 by mee Henery Trewe
Mashels depetey

Abraham Drake being out of the Collony"

Mass. Records, Vol. IV, pt. 2, p. 70, 8 Oct. 1662.

"In ans^{r} to the peticons of Vnice Cole, the inhabitants of Hampton, as also the peticon of Wm Salter, all in relation to the sajd Vnice Cole, the Court doe order, that the sajd Vnice Cole pay what is due on arreares to the keeper, & be released the prison, on condicon that she depart, wthin one month after her release, out of this jurisdiction, & not to returne againe on poenalty of hir former sentenc being executed against hir."

Same, p. 106, 18 May 1664.

"In ans^{r} to the petition of Wm Salter, it is ordered . . . and that the selectmen of Hampton shall speedily pay him what, vpon just account, is due to him respecting the charge of Vnice Cole," &c.

Same, p. 149, 3 May, 1665.

"In ans^{r} to the peticon of Vnice Cole, it is ordered, that she may haue hir liberty vpon hir security to depart from. & abide out of this jurisdiction, according to the former fauo^{r} of this Court."

CXXX.

[Court Files, Suffolk, No. 1248 5th & 6th papers.]

Boston 27 October 1673

Wee the Grand Jury for ye Court of Assistants for ye Massachusetts Colony in New England Doe Indict Lodwick ffowler of Portsmouth on Puscataq Riuer by name of Lodwick ffowler for Killing John Ellis on or about the 12th of September last (the said Lodwick ffowler being upon the Watch) by his Gunn or Musquet goeing off — & soe leaue him to further Tryall.

Hugh Mason foreman

Boston 28th Octo: 1673

Wee the Jury for Tryalls this present Court of Assistants do fynde Lodowick ffowler Guilty according to Indictm^{t}.

John C[orney*] in the name of the rest

NOTE.

There are in the case two petitions, one to the Court of Assistants by which it seems that he was fined ten pounds, and the other to the General Court asking for a trial of his case and claiming that the shooting was accidental — This is also some evidence in the case.

CXXXI.

[Mass. Archives, Vol. 48, No. 138.]

25 8 1673 To m^{r} Thomas Bercher m^{r} Isaac Robenson and the rest of the subscribers of a petition sent from Martens Vinyard vnto the honord Gouernour and Assist. of the Massachusets

Gent men

y^{rs} of the 15 present we recd by witch we vnderstand that there is a present differencs betwixt your selves and your Ancient and long continued Governour the whitch is very grievous to vs. but how to help wee kno not. for at such a time as this is to set in with a divided people we se not sufficient reson, nor to take vpon vs the Govern^{t} of any people vpon the request of a part of them. and whereas you say your day for Choycs is past, y^{t} holds forth you had a day appoynted for Election but why you proceeded not in that work we vnderstand not and if it were hindered by yourselves, you may seriously Consider whether the grete and many difficultyes y^{-} are vnder may not now be best Eased by your quiet yealding vnto your former Governo^{r}, and your one holesum lawes you have lived so long vnder. vntell you vnderstand his Majests pleasure whether to Establiesh your one Govern^{t} or to settell you vnder sum other of Collenyes in these parts. ~~And if you were vnder any difficultyes of any farren Enemy we should not be wanting on our parts to leand you Assist^{c}~~. but to shew our selfes siding in a divission amonxt our ffriends and country men we are all to geather Indisposed vnto. but earnestly desire your coomfertable closing to geather as in your best dayes.† Not els but our respects to you all. Remajne yor very lo freinds

The Court of Assists.

Past by the Court of Assistants the 31th of october 1673 as Attests

Edw. Rawson Secret^{y}. 31 October 1673

---

* Or Comey.

† From here is in Rawson's hand. The previous part is in a different hand.

CXXXII.

[Court Files, Suffolk, No. 1255.]

To the Honora^ble^. the Governo^r^ & Magestrates now assembled in Boston

The Petition of Thomas Willett

humbly sheweth

That whereas in the late mutations & change of Affaires which, by the providence of God, is come to pass amongst the English inhabiting & trading at New Yorke & the places adjacent by reason of the Dutch who haue againe reduced those parts under theire Comands as is well known unto your Hono^rs^ by reason whereof many of the Inhabitants of the Vnited Colonys doe already suffer & are more and more like soe to doe both in their persons & Estates; amongst whom yor Peticoner is noe small sufferer, in that the Dutch that are or haue been there Comand^rs^ in cheife haue seized a considerable part of the Estate of yor Peticoner to the vallue of three hundred & ffifty pounds sterling in Beavo^r^ (at leaste) notwithstanding theire proclamacon to the contrary in the generall, & theire promiss to myselfe yor Peticoner in perticuler vizt. that though they had made some Arrest of my goods for the present, yet when they should know & understand that yor. Hono^rs^. & those who are in power in these parts, did not make seizure & confiscation of the Estates perteining to the Dutch that were here: but that yor Hono^rs^. did suffer those men with sloopes & goods that were here to goe hence in peace, that then they would likewise withold nothing from yor Petition^r^. but release all that they had seized: so that yor Petition^r^ may justly feare they will also seize both his houses & debts that are in those parts.

The premisses considered yor Peticoner doth most humbly request yor Hono^rs^ to grant him an Order that he may haue the Liberty to Arrest & secure soe much of the Estate perteining to the Dutch as hee can finde in this Colony, which may remaine under the custody of Authority to bee responsible for soe much as they haue seized of the Estate of yor Petitioner as aforesaid And yor Peticoner shall ever pray

11: november 1673

In Ans^r^ to this peticon the Court declares they know not of any estate of the Dutch nation to be heere but if the peticoner doth the law is open for him to make vse [of for] his reparation

E: R: R.

CXXXIII.

[Court Files, Suffolk, No. 1254.]

[The five papers in this case relate to the trial of Peter Croy accused of committing rape. The first paper is a warrant, dated 11 Nov. 1673, to summon a jury to examine the body of the woman with the return endorsed thereon. The second paper is the indictment by the grandjury, and also a special verdict by the jury at the trial to the effect that if the evidence as to the condition of the body and other circumstantial evidence together with the crying out of the woman herself against the accused "amount unto two legall evidences or equivalent thereunto then wee finde Peter Croy guilty according to the indictment, but if not not guilty." The other papers contain a statement by the accused and several depositions in the case. The judgment of the Court does not appear.]

[Court Files, Suffolk, No. 1254, second paper.]

Wee the Grand Jury of the Massachusetts Jurisdiction or Colony in New England doe Indict Peeter Croy of Ipswich: frenchman. — by the name of Peeter Croy for not having the feare of God before his eyes & being instigated by the Divil. did on or about the 15th. of october last, Comitt a Rape on the body of Sarah Lambert in the open feild Contrary to the peace of our Soveraigne Lord the King his Croune & Dignity the lawes of God & of this Jurisdiction —

A true bill
John Parpoint in the name of
the rest.
N. 64

The Jury finde by Evidence the Body of Sarah Lambert defloured by Peter Croy or some other: and the Party defloured affirminge it to be by the said Croy; one Positive Evidence expressinge the beholding accions tending to the same & hearinge Sarah Lambert to cry out: with other Circumstantiall Evidence; wch. if all amount unto two legall Evidences; or equivalent thereunto. Then wee finde Peter Croy guilty according to the tenor of this Inditement; But if not not guilty.

Simon Lynde, Fore[ ]

(See also LXXXV.)

Court Files (Suffolk) No. 65414, part 1.

Suffolk, ss. To the Hon°. his Majestys Justices of the Court of General Sessions of the peace for the County of Suffolk July 1749.

The Memorial of Middlecott Cooke & Ezekiel Goldthwait Clerks of said Court.

Humbly Shews,

That when the Town house was Consum'd in Decem^r. 1747 your Mem° took all possible pains to preserve the Publick Records and Files of the County then in their Office, that in removing the same out of the Town house the Files of writs Executions & other Papers belonging to the County were most of 'em broke, & so Intermix'd that there was scarce a whole file of Papers together for near Seventy or Eighty years past, that upon your Mem°. Informing your Honours thereof, you were pleas'd to order them to Sort said Files & put 'em into order, which your Mem°. have accordingly done and in doing thereof have taken great care and been put to a considerable Expence of time.

Your Mem°. would therefore pray your Honours will be pleas'd to make them such an allowance for the matters aforesaid as you shall Judge reasonable.

Middlecott Cooke
Ezek^l. Goldthwait.

[part 2 of No. 65414.]

Suffolk ss. At a Court of General Sessions of the peace held at Boston for s^d County on Friday the 28 day of July 1749.

Samuel Welles Samuel Watts Samuel White Joseph Heath & Samuel Miller Esq^rs. are appointed a Committee to take the said Memorial into Consideration and report to the Court what they think reasonable to be allowed for the Services therein mentioned.

Att^r. Middlecott Cooke Cler.

The Committee appointed to Consider of the foregoing petition are Humbly of opinion that there be allowd and paid out of the County Treasury sixty five pounds Bills of the last Emision to Mes^rs. Middlecott Cooke & Ezek^l Goldthwait for there services as set forth in s^d petition which is Humbly submitted.

℘ Saml Watts
℘ order

On back

Cooke & Goldthwaits Mem°.
Report Accepted

INDEX.

INDEX.

PAGE

ABBOT, (ABBOTT, &c.), THOMAS 29
dep. 30–32
ACIE, WILLIAM, dep. 81
ACT of Oct. 19, 1652, as to Indian titles, cited 50
ACTIONS, &c.
accounts 12, 13, 67, 137, 138, 147, 197–199, 203–205, 207, 210, 220–222, 242–246
annulments 67, 68, 131, 132
apprenticeship 23
awards 38, 39, 112, 117, 203
bond, non-performance 250
bondservant 15
damages, killing of a mare by a bull 13–15
deceased wife's sister, negatived 202
defamation 152–154
detaining, cargo of coal 42–46
gift of money 121–129
money received for 129, 130
profits on 32000 lbs. of sugar 181–185
divorces 146, 252, 253
execution, irregularly levied 170, 171
foreclosure, refusal to yield up a house 190
mill, carried away, to avoid 185–187
fraudulent sale, to avoid creditors 132–134
governorship of "Martens Vinyard" 256
guardianships 15, 19–21, 137, 143, 144
levy, on any Dutch goods in colony 257
minister's salary 252
partnerships 130, 131, 150
payment, for fagots 86–90
on mortgage (usurous) 163–166
possession of, farm, &c., at Lynn 9–11
houses, lands, &c. 12, 34, 70–74, 106, 141, 146, 149–151
Iron Works, &c. 166–168
mills, &c., at Boston 39–42
Nahant 46–59
Plains Farm 1–5
Pond Farm 5–8
warehouse, &c. 148

PAGE

ACTIONS, &c., *continued.*
pulling down a frame, &c. 244, 245
prisoners, arrested while in prison 141, 142
diet and lodging of 141, 142
replevin 148
review 14, 47–49, 149, 198, 207, 243
strong waters, license to retail 13
town meetings, (rival) declared illegal 147
trespass, taking hay, &c. 74–86, 170, 171
possession of house, &c. 117–120
vessels, brought in by crews 211, 227, 240–242
mutineers 229–232, 236–238
captured by Dutch, recaptured, &c. 227–239
detaining part of venture on 246–251
disposing of part of 168, 169
"malignant" ship Gilbert, seized, &c. 11, 12
sale of, (suspicious), stopped 211
salvage of 226, 227
taking, without order 140
wages of crews 16–18, 211, 227, 240–242
widow's portion 90–93, 208
ADAMS (ADDAMS)
ALEXANDER 45
ROBERT, house in Newbury 109
SAMUEL, mortgage, Sampson Shoare to 73, 74
deed of same by, to Thomas Dyre 72
(assignee of) vs. Sampson Shoare 70–74
ADDINGTON, ISAAC, clerk, copies 68, 205–250
et al, auditors, accounts of ship Planter 16
ADMIRALTY, High Court of, case referred to 12
AGAWAM (AGAWAME), Sagamore of 49, 50, 55
ALCOCK, MR. [JOHN], chirurgeon 26, 27
ALFORD, WILLIAM 254
ALLEN, [BOZOON], et al, auditors, accounts of ship Planter 16
HANNAH, et al, summoned 225
JOHN 179
CAPT. JOHN, et al, committee to repair Town House . . . 197
ALLEY, HUGH, dep. 3
ALLHALLOWES in the Wall, London 6, 7
AMENSEENE, JOHN, to transport John Johnson (Dutch prisoner) to Boston 231
ANDOVER (ANDIVER) 156
constable of 152, 159
ANDREWES, MRS. RENEW, dep. 28, 29
ANGIER, EDMOND, vs. William Bordman (admr. of Stephen Day) . 197–199
ANABAPTISTS 171–178, 213, 215
ANNIBAL (ANNIBALL, &c.)
JOHN, dep. 226
et al, summoned 225

PAGE
Annuity, for three years, purchased 164
Anthony (Antonio), ship (*See* St. Anthony)
Apprenticeship, for nine years 23
Archard, Samuel, vs. Edward Lane 67
Archer, Goody 158
Armitage (Armitege)
Godfrey, et al, jury of inquest 60
Joseph 53, 54
et al, vs. Thomas Dexter 46, 48, 50
et als, sureties for Richard Coy 118
Armstrong (Armsetrong), Matthew, vs. Thomas Hallet, et al . 129, 130
Arrest, of prisoner in prison 141, 142
Ashby, Anthony, vs. Edith Crafford, burning his house . . . 179, 180
Ashdon, Henry, vs. James Jarret 220
Aspinwall, William, covenant (unrecorded) remembered by . . . 20
Notarial Book 11–13, 16
recorder, did not observe "the punctillio of the law" 41
Assistants (*See* Court of Assistants)
Atkinson, Theodore, vs. Thomas Deane (attorney) 148
vs. John Williams 137, 138, 147
203–207, 215, 216
et al, witnesses 210
Atwater, Joshua, et al, "chief promoter of scandalous & reproachfull petition" 178
Axey, James, et al, commissioners 57

Bacon, Daniel, Sr., (wife of) assaulted by an Indian 210
Richard 241
Baker (Bacor)
John 45
Nathaniel, dep. 51
Thomas 45
William 235, 241
Balch, John 58
Bankes (Bancks)
Mrs. Lydia, vs. Abraham Oatley 1
vs. admrs. of John Humphrey 1
grants to Moses Maverick, et al, Plains Farm . . 2
Bant (Prant)
Edward, et al, petition for salvage of ship Providence, retaken from the Dutch 226, 227
declaration as to same 234, 235
ship, goods and prisoners secured 228, 230
salvage granted 227
Baptism 174, 176, 250
Barbados (Barbadoes) 181, 238, 246–248
Barber, William, et al, grantees Plains Farm 4

PAGE

BAREFOOT, CAPT. WALTER, vs. Joseph Davis 194
profane swearing, &c. 211, 212
to return to his family in England, or pay penalty 212
debarred from practising chirurgery, &c. 212
to abstain from Mrs. Hilton's company 212
charges for apprehending, &c. 239, 240
BARKER, JOHN, testimony 61
BARNES, RICHARD, granted £20 by his mother, Anne Barnes 20
granted £16, &c., by his grandmother, Agnes Bent . 19, 20
guardian of, John Grout 15
apprenticed to his father-in-law, Thomas Blanchard . 20
vs. Thomas Blanchard 15, 19–21
BARNSTABLE (BASTABLE) 69
BARRE, JOHN, wages 18
BARTHOLOMEW (BARTHOLMEW), WILLIAM 118
dep. 120
BARTLETT, JOSEPH, vs. John Clarke 244
BARTOLL, JOHN, et al, vs. admrs. of John Humphrey, Plains Farm . . 2, 4
BASSETT, WILLIAM, et al, vs. admrs. of Thomas Dexter, Sr. 47–59
BASTER, JOHN 62
BATCHELOR, [STEPHEN] 218
BATTER, EDMOND, commissioner 58
et al, admrs. of John Humphrey 2, 10
vs. Edward Collins, et al, excrs. of Henry Dunster . . 9–11
vs. Moses Maverick, et al, Plains Farm 2–5
BEARD, THOMAS, land 143
BELL, THOMAS, et al, grantees, mills, &c., of Edward Gibbons . . . 40
Sr., vs. estate of Edward Gibbons 40–42
BELLINGHAM, RICHARD, governor 248
deps. before 61–63
examines Frank Negro 194
orders adulteresses to prison 193
remembers unrecorded covenant 20
signs answer and order of Court 10–12
BENCH AND JURY, decision by 40, 41
determination by bench 132
disagreement 37, 130, 170, 189, 190
legality of judgment left to bench 42
refusal of verdict by bench 71
BENCH OF MAGISTRATES, i. e., the Court 40, 41
BENDALL, FREEGRACE, clerk 247
BENNETT (BENNIT, &c.)
HENRY, vs. William Fellows 74–86
jury's verdict questioned, omission of an "s" 81, 83
slandering, &c., the Court 74, 75
MARGARET, (in behalf of daughter) pet. for annulment, denied 131, 132
SAMUEL, agrees to pay for wind-mill on Sagamore Hill, Lynn . 9, 11

PAGE
BENT, AGNES, grants £16, &c., to her grandson, Richard Barnes . . 19, 20
excrs. of, vs. Thomas Blanchard 21
JOHN, and John Grout (guardian) agreement 19
and Thomas Blauncher, covenant 19, 20
money and goods committed to trust of 20
BERCHER, THOMAS, et al, of "Martens Vinyard", pet. for interference with their governor, denied 256
BERRY, WILLIAM, wages 18
BETTS, [ELIZABETH] 26
JOHN, assaulted his servant, who later died 24–34
BETTY, (Indian girl), ravished 216
BIDFILLD, SAMUEL, et al, jury of inquest 60
BISHOP, GEORGE, letter of William Leddra (Quaker) printed by . . 110
"New England Judged, by the Spirit of the Lord", ed. of 1703, cited 109
NATHANIEL, constable 172
THOMAS (excrs. of) vs. Richard Saltonstall 251
BISSE, JEMIMA, summoned 225
BLACK WILL (BLACK WILLIAM, DUKE WILLIAM), Indian
sold Nahant to Thomas Dexter for suit of clothes . 49, 51, 52, 54, 55
&c., to William Witter for two pestle-stones . . 59
BLAGUE, HENRY, et al, jury of inquest 60
BLANCHARD (BLAUNCHER, &c.), Thomas, vs. Richard Barnes . . 15, 19–21
said Barnes not to be disposed of, without consent of . . . 15
and John Bent, covenant 19, 20
pet. 20, 21
"BLOTS AND BLURS ON THE BILL", cause special verdict . . . 208–210
BOLARD, MR., now bound for Virginia 223
BOLTER (BOULTER), NATHANIEL, vs. Town of Hampton . . . 141, 146
vs. Capt. Brian Pendleton 185, 186
BOND, forfeiture of, for failure to prosecute 83, 86
non-performance of 249–251
BONNER, JOHN, vs. Henry Lawton 246–249
bond of, for appeal 249
vs. Benjamin Gibbs and Henry Lawton 249, 250
BORDMAN, WILLIAM, (admr. of Stephen Day), vs. Edmond Angier . 197–199
BOSTON
Anabaptists 175, 177
Church of Christ, First 207
Common 210
Conduit St. 69, 70, 72
constables 68, 71, 172, 226
cove 70
dock 91
elders, meeting at 175
gaol (prison) 37, 99, 107, 108, 111, 172, 193, 194
house of correction 97, 99, 109, 139, 153, 219

PAGE

BOSTON, *continued.*
lecture day 25
marshal 87
Neck, Indian found dead on 223
Quakers 69
selectmen 197
Town House 196, 197
treasurer 197
venire for special Court at 179
water-mills, &c. 40, 41
West End of 209
BOSTON ATHENAEUM, Aspinwall Notarial Book at 11, 209
BOULTER (*See* BOLTER)
BOWEN (BOWIN, &c.)
ANNIE, ISRAEL, et al, summoned 225
THOMAS, et al, grantees Plains Farm 4
BRACKETT (BRACKET), PETER, et als
appraisers, estate of Capt. John Williams 206
John Dinely 209
sureties for Theodore Atkinson 216
BRADBURY, THOMAS, commissioner 65
recorder 141, 144, 146, 154, 194
BRADFORD, [WILLIAM], et als, empowered to release Quakers 98
BRADSTREET (BRADSTRET, &c.), SIMON 83, 154, 156, 157
vs. James Everell 163–166
James Pecker 200, 201
BRAINTREE (BRANTREY) 19
BRATTLE (BRATLE), THOMAS 137, 183, 203–205
BRECK, EDWARD 59, 63
BREEDON, CAPT. THOMAS 166
BREND, WILLIAM, et al, (Quakers) 97, 109
BRIDGES (BRIDGE)
JOHN 33
MATTHEW, (assignee) vs. Thomas Edsell 222
CAPT. ROBERT, dep. 13, 14
ment. 23
BRIDGHAM (BRIGHAM), HENRY 183
et al, appraisers 39
BRIGGS, THOMAS, et al, summoned 225
BRISCO (RISCO), ROBERT 251, 252
BROOKING, ELIZABETH, JOHN, et al, summoned 225
BROUGHTON, THOMAS, assignment, benefit of creditors 132
ment. 113
vs. John Checkley, creditor 132–134
BROWN (BROWNE, &c.)
ABRAHAM, (atty.), vs. Matthew Armstrong 129, 130
EDWARD, marshal 84
ELIZABETH, oath 146

PAGE

BROWN (BROWNE), &c., *continued.*
GEORGE, constable 158
JOHN, town clerk 5
WILLIAM, vs. Richard Margerum 38, 39
BUCKMINSTER, ELIZABETH, et al, petition of, and answer 208
BULLEN (BULLINES, &c.), BETHIAH (wife of John), adultery . . 191–193
BURGES, RICHARD, wages 18
BURKE, WALTER, vs. Michael White 180
BURLEY, JOHN 233
BURRELL, JOHN, et al, vs. admrs. of Thomas Dexter, Sr. 47–59
BURSLY, SARAH, raped 191
BURT, EDWARD, certification 87
BUSBY, ABRAHAM, vs. William Nickerson 121–129
answers to reasons of said Nickerson 121–126
BRIDGET, deed of gift to her children . . . 121, 122, 126–128
estate of, administration granted to son, Abraham Busby . . 128
JOHN 126
NICHOLAS 128
BUTTON (BUTTEN, &c.)
ELIZABETH, dep. 157
MATTHIAS, dep. 161
et al, summoned 151, 158
vs. John Godfrey 212, 213
SARAH, summoned 157, 158

CALLICOTT (*See* COLLECOT)
CAMBRIDGE 24, 25, 99, 112, 171, 210, 238
constables 112, 210
inhabitants, pet. for Anabaptists 177
prison 214, 215
CANNIDGE (CANNEDGE, &c.), MATTHEW, dies as result of assault by Gregory Cassell 59–63
CAPE COD 224
CAPE DE VERD ISLAND 238
CAPES OF VIRGINIA, captures off 226, 227, 234, 236, 239
CARIBA (CARIBEE) ISLANDS 217
CARLTON, [EDWARD], et al 218
CARMAN, JOHN, gunner 17, 18
CARPENTER, ALICE, et al, summoned 225
CARR (CARRE, &c.), GEORGE 63, 64, 66
CARRELL, ANTHONY, et als, sureties for Henry Leonard 246
CARTER, ANN, dep. 92
CARY, JAMES, et al, to appear before Court 178
CASSELL (CASTLE, &c.), GREGORY, accused of causing death of Matthew Cannidge 59–63
released on bond of £100 60
CATCH (*See* VESSELS)
CEAPE, CHARLES 241

PAGE

CHADLEIGH, CHRISTOPHER . . . 9
CHADWELL, ABIGAIL, dep. . . . 191
CHADWICK, CHARLES, foreman of jury . . . 132
CHAMPION (CHAMPYN), JOHN, dep. . . . 233
CHANDLER, THOMAS, vs. Job Tyler . . . 161, 162
et als, sureties for Henry Leonard . . . 246
CHANTRY, JOHN (master of ketch Truelove), censured for running down shallop . . . 224
CHAPMAN, "that was willing to give the full worth" . . . 9
CHARD, WILLIAM, certification . . . 48
CHARLES II, letter as to toleration cited . . . 173
CHARLES, WILLIAM, et al, grantees Plains Farm . . . 4
dep. . . . 131, 132
CHARLESTOWN (CHARLESTON, &c.) . . . 34, 72–74, 172, 178, 179, 191, 214
constables . . . 172, 177
CHARTER OF MASSACHUSETTS BAY COLONY
"may be upheld & maintained" . . . 196
"principal end and foundation was and is freedom and liberty of conscience" . . . 173
"proceedings were contrary to" . . . 195
CHEBACO (CHIBACTOE, &c.) CREEK . . . 76, 85, 86
CHECKLEY (CHECKLY, &c.)
ANTHONY, juryman . . . 248
JOHN, vs. Thomas Broughton . . . 132–134
CHEEVER, EZEKIELL, vs. Samuel Heford . . . 117–120
CHESHOLME, THOMAS, constable . . . 112
CHICHESTER, WILLIAM, et al, grantees Plains Farm . . . 5
CHIDLEY, JOHN, vs. John Coggan . . . 22
CHILD, ALLWIN . . . 229, 230
CHILSON, WALSINGHAM, et al, grantees Plains Farm . . . 4
CHIRURGEONS AND PHYSICIANS . . . 17, 18, 26–28, 62, 211, 212
CHUBB, THOMAS, (daughter of), indicted . . . 150
CHURCH, RICHARD, of Hingham . . . 52
CHURCH OF CHRIST . . . 172–176, 207, 213
ENGLAND . . . 6, 7
CLARK (CLARKE, &c.)
CHRISTOPHER . . . 248
EDWARD, dep. . . . 157
HUGH, et al . . . 208, 244, 245
JOHN, vs. Joseph Bartlett . . . 244, 245
MR. JOHN, chirurgeon, &c., attends Robert Knight . . . 26, 28
et als, view the body of Matthew Cannidge . . . 62
JONAS, foreman of jury . . . 242, 254
CAPT. (MAJ.) THOMAS, assistant . . . 238
commissioner . . . 167, 226
grantee, mills in Boston . . . 41, 42
protest, ship Gilbert . . . 12[illegible]
vs. Capt. William Davis . . . 130, 131, 150, 185

PAGE

Clements (Clemens)
Job, land of . . . 143
William, vs. William Salter . . . 141
Clifford (Clyfford), Bridget and Sarah, summoned . . . 254, 255
Coal, cargo of . . . 42–46
Coates (Coats), Robert, et al, vs. admrs. of Thomas Dexter, Sr. . 46, 48, 50
Cobbet (Cobbitt, &c.), Samuel . . . 56, 57
et al, vs. admrs. of Thomas Dexter, Sr. . . . 47
Coddington, William, dep. gov. of Rhode Island . . . 236
Codner, John, evidence . . . 131, 132
Coggan, John, vs. John Hatley . . . 22, 23
vs. Mary Godfrey (maidservant) . . . 24
Colcord, Edward, "reviling authority" . . . 217–220
vs. Christopher Palmer . . . 170
Cole, Unice (Eunice), "familiarity with the Divill," i. e., witchcraft 253–255
Coledome (Couldum), Clement, deps. . . . 11, 53
Coleman, Thomas, et al, witnesses . . . 254
Collecot (Callicott, &c.), Richard, foreman of jury . . 87, 179, 180
Collins, Benjamin, et als, vs. John Fletcher et als . . . 220
Edward, et als (excrs. of Henry Dunster), vs. admrs. of John Humphrey . . . 9–11
vs. Thomas Gleison . . . 112–117
Isaac, et al, appraisers . . . 39
Commonwealth, i. e., [Slandtwelvaers], Dutch frigate . . . 226–239
Connecticut (Conecticott) . . . 73
Conney (Corney, &c.), John, foreman of jury . . . 256
et al, appraisers . . . 209
Constables:
Andover . . . 159
Boston . . . 68, 71, 172, 226
Cambridge . . . 112, 210
Charlestown . . . 172, 177
Hampton . . . 219, 220
Haverhill . . . 152, 153, 158
Lynn . . . 47
Salem . . . 98
Watertown . . . 21
Woburn . . . 147
illegally chosen . . . 147
loses charges for neglect of duty . . . 219, 220
Contempt of Court, 20 stripes . . . 68
Converse, Josiah, constable . . . 147
Convoy of merchant ships from Plymouth (England) . . . 232
Cook (Cooke)
Aaron . . . 73
Edmund, et al, mutineers . . . 237
Elisha, clerk . . . 4, 93, 94, 96, 97
custodian of records of Court of Assistants in 1716 . . . 9

PAGE

Cook (Cooke), *continued.*
Capt. George, to convey house, &c., to Edward Park 12
et al, committees of the Court 9
Middlecott, et als, clerks, memorial as to Suffolk County records and files rescued in 1747 259
Richard, et al, grantees Plains Farm 4
Lt. Richard, foreman of jury 42, 145
grantor, Iron Works land 167
vs. John Hoare 196
vs. Sampson Shoare 71, 74
et als, grantees, to satisfy John Checkley 132
sureties for John Bonner 249
Sampson Shoare 72
Cooper, Thomas 8
Corn, payments made in 51, 73
Cornelisse, Jop, et al, crew of Dutch frigate 234
Corwithen (Corwithy)
David, et al, grantees Plains Farm 4
Frances, widow, married to Edward Rolph 222
Country Pay 208
County Courts
Essex, copy of record, 1658 97
records and files, 1657–1678, cited 2–179
Middlesex, copies from files, 1653–1673 . . . . 9, 15, 19, 34, 38
records and files, 1652–1673, cited 9–249
Norfolk, records and files, 1662–1672, cited 143–220
files at New Hampshire Archives 150, 211
Suffolk, copies of records, 1656–1673 . . . . 61, 71, 91, 92, 155, 228, 230, 242, 243
records and files, 1654–1673, cited 39–251
saved from fire of 1747 250
Court of Assistants
puts question of freight up to General Court 214
records of, First Book, in custody of Elisha Cook, 1716 . . . 97
copies from 181, 213, 214, 246–248
fragments of 1
Second Book, 1673–1692 97
sentence of death by 135
respited by 136
nulled by General Court 136
Cox, John, ketch of, taken by the Dutch 234
said ketch given to Capt. Thomas Raddon and Joseph Hicks 234, 235
Ralph, wages 18
Robert 241
Coy, Martha, et als, witnesses, letter of attorney 118
Matthew, dep. 61, 62
Richard, letter of attorney, from Samuel Herford 118
(attorney), vs. Ezekiel Cheever 117–120

PAGE
CRACKBONE (CRACBONE), GILBERT, testimony 27, 28
CRAFFORD (CRAFORD), EDITH, (wife of Mordecai), accused of burning house 179, 180
CRAYSE, JOSEPH 235
CREEK (CREEKE)
DEBORAH, EDWARD, et al, summoned 193
CRIMES, &c.
adultery 150, 151, 191–193
attempt to stab brother 139
barratry 215, 216
bestiality 66, 67
blasphemy, &c. 34–38, 211, 212
burglary, &c. 135, 136
burning dwelling house 179, 180
conspiracy (gaol-breaking) 104
contempt of authority 138, 139
court 68
"endeavouring to disturb his majesties government here settled" 217
false accusation of a capital crime 66, 67
"gemester at dyce" 201
"great incivillity" with Indian squaw 222
"horrid vice" 202, 203
impeachment of magistrates, &c. 195, 196
"kicking his sister upon the belly" 145
murder 25–34, 59–63, 63–66, 222, 223, 255, 256
mutiny and piracy 229–232, 236–238
"playing passage, but not for money" 201
Quakers 68–70, 93–111
rape 191, 199, 200, 210, 216, 217, 258
rayling and reviling natural father 144, 145
rending from (renouncing) the Church of Christ, (Anabaptists) 171–178
213–215
reviling authority of courts, &c. 217–220
running down and sinking a shallop 224
slander 137
slandering and openly traducing courts, &c. 74–77, 86
treason 187, 188, 207
villifying, &c., natural parents 138, 139
wickedly and perniciously subborning witnesses 153
witchcraft 151–163, 253–255
CRITCHLY (CRITCHLIE), RICHARD 209
CROMWELL, OLIVER, protector, &c. 36
CROSSE, SUSANNA, et al, summoned 225
CROUCHER, WILLIAM, wages 18
CROY, PETER, rape 258
CUPPIE (*See* GUPPY)
CURTICE, RICHARD, et al, grantees Plains Farm 4
CUSHING, DANIEL 149
CUTT, RICHARD, commissioner 143
CUTTER, RICHARD, et al, goods of Thomas Gleison in hands of, attached 112

PAGE

DALTON, SAMUEL 144
DANE (*See* DEANE)
DAND, JOHN, et als, witnesses to deed, John Milam to Edward Gibbons 41
DANFORTH (DANFORD), THOMAS
recorder . . . 112, 113, 115–117, 174, 183, 198, 210, 222, 238, 250
et al, committee on Town House repairs 197
et als, arbitrators Dunster estate vs. Gleison 112, 115
award in same 116
commissioners 134
DAVIS (DAUIS)
EPHRAIM, et al, summoned 158
JOSEPH, vs. Capt. Walter Barefoot 194
MR. JOSEPH, payment to, secured by mortgage 10
(estate of), vs. estate of Henry Dunster 9
NICHOLAS, et al, (Quakers) committed to prison 68, 69
banished on pain of death 68, 69
CAPT. WILLIAM, dep. 131
vs. Capt. Thomas Clarke 130, 131, 150, 185
estate of John Dinely 208–210, 242–244
DAVY, HUMPHREY, et al, commissioners 134
DAY, STEPHEN, (estate of), vs. Edmond Angier 197–199
DEACON, GEORGE 235
JOHN 3
DEANE (DANE)
FRANCIS, summoned 159
SILVESTER, (atty. of), vs. Theodore Atkinson 148
THOMAS 148, 191, 192, 250
DECEASED WIFE'S SISTER, negatived 202
DECGENS (ketch) taken by the Dutch and given away 234, 235
DEDHAM, &c., venires for special Court of Assistants 179
DEERING (DERING)
HENRY, et als, to take account of ship Providence, inventory
goods, &c. 228, 230, 231
(atty. to John Fletcher) vs. John Eaton, et als . 220
"defendant", defined 183
DELINCOURT (DE LINQUORT) (*See* LINCOURT, &c.)
DENISON, MAJ. GEN. DANIEL 82
dep. by 78, 85, 86
deps. before 53, 154–156, 158
receives reasons of appeal 51
et als, examination before 66
given land by Town of Ipswich 85
oaths before 118
DENNUM (*See* DUNNUM)
DEPUTY GOVERNORS:
John Endicott 23
John Leverett 231, 238, 239, 248
John Winthrop 12

PAGE

DEPUTY GOVERNORS, *continued.*
prisoners to appear before 98, 231
examined by 238, 239
et al, dec. by 91
grant administration 128
pets. to 13, 20, 107, 108, 227, 240, 241
returns to 228, 230
DEVONSHIRE (England) 231
DEXTER, THOMAS 5
bought Nahant, from Black William for suit of clothes . 49, 51, 54, 55
yielded his rights to Town of Lynn 52, 53, 56
vs. Town of Lynn for Nahant, 1657 46–59
sons-in-law 48, 51
JR., et als, (admrs.) vs. Town of Lynn for same, 1678 . 47–53
DIAR (*See* DYER)
DIVEREUXES Farm (Marblehead) 4
DINELY, FATHERGONE (admr. of John) vs. (atty. of) Christopher Stenwicke 208–210, 242, 243
JOHN, deceased, late of Virginia 209
DIXY, WILLIAM, dep. 54
DOLIBER, JOSEPH, et al, grantees Plains Farm 4
DORCHESTER, &c., venires for special Court of Assistants 179
mentioned 158
DOUNE (DOUNES), EDMOND, beaver skins &c., stolen from 154
et als, vs. William Greenough 168, 169
DOVER (New Hampshire) 240
land at, levied on 142–144
petition of inhabitants refused 217
(England), ship Gilbert of, seized as a "malignant" 11, 12
mayor of, certifies as to same 11
DOWNING, [EMANUEL], land of 2
DRAKE (DRAK), ABRAHAM 255
summoned 254
DRINKER, EDWARD, et al, Anabaptists 171–178
DRIUER, ROBERT, dep. 58
DRURY, HUGH, et al, jury of inquest 60
DUBLIN (Ireland) 246
DUDLEY (DUDLY, &c.)
SAMUEL, et al, to examine into the stinting of the Commons at Hampton 28
et als, land given to, by Town of Ipswich 85
ment. 77, 80, 82, 84–86
THOMAS, governor 10, 23
DUDSON, JOSEPH 248
DUKE WILLIAM (*See* BLACK WILL)
DUNCAN, NATHANIEL, auditor general, et al, to examine ships' accounts 16
commissioner, appraisers sworn before 39
DUNNUM (DENNUM, &c.), ALEXANDER, summoned 254, 255

PAGE

DUNSTER, HENRY, (execrs. of) vs. admrs. of John Humphrey 9–11
vs. Thomas Gleison 112–117
DURAND, [WILLIAM], scrivener 20
DUTCH
captain's bill of gift for prize 234, 235
colours 238
expedition against 38
frigate Slandtwelvaers (*See* LINCOURT, &c.)
goods, levy on any in colony 257
prisoners 227, 228, 231, 238, 239
ship Lenham brought into Piscataway 211
sale of, stopped 211
DYER (DYAR, &c.), MARY and WILLIAM, et al, (Quakers) 68, 69
THOMAS, Sampson Shoare mort. to Samuel Adams 73, 74
Samuel Adams sells to Thomas Dyer 72
(atty. to Samuel Adams) vs. Sampson Shoare . . . 70–74
(atty. to Town of Weymouth) vs. James Lovell . 149, 150

EASTON, NICHOLAS, gov. of Rhode Island 236
EATON (EATEN)
JABEZ, et al, summoned 225
JOHN, et als, vs. Henry Dering (atty. to John Fletcher) . . . 220
SAMUEL, et al, mariners, censured 224
[THEOPHILUS] and his company 57
EBORN, MOSES, lands of 8
EDCOCKE, GEORGE, et als, witnesses 116
EDMONDS, WILLIAM, dep. 58
EDMONDSTOUN, ANDREW 241
EDSELL (EDSILL, &c.), THOMAS, vs. Matthew Bridge 221, 222
vs. Henry Harris 220, 221
EDWARDS, i. e. "S. EDWDS" 214
ELA (ELAH, &c.), DANIEL, vs. John Godfrey 151, 152
ELLIOT, JACOB 209
ELLIS, JOHN, killed by Lodwick Fowler 255, 256
ENDICOTT (ENDECOTT), JOHN 10, 23, 24
gov., sentenced William Leddra to death 94, 96
ENGLAND, laws of 98, 109
ment. 3, 12, 16, 20, 36, 37, 91, 93, 98, 99, 107–109
120, 212, 230, 231, 233, 241, 246
ENGLISH GOODS 221
ENGLISHMEN 232, 235, 237, 239, 257
EVERELL (EVERILL, &c.), JAMES, vs. Simon Bradstreet 163–165
ment. 151, 191, 192, 210, 211
et al, jury of inquest 60
EXETER (EXITER) River (New Hampshire) 143, 171

FARNHAM (FARNEHAM), JOHN, et al, (Anabaptists) 176–178
FARR, GEORGE, testimony 54, 57

PAGE

FARRY (*See* TERRY)
FAWER, BARNABAS, et al, jury of inquest 60
FELLOWS (FELLOWES), WILLIAM, vs. Henry Bennet 74–86
jury's verdict questioned, omission of an "s" 81, 83
FEN, ROBERT, et al, vs. Thomas Gainer 16–18
FERO, ANTONI, et al, crew of Dutch frigate 234
FIFIELD, WILLIAM, et als, appraisers 186
FITCH, THOMAS 222
FLETCHER, EDWARD 137
JOHN (atty. of), vs. John Eaton, et als 220
FLUSHING (The Netherlands) 226, 238, 239
FLYNT, [THOMAS], assistant 23
FOOTE, JOSHUA, vs. George Foxcroft 12, 13
FORREST (FOREST, &c.), WILLIAM, et al, pirates . . . 229–232, 236–238
FORREST RIVER (Salem and Marblehead) 3
FOSTER, CAPT. [HOPESTILL] committee to repair Town House . . . 197
THOMAS, wages 18
FOWLER, LODWICK, indicted for murder of John Ellis 255
FOXCROFT, GEORGE, vs. Joshua Foote 12, 13
FRANK NEGRO, conspiracy 194
FREEMAN, disfranchised, re-enfranchised 175, 207
FREESE, JAMES, testimony 64, 65
FREIGHT, question as to, put to General Court 214
FREIND (FRENDE), JOHN, grantee 3
FRENCH, DELIVERANCE, (wife of John) adultery 150
RICHARD, dep. 29
WILLIAM, test. 33, 34
FRIGATE (*See* VESSELS)
FROTHINGHAM, WILLIAM, land of 34
FRYER, NATHANIEL 150
Dutch prisoners secured in warehouse of 227
ship Providence in custody of 228–230
wages of seamen of, to be paid by 233
FURNIS DAM, &c., appraisal 167

GAGE, JOHN, lot layer, of Ipswich 77, 80, 83, 156
dep. as to laying out lot 85
testimony by, ment. 76, 78, 79, 81, 83
GAINER, THOMAS, vs. Robert Fen et al 16–18
GALLIOTT (ship) laden with coal 42–46
GALLOP, NATHANIEL, et als, dep. 60
SAMUEL, et als, dep. 60
GARDINER, THOMAS, et als, committee to divide estate 208
GEDNEY, BARTHOLOMEW, deed from Richard and Judith Hancock . . 7, 8
GENERAL COURT
annuls capital sentence of Court of Assistants 136
concur in making it unlawful to ask counsel of magistrates . . 21, 22

PAGE

GENERAL COURT, *continued.*
questions put to:
deceased wife's sister 202
freight 214
treason 187
"& ye word of God" to determine degree of crime 199
GEORGE (GEORG), JOHN, et al (Anabaptists) 172–178
(Indian) 52
GEREARDY, JOHN 44
vs. Robert Pateshall 42
GERISH, CAPTAIN, ment. 109
GERRITS, PIETER, et al, crew of Dutch frigate 234
GIBBON (GIBBONS, &c.)
EDMUND, vs. Peleg Sanford 181–185
MAJ. GEN. EDWARD
purchases ship Planter 17
part of water mills 39–41
vs. Thomas Clarke, ship Gilbert 11, 12
warehouse of 70
estate of, adm. granted to Thomas Lake et al 40
(admrs. of) vs. attys. of Thomas Bell, Sr. 39–42
GIBBS, BENJAMIN, et als, vs. John Bonner 249
GIFFORD (GIFFARD), JOHN, pet. and appraisal of Iron Works 166
GILBERT ("malignant" ship), seized at Boston, protest, &c. 11, 12
GIPSON, JOHN 235
GLEISON (GLEEZON), THOMAS, note, payable in wheat 116
(excrs.) of, vs. Henry Dunster 112–117
GLOVER, JOSE, vs. Henry Dunster 9
"GOD, ye word of," "and ye General Court" to determine degree of crime 199
GODFREY (GODFRY, &c.)
JOHN, accused of witchcraft by John Rimington et als . . . 151–162
suspiciously but not legally guilty 151, 152
subborning witnesses, &c. 152–161
vs. Matthias Button 212
Daniel Ela 151–161
John Rimington, et ux. 190
MARY, (maidservant) vs. John Coggan 24
PETER, evidence 155
WILLIAM 226
GOLDEN FOX (ship) 194
GOLDING, PETER, (assignee of) vs. Thomas Edsell 221, 222
GOLDTHWAITE, EZEKIEL, et als, memorial of, as to records and files rescued
in 1747 259
GOODEN (GOODINE, &c.), WILLIAM, vs. Thomas Hawkins 86–90
GOOKIN, (GOOGIN, &c.), CAPT. DANIEL, assistant 183
testimony before 33, 134
et als, arbitrators, award of 116
issue warrant for an Indian 21

PAGE

GOULD (GOLD, &c.)
THOMAS, et al, (Anabaptists) 171–178, 213, 215
ZACCHEUS, lessee Plains Farm 4
GOVERNORS:
Richard Bellingham 248
Thomas Dudley 23
John Endicott 94, 96
admonishment by 175, 195
deed acknowledged before 73
examination by 94, 96, 194
ment. 23, 57, 128, 177, 202
security given to 177
sentence by 93–96
speech against 68
et al, define "widow's thirds" 91
grant administration 128
letters from Quakers to 99–108
pets. to . . . 13, 182, 183, 202, 224, 229, 230, 240, 241, 256, 257
prisoner to clear himself of money before 130
GRAND JURY 35, 59, 63, 151, 179, 187, 194, 253, 255, 258
GRAUES, MARK, dep. 55
SAMUEL, dep. 85
GREAT BAY (Dover, N. H.) 143
GREAT ISLAND (Piscataqua River, N. H.) 239
GREGORY, EDWARD 241
GRELE, ANDREW, et als, dep. 154
GREEN (GREENE)
HANNAH, et al, of London, dep. 6, 7
JAMES 89, 90
JOHN 6
NATHANIEL 248
GREENLAND (GREENELAND), HENRY, sale of Dutch ship Lenham to, nulled 211
"endeavoring to disturb his majesties government here settled" . 217
pet. of inhabitants of Dover (N. H.), &c., denied 217
wife Mary, allowed provisionally 217
GREENOUGH, WILLIAM, vs. Edmond Doune and Thomas Kellond . 168, 169
GRIDLEY, BELIEF, reviling his father, &c. 144, 145
GRIFFING, JOHN, dep. 155
GROSS (GROSSE, &c.)
CLEMENT, vs. Jeremiah Houchin, et als, guardians of children of Edmond 90–93
EDMOND, deceased 91–93
children of, Isaac, John and Susannah 90–93
husband of his relict, Samuel Sheares 91

PAGE

GROSS (GROSSE. &c.), *continued.*
RICHARD, of ship Providence 233
GROUT, JOHN (guardian of Richard Barnes) and John Bent, agreement 19
guardianship resigned by 15
deed of gift from his mother-in-law, Bridget Busby . . 127
SARAH, deed of gift from her mother 126, 127
GROYNE, THE (i. e., Corunna), Spain 232, 238, 239
GRUBB, THOMAS, et al, summoned 177, 178
GUILDHALL (London) 6
GUPPY (GUPPI, &c.), REUBEN, accused Richard Pitfold of bestiality . 66
to be whipped, &c., same, not true 67
GURDEN, MR., farm of 80

HADDOCK, CAPTAIN 236
HADLEY, GEORGE, delivers land to Robert Hasseltine 136
ment. 120
HAITFEILD, JONATHAN, et al, took oath 38
HALL, THOMAS, et al, goods of Thomas Gleison in hands of attached . 112
HALLETT, JOHN, et als, vs. Matthew Armestrong 129, 130
HALSALL, GEORGE 45
HAMOND, CAPT. LAWRENCE, et al, to examine accounts 204
HAMPSHIRE (England) 20
HAMPTON, (New Hampshire)
commons, Edward Colcord, et als, as to stinting 218
marshal 143
pets. of inhabitants, as to Edward Colcord 219
as to Unice Cole 255
vs. Nathaniel Boulter 146
witchcraft, Unice Cole "not legally guilty" 253–255
HANCOCK, RICHARD, and Judith Winthrop married 6, 7
grant part of Pond Farm to Bartholomew Gedney 7
to John Pudney 8
same reconveyed by Pudney to . . 8
et al, lease Pond Farm to Pudney 8
Judith, dep. as to marriage of Margaret 7
and Margaret, only children of Stephen Winthrop, dec'd 6
HARKER, WILLIAM, dep. 57
HARRENDINE, ELIZABETH, summoned 225
HARRIS, HENRY, dep. 239
ment. 221
vs. Thomas Edsill 220, 221
WILLIAM 8
HARTT, JOHN, et al, grantees Plains Farm 4
HASELWOOD, RICHARD, wages 18
HASSELTINE (HAZELINE), ROBERT, vs. George Hadley 136
HATHORNE (HAWTHORNE, &c.)
JOHN, vs. Andrew Mansfield 137

PAGE

HATHORNE (HAWTHORNE, &c.), *continued.*
MAJ. WILLIAM, assistant 167, 183
atty. for Mrs. Lydia Bankes 2
sells Plains Farm 4, 5
daughter Sarah divorced 146
evidence before 52, 131, 132
issues warrant for William Leddra 98
ment. 216
to oversee whipping, &c. 67
HATLEY, JOHN, vs. John Coggan 22, 23
HAVERHILL (HAUERHILL), constables 152, 153, 158
marshal 152
ment. 158, 159
HAWARD (*See* HOWARD)
HAWEN (*See* HOWEN)
HAWKINS (HAWKINGS, &c.), THOMAS, purchases coal 45
vs. William Gooden, payment for fagots 86–90
HAWKS, JOHN 168
HAWTHORNE (HAUTHORN, &c.) (*See* HATHORNE)
HAZELINE (*See* HASSELTINE)
HEATH, JOSEPH, et al, committee on early court files 259
HENLY, GEORGE, et al, summoned 225
HELWIS, EDWARD, wife Sarah granted divorce 146
HERFORD (HEFORD, &c.), SAMUEL, vs. Ezekiel Cheever 117–120
HIBBINS (HIBBINES), WILLIAM, assistant 23
et al, committees of the Court vs. estate of Joseph Davis . . 9
pet. as to wind-mill at Lynn 10
HICKES (*See* HIX)
HILL (HILLS)
JOSEPH, et als, (excrs. of Henry Dunster)
vs. admrs. of John Humphrey 10
Thomas Gleison 112–117
VALENTINE 131
HILMAN, HANNAH, et al, summoned 225
HILTON, MRS. [CATHERINE] 212
HINGHAM 52
HITHER STONES MEADOW (Lynn) 7
HIX (HICKES)
JOSEPH, et als, ketch Decgens given to, by Dutch captain . 234, 235
RICHARD, master of the "James and John" 169
THOMAS, et al, grantees Plains Farm 4
HOAKSEY (HOKESEY), JOHN, servant 247
HOARE, JOHN, (agent) vs. Lt. Richard Cooke 196
impeaches magistrates et al 195, 196
complaints groundless and unjust, fined £50 196
withdraws from Court before sentence, &c. 196

PAGE

HOARE, JOHN, (agent) vs. Lt. Richard Cooke, *continued.*
released (on pet.), fine abated £20 196
on pet. of his wife (Alice), abated on payment of £10 . . . 196
acknowledges errors, asking compassion, &c. 196
granted, to be severely admonished in open Court, &c. . . . 196
HOBS, GOODWIFE 254
HODGES, HUMPHREY, et als, sureties for John Bonner 249
HOLDER, CHRISTOPHER, (Quaker) 99–111
letter to governor et al, from Rhode Island 104, 105
facsimile of 106
letter to governor et al, from common gaol in Boston . . . 107
facsimile of 108
banished on next ship, on pain of death 109
allowed one day a week to go about his business, with keeper, at own charge 109
HOLDRIGE, WILLIAM, (wife of) summoned 158
HOLT, RICHARD, boatswain 17, 18
HOLYOKE, EDWARD, testimony 53
HOOKE, CHARLES, vs. William Osbourne, apprenticeship 23
HOPE (catch) 140
HORRIL (HORRELL, &c.), HENRY, drowned in Salisbury River . . . 63–66
HOSKINS, RICHARD, oath 146
HOWARD, ROBERT, et als, witnesses 210
SAMUEL, dep. 88, 89
WILLIAM, dep. 159
pet. in hand of 203
to appear before court 177, 178
HOWEN (HAWEN), JOHN, et al, summoned 225
HOWCHINE (HOUCHIN, &c.), JEREMIAH, commissioner 184
et al, guardians, vs. Clement Grosse 90–93
HUBBARD (HUBERD, &c.)
JAMES 115
land of 34
et als, dep. 116, 117
CAPT. JOSHUA, testimony before 52, 53
HUCHISON (*See* HUTCHINSON)
HUDSON, ELIZABETH (wife of Nathaniel), adulteress 192, 193
FRANCIS, oath 92
WILLIAM, et al, sureties 72
HUES, MR. (agent for Joshua Foote) 13
HUGGINS, ANN, summoned 254, 255
HULL, JOHN 183
et al, witness deed of gift of Bridget Busby 127, 128
HUMFRY (HUMPHREY, &c.), JOHN 49, 52, 53, 57
granted Plains Farm until inhabitants of Marblehead need it . 1, 2
(admrs. of) vs. Moses Maverick et al, for same 1–5
excrs. of Henry Dunster 9–11

PAGE

HUMFRY (HUMPHREY, &c.), JOHN, *continued.*
granted Pond Farm (Saugus and Salem) 6
loses it to Robert Saltonstall by execution 5, 6
Saltonstall sells to Stephen Winthrop 6
Winthrop heirs sell to James Menzies et al 6–8
Menzies vs. John Pudney et al for same 5–8
HUTCHINSON (HUCHISON)
CAPT. EDWARD, surety for Peleg Sandford, bond £500 181
prisoner for payment of same, asks release 181, 182
released, bond still in force 183, 184
writ served on said Sandford for 184
et al, signers of "scandalous & reproachful petition" 177
to appear before court, &c. 178
et als, books, &c., of Edward Nailer to be delivered to 225
said books, &c., to be delivered by, to Mrs. Catherine Nanny . 253
commissioners, Nanny vs. Nailer 226
FRANCIS 168

IGNORANCE, jury of life and death acquits upon point of 35
INDIAN TESTIMONY, validity of, questioned by grand jury 222
INDIANS:
Betty (praying), raped 216, 217
Black Will (Black William, Duke William), sells Nahant, &c. . 49, 51
52, 54, 59
Humphrey, acquitted of murder 222, 223
John 49
Pabatlough (Pabatuhoh, &c.), Samuel, found dead 223
Pabatucloh (Paupachokow) et als, accused of murder . . . 222, 223
Sagamores:
of Agawam 55
George 49–52, 55
James 49, 54
Samuel, attempt to ravish 210
Sarah (squaw), Samuel Judkins's "great incivility" with . . . 222
Twenty Rod, rape of an Indian child 216, 217
William, of Natick 210
INGALLS, FRANCIS, deed from Increase Nowell and Henry Dunster . . 10, 11
INGRAM, RALPH, et als, vs. Ephraim Turner 212
INQUESTS (*See* JURY OF)
IPSWICH 15, 152, 154, 156, 157, 258
free school in, donations for site 120
land given by, to Maj. Gen. Denison and Mr. Dudley 85
marshal of 83, 119
IRELAND 246–248
Edward Helwis, sergeant to a foot company in, bigamist 146
IRESON, EDWARD, testimony 56
IRON WORKS, agent for (William Osborne) vs. Charles Hooke, apprentice, 23
Capt. Thomas Breedon vs. John Giffard 166–168

PAGE

Isack (Isake), Thomas, et als, vs. Matthew Armestrong 129, 130
Isle of Sables 169

Jackson, Edmond, oath 92
Edward, grand jury 24
John, Sr., summoned 210
Jacob, Richard 77
James, Erasmus, et al, grantees Plains Farm 5
Henry, et al, mariners, censured 224
James Sagamore (Indian) 49, 54
James & John (vessel) 169
Jamaica 129
Jarrett (Jarret, &c.), James, servant 247
vs. Henry Ashden 220
Jeannison, Patrick, rape of a child 199, 200
John (Indian) 49
Johnson, Francis, commissioner, oaths before 49, 54–56
Isaac 54, 58
John, Dutch prisoner, brought to Piscataqua 231
dep. at Great Island 239
to be transported to Boston 231
examination by John Leverett, dep. gov. 238, 239
Joseph, dep. 159
summoned 158
Thomas, constable 159
William, vs. Town of Woburn 34
Jorey, John 233
Joy (Joye), Thomas, et al, appraisers, Iron Works 167
estate of William Browne 39
Joyce, William, wages 18
Joyliffe, John, deed from Robert Pateshall 42
et al, to examine accounts 204
Judkins, Samuel, "great incivility" with Indian squaw 222
Juries:
grand, indictments, &c. 24, 35, 59, 63, 93, 144, 145
179, 180, 187, 192, 194, 199, 200, 210
211, 213, 214, 216, 222, 253, 255, 256
leaving out words in indictment, causes dissent 34, 35
of inquest 59, 60, 223
of life and death 34
verdict, changed by an "s" 81–83
special 13, 39, 42, 87, 90, 91, 132, 141, 192, 205, 254
Jury and Bench (*See* Bench and Jury)
Jurisdiction (i. e., Commonwealth), Quakers banished from 68, 69
93, 95, 109

Keayne (Keene)
"Mrs. Anna," lately married to Edward Laine, annulment . . . 67, 68
et al, summoned 225
Capt. Robert, Town House in Boston founded by the late . . . 197

PAGE
KELLOND, THOMAS 187
et als, vs. William Greenough 168, 189, 190
KELLY, ROGER, committed for taking catch, without order . . . 140
vs. Benjamin Ward 140
KEMBLE, HENRY 45
KENNISTON, JOHN, execution against 150
KENRICK, ANNE and JOHN, children of, choose guardian 137
ELIJAH and MARIA, choose Peter Oliver 137
KERTLAND, NATHANIEL, et al, vs. admrs. of Thomas Dexter, Sr. . . . 46–59
KETCH (*See* VESSELS)
KETLE, [ESTHER], statement by 191
KEYSAR (KEASER, &c.), GEORGE 46, 48, 50, 54
dep. 52
et al, vs. Thomas Dexter 46–59
KILCUP, [WILLIAM] 167
KILLING of a mare by a bull 13–15
KILVERT, ROGER, goods of, detained by Robert Pateshall 42, 43
vs. John Gerardy 42–46
KING, DANIEL, dep. 58
vs. George Taylor, "mare killed by a bull" 13–15
HENRY, mate of ship Providence, lately taken by and from the Dutch 227, 228
et al, portlage bill, wages allowed 233
declaration as to occurrences on 232, 233
RALPH, et al, vs. admrs. of Thomas Dexter, Sr. 47–59
WILLIAM, wages 18
KNIGHT, ABRAHAM, wages 18
ANNE, testimony 14, 15
ROBERT (servant to John Betts), murderously assaulted by him 24–33
vs. John Treworthy, et al 16
et al, appraisers, Iron Works 167

LABORNE, ALEXANDER 142
LAKE, CAPT. THOMAS, et al, admrs. of Edward Gibbons, vs. attys. of Thomas Bell 40–42
to examine accounts 204
et als, to receive books, &c., of Edward Nailer . . 225
to deliver same to Mrs. Catherine Nanny . 253
LAMBERT, MICHAEL 54, 55
SARAH, raped 258
LANE (LAINE)
MRS. ANNA, vs. Edward, annulment granted 67, 68
EDWARD, pet. to General Court ment. 68
vs. Samuel Archard 67
and Anna Keayne, marriage contract, ment. 68
LANGSTAR, HENRY 150
LAREMITT, WILLIAM 142
LAUGHTON (*See* LAWTON)

PAGE

LAUSON, CHRISTOPHER, et al, summoned 225
LAWS:
against Quakers, made in Oct., 1658, cited 69
being according to God's word, cited 50
books of, cited 31, 78, 118, 122, 150
counsel, in matters of, not to be given by magistrates . . . 21, 22
now divers worthy men able to give . . 21
which require satisfaction by service where estate cannot be found, cited 134
LAWTON (LAUGHTON, &c.)
HENRY, vs. John Bonner 246–249
THOMAS, commissioner, deps. before 56–59
LAYTON (LEIGHTON, &c.), THOMAS, et al, vs. admrs. of Thomas Dexter 46–59
LEADER, RICHARD 59
LECHFORD, THOMAS, Note Book 4
LEDDRA (LUTHERWAY, &c.) WILLIAM (Quaker) 93–111
Salem, 1658 97
Plymouth, 1658, 1659 . . . . 97, 98
Salem, 1660 98
arrested and brought to Boston, 1660 98
banished on pain of death 93
returns to Boston, imprisoned, &c. 93
sentenced to death by Gov. Endicott 93, 94
facsimile of sentence 95, 96
last words those of Stephen the Martyr 99
letters:
from "ye Prison: Plymouth", 1659 99–103
facsimile of 103
"Boston-Gaol" the day before his execution . . 110, 111
LEECH, JOHN, of London, et al, dep. 6
LEGG (LEG, &c.)
JOHN, et al, grantees Plains Farm 4
dep. 49, 57
testimony 50, 55
SAMUEL 209
LEIGH, JOHN, et als, bondsmen for Richard Coy 118
LENHAM (ship), sale of, stopped 211
LEONARD (LENNARD), HENRY, vs. Andrew (Ambrose) Makefashion . . 245
LEVERETT (LEUERETT), HUDSON, house of 206
JOHN, assistant, evidence of Sir Thomas Temple, before 188
major general, commissioner 134, 137, 203–205
governor
dep. before 236
examination before 238, 239
petition to 231
LEWIS (LEWES)
JOHN, prosecutes Robert Quimby for murder 64–66
et al, vs. admrs. of Thomas Dexter, Sr. 47

PAGE

LEWIS (LEWES), *continued.*
JONAS, dep. 235
PHILIP 150
LIDGETT (LIDGET), PETER 183
discharged as surety for Michael White 180
et al, award to Capt. John Bonner, not performed 251
LIME (*See* LYME)
LINCOURT (LINCORT, &c.), CAPT. CORNELIUS DE 226–239
commander of Dutch frigate [Slandtwelvaers] i. e., Commonwealth 226–239
takes ketch Decgens of Boston, Capt. Cox 234
gives her to Capt. Thomas Raddon et als 234, 235
bill of gift, Dutch and English 234, 235
takes ship Providence 226, 227
prize ship Providence takes ship Little Barkley 226
retaken and brought to Piscataqua, 226–228, 230
delivered to Capt. Thomas Raddon . 230, 231
Little Barkley runs away with captors 226
declaration of occurrences on the Frigate 238, 239
Little Barkley . . . 234, 235
Providence 232–236
LINDSEY (LINDSY, &c.)
CHRISTOPHER, dep. 49
ment. 54–56
FRANCIS 54
LISBON (LESBON, &c.) Portugal 229, 236, 237
LITTLE (LITLE), MARY, et al, summoned 225, 226
LITTLE BARKLEY (ship), taken by Dutch, runs away, &c. . . . 226–228, 230
234, 235
LITTLETON, WALTER, master in chancery 146
LIVERPOOL (England) 246
LONDON (England) 6, 7, 12, 16, 234
LORD, ROBERT, clerk 11, 82, 84, 86, 117–120, 153
marshal 117–120
LOVEL (LOVELL, &c.), JAMES, vs. Thomas Dyer, attorney, Town of Weymouth 149
LOW, JOHN, land of 70
LYME (LIME) England 240, 241
LYNDE, SIMON 248, 258
THOMAS, land of 34
LYNDON, AUGUSTIN 248
LYNN (LINN, &c.)
common land near meeting-house 48
constable of 47
Humfry's or Pond Farm, litigation, 1642–1695 5–9
Farm, &c., Sagamore Hill, litigation 9–11
meeting-house 48

PAGE

LYNN (LINN, &c.), *continued.*
Nahant, bought for suit of clothes 49, 51, 54, 55
rights in, yielded to Town 52, 53, 56
Sagamore Hill and Swampscoat bought for two pestle stones 59
Sagamore Hill, litigation 9–11
Saugus 51, 52, 54, 57, 59
selectmen vs. Thomas Dexter, Sr. for Nahant 46–59
estate of same for Nahant 47–53
tide-mill 11
water-mill 9–11
frozen in winter, no water in summer 11
wind-mill 9–11
much use in the town 11
sold to Samuel Bennet, 1644 9–11
worth £100 sterling 11
LYNNFIELD 6
LYON, JOHN, et al, grantees Plains Farm 4

MACKINTIRE, DANIEL, et al, vs. James Menzies 8
MAGISTRATES:
counsel in cases likely to come before them not to be given . . 21, 22
direction to be given to courts or officers 21
impeached, &c., by John Hoare 195, 196
mortgage (not acknowledged before) recorded 39–42
MAID (MAIDE), JOSHUA, wages 17
MAIDSERVANT, imprisoned, to serve additional time with her master . 24
MAKEFASHION (MAKFASHION), ANDREW (AMBROSE), vs. Henry Leonard 245, 246
MALAGA (Spain) 238
MALDEN (MALDON, &c.) 88, 90
MANNINGE (MANING), DANIEL 158
WILLIAM, testimony 27
MANSFIELD, ANDREW, vs. John Hathorne, slander 137
et al, vs. admrs. of Thomas Dexter, Sr. 47–59
MAPLE, GREGORY 241
MARBLEHEAD 51, 131, 132
Plains Farm, grantees, 1646 . . . . 4, 5
Humfry estate vs. proprietors of 1–5
town clerk, John Browne 5
town records, extraet from 4, 5
MARGERUM (MARJERUM), RICHARD, pet. of and answer 39
vs. William Browne 38, 39
MARRIAGE OF DECEASED WIFE'S SISTER, negatived 202
MARSHAL:
of Boston (Suffolk County) . . . 38, 39, 47, 67, 70–72, 87, 121, 148, 247
Ipswich 83, 119
Norfolk County 254
Salem 152

PAGE

MARSHAL GENERAL, Edward Michelson
deputies 171, 186
executions to be served by 205, 209, 210, 221
or his deputies 133, 149, 150, 184, 186
to carry out punishments, with guard, &c. 139, 145
MARSHALL, ROBERT 219
CAPT. THOMAS, commissioner 49, 57
et al, vs. admrs. of Thomas Dexter, Sr. . . 47–59
"MARTENS VINYARD," interference in government, refused . . . 256
MASON, ARTHUR, accused of treason 187, 188
disfranchisement taken off 207
et al, surety for Jonathan Parker 135
bond extinguished 136
HUGH, foreman, grand jury 194, 222, 255
JOHN, et al, summoned 254, 255
[RALPH] 226
MATSON, THOMAS, et als, sureties for Theodore Atkinson 216
MATTOCKE, JAMES, et al, jury of inquest 60
MAVERICK, MOSES, et al, grantees Plains Farm 2, 4, 5
vs. admrs. John Humphrey 1–5
MAY, JOHN 235
MEADE, CAPT. WILLIAM, et als vs. Ephraim Turner 212
MEARES (MEERES), JAMES 210, 243
MELLONS, JOHN, JR., et al, mariners, censured 224
MENATOMY (MENATTOMY), mill at 116
MENZIES, JAMES, grantee Pond Farm 7
vs. John Pudney et al, possession of same 5–8
MERRIMAC (MERAYMAK) RIVER 156
MERRITT, NICHOLAS, et al, grantees Plains Farm 4
METCALFE, JOSEPH, et al, jurymen, dep. as to action of 81
MICHELL, THOMAS, testimony 60
MICHELSON (MITCHELSON), EDWARD (*See* MARSHAL GENERAL)
MILAN (MILLAM), JOHN, sells water mills to Edward Gibbons . . . 39
MILLER, SAMUEL, et al, committee on early court files 259
THOMAS, vs. Robert Brisco 251, 252
MILLS, JAMES, et al, witnesses, deed Milam to Gibbons 41
MILLS (tide water, wind) 9–11, 39–42, 185–187
MINISTER'S SALARY 252
MONHIGGIN (MONHEGAN) ISLAND (Maine) 193, 220, 221, 242
murderous assault at 59–63
MOODY, LADY DEBORAH of Swampscutt Farm 4
MOORE (MORE)
GOULDING 28
MARY 226
THOMAS, et al, sureties on bond 48
MORSE, JOHN 206
MORTGAGE recorded but not acknowledged, legality questioned . . 39–41

PAGE
MOULDER, MRS. [CHRISTIAN], summoned 226
MOULTON, JOHN, et als, pet. 218
MUNNINGS, GEORGE, prison keeper, to answer for escape of Benjamin Saucer 37

NAHANT (NAHAUNT, &c.)
bought of Black William, for suit of clothes . . 49, 51, 52, 54, 55
two pestle-stones 59
common plantation, &c., of Lynn 53, 56, 57
fencing of, pasturing, &c. 49, 56–59
pine trees, runnings out of 59
proprietors yield rights to Lynn 52, 53, 56
selectmen of Lynn vs. Thomas Dexter for 46–59
estate of same 47–53
wolves, driven from, by train band 56
NANNY, MRS. CATHERINE (daughter of John Wheelwright), late wife of Edward Nailer 224–226, 252, 253
NASH, GOODMAN, testimony 5
NATICK INDIAN 210
NAYLOR (NAILER), EDWARD, breach of marriage covenant, &c. . 224–226, 253
divorced by his wife [Catherine] Nanny 252, 253
late wife granted books, &c. 225, 253
banishment modified 225, 253
granted custody of his children 253
NEAFFE, MARY (wife of William), summoned 158
NEEDOM, WILLIAM 232
NEGRO, FRANK, conspiracy 194
NEGUS, BENJAMIN, to appear before Court 178
JONATHAN, ment. 71, 87–90
testimony 53
NEWBURY (NEWBERRY, &c.)
meeting-house 156
minister, Rev. Benjamin Woodbridge
pets. General Court for salary 252
referred to selectmen 252
Plain 159
Quaker conference with "priest" at 109
witchcraft, John Godfrey of, "not legally guilty" 151–161
"NEW ENGLAND Judged, by the Spirit of the Lord", ed. of 1703, cited 109
NEWFOUNDLAND 237
NEW PLIMOUTH (*See* PLYMOUTH)
NEWPORT (Rhode Island) 236
NEW YORK (NEW YORKE) 209, 243, 257
NICKERSON, ANNA, deed of gift from her mother, Bridget Busby . . . 126
WILLIAM, vs. Abraham Busby, admr. of Bridget Busby 121–129
NICHOLLS, MR. 116
RANDAL, to appear before Court 187

PAGE

NICHOLSON (NICKOLSON)
EDMUND, et al, grantees Plains Farm 4
JOSEPH (and wife Jane), Quakers, banished 93–95
NON SUIT, because attachment was made by wrong clerk 48
NORFOLK COUNTY 254
NORMAN, RICHARD, SR., et al, grantees Plains Farm 4
NORTHY, JOHN, et al, grantees Plains Farm 4
NORTON, FRANCIS, et als, witnesses, deed Addams to Dyer . . . 72
HUMPHREY 69
NORWICH (England) 238
NOWELL, INCREASE, assistant and secretary 1–39
Court record and files in his custody 1, 39
evidence before 26–30, 32, 38
grants guardianship, &c. 15, 19
signs agreement "that ye bull did kill ye mare" 14
consent to verdict of jury of life and death 35
executions for Court 18, 38
license to sell strong waters 12, 13
orders of Court 22, 23
takes mortgage on Humfry's Farm for 21 years, 1641 . . . 10, 11
et al, committees of Court, estate of Joseph Davis 9
John Humfry 9–11
pet. to sell wind-mill, &c., recommended 9, 10
sell farm to Francis Ingalls 10
NOYES (NOICE), PETER, witness, &c. 19–21

OLIVER (OLLIVER, &c.)
CAPT. JAMES, "only one man in Boston" that cannot examine accounts of Capt. Williams 138
payment of balance on bond to 136
son-in-law of Thomas Dexter, Sr. 51
surety for Clement Grosse 92
et al, sign "scandalous & reproachfull petition" 177, 178
et als, admrs. of Thomas Dexter, Sr., vs. Town of Lynn . . 47–53
PETER, guardian of Elijah and Maria Kenrick 137
ORANGE, William III, Prince of, commission from 232, 234, 239
ORCHARD, THOMAS, mate of ship William & John 236, 241
ORDNANCE, twenty pieces of 232
ORDWAY, JAMES, dep. 155
OSBORN (OSBRONE, &c.)
THOMAS, and Thomas Gould (Anabaptists) 171–178
WILLIAM, agent for Iron Works, vs. Charles Hooke 23
late commander of ship William & John 240, 241
OTLEY (OATLY, &c.)
ABRAHAM, vs. Mrs. Lydia Bancks 1
ADAM, agent for John Humfry, sells house to pay carpenter . . 3
sent cattle to Farmer Dexter to prevent seizure 5
suggests selling wind-mill to pay debts 9

PAGE
PABATLOUGH (PABATUHOH, &c.), SAMUEL (Indian), found dead 223
PABATUCLOH (PAUPACHOKOW), et als, accused of killing 223
PADDY, WILLIAM, excr. of, (Capt. William Davis) vs. Capt. Thomas Clarke 130, 131, 150, 185
PAGE (PAIGE), NICHOLAS, dep. 188
et als, sureties 243
witnesses 210
PAINE (PAYNE, &c.)
JOHN 141, 237
et als, sureties for Jonathan Parker, burglar, &c. 135
bond extinguished 136
ROBERT, dep. 120
WILLIAM 120, 218
PALMER, CHRISTOPHER, deputy marshal general . . . 143, 170, 171, 219
executions irregularly levied by 170, 171
vs. Edward Colcord 170
vs. Capt. Richard Waldern 170, 171
PARK (PARKS, &c.)
EDWARD, to receive house and land from Capt. George Cooke . 12
WILLIAM, foreman, grand jury 187
guardian, Samuel and Hannah Scarborough 137
et als, to repair Town House 197
PARKER, JONATHAN, burglary, &c. 135, 136
defence, unlocked door, &c. 135
sentenced 135
pet. for suspension 135
respited on bond of £200 135
annulled on payment of £40 136
bond extinguished 136
payment of £40 by sureties nulled 136
NATHAN, summoned 159
PAUL, "gemester at dice" 201, 202
RICHARD, commissioner 53, 206, 209
et al, sureties for Jonathan Parker, &c. 135, 136
PARPOINT, JOHN 258
PATTESHALL (PATESHALL, &c.), ROBERT, vs. John Gerardie 42–45
PEABODY 6
PEACH, JOHN, et al vs. admrs. of John Humphrey 2
SR., et al, grantees Plains Farm 4
PECKER, JAMES, vs. Simon Bradstreet et al 200, 201
PEIRCE (PEARCE, &c.)
THOMAS, dep. 27
WILLIAM, et al, witnesses to deed of gift by Bridget Busby . 127, 128
PEIRSON, PETER, et als (Quakers), imprisoned at Plymouth . . . 97, 98
PEKET (PICKARD), JOHN, mutineer 237, 238
PELHAM, HERBERT, et al, orders of Court by 10, 12
PENDLETON, CAPT. BRIAN, vs. Nathaniel Boulter 185
CAPT. JAMES, agent and attorney to above 185

PAGE
PERCIVALL, JOHN, "parish clark", London, dep. 7
PERINS, HUGH, et al, mariners, censured 224
PERKINS, ABRAHAM, deputy marshal general 186
Sr., summoned 254, 255
MARY (wife of Jacob), summoned 254, 255
PERRY, JOHN, wages 18
PESTLE STONES, Nahant, &c., sold for two 59
PETER, [REV. HUGH], farm of 2–4
PETUXIN RIVER (Virginia) 232, 234
PHELPS, NICHOLAS, disorderly meeting at house of 97
PHILLIPS, JOHN, et al, jury of inquest 60
NICHOLAS 165
PHIPS (PHIPPS)
SAMUEL, clerk 34
SOLOMON, to appear before Court 178
PHYSICIANS AND CHIRURGEONS 17, 18, 26–28, 62, 211, 212
PICKARD, JOHN, deputy marshal general 136
PICKMAN, NATHANIEL, dep. 3
PIKE, ROBERT, commissioner 157
dep. 157
PISCATAQUA (PISCATAQUAY, &c.) RIVER (N. H.), ships brought to . . 211
226–239
PITFOLD, RICHARD, falsely accused of bestiality 66
PLACE, PETER, jury of inquest 60
PLAINS FARM (Marblehead) 1–5
granted to John Humphrey, 1635 1
leased to Zaccheus Goold, 1640 4
sold to Moses Maverick, et al, 1645 2
grantees, list of, 1646 . . . . 4, 5
PLANTER (ship), seamen of, vs. Robert Risbie et al, wages 16–18
PLYMOUTH (PLIMOUTH)
mutineers break prison at 229
Quakers, imprisoned at, refuse to depart 97, 98
re-imprisoned 97, 98
agree to depart, released 98
letter of William Leddra, from "Ye Prison: Plymouth" . . 99–103
PLYMOUTH (England) 231, 232, 235, 236
POLLARD, WILLIAM, et al, examination of 194
POND (HUMPHREY'S) FARM (Saugus and Salem) 5–8
granted to John Humphrey, 1635 6
portion obtained by Robert Saltonstall, 1642 6
sold to Stephen Winthrop, 1645 6
sold to James Menzies, 1698 6
PORTER, EDWARD, foreman of jury 145
JOHN, JR., rebellious carriages to his parents, &c. 138, 139
PORTLAGE BILL 233
PORTSMOUTH (New Hampshire) 150, 217, 255
PORTUGAL (PORTUNGALL, &c.) 231, 236, 237

PAGE

POTTELL, JOHN, committed for murder, escaped 194
PRANT (*See* BANT)
"PRESSE", secretary to send sentence of Anabaptists to 177
PRICE, WALTER, et als, deed from Thomas Broughton 132
PRINCE WILLIAM III, of Orange, commission from 232, 234, 239
PRISONER, allowed one day a week to go about his business, with keeper, at his charge 109
PROVIDENCE (ship), taken, retaken, &c., . . . 227, 228, 230, 232, 235, 236, 239
PRYNNE, NICHOLAS, commander of ship [Little] Barkley 234
PUDNEY, JOHN, grantee and grantor, part of Pond Farm 8
et al, vs. James Menzies, possession of same 5–8
PULSIFER, [DAVID], copies by 222, 244
PUNISHMENTS:
abstaining from Mrs. Hilton's company 212
acknowledge offence publicly or pay fine 74, 75, 137
admonished by governor in open Court 188, 195
(severely) for running down and sinking a shallop at anchor 224
banished to 10 miles from Boston 223, 224
from jurisdiction 177, 201, 212, 217, 224, 255
on penalty of death for return 68, 69, 93, 95
death 135, 136, 200
sentenced by governor 93–96
debarred from admission as attorney or surety in any legal process, 217
practice as chirurgeon, &c. 212
deported at country's charge 224
"disabled from pleading any cases but his own" 196
disfranchised 173, 187, 207
fined 74, 75, 137, 139, 153, 155, 171, 192, 193, 201, 212, 217
house of correction 97, 219
closely and safely, house diet only 139
prison 68, 69, 107–109, 155, 172
sentence of Anabaptists sent to the press 177
(capital) respited and nulled 135, 136
sold for life to some of the Cariba Islands 217
stand on Lecture Day, one hour
on gallows ladder with rope about neck . 25, 130, 192, 193
pillory with inscription in capitals 145, 153
to carry it peacefully with all men 212, 215
to return to family in England or pay fine 212
unhibbeted and disabled from suing in any court 215
wear a rope around his neck, outside his clothes 203
whipped severely (10 to 39 stripes) . 25, 67, 68, 139, 145, 192, 193
10 stripes or fined £10 . . . . 192, 193
tied to a great gun and 139
PUTNAM, JOHN, dep. 34

PAGE

QUAKERS:
Brend, William 97, 109
Davis, Nicholas 68, 69
Dyer, William and Mary 68, 69
Holder, Christopher 99–111
Leddra, William 93–111
Nicholson, Joseph and Jane 93–95
Peirson, Peter 97, 98
Robinson, William 68–70, 97
Scott, Patience 68, 69
Stephenson, Marmaduke 68, 69
law against 69, 93, 95
letters from 99–111
liberty to pass to England 93, 95
QUAMSCOTT PATENT, land, &c., of Capt. Richard Waldern's at . . . 144
QUIMBY (QUENBY), ROBERT (ROBBIN), accused by John Lewis of drowning Henry Horril 63–66
grand jury "cannot find [him] guilty" 65

RADDEN (RADDON)
ROBERT, of ship Providence 235
CAPT. THOMAS, master of ship Providence, taken by Dutch, retaken, &c. 230–235
with part of crew carried off by Capt. Lincourt . . . 232, 233
given ketch Decgens by Capt. Lincourt 234, 235
declaration by members of crew 235
petition for custody of the Providence, granted . . . 230, 231
gives bond for £500 to answer to charge of not seizing the Antonio 231, 232
RAINSBOROUGH, WILLIAM, et al, dep. 6
RAM ISLAND (Salisbury) 65
RAMSDELL, JOHN 55
dep. 48, 49
et als vs. Henry Leonard 245
RAUSE, FAITHFUL, et al, witnesses, deed Samuel Addams to Thomas Dyer, 72
RAWLINGS, JOSEPH, et al, mariners, censured 224
RAWSON, EDWARD, recorder and secretary
allows bill of charges 46
appoints guardians 137
copies, &c., by 1–257
dep. before 60
endorsement by 75
oath before 128
paper in hand of 69
reasons of appeal received by 124

PAGE

Rawson, Edward, recorder and secretary, *continued.*
signs determination of bench . . . 133
execution . . . 67
order of Court . . . 135
records . . . 25, 40
warrant . . . 68, 69
Read, Mary, et al, summoned . . . 225
Philip, chirurgeon, &c., blasphemy, &c. . . . 211
Thomas, deputy marshal . . . 144
Recorder (William Aspinwall) did not observe "the punctillio of the law" . . . 41
Records and Files removed when Town House was consumed December, 1747 . . . 259
Recovery (catch) . . . 246–249
Redknap, Joseph, deps. . . . 56–59
Redman, John
atty. for Town of Hampton vs. Nicholas Boulter . . . 141, 146
Christopher Palmer vs. Capt. Richard Walderne . . . 170
deputy marshal general . . . 239
Remington (Rimington, &c.)
Abigail, dep. as to son John, and John Godfrey . . . 161
John and Abigail, vs. John Godfrey, foreclosure . . . 190
et als, accuse John Godfrey of witchcraft . . . 151–161
Jr., dep. as to John Godfrey . . . 160, 161
ment. . . . 158–161
Respite, in Capital Case, granted . . . 135
Rhode (Road) Island . . . 69, 107, 108, 229, 236
Richards, Mrs., house broken into, &c. . . . 136
Edward, et als, dep. . . . 58, 59
John, (atty.) vs. Ephraim Turner . . . 212
et al, admrs. estate of Edward Gibbons . . . 40
Riches, Goodman . . . 54
Richison, Amos . . . 90, 112, 121
Ridgway, Jonathan, et al, oaths . . . 38
Risco (*See* Brisco)
Risby (Risbie), Robert, master of ship Planter, et als, vs. seamen of same . . . 16–18
Roads, Zechariah, acknowledged fault, admonished . . . 175
Robinson (Robbinson, &c.)
Isaac, et al, of "Martens Vinyard", pet. refused . . . 256
William, et al, (Quakers) . . . 68–70, 97
Roberts (Roberds)
Grace, raped . . . 199
Robert, dep. by . . . 84, 85
dep. about . . . 85
ment. . . . 76, 78, 79
Roby, Henry, constable . . . 219, 220
Rolfe, Benjamin . . . 213
Edward, indicted for having two wives, acquitted . . . 222

PAGE

ROPER, ELIZABETH and SARAH, dep. 158
SUSANNA, dep. 156
ROWLAND, RICHARD, et al, grantees Plains Farm 4
ROWLEY (ROWLY) 156, 158
ROXBURY 162
&c., venires for special Court of Assistants 179
RUSSELL, JOHN, (Anabaptist) 213–215
of Boston, et al, summoned 225
of ship Little Barkley, decl. 235, 236
RICHARD, et als, attys. for owners of ship Gilbert 11
treasurer, bonds in favor of 218, 231, 249
to deport Rebecca Turner 223, 224
WILLIAM, et al, goods of Thomas Gleison in hands of, attached 112
RUSHWORTH, EDWARD, account presented 217
RUST, [NATHANIEL, et ux] 156
RUTTER, JOHN, et al, sign covenant 19
(wife of) et als, excrs. of Alice Bent, vs. Thomas Blancherd . . 21

S. & EDWARDS, question as to case of 214
SABLES, Isle of 169
SACER (*See* SAUCER)
SADLER, [RICHARD] 54
SAFFIN (SAFFYN, &c.), JOHN, foreman of jury 151
vs. Edward Ting 168, 169
et als, sureties for Benjamin Gibbs 251
SAGAMORE (SAGOMORE) HILL, (Lynn) 10, 11, 59
SAGAMORES:
of Agawam 49, 55
GEORGE 49–52, 55
JAMES 49, 54
ST. ANTHONY (SAN ANTONIO) (ship), piratically seized by crew 229–232, 236–238
ST. BUTTOLPHS WITHOUT ALGATE (London) 7
ST. MARGARETS (Westminster) 6
SALE, THOMAS, et als, witnesses 118
SALEM 2, 8, 39, 53, 58, 67, 97, 98, 146, 152
constable of 98
house burned at 179, 180
inhabitants hire pasturage at Nahant 51, 52
marshal of 152
Plains Farm, litigation 1–5
Pond (Humfry's) Farm, litigation 5–9
Quakers at 97, 98, 109
SALISBURY (SALUSBURY, &c.) 254, 255
SALISBURY RIVER, Henry Horrell drowned in 63–66
SALMON, DANIEL, deps. 2, 55, 56
SALTER, JABEZ, et al, summoned 225
WILLIAM, prison keeper 141, 142, 184, 229, 255
vs. William Clements, prisoners' board, &c. 141

PAGE

SALTONSTALL (SALTINGSTON)
RICHARD, ESQ., assistant 10
tenant of, (William Fellows) vs. Henry Bennett 75–86
SIR RICHARD 58
ROBERT, vs. estate of John Humfry 5
sells Pond Farm to Stephen Winthrop 6
SALVAGE, for bringing in ship Providence, allowed 226, 227
SAMUEL (Indian), attempted rape 210
SANBORN (SANBOURNE), JOHN 146, 218
et al, appraisers, house of Nathaniel Boulter 186
SANDEN, ARTHUR, et al, grantees Plains Farm 4
SANDY POINT, "nere Exiter River" (New Hampshire) 171
SANDYS, JOHN, et als, sureties for Fathergone Dinely 243
SANFORD (SANDFORD), PELEG, vs. Edmund Gibbons 181–185
defaults bond 183, 184
SARAH (Indian squaw), "incivility" of Samuel Judkins with . . 222, 223
SAUCER (SACER), BENJAMIN, blasphemy, breaking gaol, &c. . . . 34–38
SAUGUS (SAUGUST), "now called Linn" 51, 52, 54, 57, 59
SAUNDERSON, ROBERT, et al, witnesses, deed of Bridget Busby . . 127, 128
SAVAGE, CAPT. THOMAS, house of, fired by Edith Craford 179
SAVERY, KATHERINE, deed of gift from her mother 126
SCARBOROUGH, JOHN and MARY, children of, to choose guardian . . 137
HANNAH and SAMUEL, choose William Parks . . . 137
SCARLET, SAMUEL 248
SCHOOL (free), Ipswich 120
SCIDDALL, FRANCIS, servant 247
SCILLY (SILLY), England 232
SCOTT, PATIENCE, et al, (Quakers), committed 69
THOMAS, (atty. to John Gerardy) vs. Robert Patteshall . . . 42–46
bill of charges for coal 46
SCOTTOW, JOSHUA, dep., deed, Samuel Shoare to Samuel Addams . . 73
writing drawn up by 73
et al, admrs. Edward Gibbons, vs. Anthony Stoddard et al . . 40–42
SECRETARY, granted executions illegally, charged 182
to renew executions on judgments 133
to send sentence against Anabaptists "to the presse" . . . 177
SEDGWICK (SEDGWICKE), MAJ. ROBERT, "commander in chefe of this fleet" 38
to deliver Benjamin Saucer, blasphemer, to prison keeper . . 38
SEELY, JOHN, et al, summoned 225
SENDALL, SAMUEL, dep. as to agreement with Sampson Shoare . . . 73, 74
et al, jury of inquest 60
et als, appraisers 73, 74
SENNET, JOHN, et al, deposed as to declaration 233
SENTENCE (CAPITAL), respited and nulled 135
SERGEANT (SERJANT, &c.)
LEONARD, chirurgeon of ship Planter 17, 18
STEPHEN, beaver skins, &c., of, stolen 154

PAGE
Severance (Severonce, &c.), John . . . 156, 157
Severs, Thomas, et al, crew of Dutch frigate . . . 234
Sewall (Sewel)
Mitchell, clerk . . . 213
Stephen, clerk . . . 5, 6
Sexton, Thomas, et al, examined by governor . . . 194
Shallop (*See* Vessels)
Shapleigh (Shapley), Nicholas, vs. Robert Knight . . . 16
Sharp, [Samuel] . . . 53
Shaw, Elizabeth, summoned . . . 254, 255
Sheares, Samuel, husband to relict of Edward Grosse . . . 91
Shepard, Thomas, et al, summoned . . . 193
Sherman, John . . . 216
Ships (*See* Vessels)
Shoare, Sampson, vs. Thomas Dyer (assignee of Samuel Adams) . . . 70–74
mort. to Samuel Adams . . . 73, 74
considers selling to Samuel Sendall . . . 73, 74
Samuel Adams sells to Thomas Dyer . . . 72
Short, John . . . 61, 62
Shorthose, Robert, land of . . . 34
Shrimpton (Shrempton), Henry, assignment to . . . 115, 116
Shute, Elizabeth, et al, summoned . . . 225
Sibermyen [?] . . . 234
Sibley, John, testimony . . . 58
Simes, Mrs. Sarah . . . 36
Simonds, Samuel, et al, answer to pet. of Increase Nowell et al . . . 10
Simple (Simpull), John, rape . . . 191
Skerries, Francis . . . 152, 154
Slandtwelvaers, i. e., Commonwealth, Dutch frigate . . . 226–239
Sloop (*See* Vessels)
Smith (Smyth)
Anne, summoned . . . 254, 255
Anne Kenrick (formerly), children of, choose guardian . . . 137
George, wages . . . 18
James, et al, grantees Plains Farm . . . 4
John, constable . . . 172
et al, pirates . . . 229–232, 236–238
Mary Scarborough (formerly), children of, choose guardian . . . 137
Thomas . . . 2
Somerby, Abiel, dep. . . . 155
Anthony, et al, selectmen of Newbury . . . 252
Southworth, Constant, et als empowered to release Quakers . . . 98
Sparke, John, wages . . . 18
Spencer, [John] . . . 159
Spittlefields, (London) . . . 7
Sprague, Mary, dep. . . . 191
Squamscott Patent (*See* Quamscott)
Squier, George . . . 241

PAGE

STACEY (STASY)
HENRY, et al, grantees Plains Farm 4
JOHN, SR., et al, grantees Plains Farm 5
WILLIAM, "horrid vice", pet. to take rope off his neck, denied 202, 203
STAFFORD, FRANCIS, servant 247
STANNION (STANION), JOHN 219
sworn to appraise goods and lands 143
STARR, MR. COMFORT, chirurgeon, &c., et als, viewed body of Matthew Cannidge 62
STEBBYN (STEBBYM), JOHN 248
STENWICKE (STEENWICKE, &c.), CORNELIUS, vs. admr. of John Dinely 208–210, 242, 243
STEPHEN (the martyr) quoted by William Leddra before his death . . 99
STEPHENSON, MARMADUKE, et al, (Quakers) 68, 69
STEPNEY (England) 7
STILEMAN, ELIAS, clerk 49, 54, 55, 57, 58
commissioner 239
et al, to take account of ship Providence, inventory goods, &c. . 228, 230, 231
STILTSON, WILLIAM, et al, to repair Town House 197
STINTED COMMONS 218
STODDARD, ANTHONY, assistant 183
receives reasons of appeal 89
commissioner, evidence before 128
et al, grantees one eighth of water-mills 40
vs. admrs. of Edward Gibbons, possession of same 40–42
to consider necessary repairs on Town House 197
STOUGHTON, WILLIAM, assistant 238
atty. of Richard Saltonstall, vs. Thomas Bishop 251
STRONG WATERS, pet. by William Toy, distiller, to retail 13
SUDBURY 19
SUFFOLK COUNTY 243, 244, 251
committee to repair Town House 197
files and records removed when Town House was consumed in 1747 259
marshal 38, 39, 47, 67, 70–72, 87, 121, 148, 247
to bear one fourth of expense of repairing Town House . . . 197
SUGAR (32,000 lbs.) litigation over 181–185
SUNTAUG LAKE 5, 6
SWAMPSCUTT (SWAMPSCOAT) farm, "where the Lady Moody lived" . . 4
Nahant and Sagamore Hill bought for two pestle stones . . . 59
SWAN (SWANN, &c.)
ELIZABETH, summoned 158
JOHN, et al, goods of Thomas Gleison in hands of, attached . . 112
RICHARD, et al, jurymen, dep. as to verdict of 81
ROBERT, summoned 151, 158
SWEET, RICHARD 241
SWETT, STEPHEN 155

PAGE
SWITZER (SUITZER), BENJAMIN, et als, chief promoters of "scandalous & reproachfull petition" 178
SYMONDS (SYMONS)
SAMUEL 82, 83, 183
assistant 23, 66
agreement against counselling inhabitants, in hand of . . 22
dep. before 158
oath before 81
receives reasons of appeal 77
et al, examines murderer 66
bond for prosecution of, before 66
WILLIAM, et al, summoned 151, 158
SYMSON, FRANCIS, et al, grantees Plains Farm 4

TARBOX, JOHN 59
TAYLOR (TAYLOUR, &c.), GEORGE 233, 235
vs. Daniel King, "mare killed by a bull" 13–15
TEMPLE, SIR THOMAS, prisoners committed for, re-arrested while in gaol, 142
evidence as to Arthur Mason sent by 188
TERRY (TARRY, &c.), JOHN, master of ship Antonio, et al, forced to long boat by mutinous crew 229, 231, 236–238
THOMAS, [ALICE], shop of 226
EVAN 45
TIDD, JOSHUA 216
TIDE-MILLS (*See* BOSTON and LYNN)
TILER (*See* TYLER)
TING (*See* TYNG)
TOOLEY (TOOLLY), JOHN, of ship Antonio, declaration as to mutiny . 236–238
TORREY, WILLIAM, clerk of deputies . . 25, 36, 37, 184, 189, 199, 202
TORTOODARS (TORTUGAS) 130
TOWN MEETINGS (rival), nullified 147
TOY (TOYE), WILLIAM, distiller of strong waters, pet. to retail . . . 13
TRAIN BAND drives wolves out of Nahant 56
TRASKE, CAPT. WILLIAM, dep. 50, 58
TRAUIS, RICHARD 221
TRERICE (TRERISE)
NICHOLAS, administration granted to widow Rebecca 34
MRS. REBECCA, deeds land to William Johnson 34
TREASURER 181, 196, 246, 249
Richard Russell 223
bonds in favor of 92, 171, 218, 245
payment to 136
to pay one half costs of repairing Town House 19
costs to Capt. Richard Walderne 171
witnesses 152
TREW, HENRY, deputy marshal 255
TREWORTHY, JOHN, NICHOLAS, et als vs. Robert Knight 16

PAGE

Trickey, Thomas 241
Truelove (ketch), crew censured for running down shallop 224
Turell, (Turille, &c.)
Daniel, jury of inquest 60
Mary, et al, summoned 225, 226
Rebecca, deported to Virginia 223
Turner (Turnor)
Ephraim, dep. of, ment. 184
vs. atty. of Capt. William Meade et als 212
Capt. [Nathaniel] 49, 53, 57
Lt. Robert, meeting at tavern of 138
William, et al (Anabaptists) 172–178
Turpin, Peter, adultery with Bethiah Bullen and Elizabeth Hudson 191–193
Turyn, Daniel 45
Twenty Rod (Indian), rape 216
Twist, Peter 7, 8
Tyler (Tiler), Job, et als, accuse John Godfrey of witchcraft . . 151–161
Tyleston, Thomas 248
Tyng (Tynge, &c.)
Edward, assistant 52, 183, 248
dep. before 52
examination of murderer by 223
et al, examination by 238
vs. James Pecker 200, 201
John Saffin 168, 169
Jonathan, et al, sureties for Lt. Richard Way 47

Usher (Vsher)
Hezekiah 183
et al vs. estate of Edward Gibbons 39–42
John, et al, sureties for Cornelius Stenwicke 243
Usury 164

Vaine, Henry, testimony by 53, 54
Verdicts (Special) 13, 39, 40, 42, 90, 91, 132, 133, 186, 205
Veren, Hilliard, clerk 2, 3, 52–59, 139, 153, 157
Vessels:
—— fishing shallop 224
—— galliott 42–46
—— sloop 238
Commonwealth (*See* Slandtwelvaers)
Decgens (ketch) 234, 235
Gilbert (ship) 11, 12
Golden Fox (ship) 194
Hope (catch) 140
James & John 169
Lenham (ship) 211
Little Barkley (ship) 226–228, 230, 234, 235

PAGE

VESSELS, *continued.*
Planter (ship) . . . 16–18
Providence (ship) . . . 227, 228, 230, 232, 233, 236, 239
Recovery (catch) . . . 246–249
St. Anthony, i. e., San Antonio (ship) . . . 229–232, 236–238
Slandtwelvaers, i. e., Commonwealth (frigate) . . . 226–239
Truelove (ketch) . . . 224
William & John (ship) . . . 240, 241
William & Thomas (ship) . . . 131
VIALLS, JOHN, public house . . . 187
"VIEW OF YE BODY" by chirurgeons . . . 62
VIRGINIA (VIRGINEA) . . . 209, 223, 224, 228, 230, 232
234, 235, 239, 241, 246
Capes of, (ships taken off) . . . 226, 227, 234, 236, 239
deportation to . . . 223
Petuxine River . . . 232
River . . . 234

WADE, JONATHAN, SR., dep. . . . 85
farm of . . . 77–79, 82, 84, 85
testimony of . . . 77, 78, 80
WAITE (WAYTE, &c.)
JOHN, testimony . . . 89–91
writ by . . . 112
SERGT. RETURN, summons accuser of Arthur Mason to Gov. Bellingham . . . 188
marshal general's deputy, assigned . . . 193
return of writ by . . . 193
RICHARD, marshal, bond in favor of . . . 87
executions by . . . 38, 39, 71, 72, 121, 148
general's deputy . . . 67
WALDERN (WALDRON, &c.), CAPT. RICHARD, vs. Christopher Palmer 170, 171
Israel Wight . . . 142–144
WALES, NATHANIEL, et al, jury of inquest . . . 60
WALKER, CAPT. RICHARD, dep. as to appraisal of Iron Works . . . 166, 167
testimony . . . 52
et al, appraisers . . . 166, 167
vs. admrs. of Thomas Dexter, Sr. . . . 46–59
WALL, JACOB, et al, crew of Dutch frigate . . . 234
WALLS CREEKE, (Dover, N. H.) . . . 143
WALTER (WALTERS), ELIZABETH, et al, summoned . . . 225
WALTON (WALTOWN), WILLIAM, et al, grantees Plains Farm . . . 4
WARD
BENJAMIN, vs. Roger Kelly . . . 140
HENRY . . . 6
MARGARET (WINTHROP), widow, marriage to Edmund Willie . . . 6, 7
SAMUEL, oath . . . 173
WARREN, PETER, testimony . . . 62, 63

PAGE

WATER-MILLS (*See* LYNN)
WATERTOWN (WATERTOUNE, &c.), constable 210
venires for a special Court of Assistants 179
WATTS, SAMUEL, et al, committee on early court files, &c. 259
WAY (WAYE), LT. RICHARD
power of attorney from Capt. James Oliver, admr. 51
vs. Town of Lynn 47–59
signed "scandalous & reproachfull petition" 177, 178
WAY-HILL, Hampshire, (England) 20
WEBB, JOSEPH, clerk 5, 6
marshal 48
et als, sureties 47
WEDGWOODE, [MARY] 254
WELLS, SAMUEL, et al, committee on early court files, &c. 259
WENHAM (WEANAM) 120
WESTMINSTER (England) 6, 7, 146
WEYMOUTH (WEIMOUTH) 72, 73
(by its atty.) vs. James Lovel 149, 150
WHARTON, RICHARD, constable 226
et als, sureties 251
WHEAT, payment in 116
WHEELWRIGHT, JOHN, (books, &c., belonging to his daughter, Catherine Nanny) 252, 253
WHETCOMBE, JAMES, et al, jurymen 248
WHITE
MARY, accused of lewd behaviour 132
vs. Elias, annulment, denied 131, 132
MICHAEL vs. Walter Burke 180
WHITICKER (WHITACRE), ABRAHAM and ELIZABETH, dep. 154
summoned . . 158
WHITING (WHITEING), SAMUEL, SR., testimony 57
WHITMORE (WHITMOR), FRANCIS 115
dep. 116, 117
et al, witnesses 116
WHITNEY, JOHN, et al, summoned 210
WHITTIER (WHITT:HAIRE), ABRAHAM, et al, grantees Plains Farm . . 4
THOMAS, constable 152, 153
"WIDOW'S PORTION" 90–93, 208
WIGGIN (WIGGEN, &c.)
ANDREW, land of 143
CAPT. THOMAS, assistant 23
JR., et al, appraisers 143
WIGHT (WEIGHT), ISRAEL, vs. Capt. Richard Walderne . . . 142–144, 170
WILD, WILLIAM, affirmation 85
WILKINS, PRUDENCE, land of 34
WILLET, CAPT. THOMAS
pet. to levy on any Dutch goods in colony 257

PAGE

WILLET, CAPT. THOMAS, *continued.*
et al, (excrs. of William Paddy) vs. Capt. Thomas Clarke . . 185
WILLEY (WILLIE), EDMOND and MARGARET (WINTHROP) WARD married . 7
et al, lease Pond Farm to John Pudney 8
EDMOND (atty.) sells one half of Pond Farm to James Menzies 7
MARGARET
gives power of attorney to her husband Edmund . . . . –. 7
and her sister, Judith Hancock, only heirs of Stephen Winthrop 6
WILLIAM (Natick Indian) 210
WILLIAM & JOHN, (ship), pet. of crew for relief 240, 241
WILLIAM & THOMAS, (ship), Matthew Armstrong, late master of . . 130
WILLIAMS (WILLIAM, &c.)
JOHN 53
CAPT. JOHN, vs. Theodore Atkinson 137, 138, 147
203–207, 215, 216
JOSEPH, (negro), et al, mariners, censured 224
NATHANIEL, et als, (guardians) vs. Clement Grosse 90–93
WILLIAMSON, ANN, dep. 29
WILSON, ALEXANDER, et al, pirates 229–232, 236–238
WIND-MILLS (*See* LYNN)
WING, JOSEPH, et al, mariners, censured 224
WINSLEY, EPHRAIM, et al, summoned 254, 255
WINTER, WILLIAM, dep. 49, 55
WINSHIP, EDWARD, LT., et al, goods of Thomas Gleison in hands of, attached 112

WINTHROP (WINTHROPE)
JOHN, deputy governor 6, 10, 12
governor 17
JUDITH, marries Richard Hancock 6, 7
MARGARET, marries Henry Ward 6
then Capt. Edmund Willie 7
STEPHEN, ESQR., buys Humfry's or Pond Farm 6
of James Street, Westminster, deceased . . 7
daughters, Margaret and Judith, only children . 6
divide, lease and sell said farm . . 7, 8

WISWALL (WISEWALL, &c.)
ENOCH 248
JOHN, et al, commissioners 134
NOAH 244

WITCHCRAFT
UNICE, (EUNICE) COLE, not legally guilty, but just grounds for vehement suspicion 253–255
JOHN GODFREY, not legally but suspiciously guilty, discharged, 151–161
WITT, JOHN, testimony 55

PAGE

WITTER, WILLIAM, buys Nahant, &c., from Black Will 59
testimony 50, 59
WOBURN (WOOBORNE, &c.) 114
Anabaptists 213, 214
constable of 147
town meetings (rival) illegal 147
new to be called 147
vs. William Johnson 34
WOLVES driven from Nahant by Train Band 56
WOOD, ALEXANDER, vs. John Chantry et al, of ketch Truelove for running down his shallop. 224
WOODBRIDGE, REV. BENJAMIN, (of Newbury) petition for his salary . 252
WOODMANSEY, JOHN, vs. William Salter, diet, etc., of prisoners . . . 142
WOODY (WOODEY, &c.)
DORCAS, et al, summoned 225
ISAAC, testimony 74
RICHARD, testimony of, ment. 50
son-in-law of Thomas Dexter, Sr., surety 48
WORCESTER, WILLIAM, testimony 15
WYBORN, THOMAS 195

YALE, MR., (agent for George Foxcroft), ment. 12, 13
YEOMANS, EDWARD, summoned 151, 158
YORK COUNTY (Yorkshire) 217, 218